NEW WORLD

THE FIRST PICTURES OF AMERICA

Edited by

STEFAN LORANT

The theme of this extraordinary book, THE NEW WORLD, is the vast virgin forest of North America and the attempt of the French and English to settle there. Eyewitness accounts, breathing the freshness of the events, give a clear impression of what life here was like—only seventy years after Columbus landed on the shores of the new continent.

But most fascinating are the illustrations.

Sixty-three watercolors—all reproduced in this volume in their original color—were drawn by the governor of Raleigh's second colony on Roanoke Island, John White, the grandfather of Virginia Dare. White drew the New World as he saw it; he sketched the Indians, their customs and habits, and painted the birds and flowers of the country. His drawings, made between 1585 and 1587—thirty-five years before the Pilgrims disembarked on the shores of Massachusetts—are the earliest authentic representations of aboriginal life in North America. (Additional figure drawings by White are reproduced in black and white; thus the reader can find all seventy-five drawings by him within the covers of this volume.)

Theodore De Bry, the Flemish artist, made twenty-three engravings after John White for his book on Virginia, which he issued in 1590. Each of these superb engravings is reproduced in THE NEW WORLD, so comparison can be made with John White's originals.

Another series of De Bry's engravings—forty-three of them—depict the life of the first French colony on the shores of the St. John's River. These engravings were made after paintings of Jacques Le Moyne de Morgues, who came to the Florida colony with Jean Ribaut and who had the good fortune to escape the massacre. The one surviving painting of Le Moyne was discovered by the editor of this volume and is reproduced in its original colors.

Thus THE NEW WORLD offers five different books in one: first, John White's drawings, sketched in Virginia about 1585; second, Theodore De Bry's twenty-three engravings of the Florida Colony; third, De Bry's forty-three engravings of the Virginia Colony; fourth, Thomas Hariot's "New found land of Virginia" (first published in London in 1588); and fifth, eyewitness accounts of Jacques Le Moyne de Morgues, Nicolas Le Challeux, Arthur Barlowe, Ralph Lane, and John White.

Jacket by Barbara Koontz

OTHER BOOKS BY STEFAN LORANT:

I WAS HITLER'S PRISONER (1935)

LINCOLN, HIS LIFE IN PHOTOGRAPHS (1941)

F. D. R., A PICTORIAL BIOGRAPHY (1950)

THE PRESIDENCY (1951)

LINCOLN, A PICTURE STORY OF HIS LIFE (1952)

THE LIFE OF ABRAHAM LINCOLN (1954)

THE LIFE AND TIMES OF THEODORE ROOSEVELT (1959)

PITTSBURGH, THE STORY OF AN AMERICAN CITY (1964)

THE NEW WORLD

THE FIRST PICTURES OF AMERICA

MADE BY JOHN WHITE AND JACQUES LE MOYNE
AND ENGRAVED BY THEODORE DE BRY

WITH CONTEMPORARY NARRATIVES
OF THE FRENCH SETTLEMENTS IN FLORIDA
1562-1565
AND THE ENGLISH COLONIES IN VIRGINIA
1585-1590

A NEW, REVISED EDITION

EDITED AND ANNOTATED BY

STEFAN LORANT

DUELL, SLOAN AND PEARCE · NEW YORK

LIBRARY OF CONGRESS CATALOG CARD NUMBER: 65-26310
PRINTED IN THE UNITED STATES OF AMERICA
BY THE BECK ENGRAVING COMPANY, INC., PHILADELPHIA
FOR MEREDITH PRESS

FIRST REVISED EDITION

CONTENTS

ILLUSTRATIONS

LIST OF ILLUSTRATIONS

THEODORE DE BRY'S ENGRAVINGS FOR HIS FLORIDA VOLUME, ISSUED IN 1591

MADE AFTER THE PAINTINGS OF JACQUES LE MOYNE DE MORGUES

THE 75 WATERCOLORS OF JOHN WHITE

THEODORE DE BRY'S ENGRAVINGS FOR HIS VIRGINIA VOLUME, ISSUED IN 1590

MADE AFTER THE WATERCOLORS OF JOHN WHITE

NOTES ON THIS BOOK

"IN THIS VOLUME," so I wrote in the Foreword of the 1946 edition, "I have attempted to recreate—through contemporary narratives and pictures—the story of the first abortive French and English settlements on the eastern shores of North America." That sentence still holds for this revised and enlarged edition.

The book is divided into two parts; the first deals with the French settlements in Florida during the years 1562–1565, the second with the attempted colonization of Virginia between the years of 1584 and 1590.

About the French efforts:

In 1562 the Huguenot leader Gaspard de Coligny dispatched a small party to the New World under the command of the valiant soldier Jean Ribaut. The Frenchmen landed on the shores of the St. John's River of South Carolina. Ribaut found the land so desirable that he left thirty soldiers behind to hold it for France while he returned home for supplies and reinforcements. But when he reached France, the country was in the throes of a religious civil war, and he was unable to leave for the New World.

After the restoration of peace, another Huguenot colony sailed to Florida, this time under the command of René de Laudonnière, as Ribaut was at that time a prisoner of the English in the Tower of London. When he was freed, Admiral Coligny sent him to America to take over the colony's command from Laudonnière.

Philip II, the Spanish monarch, watched with growing alarm the intrusions on territory that he regarded as his. Thus in the summer of 1565 he ordered an armed fleet under Pedro Menéndez de Avilés to clear Florida of the French invaders. Menéndez took Fort Caroline, wiping out its defenders. Some of the French ships perished in a tempest; most of the French soldiers were massacred by the Spaniards.

Among the handful of Frenchmen who saved their lives was the carpenter Nicolas Le Challeux, and he later related his experiences. (His narrative is on pages 88—116.) Another of the men who escaped the Spanish sword was the artist Jacques Le Moyne de Morgues, who drew pictures and described the dramatic events. (His narrative is on pages 33—86).

Of Le Moyne's pictures only one has come down to us. I found it in the possession of the late James Hazen Hyde of New York, and he gave me permission to reproduce it. (It appears in full color on page 32.)

Though Le Moyne's other originals have been lost, his paintings were engraved by the Flemish artist Theodore De Bry for the second volume of his series of illustrated voyages, which he issued in 1591. (All forty-three engravings of De Bry's are printed on pages 34—199.)

Thus, the two French narratives—Le Moyne's and Le Challeux's—with the engravings of De Bry after Le Moyne, make up the first part of this volume.

The second part of the book describes and illustrates the efforts of the English to settle in the New World. Raleigh and Hakluyt dreamed of the colonization of America on a vast scale. To tell the story of those early English settlements all the known early narratives and eyewitness accounts are reprinted. As this book is intended for the general reader and not for the historian, I thought it permissible to modernize the Elizabethan words and phrases and to standardize the capriciousness of the Elizabethan spelling. Mrs. James Hulbert (Lucille Grigorieff), an outstanding Elizabethan scholar, was responsible for the transposition of the text. Those who would like to consult the original versions can easily find them. They are listed in the Bibliography.

This is the outline of the English attempts to establish a settlement in the New World:

The freshly knighted Walter Raleigh, who, after the loss of his half-brother Sir Humphrey Gilbert at sea, was given a patent by the Queen for the exploration and profitable colonization of North America, dispatched two small ships under the command of Philip Amadas and Arthur Barlowe in 1584. The captains were to explore the land of the new continent, make investigations of its resources, and ascertain the feasibility of a settlement. On their return Barlowe submitted to Raleigh his report. (It is printed on pages 125–133.)

Raleigh then outfitted an expedition which he sent to the New World a year later. The majority of the 107 men—the first English settlers in America — were soldiers, though there was a sprinkling of merchants and specialists among them, like Thomas Hariot the scientist, Joachim Ganz the metallurgist, John White the artist. The colonists stayed at Roanoke Island for a year, and when their supplies ran out they returned in Drake's ship to England. Fifteen men were left behind to hold the country for England; what their fate was is lost in the mist of history. (Ralph Lane's report to Raleigh about his 1585 adventure is on pages 135–149.)

Thomas Hariot wrote a narrative on the newly found land of Virginia which was first published in London in 1588 and reprinted two years later in De Bry's Virginia volume. (It is on pages 227–277.) The colonists' return with Drake was written up by an anonymous writer in 1586. (See pages 151–153.)

In 1587 Raleigh sent out another colony, this time under the governorship of John White, to establish a settlement on Chesapeake Bay. However, White settled on Roanoke Island. When difficulties arose, he returned to England. Not until 1590 was he able to reach the New World again. Arriving at the spot where he had left his men he could not find them. What happened to that "lost colony" still haunts our imagination.

White described his voyage and his search for the colonists in a letter and report to Richard Hakluyt. (It is on pages 167–179.)

During his stay in America White sketched the Indians who lived near the coast where the English attempted to settle; he pictured the southeastern Algonkians, their villages, their customs, their habits. He also made drawings of the plants, fruits, fish, birds, and animals. They were delightful pictures, but no works of art.[1]

On his return to England he probably took with him these sketches, from which he then made his final renderings at leisure. (The story

1. Much nonsense has been written about White's artistic ability. Instant experts tried to make him out as a great artist. That he was not. But he was a fairly competent craftsman, who could draw figures of animals and plants without much distortion, even though his perspectives are poor and his figures reveal an obvious lack of anatomical knowledge.

Whether he had proper art training we do not know. That he studied the works of the great masters—of Leonardo da Vinci, of Albrecht Dürer, of Hans Holbein—and that he looked at the illustrations in old chronicles and costume and travel books we may assume. He must have been familiar with the drawings of the Flemish Lucas de Heere, who lived in London between the late 1560's and early 1570's, for his Eskimo drawings show great similarity with de Heere's Eskimos. Nicolas de Nicolay's Turkish and Oriental figures in his 1586 volume *Navigations et peregrinations orientales* may have been another influence.

Laurence Binyon, who forty years ago analyzed White's artistry, came to the conclusion that the paramount interest in his drawings was "not artistic"; their main value was for the ethnologist and historian. John Canaday, the eminent art critic of the *New York Times,* voiced a similar opinion when he wrote in his newspaper on March 18, 1965 that the drawings "are not fine art in the usual sense, but they are an extraordinarily engaging group of pictures. Created as the kind of documentary record that today would be supplied by the camera. . . . White was no Audubon, and his paintings of birds, fish and butterflies are beautifully patterned simply because nature patterned these creatures beautifully in the first place."

of the drawings is on pages 180–184.)

Until the publication of this volume, these important representations of early American life had never before been printed in their entirety and in their original colors. (They were and are so printed on pages 185–244.)[2]

White's original work, which the British Museum acquired in 1866 from the American antiquarian Henry Stevens, bound in a single volume, numbered 75 drawings. Of these 63, pertaining to America (including also the pictures of two European birds) are printed in full color, while his twelve figure drawings, which have no connection with the English settlements, are printed in black and white (see page 183).

For this edition some of the text, editorial notes and color reproductions have been revised. In the nomenclature of natural history subjects I originally followed the British Museum Catalogue of 1907. Since then the Museum has revised and reinterpreted Laurence Binyon's descriptions; I have followed these revisions.

In the Bibliography I have added some of the important works relating to the subject which have appeared since the original publication of this volume.

"Farview," Lenox, Massachusetts
June 10, 1965

STEFAN LORANT

[2]Although—as the Keeper of Prints and Drawings of the British Museum in his *Preface* to that institution's $225 edition of John White's drawings noted—"no process yet devised can reproduce watercolour in exact facsimile," the reproductions of White's pictures in this volume are as faithful to the originals as could be made by one of America's outstanding printing firms—the Beck Engraving Company in Philadelphia.

We do not really know the "exact" original colors of White's drawings. In the fire of 1865 at Sotheby's when the drawings were soaked in water and left offsets on the intervening pages, much damage was done to the colors. "A glance at the offsets which then resulted shows clearly that many lost a considerable amount of pigment. Before this the drawings must have given a much stronger, more vivid and finished impression," wrote the experts of the British Museum (*The American Drawings of John White,* Vol. I, p. 28). As time passed some further rubbing occurred. Continued the experts: "This was negligible for the Indian drawings, most of which were inlaid, but greater for the natural history drawings. . . ."

Still one has the feeling that the colors on the whole remained substantially the same.

THE CHIEF CHARACTERS IN THE FLORIDA CONTROVERSY

THE FRENCH

Catherine de' Medici
1519-89

Wife of Henry II and mother of three French Kings: Francis II, Charles IX, and Henry III. After the death of her first son in 1560, she became the guardian of ten-year-old Charles IX. From then until her death she was the real power, striving by every subtle art to hold the balance between Huguenots and Catholics.

Charles IX
1550-74

Second son of Henry II and Catherine de' Medici. He succeeded his brother, Francis II, to the throne when he was only ten years old. During his reign France was in the throes of religious and civil war. Charles IX had not much influence in the affairs of the state. He was a weak puppet in the hands of his mother.

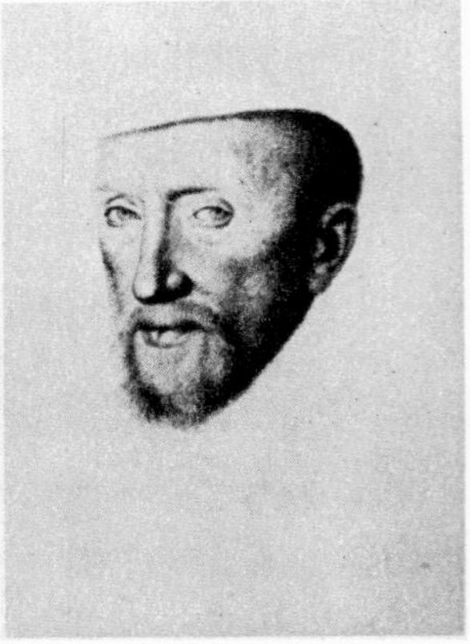

Gaspard de Coligny
1516-72

One of the leaders of the Huguenots. He was mainly responsible for the first French settlements in the New World. For a long time Coligny was an adviser of Catherine de' Medici, which did not deter the Queen Mother from allowing his murder in the massacre of St. Bartholomew on August 24, 1572.

René de Laudonnière
?-1582

He was commander of the French colony in Florida in 1564. When the Spaniards attacked the French Fort Caroline, Laudonnière escaped on one of the French vessels and reached England in October, 1565. A few months later he returned to France but was coldly received by the Court and died in obscurity.

THE SPANIARDS

Philip II
1527-98

King of Spain, champion of the Roman Catholic world, more powerful than the Pope himself. He followed his father, Charles V, to the throne in 1556. After the death of his first two wives—Mary of Portugal and Mary Tudor of England—he married Elizabeth, daughter of Henry II and Catherine de' Medici.

Elizabeth Valois
1546-68

She married Philip II in 1559. During the marriage celebrations her father Henry II, was wounded in a tournament and died. Elizabeth was a true daughter of Catherine de' Medici. She kept her mother regularly informed of her husband's intentions through Fourquevaux, the French Ambassador.

The Duke of Alba
1508-83

The scourge of the Netherlands, trusted adviser of Philip II, who accompanied Queen Isabella (Elizabeth Valois) to the Bayonne Conference. Alba, President of the Council of Blood, the high tribunal against the heretics, was the power behind the throne in the Florida controversy between Spain and France.

Menéndez de Avilés
1519-74

A very able naval officer, commander of the Spanish fleet which Philip II sent to the New World to clear Florida of the heretics. Menéndez attacked and captured the French fort, killing its defenders. When Ribaut's ships were wrecked and Menéndez came upon the survivors, he massacred all the Frenchmen.

NOTES ON THE FRENCH SETTLEMENTS IN FLORIDA

1562—1565

THE struggle between Spain and France for a small stretch of land in the wilderness of the New World has all the elements of a Shakespearean drama: politics, romance, war, adventure, murder.

Its setting is a huge and unknown continent, a vast country of uncertain boundaries—Florida. The Spaniards of that day understood by Florida the whole country extending from the Atlantic on the east to the longitude of New Mexico on the west, and from the Gulf of Mexico and the River of Palms indefinitely northward towards the Polar Sea. All of this enormous territory belonged to Spain by right of discovery, conquest, and papal patent.

Since Ponce de Léon first set foot in Florida[1] in his quest for the fountain of youth, Spain had made many attempts to settle on the eastern seaboard of North America. Francis de Garay and Vásquez de Ayllón sent their expeditions there, exploring the coast; Narváez and De Soto followed, searching for gold. Cancello, the Dominican monk, and others came to convert the savages to the true faith. Guido de las Bazares looked for a site to establish a settlement; Tristan de Luna landed with his colonists. Most of them lost their lives, and the remainder came away disillusioned. They did not discover gold; they did not find treasure. Their search ended in frustration; their sacrifices were in vain.

After the De Luna expedition Philip II, disappointed and discouraged, proclaimed that no further attempts should be made to colonize the eastern coast of Florida. This was on September 23, 1561. By then Spain had no fear that any of her rivals would challenge her in Florida.

But Philip was mistaken. Even while he was making his announcement, French seamen were preparing to sail there.

Why France Wanted Florida

France had already cast covetous eyes upon the narrow strip of soil upon the Atlantic coast. Her reasons were not far to seek. These shores were of great strategic importance, for through the narrow Straits of Florida, or the Bahama Channel, as it was then called, passed the Spanish treasure ships on their return from the Indies. If France could gain a foothold on that coast, all the Spanish galleons and their riches would be at her mercy. And what riches they were! At least ten to fifteen million dollars' worth of gold and jewels were carried yearly to Spain in those ships.[2]

The passage through the narrow channel was hazardous. Violent tempests and perilous reefs endangered the Spanish ships. Many of them were wrecked on the rocks. If they should be harassed, not only by the elements but also by the enemy, not many of them would reach home.

Could Spain tolerate a foreign power in the Florida Straits? Never! She might temporarily abandon the idea of a permanent settlement, but she could not allow France to occupy the coast.

The real deep-rooted cause of the controversy was, that Spain feared to lose her gold. But since kings and statesmen often do not care to admit their more prosaic and sordid reasons for going to war,

1. As Ponce de Léon discovered land on Easter Sunday, March 27, 1513 he named it Pascua Florida, the Spanish name for Easter Sunday.

2. Navarette, in his *Conservación de monarquias* (Madrid, 1626), p. 143, writes that between the years 1519 and 1617 Spain imported 1536 millions registered gold and silver.

in the struggle for Florida the religious controversy between Spain and France was emphasized rather than the fight for gold.

Dramatis Personae

The chief characters in the struggle are worthy of a Shakespeare's imagination. First the Spanish monarch Philip II. Not brilliant, yet tenacious, hard-working, and jealous of his authority, he watched personally over every detail of his administration, making notes, drafting dispatches, and receiving the communications of his ambassadors. Often slow in making decisions, a man of many hesitations and contradictions, he was, nevertheless, single-minded in his ultimate goal: to restore Catholicism in the world, under the leadership of Spain, and to uphold the medieval ways of life. He was for Spain first and last, and this Spain of his meant formality, bigotry, cruelty, and the Inquisition. Philip acknowledged only one God and one religion and looked with horror upon all those who would form a personal opinion upon God and faith and thus bring chaos into the world. He believed in God, on Whose will alone success and failure depended, and he believed that unity of religion was indispensable to the maintenance and authority of the state and order.

His private life was a mirror reflecting the interests of his realm. He married first his cousin Mary of Portugal, who died soon after giving birth to a son, Don Carlos. For fifteen years Philip remained a widower. Then he married again—this time Mary Tudor (Bloody Mary) in order to gain England's support against Spain's enemies in Europe. When Mary died, in 1558, Philip made advances to Queen Elizabeth, but, realizing England's weakness, he married instead—four months after the signing of the Peace of Le Cateau-Cambrésis (April 2, 1559)—Elizabeth Valois (Isabella of the Peace), daughter of the French king, Henry II.

He thus became the son-in-law of his adversary in the Florida conflict: Catherine de' Medici, mother of three successive French kings—Francis II, Charles IX, Henry III. Within a year Catherine lost both her husband, Henry II, and her son Francis II. But with the accession of her ten-year-old son, Charles IX, in 1560, she became the real power in France. A compromiser, a politician, an appeaser, a double dealer, she had learned the art of politics from Machiavelli; friendship, loyalty, good faith had no real meaning for her. She courted power. She had lived her whole life in the shadow of her husband's mistress, so that when power came to her at last, she held onto it with every ounce of her boundless energy. Under Catherine the country went through a turbulent period of religious wars. Huguenots[3] and Catholics fought each other on the battlefield, while she held the throne of France firmly for her son, turning her ear now to the Catholics, now to the Huguenots. Parkman describes her as a woman of "mean spirit, bad heart and fathomless depths of duplicity." But Balzac, who studied her character with less bias, believed that she was one of the greatest of French rulers.

These were the chief antagonists in the drama: Philip II for Spain; Catherine de' Medici for France. But their will was carried out by others.

It was Gaspard de Coligny, valiant leader of the French Huguenots, who resolved to plant a Huguenot colony in Florida and challenge Spanish supremacy there. Coligny hated Spain, not only as the foe with whom France was continually at war but also as the bulwark of bigotry, of fanatic Catholicism, and as the cruel enemy of the reformed religion. His counterpart on the Spanish side was the Duke of Alba, cruel and reactionary adviser of Philip II.

Yet even more vital than the parts played by Coligny and Alba were those of the men who commanded the troups, Jean Ribaut and René de Laudonnière upon the French side, and Pedro Menéndez de Avilés upon the Spanish.

Ribaut Sails to Florida

The struggle for Florida began with the departure of two small ships[4] from the French harbor of Havre de Grace in February, 1562. France was on the verge of civil war. Catholics and Huguenots were soon to meet on the battlefield.

Crowded on the boats were one hundred and fifty persons. They had been recruited by Admiral Coligny, who had organized the expedition, outfitted the boats, appointed the commander, and given orders to sail to Florida.

3. French Protestants of the 16th and 17th centuries. The word Huguenot, *eiguenot*, comes from the German *Eidgenossen* (*eid*—oath; *genossen*—comrades). It was applied to the Genevese when they joined the Swiss confederation.

4. One was 160 tons; the other 60 tons; their names are not recorded.

Once before Coligny had attempted to plant a Huguenot settlement in the new world. It was in 1555 on the shores of Brazil under Villagagnon's leadership. At that time his plan had ended in dismal failure. But now the leader of the expedition was Jean Ribaut, "a man in trueth expert in sea causes," a devout Protestant, a courageous soldier, and a stanch patriot—a man very different from Villagagnon.

The two small French ships reached the Florida coast on April 30, 1562, and cast anchor in the neighborhood of the present site of St. Augustine. Ribaut "veewed the coast all along with an inspeakeable pleasure of thoderiferous smell and bewtye of the same."[5] The Frenchmen rowed to the shore, where "a good numbre of the Indians, inhabytants there," welcomed them "withowt any taken of feare or dowbte." They were "all naked and of a goodly stature, mighty, faire and aswell shapen and proportioned of bodye as any people in all the worlde, very gentill, curtious and of a good nature."

As it was the first day of May, the French commander named the stream the River of May (the St. John's). Ribaut and his companions, after the long and tedious ocean journey, were overcome with joy. The country seemed to them "the fairest, frutefullest and pleasantest of all the worlde, habonding in honney, veneson, wildfoule, forrestes, woodes of all sortes, palme trees, cipers, ceders, bayes, the hiest, greatest and fairest vynes in all the wourld with grapes accordingly, which naturally and withowt mans helpe and tryming growe to the top of okes and other trees that be of a wonderfull greatnes and height." Ribaut's narrative records with vivid freshness that first happy day in the new world. "The sight of the faire medowes is a pleasure not able to be expressed with tonge," he writes, "full of herons, corleux, bitters, mallardes, egertes, woodkockes, and of all other kinde of smale birdes, with hartes, hyndes, buckes, wild swyne, and sondery other wild beastes as we perceved well bothe then by there foteing there and also afterwardes in other places by ther crye and brayeng which we herde in the night tyme. Also there be cunys, hares, guynia cockes in mervelus numbre, a great dele fairer and better then be oures, silke wormes, and to be shorte it is a thinge inspeakable, the comodities that be sene there and shalbe founde more and more in this incomperable lande, never as yet broken with plowe irons, bringing fourthe all thinges according to his first nature, whereof the eternall God endued yt."

At nightfall the French rowed back to their ship, but next morning they returned to the land, carrying with them a stone, "in which pillar the Armes of France were carved and engraved."[6] They put up the stone near the mouth of the river, thus taking possession of the country for the French crown. After this ceremony they sailed seven leagues[7] farther along the coast and found "a great opening or bay"; here they cast anchor, explored the river mouth, and gave the stream the name Seine (the St. Mary's). They moved on, discovered seven more rivers (see pages 41, 43), and stopped at a large harbor in a great stream, which they named Port Royal (the Broad River of South Carolina). The Frenchmen roamed over the countryside, and with each step their enthusiasm grew. Ribaut wondered over the "aboundaunce of fishe as is increadeble"; he marveled that there were "havens, rivers and islandes of suche frutefullness as cannot with tonge be expressed, and where in shorte tyme great and precyous comodyties might be found"; he spoke delightedly of "gold, silver, pearls, turquoise," and he asserted with an ultimate assurance that the land "lacketh nothing." For two weeks the Frenchmen explored this earthly Paradise. They erected another column "in a comodyous pleasaunt and high place, at the entrye of a faire great river" (probably Skull Creek). Then it was time to sail for home.

Ribaut had come to Florida to explore the country, not to settle it; but now that he had seen the richness of the land, he spun dreams of the "great good and comodyties that may be brought thence into France, if we leve a nombre of men there, that may fortifye and so provide themselves of thinges necessarye, for in all newe discovers yt is the chef and best thinge that may be don at the begining, to fortifye and people the country which is the true and chef possesion." He then made a speech to his men. He appealed to their patriotism and asked for volunteers to hold the land for France.

5. This and the following quotations are from Jean Ribaut, *The Whole & True Discouerye of Terra Florida*, published in London in the spring of 1563 (see Bibliography).

6. René de Laudonnière in Hakluyt's *Principal Navigations* (MacLehose, N. Y. 1905), VIII, 457-58.

7. A nautical, or marine, league is 3.45 miles.

Every one of the soldiers wished to stay. Ribaut selected thirty men,[8] who were to remain in Florida "of their one fre and good willes." He appointed as their captain Albert de la Pierria. As the soldiers had asked Ribaut to build them a fort, a site was chosen near the creek Chenonceau,[9] and there on an island (Parris Island) a fort was built. It was named Charlesfort in honor of twelve-year-old Charles IX, King of France.

Ribaut left the soldiers food and ammunition, then, on June 11, he set sail, promising to return within six months with supplies and other necessities. The men watched the ships as they became smaller and smaller and disappeared below the horizon, leaving them alone in the vast and unknown land—the only white men between the North Pole and Mexico.

They completed the fort, went hunting and fishing, visited the Indians, and attended their feasts. But they had neither planted maize nor cultivated the soil, so confident were they that their leader would soon return.

Yet one month followed another, and there was no sign of Ribaut. "Their victualles beganne to waxe short, which forced them to have recourse unto their neighbours, and to pray them to succour them in their necessitie."[10] The Indians helped them at first; the amount was not much, for the new harvest had not yet come in. Then the French set out and went into that part of the country where Ouadé and Couëxis lived. These chieftains filled their canoe with maize and beans. But their joy was short-lived, for a fire destroyed Charlesfort and all their newly acquired stock. They "found themselves in such extremitie, that without the ayd of Almighty God, the onely searcher of the hearts and thoughts of men, which never forsaketh those that seeke him in their afflictions, they had bene quite and cleane out of all hope."

The soldiers' anger turned against their captain, who had exiled one of their comrades—La Chere—to a neighboring island, where the unlucky soldier was slowly starving to death, and who had hanged another man with his own hands "for a smal fault." Starvation and solitude must have preyed heavily on Captain Albert's mind. He threatened to kill everyone who would not obey. The soldiers "fell into a mutinie, because that many times he put his threatenings in execution: wherupon they so chased him, that at the last they put him to death." The captain out of the way, they rescued the half-starved La Chere from his island and chose Nicholas Barré as their new leader.

But what had happened to Ribaut? Why did he not return? Weeks grew to months. The tired, hungry, homesick soldiers, oppressed, lonely, and dejected, were on the verge of despair. They had only one thought—to leave their bleak and inhospitable surroundings and to return home. Yet how? They had no ships.

In their desperation "they began to build a smal Pinnesse." They lacked cordage and sails. Chief Audusta visited them and promised enough cordage "as should suffice to furnish the Pinnesse with tackling." They searched for moss, and with it they calked their boat. They made sails out of their shirts and sheets. And when this crazy, patched-up, fragile brigantine was ready, they placed in it "their artillerie, their forge, and other munitions of warre which Captaine Ribault had left them, and then as much mill as they could gather together. But being drunken with the too excessive joy, which they had conceived for their returning into France, or rather deprived of all foresight & consideration, without regarding the inconstancie of the winds, which change in a moment, they put themselves to sea, and with so slender victuals, that the end of their interprise became unluckly and unfortunate." They had gone only a third of the way when such a calm descended "that in three weekes they sailed not above five and twentie leagues."

The supplies gone, "every man was constrained to eate not past twelve graines of mill by the day." And even this slim ration was soon used up. Now "they had nothing for their more assured refuge but their shooes and leather jerkins which they did eat." To still their thirst "some of them dranke the sea water, others did drink their owne urine." The weak among them died. And as if hunger and thirst were not enough the boat began to leak. More

8. This number varies in the different narratives. Laudonnière speaks of 28; in Hakluyt's English translation there are 26; Guillaume Rouffi, the French boy, says there were 26; while in Chantone's, the Spanish ambassador's report to Philip II the number is 25.

9. Probably Archer's Creek, six miles from the present town of Beaufort, S. C.

10. This and the following quotations are from Laudonnière's narrative (printed in English in Hakluyt's *Principal Navigations*, MacLehose edition), VIII, 480-86.

dead than alive, the survivors had to bail out the water "that on al sides entred into their Barke."

Still worse was to come. "After they had eaten up their shooes and their leather jerkins, there arose so boystrous a winde and so contrary to their course, that in the turning of a hande, the waves filled their vessel halfe full of water and brused it upon the one side."

All hope had now left them. They lay in the bottom of the boat, waiting for the end. The waves tossed their rickety brigantine mercilessly. Suddenly one of the soldiers spoke up. He implored his comrades not to despair. He assured them that if the wind changed, in three more days they would reach land. The men went on bailing, starving for three more days. Still all they saw was water, water everywhere, and no land in sight.

They were crazy with hunger. In their "despaire certaine among them made this motion that it was better that one man should dye, then that so many men should perish: they agreed therefore that one should die to sustaine the others." The lot fell on La Chere, the wretched soldier whom they had rescued from starvation only a short time before. They killed him, and his "flesh was devided equally among his fellowes."

And then they saw land. But by that time they had not the strength to navigate their vessel. Their boat drifted rudderless on the waves.

They were found by an English ship; the men were given food and drink. The feeble and the sick were put ashore at Corunna; the others were taken to England, where they met not only the highest in society, but Queen Elizabeth herself. And through their tales the English learned of the French settlement in the New World.

The Spanish Burn Charlesfort

What was Spain's reaction to the news that French ships had sailed to Florida? When Chantone, the Spanish ambassador in France, heard of Ribaut's preparations, he immediately repaired to the court and obtained an interview with the Queen Mother,[11] reminding her that Florida belonged to Spain and that no Frenchmen had the right to go there. Catherine de' Medici reassured the ambassador that nothing would be done to the detriment of Philip's interests, and she promised a written reply to Chantone's protest. But the Spanish ambassador was not so easily taken in. He knew how little Catherine's words could be trusted. The Queen professed to have no knowledge of the expedition, though it was common gossip that she not only knew about it but had even invested 1,000 ducats of her own money to outfit the ships. Chantone had spies in every French port; they watched all ships and made their observations to the ambassador, who in turn sent these reports to his King. Philip II transmitted them to the Council of the Indies and asked for advice. Yet even before the Council could discuss the matter Ribaut had sailed.

At the French court the Spanish diplomatic representations continued. Chantone pressed hard for an answer. Still Catherine remained silent. Chantone, losing patience, told her bluntly that as he had not received a satisfactory promise from her regarding Florida, his King "would adopt measures for getting possession of those who had gone there in order to chastise them."[12]

It was long before Chantone was able to obtain a complete report on Ribaut's venture. Not until January of the following year did he send to Philip a full account of the French expedition, revealing the number of men Ribaut had left in Florida, describing the places they had visited, and disclosing the names of the persons at the French court who were behind the undertaking.

With Chantone's report before him, Philip decided to act. Florida was to be cleared of "the French who had gone to settle there." They were to be expelled "to avoid the robberies to which the fleets and single vessels coming from the Indies were exposed by the nearness of such settlements."[13] He ordered the Governor of Cuba to equip a ship and dispatch an armed force. They were to remove Ribaut's columns, destroy the French fort, and if they found the settlers, to deal with them as they thought just.

In May, 1564, twenty-five Spanish soldiers under the command of Don Hernando de Manrique de Rojas left in the frigate *Nuestra Señora de la Concepción* to clear Florida of the intruders. The governor thought twenty-five men would be sufficient to free the continent of the invaders. But

11. January 23, 1562.
12. Chantone to Philip II, May 7, 1562, MS Arch. Nat., Paris, K, 1497 (29).

13. Memorial de Pero Menéndez de Avilés in Ruidíaz, *La Florida*, II, 320 (see Bibliography).

when Manrique de Rojas reached Florida, Ribaut's small colony had already left Charlesfort.

The Spanish commander made a careful search along the coast. He found among the Indians a sixteen-year-old French youngster, Guillaume Rouffi, who had remained in the New World because he believed life in the wilderness was better than the mad crossing of the ocean without a seaworthy boat and experienced navigators. Rouffi led Manrique de Rojas to the fort and showed him the spot where Ribaut had erected his column. The Spanish commander acted without hesitation; he burned Charlesfort, took the column onto his boat, and, with Rouffi on board, he sailed to Havana.

Ribaut Is Caught by the English

But where was Ribaut? Two years had passed since he had left Florida. He reached France on July 20, 1562. By that time the country was in the throes of civil and religious wars. Admiral Coligny, leader of the Huguenot forces, had far greater matters to care for than the soldiers whom Ribaut had left in the Florida wilderness. Great as were Ribaut's efforts, there was no hope of sending relief to the colonists.

Ribaut fought with the Huguenots in the defense of Dieppe, and when that city surrendered, he fled to England.

He did not forget the men whom he had left in Charlesfort. He wrote a book on his voyage to Florida and published it in London in May, 1563 (see Bibliography). He had an interview with Queen Elizabeth, told her of the new world, of its wealth and riches, and asked for her assistance. Elizabeth was cautious; Philip's spies were everywhere, and she did not dare to help Ribaut openly, but she encouraged him to proceed with his preparations. There was a tale, which Ribaut later denied, that the Queen had offered him a pension of three hundred ducats and a house if he would help England to take possession of Florida.

The same month in which his book left the press Ribaut was busy outfitting a fleet. His partner in the enterprise was the notorious Thomas Stukeley, an unscrupulous young adventurer.

Bishop Quadra, Philip's "ear" in England, wrote worried letters to his King about the prospective English colony in Florida. He reported that Stukeley and Ribaut intended to go to Charlesfort, which Stukeley would take over for his Queen.

But this was not to be. Jean Ribaut was caught on board a Flemish vessel attempting to escape from Gravesend with the three French pilots who were to have guided the expedition to Florida. The pilots were put back onto the boats in shackles; Ribaut was thrown into prison.

What were the reasons which prompted Ribaut to flee from England? Quadra, the Spanish ambassador at Elizabeth's court, in a letter to Philip II gives this explanation: Ribaut had promised to deliver Charlesfort to Stukeley, but had repented of this promise and had therefore tried to escape.

A New Huguenot Colony Sails to Florida

The Peace of Amboise in 1563, marked the temporary end of the war between Catholics and Huguenots. Coligny returned to the court; soon he was making preparations for sending a fresh Huguenot colony to Florida, seeking "new means of traffic and profit in strange lands."

As Ribaut was still imprisoned in England, Admiral Coligny chose René de Laudonnière, who had been Ribaut's lieutenant on the first voyage, to lead the expedition.

Under Laudonnière's command, three ships,[14] with three hundred men, left Havre de Grace; there were also four women on board. They sailed on April 22, 1564 (one day before Shakespeare was born) and reached the Florida coast two months later, June 22. They landed "about thirtie leagues above the River of May."[15]

Three days later they cast anchor at the mouth of the River of May and went ashore almost at the same spot where Ribaut had disembarked two years before.[16] Indians emerged from the woods to greet them. "Amy, amy!" (friend) called out Chief Saturiba, and he led the French to Ribaut's column,[17] which the natives worshipped as an idol (see page 51). Athore, Saturiba's eldest son, gave Laudonnière a wedge of silver, "in recompense whereof" the French commander "gave him a cutting hooke and some other better present."

14. The *Isabella*, the *Little Breton*, and the *Faulcon*, the first only sixty, the second eighty, and the last—a man-of-war—three hundred tons.

15. This and the following quotations are from Laudonnière's narrative as reprinted in Hakluyt's *Principal Navigations* (MacLehose edition), IX, 5-15.

16. Near the present-day village of Mayport.

17. It was the second column, which Manrique de Rojas did not discover.

The next morning the French rowed up the river. Natives flocked to the shores of the stream, watching the strangers with curious eyes.

Laudonnière ascended a hill, which is now called St. John's Bluff, and viewed the land. He saw "nothing else but Cedars, Palme, and Baytrees of so sovereigne odour, that Baulme smelleth nothing like in comparison," and for him the place seemed "so pleasant that those which are melancholicke would be inforced to change their humour."

Returning to the river mouth, the French found Saturiba waiting for them. Laudonnière was anxious to learn from the Indian the source of the silver which had been given him. Saturiba told him that it came from a region called Thimogoa, whose people were his "most ancient and naturall enemies." Laudonnière, his mind on the silver, promised Saturiba the help of his harquebusiers[18] whenever the chief was ready to attack the Thimogoas.

The region around the River of May seemed the best spot for a settlement, as "the country abounded in Maiz and corne, besides the Golde and Silver that was found there." Laudonnière marked off a triangle where a fort was to be erected. Saturiba, "with whom friendship increased as the dayes increased," commanded his subjects to help with the building, and in a short time Fort Caroline, named in honor of the French king, was finished.

Alliances with Rival Chieftains—for Gold

The fort had scarcely been completed, when Laudonnière, not disposed to "lose a minute of an houre, without imploying of the same in some vertuous exercise," dispatched Ottigny, his lieutenant, to find out "what this Thimogoa might be, whereof the Paracoussy Saturiba has spoken to us so often."[19]

Ottigny pushed twenty leagues farther up the river, where he came upon a group of Indians. He approached them with presents and asked them whether they had gold and silver, but "they tolde him they had none as then: and that if he would send one of his men with them, they would bring him without danger into a place where they might have some." One of Ottigny's soldiers was willing to accompany the natives; when he returned, he spoke of a Chief Mayrra, "rich in Gold and Silver . . . and that for small quantitie of marchandise enough might he had of him." The soldier implored Ottigny to allow him to remain behind to find out more about the gold.

A fortnight later Captain Vasseur and Sergeant La Caille left Fort Caroline to look for this soldier. After two days' journey they came to the village of Chief Molloua, where they found their man laden "with five or sixe pounds weight of silver which he had trucked and traffiqued with Indians." Molloua feasted the French with bread and fish, and as time passed his tongue loosened and he became talkative. He told Vasseur and La Caille that he was but one of the forty vassals of the great Chief Holata Outina, whose mightiest enemy was Saturiba. This King had "under his obeyance thirtie other Paracoussies,"[20] and his main allies were Chiefs Potanou, Onatheaqua, and Oustaca, of whom Potanou was the most dangerous.

But what interested the Frenchmen more than the description of the chiefs was Molloua's talk of the gold and silver which could be found in the Apalatcy (Appalachian) Mountains. Vasseur and La Caille were so impressed by the tales of gold that they promised Molloua French help in subduing the inhabitants of these mountains.

That was how the French made alliances. Laudonnière had pledged his word to Saturiba, and now Vasseur and La Caille promised French assistance to Outina, Saturiba's greatest enemy!

In August, Saturiba sent his envoys to Laudonnière, reminding him of the pact whereby he was "friend to his friendes and enemie unto his enemies," and asking him to join with his harquebusiers in a war against Outina (see page 57). Laudonnière hedged. He used polite words. He told the envoys "that for this [Saturiba's] amitie I would not purchase the enmitie of the other, and that albeit I would, yet notwithstanding I wanted meanes to doe it."

Translated into simple words this meant: no help. Now that Laudonnière knew of the gold in

18. A soldier armed with a harquebus—or arquebus—the portable firearm of the 15th and 16th centuries. At first a harquebus was so heavy that it could be fired only from a support, but at the time of this narrative harquebuses were already made with a bent stock and a larger butt so that they could be fired from the shoulder.

19. This and the following quotations are from Laudonnière's narrative, Hakluyt (MacLehose, N. Y. 1905), IX, 19-34.

20. The title of the chief was *paracusi* or *paracoussy*, and when one referred to him as a war leader, one called him *urriparacusi, urri* or *iri* meaning war.

the Apalatcy Mountains, he could ill afford to go to war against Outina. He needed that chief's good will, as the only road to the Apalatcys—so Laudonnière thought—led through Outina's territory.

For Saturiba it was too late to postpone his war. His army was ready, his supplies assembled. He would march against Outina even without French help. He raided Outina's village, surprised the enemy, and "cut them all in pieces, except the women and little children."

When Laudonnière learned of Saturiba's victory and that the chief had captured and brought home with him a few of Outina's men, an idea came to him. To his unimaginative mind it seemed a stroke of genius. He would ask Saturiba for two of his prisoners, return them to Outina, and thus gain that chief as an ally.

What a naïve plan this was! Laudonnière did not hesitate to alienate Saturiba, who had helped him with food, even though he had not yet secured the friendship of Outina.

Laudonnière asked Saturiba for the prisoners. The enraged chief replied that he would not grant favors to one who had broken his oath to him. Laudonnière was deeply offended; he set out with twenty harquebusiers, and Saturiba, though "angry at the heart," was forced to surrender his prisoners.

On September 10 Captain Vasseur and Ensign Arlac, with ten harquebusiers, escorted the two men back to Outina's village. They were gratefully received by the chief, who shrewdly asked the French "to ayde and assist him in battaile against one of his enemies called Potanou, whereunto Monsieur de Arlac consented willingly." Arlac remained with half of his force to help Outina, while the other five soldiers, with Captain Vasseur, returned to Fort Caroline.

Outina assembled his force, went to war, and with the assistance of the French harquebusiers, who "slew many of his enemies," won a victory over Potanou (see page 61).

Discontent at Fort Caroline

With the approach of winter, life in Fort Caroline became harsh. Food was scarce; the men were put on half rations. Their work was strenuous, the surroundings bleak, and the newness and excitement of the strange country had worn thin. They complained of Laudonnière. They accused him of being tyrannical to the men; they held against him that he was under the influence of a few select officers. But their main grievance was that Laudonnière kept them from going in search of gold.

Most of them had come to the New World rather to seek for gold than—as future historians were to declare—to found a Protestant settlement. It was the hope of getting rich that made them ready to endure hardships. If it had been otherwise, they would surely at least have brought a minister with them.

One of the soldiers, a fellow named La Roquette, bragged "that hee was a great Magician, and that by the secrets of Art-magicke he had discovered a Mine of gold and silver farre up within the River,"[21] and he promised everyone who would come with him ten thousand crowns. The men believed this nonsense. They listened to De Gièvre,[22] another nobleman, who told them that as Laudonnière had made them work, instead of letting them discover the treasure, they should put the commander "out of the way and to choose another Captaine."

But in Laudonnière's presence the same De Gièvre professed loyalty and asked the commander in the name of the soldiers to "conduct them to the Countreys where the Mine was." Laudonnière refused until they should settle "the Fortresse in such estate, that those which were to stay at home behind should remaine in securitie against the Indians which might surprise them."

Then Laudonnière fell ill. The "loyal" De Gièvre incited the men to kill their commander, and when they hesitated, he approached the apothecary and tried to persuade him to put poison in Laudonnière's medicine. Failing in this effort, De Gièvre asked the apothecary for "a little Arsenike or quicke Silver," which he himself would put in the commander's drink. But as the apothecary refused to give the poison, De Gièvre had to think of other means to kill Laudonnière. His next plan was to hide a barrel of gunpowder under the commander's bed "and by a traine to set it on fire."

Had it not been for De Marrilac, a nobleman with a desire to return to France, Laudonnière would, indeed, have been blown to pieces. But in return for a passage home in one of the next ships, De Marrilac revealed the conspiracy.

21. This and following quotations are from Laudonnière's narrative, Hakluyt (MacLehose, N. Y., 1905), IX, 35-48.

22. In Laudonnière's narrative this nobleman is called Le Genre.

Already, two of Laudonnière's ships, the *Isabella* and the *Faulcon*, had returned to France. The third —the *Little Breton*—was still at anchor opposite the fort. And there was another small vessel besides in which Captain Bourdet[23] had come to Florida in September to visit the colonists. He stayed with Laudonnière for two months. On November 10 he was ready to leave for the return voyage. Laudonnière asked him "to carry home with him some sixe or seven Souldiers," the chief troublemakers among the colonists. The captain took with him the dissatisfied soldiers and in return left a few of his own sailors with Laudonnière. This exchange proved disastrous to the colony. Bourdet's men caused more trouble to Laudonnière than the soldiers whom he had sent back to France. They rallied the discontented element, and, three days after Bourdet left, two of them stole a bark, were joined by thirteen colonists, and sailed away. The deserters headed for the West Indies. Off the coast of Cuba they seized a Spanish treasure ship, and in it they sailed on. But while they were ashore searching for fresh water, their prisoner—the vessel's Spanish captain—escaped with the craft, reached Havana, where he sounded the alarm. The Spaniards captured the Frenchmen, questioned them, and from their answers learned the story of the French settlement in Florida.

This first desertion was followed by others. Two of Bourdet's Flemish carpenters stole another bark. Before they departed in it they "cut the cables of the Barke, and of the Shipboate, that it might goe away with the tyde," so that they could not be pursued. Now the settlers were without ships. Laudonnière ordered his men to build two new vessels— one thirty-five, the other thirty-six feet long. The boats were nearly completed, "when ambition and avarice, the mother of all mischiefe, tooke roote in the hearts of foure or five souldiers which could not away with the worke and paines taking." They told the others "that it was a vile thing for men of honest parentage, as they were, to moyle themselves thus with abject and base worke, seeing they had the best occasion of the worlde offered them to make themselves all riche." And they suggested that they only had "to arme the two Barkes which were in building, and to furnish them with good men: and then to saile unto Peru, and the other Isles of the Antilles, where every Souldier might easily enrich himselfe with tenne thousand Crownes."

The seeds of rebellion grew. Behind the chief spokesmen for the malcontents—De Fourneaux, Stephen of Genoa, and La Croix—sixty-six colonists rallied. They drew up a paper listing their grievances and demands, and on a Sunday morning La Caille read this to Laudonnière. The men asked the commander to allow them to sail to New Spain for supplies. Laudonnière, who "feared greatly, that under pretence of searching victuals, they would enterprise somewhat against the King of Spaines Subjects," refused their request. He would not disobey his Queen's instructions. For Catherine had warned him "very expressly, to doe no kind of wrong to the King of Spaines Subjects, nor any thing whereof he might conceive any jelousie." He did, however, tell the men that as soon as the two boats were ready, they could go and barter with the Indians for provisions (see page 46).

A week later Laudonnière fell sick again. The mutineers thought their time had come.[24] Late at night Fourneaux, followed by twenty harquebusiers, broke into Laudonnière's house and told the commander that the men "would goe to New Spaine to seeke their adventure." The soldiers seized the guns and ammunition and took the commander into custody. Laudonnière complains that "they layd hands on mee and carried mee very sicke, as I was, prisoner into a shippe which rode at ancker in the middest of the River." While Fourneaux was arresting Laudonnière, the other conspirators disarmed the loyal officers and soldiers. Now the fort was in the hands of the conspirators.

De Fourneaux concocted an order on parchment in which Laudonnière authorized his men to sail to New Spain for provisions. Laudonnière was asked to sign the paper. He was told—so he relates— "that if I made any difficulty they would all come and cut my throat in the shippe." Rather than this, he affixed his signature.

The conspirators then completed the two small vessels, took arms and ammunition aboard, compelled Captain Vasseur to deliver to them the flag of his ship, and forced Trenchant, "an honest and skilfull Pilot," and other loyal sailors to join them and navigate the vessels. They planned "to saile unto a place of the Antilles called Leauguave, be-

23. Probably a private adventurer who came to Florida in search of gold.

24. Le Moyne describes the conspiracy in detail (see pages 50-51).

longing unto the king of Spaine, and there to goe on land on Christmasse night, with intention to enter into the Church while the Masse was sayd after midnight, and to murder all those that they found there."

On December 8 they left the fort. As soon as they had gone, the loyal officers freed Laudonnière from the ship. The commander at once "ordained new Captaines to command the troops" and took the oath of the men that they would obey their officers' orders. With proud satisfaction Laudonnière notes: "After the departure of my mutinous companions I was as well obeyed as ever was Captaine in place where he commanded."

Making Friends and Enemies

The old year ran out; a new one came in. The Indians left for the forests; the colonists were without food. Now the French had to pay for their shortsighted policy. They had come to the New World for gold and treasures; they had come to conquer. They had neither sowed nor planted. They had relied on supplies from France, and when no relief came their colony faced starvation.

Their dealings with the natives had been unfortunate. They had driven the Indians, who at first had been so friendly toward them, into hostility.

Saturiba and his tribe withdrew from their neighborhood after the great storm in August. At that time lightning caused such a fire that more than five hundred acres of land were devastated and the dwellings of the Indians were burned down. Saturiba thought it was not the elements, but the French guns which had caused the holocaust, and he sent six of his men to Laudonnière asking him to cease cannonading his country. Laudonnière, instead of telling them the truth, strengthened the Indians in their belief in the destructive power of the French.

For Saturiba this was the end. He had had enough of Laudonnière's betrayals, enough of the man who had broken his oath as an ally, taken away his prisoners and sent them back to Outina, and who had now burned his village.

Saturiba was not the only chief to turn hostile toward the French. Potanou also hated them, for the harquebusiers had killed many of his subjects.

Wherever they went, the French aroused resentment. One of them, La Roche Ferrière, who journeyed as far as the Apalatcy Mountains, bartering and trading with the natives, carried himself with such an air that the natives called him "Thimogoa" (enemy). Another, Pierre Gambié, who had gone to live with Chief Adelano and had married the chief's daughter, was so harsh and despotic, that the natives murdered him (see page 119).

Having lost old friends, Laudonnière hoped to win new ones. As soon as the two barks were ready, Vasseur set out to visit Audusta. This generous chief gave the Frenchmen beans and other vegetables, besides stags, skins, and furs.

Then they visited the widow of Chief Hiouacara, who lived twelve leagues north from the fort. She was "the most beautiful of all the Indians . . . yea, and her subjects honour her so much, that almost continually they beare her on their shoulders, and will not suffer her to go on foot." She proved as goodhearted as she was beautiful and filled the French barks with food.

When hunger pinched again, Laudonnière sent his men to King Outina, whom he had helped to win victories over his enemies, yet this chief gave only a small amount of maize, and for it the French had to pay twice as much in merchandise as it was worth. Outina let Laudonnière know that if the French aided him in his war against Astina, they would find all the maize they needed in that chieftain's village. Laudonnière therefore sent out Ottigny and Vasseur with a few harquebusiers, but when the French soldiers reached Outina's place, they found that the chief had no desire to attack Astina, but wanted the French harquebusiers to wage war against his other enemies.

The Frenchmen, "almost dead for hunger," were infuriated by this deception, and when they returned to the fort, asked Laudonnière to "punish the boldnesse and maliciousnes of the Savages, which they could no longer endure" and "to take one of their kings prisoner." They reasoned that a captured chief could be exchanged for food. Laudonnière listened to the men's demand; he left the fort and captured Outina. He told the natives that their chief would be released if they would bring food to Fort Caroline.

The news of Outina's capture traveled throughout the land. All the chief's enemies sent envoys to Laudonnière asking him to kill Outina, and for this they were willing to give the Frenchmen food. "Subtill and craftie" Saturiba "sent twise seven or eight baskets of Maiz or of Mast," hoping that Laudonnière would hand Outina over to him; but when he found that the French commander could not be moved, he stopped sending food.

Laudonnière hoped that supplies from France would arrive by April, but May came, and as there was still no relief in sight, the colonists "fell into extreme want of victuals, constrained to eate the rootes of the earth and certaine sorrell which we found in the fields." They received some fish and a small amount of maize and beans from the Indians when they returned from the woods, without which they would have "perished with famine."

"This famine held us from the beginning of May until the middest of June. During which time the poore souldiers and handicraftsmen became as feeble as might be, and being not able to worke did nothing but goe one after another in Centinel unto the clift of an hill, situate very neere unto the Fort, to see if they might discover any French ship," writes Laudonnière.

The Indians, seeing the weakness of the colonists, sold their food for so "deere a price" that in a short time they had taken all the merchandise the French possessed. They approached close to the fort, bringing their fish in little boats, and bargaining so hard that often the soldiers had "to give away the very shirts from their backs to get one fish." And when they complained about the excessive price, the Indians replied, "If thou make so great account of thy marchandise, eat it, and we will eat our fish."

The Conspirators Return to the Fort

On the twenty-fifth of May an Indian came into the fort with a message from Chief Patica, who "had descried a shippe upon the coast." The colonists rushed to the shores in excited expectation, hoping to greet the long-awaited supply ship from France. But when they reached the water's edge they found, not the supply ship, but a Spanish brigantine, and the vessel held, not food, but the conspirators who had left the fort in December.

The deserters were brought into the fort, where they told their story. It was the usual tale of piracy. Sailing along the coast of Cuba, they had captured a brigantine. Later, at Baracou, they had taken an eighty-ton caravel, and at Cape Tiburon still another vessel, "with great store of riches, aswell of golde and silver as of merchandise and wine," and carrying the Governor of Jamaica.[25]

Yet they had been "determined to seeke more." Returning to Jamaica to exchange the Governor for ransom, fate had overtaken them. The Governor had sent his sons with a letter to his wife "to advertise her that she should make provisions of victuals to send unto him." But he also "spake unto the boyes secretly that with all diligence she should send the vessels that were in the havens neere that place to succour and rescue him."

The next morning, three Spanish sloops blocked the path of the conspirators. There was no way of escape for them. The large prize, with thirty-three Frenchmen, was forced to surrender, and soon the Spaniards had killed every one of the thirty-three.

The twenty-six men in the brigantine had seen the approaching Spanish ships. They quickly cut the cables and sailed away. With them was the pilot Trenchant, who, with other loyal sailors, had been forced to join the rebels; while the others slept, he steered the brigantine back to Fort Caroline.

Laudonnière put the four leaders[26] of the conspiracy into fetters. They were to die on the gallows "to serve for an example to the rest."

One of them protested. It was shameful to die on the gallows, he cried. Laudonnière's men agreed with him and asked the commander not to hang them, "but rather let them be shot thorow, & then afterward . . . their bodies might be hanged upon certain gibbets along the havens mouth."

This was done.

Famine

The famine in the fort continued. Laudonnière writes that one of the soldiers "gathered up among the filth of my house, all the fish bones that he could finde, which he dried and beate into powder to make bread thereof."[27]

"The effects of this hideous famine appeared incontinently among us, for our bones eftsoones beganne to cleave so neere unto the skinne, that the most part of the souldiers had their skinnes peirced thorow with them in many partes of their bodies."

25. Le Moyne says it was the Governor of Havana.
26. De Fourneaux, Stephen of Genoa, Le Croix, and Seignore.

27. This quotation and those following are from Laudonnière's narrative, Hakluyt (MacLehose, N. Y., 1905), IX, 66-80.

In desperation the men raided the Indians' fields. They found ripe maize in Enecaque. When they brought the maize to the fort, the men ate it in such haste that they "fell sicke with eating more of it then their weakened stomackes could digest."

Outina, seeing the Frenchmen's plight, asked Laudonnière to take him back to his village and exchange him for ripe maize and beans. Laudonnière set out with the chief, but the natives drove such a hard bargain that the negotiations failed. A fortnight later Laudonnière once more rowed up the river with his prisoner. This time the natives seemed more willing. For four days the bargaining went on. At last the French received the maize but when they carried it to the ships, the natives ambushed them. The fighting over, only "two men's burdens" of maize was left to Laudonnière.

In Fort Caroline the colonists watched with anxious eyes the progress of their new boat. They had had enough of the New World. They wished to return to France. But the chief carpenter now told Laudonnière that he would not be able to finish the vessel by August, as he had promised, since two of his men had been slain by the Indians. This "caused such a mutinie among the souldiers that very hardly he escaped killing." Laudonnière "appeased them." He said that all work on the new ship was to cease, and instead of building a new one the carpenters were to repair and enlarge the brigantine which the conspirators had brought back from Spain. The soldiers demolished the dwellings and dismantled the palisades, since all lumber was needed for the rebuilding of the brigantine.

Hawkins Arrives

On the third of August the dejected Laudonnière walked up the little hill overlooking the sea. How often had he scanned the horizon for sails! This time they were really there. He saw four sails on the water, coming nearer and nearer to the coast.

The ships cast anchor. They carried the English flag; they were under the command of John Hawkins and had come to the coast in search of water.

The next day Hawkins came ashore to visit Laudonnière. The old slave trader was in a generous mood. He asked the French to sail home with him. Laudonnière was hesitant to accept the offer, for he "knewe not how the case stood betweene the French and the English: and although hee promised me on his faith to put mee on land in France, before hee would touch in England, yet I stood in doubt least he would attempt somewhat in Florida in the name of his mistresse."

The French soldiers were of another opinion. Hearing that their commander had rejected Hawkins's offer, "there arose a great mutinie." They demanded that Laudonnière accept his aid.

Laudonnière asked Hawkins for a vessel, for which he wanted to pay in merchandise and silver. Hawkins was ready to make the bargain, but Laudonnière's officers advised the commander to keep the silver, "for feare lest the Queene of England seeing the same, should the rather bee encouraged to set footing there, as before she had desired." They suggested that they take the silver to France "to give encouragement unto our Princes not to leave off an enterprise of so great importance for our commonwealth," and pay Hawkins instead with artillery, "which otherwise we should be constrained to leave behind us."

Laudonnière went to see Hawkins on his ship to make the deal. He took with him a few of his officers, "all men of experience in such affaires and knowing sufficiently how to drive such a bargaine." There was no need for bargaining. John Hawkins asked only seven hundred crowns for the vessel which he would leave to the French, and it was agreed that the price could be paid in guns and gunpowder.

The English commander, "moved with pitie," gave the French food, beans, salt, and wax "to make candels," and presented them with fifty pairs of shoes, which were needed badly. For all these goods Laudonnière handed a note to Hawkins. The note was not of much value. Years later Laudonnière wrote that "untill this present I am indebted to him."

When Hawkins's fleet departed, the French busied themselves with preparations; they baked ship's biscuits and filled the casks with fresh water. On the second of August they were ready to leave, but they had to wait for a favorable wind. And when the wind came and the tide was right and they were in the act of hoisting sail to leave Fort Caroline forever, they saw seven sails approaching the shore.

The ships they now saw were under the command of Jean Ribaut, bringing the long-awaited relief. When Ribaut landed, he delivered a letter from Admiral Coligny to Laudonnière. It was couched politely, but it was firm. Laudonnière was asked to relinquish his command to Ribaut and return to France. Laudonnière was stunned. Why should he be recalled? Ribaut told him that the men who had returned to France were full of complaints and that the ships which Laudonnière had sent home had brought many dissatisfied letters to the admiral. The charges against Laudonnière were manifold. Some said that he was quick "to play the tyrant" and that he "was too cruell unto the men." It was said that he "sought to be advanced by other meanes then by My Lord Admirall" and that he "had written to many Lords of the Court, which" he "ought not to have done." And Admiral Coligny "took it very evill" that he "had carried a woman with him."[28]

Laudonnière denied all these accusations. He told Ribaut that the rumors about the woman were malicious, for she was only "a poore chambermayd," who had looked after his household and helped the soldiers when they fell sick, and he added that "all my men thought so well of her, that at one instant there were sixe or seven which did demand her of me in marriage." As to the other charges, he asserted that he had had to rule with an iron hand and enforce authority, even if his orders seemed harsh in French. But he had had no underhanded dealings with the Lords of the Council, nor had he been disloyal to Admiral Coligny.

Ribaut was easily convinced that Laudonnière was unjustly accused, and he asked him to remain with the colony and share the command. Laudonnière was willing to stay, but as to the command—it was Ribaut's.

After this, Laudonnière fell "into a melancholy" and stayed in bed for nine days.

Diplomatic Interlude

Ribaut's departure for Florida caused great excitement in Spain. Alava, the Spanish ambassador at the French Court (who had succeeded Chantone), reported to Philip II a month before Ribaut left Dieppe, that the pirates of Normandy and Brittany "were so ravenous in their greed for the Indian fleets that they threatened to create graver complications than those involved in the mere question of the title to Florida, which might even lead to a war between the two nations."[29]

The Spanish diplomats feared that once the French secured a foothold on the Florida coast, they could not only threaten Spanish shipping in the Bahama Channel but also in the event of war easily rob and plunder Cuba, Hispanola, Jamaica, and other Spanish possessions. "Act promptly, before the Admiral of France can forestall you," Ambassador Noriega urged the King,[30] "and seeing that they are Lutherans, it is not needful to leave a man alive, but to inflict an exemplary punishment, that they may remember it forever."

Philip hesitated. He asked the Duke of Alba for advice. The Duke's proposal was this: to dispatch a fleet to Florida and chase the French out of the country. But, to justify this warlike act between two countries at peace, the Council of the Indies was to issue a declaration, explaining to the world why Philip had the right to exclude the French from Florida. Yet this was only one of Alba's suggestions. The other was to settle the controversy peacefully through diplomatic negotiations. He advised Philip II to send the Spanish ambassador to the Queen Mother and demand that she recall the French ships and promise not to send more reinforcements to Florida. If Catherine refused to give a satisfactory answer, a member of the council was to be sent to France, thus giving more emphasis to Spain's determination.

Philip followed Alba's advice to the letter. By then he had already chosen the man to go to Florida to hold that land for the Spanish Crown. It was forty-seven-year-old Pedro Menéndez de Avilés, a brave and experienced seaman and a proven servant of his King. On March 20, 1565, an *asiento* was drawn up between Philip II and Menéndez.[31]

28. This quotation and those following are from Laudonnière's narrative, Hakluyt (MacLehose, N. Y., 1905), IX, 86-89.

29. Alava to Philip II, May 7, 1565, MS Arch. Nat., Paris, K, 1503 (88).

30. Noriega to Philip, March 29, 1565.

31. The *asiento* set forth in great detail the duties of Menéndez. He was to equip six sloops of 50 tons each and four smaller vessels. He was to take with him 500 men. Of these, 100 were to be soldiers, and 100 sailors; the rest were to be artisans, laborers, and farmers, yet they must know how to handle arms. Twelve members of the Society of Jesus and twelve monks of other orders were to be on board as well. He had to transport five hundred negro slaves from Spain, Portugal, the Cape de Verde Islands, or Guinea, and one-third of these were to be women. But no heretics or Jews, Moors, or Marranos were to be taken on the voyage.

As to animals, 100 pigs, 400 lambs, and some goats were to be carried.

Menéndez was to investigate the gulf coast of the peninsula, to sail from the Florida Keys as far north as Newfoundland, and to report on the ports, currents, rocks, shoals, and bays. And he was to find out "if in the said coast or land there were settlers or corsairs of other nations whatsoever not subject to

On May 5 the Council of the Indies proclaimed that Philip II was the rightful ruler of Florida, as that country had been given to him by "the bull of Pope Alexander, to whom, as Vicar of Our Saviour, it pertains to procure the conversion of all the heathen to his Holy Catholic Faith, and [who] to this end could appoint a Supreme Christian Prince over all the native Kings and Lords of all the Indies." Thus the Pope granted the Spanish King "the Lordship over all that had been or should be discovered within the limits set forth in the said bull, within which is the said Florida, and for the same reason he prohibited and was able to prohibit, under the penalties therein contained, that any other should enter them."

Furthermore, the council suggested sending a fleet, "because as the port of the French is in the Channel of Bahama, which is the passage of the Indies, it is of great importance to the service of Your Majesty to drive that people out from there."[32]

While Menéndez was preparing his fleet, Philip was engaged in giving instructions to Alava. The ambassador was to see the Queen Mother and protest to her about the occupation of a province to which the French had no right. He was to tell Catherine that "if we have dissimulated until now in urging her, or impressing matters concerning other vessels which we have heard have gone to Florida, it has been because we believed that they were corsairs, and went to rob without the orders or command of either herself or the King, her son; and that I had given orders that such should be chastised, as it is reasonable that infractors of the public peace should be, who undertake such enterprises without the order and command of their King."[33]

Philip II let his ambassador know that if Ribaut's ships had already left France, he was to remain silent. Why complain, without hope of success, when Spanish arms in Florida could settle the controversy far more effectively?

Philip's attitude was firm over the Florida issue, yet he was careful not to drive Catherine into a hostile attitude. The Bayonne Conference was to begin in a few days. Isabella[34] and the Duke of Alba were making the final preparations for the journey. They were going as Philip's envoys to confer with Catherine on a far weightier matter than Florida—the extermination of the heretics in the two countries.

As Ribaut's fleet had already sailed, Alava remained silent.

The news of Ribaut's departure reached the Spanish King after his wife and the Duke of Alba had left for Bayonne. He sent a letter after the Duke, telling him that Ribaut had left France and leaving it to his discretion to handle the issue with the French Queen.

Alba, too, chose to remain silent. He wrote to Philip on June 28 from Bayonne, explaining why he had not talked about the Florida matter to Catherine. He feared that some of the Queen's councilors "might turn against the Catholics and say to the latter: 'Since Your Majesty was somewhat offended at this, what confidence could they have that you would assist them in graver matters?' "[35]

The day after Alba wrote the letter to his King, the Spanish fleet under the command of Menéndez set sail from Cadiz. Now it was important for Spain to keep complete silence until the ships arrived in the New World. For three months neither Philip nor his ambassadors mentioned Florida. But toward the end of September, when the King was certain that Ribaut had reached the New World and that it would be too late for the French to warn him or to send assistance, Philip II wrote to his ambassador in France: "It is now my wish that you speak to the Queen Mother and say to her, that having understood that some of her subjects had gone to Florida to usurp that province, which we had discovered and possessed for so many years, I have given orders to send and chastise them as thieving pirates and perturbers of the public peace. And having made this provision I had thought to have done with it, but that the brotherly relations which I have had

Us," and if there were, he was "to drive them out by what means you see fit."

The voyage was to be made at Menéndez' own expense, though he was to receive a loan of 15,000 ducats from the King for the outfitting of his fleet. Yet, if his expedition was successful, he would be rewarded with great returns. A land grant twenty-five leagues square, two thousand ducats from the rents and products of the country, the possession of two fisheries, and permission to trade with the West Indian Islands free of duty for a certain period were some of the privileges which were granted to him under the *asiento*.

32. MS Direc. de Hidrog., Madrid, *Col. Navarrete*, XIV, Doc. 35.

33. Philip II to Alava, June 2, 1565, MS Arch. Nat., Paris, K, 1504 (2).

34. Philip's wife and Catherine's daughter.

35. Alba to Philip II, June 28, 1565, MS Arch. Nat., Paris, K, 1504 (30).

with the Most Christian King, the frankness and sincerity that should be observed with him and with her in all matters, have induced me not to conceal this from them."[36]

The ambassador was instructed to demand the withdrawal of the French subjects from Florida "for it is not becoming what with the love, conformity, and brotherly relations existing between the Most Christian King and myself, here, that our subjects yonder should go warring the one against the other. And you are to press the Queen strongly in regard to this, not with entreaties, but by showing her that it is a matter which should not and cannot be concealed, and you are to inform me what answer she gives you."

Alava delivered his master's message to Catherine on November 23. By that time Philip had already had a report of the arrival of Menéndez in Florida.

Before Catherine saw Alava she had been warned by Baron Fourquevaux, her ambassador at the court of Philip II: "I have learned from the Queen, your daughter, that which I wrote you concerning Florida in my other letter, how that this King will not suffer that the French nestle so near his conquests, so that his fleets in going and coming from New Spain are constrained to pass in front of them. For which reason if they go from France to said country, it is well for them to go with sufficient strength and equipped for defense."[37]

Fourquevaux further advised Catherine "neither to acknowledge nor disavow your subjects who are there or who may go thither, for before the conquest be decided time will pass, the which may bring this Majesty and the Germans into such difficulties, that he will abandon the said quarrel, or let it sleep."

Thus, Catherine was well prepared when the Spanish ambassador went to see her. What took place at that interview is best described in Alava's own words, for the Spanish ambassador reported in great detail to Philip his talk with the Queen Mother. He wrote that he was received by Charles IX and that the young King took him by the hand and conducted him to his mother's chambers, where he found Catherine surrounded by heretics and Catholics and many people. "She received me with the same demonstrations with which her son had received me, but not wishing to give me a private audience, saw me there, in public, drawing her son very close to her and causing me to draw near also. I began to repeat the subjects of Your Majesty's letter, when I had so severe a chill that I had to take out the paper I carried with me and begin to read it. I was as little able to do that, and finally they called L'Aubespine,[38] but not finding him, Saint Sulpice[39] had to read it. The Queen held her head so that the company could not well see her face and assumed a very melancholy expression until the subject of the Imperial alliances was reached, when she lighted up a little and said that it seemed well to her. We then began upon the matter of Florida, upon which Saint Sulpice attempted to comment before she answered. I observed that I had come to converse with them and hoped they would be contented with Saint Sulpice's reading of the paper, and so they dismissed him. The Queen would not allow me to say a word on the subject, at one moment telling me 'The subjects of my son are going only to a mountainous region called Hercules discovered by the French crown over two hundred years ago.' I turned to the King and began to enlarge upon the matter with the urgency which Your Majesty had directed me to use. The Queen's eyes kindled and she poised herself like a lioness to hear what I was saying to her son. I said in substance that it was a business of great consequence and that he should beseech his mother to weigh it well. At this she grew angry with me, and to tell Your Majesty the truth, I did the same with her, for she would not answer to the point and feigned wonder at everything I said. At last, closing her eyes, she exclaimed that for the life of her she understood nothing of this matter. By this Your Majesty can see with what sincerity she deals."[40]

A week after this interview Burdin, the King's secretary, handed Alava the official reply of the French crown. It was a typical diplomatic document, full of double meanings. While on the one hand, the answer read, it was not the French King's will and intention to allow his subjects to occupy

36. Philip II to Alava, Sept. 30, 1565, MS Arch. Nat., Paris, K, 1504 (66).

37. Fourquevaux to the Queen, Nov. 3, 1565, *Dépêches*, p. 6.

38. Claude de l'Aubespine, Secretary of State under Francis I, Henry II, Francis II, and Charles IX.

39. Jean d'Ebrard de Saint Sulpice, former French ambassador to Spain.

40. Alava to Philip II, Nov. 29, 1565, MS Arch. Nat., Paris, K, 1504 (80).

lands discovered by Spain, on the other hand France would not restrict its subjects from traveling to places that Spain had neither discovered nor taken possession of. Then, too, the country to which the Frenchmen had sailed had been discovered by none other than the French and named by them *La Tierra de los Bretones*. Yet, if French subjects transgressed on Spanish land and hindered Spanish shipping, they would receive punishment.

Alava read the reply, and his face flushed. Angrily he turned to Burdin. "Why do you want us to talk this nonsense? Whether you call it the Land of the Bretons or the Mountains of Hercules, as the Queen does, the province where the vassals of your King are going is the same which we call Florida and you New France, to which it is requested that none of the subjects of your master go."

"The French discovered the Land of the Bretons a hundred years ago, as can be seen by the maps of the newly discovered provinces," answered Burdin.

With that the argument ended.

Alava's interview with the Queen Mother shows how cleverly Catherine handled the controversy. She followed Fourquevaux's advice, evaded the real issue, and turned the Spanish complaints into a discussion on geographical boundaries.

The question now was: Where did the Land of the Bretons begin and where did it end? The southern boundaries of that country were as vague as the northern boundaries of Philip's Florida. Philip claimed the right to the whole continent to the north, and Catherine thought that by the same reckoning she could claim to be the rightful ruler of the continent to the south.

It is likely that Catherine did not know the great distance which separated the Land of the Bretons from the Florida Peninsula.

Menéndez Reaches Florida

But we are ahead of events. At the time of Alava's interview with Catherine—though neither of them then knew it—there were no more French subjects in Florida.

Let us return to Fort Caroline, which we left after Ribaut had arrived there: the colonists still engaged in bringing the supplies ashore; Laudonnière still sick in bed. The mood of the colony had changed. The men now had fresh hopes, they dreamed of gold again; with food in their stomachs, the future looked rosy.

But these peaceful days were soon over. Ribaut landed at Fort Caroline on August 28. A week later—on September 4—Menéndez' fleet found the French vessels.

The Spanish flagship drew alongside Ribaut's *Trinity*. A trumpet sounded from the *San Pelayo*, and a trumpet replied from the French flagship. Menéndez called to the French boat:

"Gentlemen, whence does this fleet come?"

"From France," a voice answered.

"What are you doing here?"

"Bringing infantry, artillery, and supplies for the fort which the King of France owns in this country and for the others which he is going to build."

"Are you Catholics or Lutherans?"

"Lutherans, and our general is Jean Ribaut."

Then the French voice began to question, and Menéndez replied:

"My name is Pedro Menéndez de Avilés; and this is the Armada of the King of Spain, who has sent me to this coast and country to burn and hang the Lutheran French who would be found there, and in the morning I shall board your ships."

A French soldier shouted: "If you are a brave man, don't wait until morning. Come on now—and you will see what we will do to you!"

Silence descended; a frightening silence.

"A stillness such as I never heard since I came to the world," says the chaplain of the Spanish fleet. Then pandemonium broke loose. Abuses, threats, foul words, obscenities flew from boat to boat.

The Spanish soldiers drew their swords, ready to jump aboard the French ships. The Spanish flagship moved nearer the *Trinity*. At that moment the cable of the *San Pelayo* caught in the capstan. Menéndez hurried down from the bridge, urging on his men to free it.

While every hand aboard the Spanish boat worked feverishly, the French "cut their cables, left their ankers, and set saile." At last the *San Pelayo* was free, and Menéndez set out after the French flagship.[41] The chase continued through the night. But the French ship had more speed. At dawn Menéndez gave up the pursuit and returned to the

41. The *Trinity* and two other French vessels turned north, pursued by the *San Pelayo* and a small patache. The fourth French ship, the *Emérillon,* turned south and was chased by three smaller Spanish boats under the command of Valdes.

From the *Pageant of America*, Copyright Yale University Press

THE EARLIEST VIEW OF ST. AUGUSTINE

From the original Mestas map in the *Archives of the Indies,* Seville. The map is dated 1595, but later research found ample evidence that it might have been drawn thirty years earlier.

In the lower left is the alarm bell hanging on a pole. Beyond it and the small protecting fort is the church building with its strange tower of chimes. Next to the church, towards the right, is the Governor's house. In the center are the fortifications; in the background the cultivated fields.

River of May to land his troops and build a fort.

When he arrived there, he saw three French boats in the river and two companies of French harquebusiers waiting for him on land. Menéndez had no desire to fight—yet. He sailed southward and cast anchor at the inlet which Laudonnière named the River of Dolphins. Here he found three of his other ships with the troops already on land and the ammunition in safety. Menéndez sent his men ashore, and they at once began to dig ditches, to throw up a breastwork of earth, to fortify a large Indian dwelling, and to build houses. Thus, St. Augustine, oldest city in the United States, was born.

The Spanish commander hastened the unloading of his supplies. Two French vessels had appeared soon after his landing, but had sailed away again. Would they return? In two days most of the supplies were on land. What was still in the holds of the ships remained there, for Menéndez ordered the *San Pelayo*[42] and the *San Salvador* to sail for Hispanola.

A few days after his vessels had left, Menéndez wrote to his King: "It will be desirable that Your Majesty give orders that I be provided with a year's supply of corn for each horse which I shall bring to these provinces. . . . And for the future, in the course of a year I will give orders to sow and plant corn so that they shall have provender here; for by no means would it do to take it from the Indians, in order not to make enemies of them; on the contrary, it will be advisable for us to feed those who have none, in order to win their love and friendship. Let Your Majesty rest assured that if I had a million more or less, I would spend it all upon this undertaking, because it is of such great service to God Our Lord, and for the increase of our Holy Catholic Faith and the service of Your Majesty. And therefore I have offered to Our Lord, that all that I shall find, win, and acquire in this world shall be for the planting of the Gospel in this land, and the enlightenment of its natives, and thus I pledge myself to Your Majesty."[43]

Ribaut Sails against the Spanish Fleet

After the chase, the French ships returned to Fort Caroline. Ribaut and his captains held council by the bedside of the sick Laudonnière. Ribaut suggested an immediate attack upon the Spanish fleet. Laudonnière advised caution; he feared that the storms so prevalent in that month might drive the French ships out to sea and that Fort Caroline would be left without defense.

But Ribaut's mind was set. He expected that Menéndez would attack Fort Caroline by land; he therefore planned to destroy the Spanish fleet while Menéndez and his soldiers were fighting for the fort. Taking with him his best soldiers, Ribaut set out with four large vessels and eight pinnaces.

"The very day that he departed, which was the tenth of September," writes Laudonnière, "there rose so great a tempest accompanied with such stormes, that the Indians themselves assured me that it was the worst weather that ever was seene on the coast."[44]

Laudonnière ordered his ill-assorted and inexperienced men to strengthen the fortifications; he "gave them to understand the necessity and inconveniences whereinto we were like to fall, aswel by the absence of our ships, as by the neereness of the Spanyards, at whose hands we could looke for no lesse than an open and sufficient proclamed war, seeing they had taken land and fortified themselves so neere unto us."

Tensely the small garrison waited. Sentinels scanned the horizon; they vigilantly watched the woods. Fog descended. Rain poured down in torrents. Night followed day, and day followed night —in all ten days had passed since Ribaut's departure. And still there was no news of him. Had he taken the Spanish fleet, or was he lost?

The Capture of Fort Caroline

When Ribaut's ships reached St. Augustine, the *San Pelayo* and the *San Salvador* had already left their anchorage. The French boats set out after them, but the Spanish ships were well away, and they soon gave up the chase. Ribaut decided to turn back, sail to St. Augustine, attack and destroy the fort. But as he approached the shore, the breeze rose to a gale, the gale to a hurricane, and his fleet was swept out to sea.

Menéndez saw the French boats carried away in the storm. He realized that Ribaut and his force could not turn back, for the wind was against them. Now was the time to attack the French fort.

On September 17 Menéndez set out from St. Augustine with five hundred soldiers. The troops waded through swamps in pouring rain, the water never lower than their knees. They blazed a path through the forest. They swam through creeks and streams.

"The rains continued as constant and heavy as if the world was again to be overwhelmed with a flood." Still the soldiers went on, marching by day, camping at night. On the third day they halted in a marshy pine grove, standing up to their waists in the muddy rain water, a quarter of a mile from Fort Caroline.

Within the fort the French were ignorant of

42. On board the *San Pelayo* were twenty-five heretics who were discovered among the crew after the Spanish fleet left Cadiz. They were to be sent to Spain. The twenty-five Lutherans knew how little their lives would be worth after they reached Spanish territory. Their only hope was to act while still at sea. They therefore killed the captain, the master, and all Catholics on board the flagship, and then crossed the ocean, reaching the coast of Denmark, where the *San Pelayo* was wrecked. Yet all of the Lutherans escaped unharmed.

43. Menéndez to Philip II, Sept. 11, 1565.

44. This quotation and those following are from Laudonnière's narrative, Hakluyt (MacLehose, N. Y., 1905), IX, 92-94.

their danger. "The night between the nineteenth and twentieth of September La Vigne kept watch with his company, wherein he used all endeavor, although it rayned without ceasing. When the day was therefore come, and that hee saw that it rayned still worse then it did before, hee pitied the Centinels so too moyled and wette; and thinking the Spanyardes woulde not have come in such a strange time, hee let them depart, and to say the trueth, hee went himselfe unto his lodging."

It was at that very hour that Menéndez called his captains to attack. Ahead of the troops went Jean François, one of the French deserters who had been captured by the Spaniards in Cuba. His hands were tied, and the end of the rope was held by Menéndez.

When day broke, the Spaniards saw Fort Caroline. Two of them pushed forward.

The French sentinel shouted: "Who goes there?"

"Frenchmen," answered the Spaniards. The sentinel spoke no more. A knife silenced him.

Menéndez gave the battle cry, "Santiago, at them! God help us! Victory!"

And the Spanish soldiers rushed toward the fort.

The trumpeters inside Fort Caroline sounded the alarm. The French came running from their quarters in the heavy rain, rising straight from their beds. Laudonnière, in a nightshirt, tried to rally his men. It was too late. The battle was over in less than an hour. Spanish flags flew over Fort Caroline. The attackers had not lost a single man, but of the 240 Frenchmen, 132 were killed.

Laudonnière escaped through the western breach in the fort, while others jumped the ditch, seeking refuge in the woods.

Outside the fort the *Pearl* and another French vessel were still at anchor; the smaller French boats were waiting farther down the river. Menéndez sent an envoy to the *Pearl*, demanding surrender. The renegade Jean François translated Menéndez' demands. He told Jacques Ribaut[45] that if he would surrender the French ships, a boat would be given to him and he would be allowed to sail with the surviving women and children to France. Jacques Ribaut refused. When the Spanish soldiers on the shore heard of Ribaut's refusal, they tore out the eyes of the French whom they had killed in the fort, and, amidst cursing and shouting, hurled them into the *Pearl*.

Then the guns of the fort were turned against the vessels. A shot sank the smaller one. Jacques Ribaut rescued its men and took his own ship down the river, where he joined the other French boats.

Menéndez wanted to return to St. Augustine at once. He feared that Ribaut would attack the fort and destroy it while he was in Fort Caroline. He called his troops together ready for an immediate march. But the exhausted soldiers demurred. They had not slept for days. They wanted rest. The order had to be changed.

And while in the fort out of a hundred Spanish mouths and noses the snores soared toward Heaven, finally acclaiming victory, in the woods the French fugitives were seeking safety. Laudonnière met a few of his soldiers who were heading toward an Indian village. Later he found the artist Le Moyne and four others wandering in the forest.

Le Moyne parted from his companions and went on alone, searching for the French boats. He came upon the tailor Grandchemin, and together they waded through swamps and morasses. But the exhausted Grandchemin could not endure it any longer. He would return to the fort and surrender. All Le Moyne's pleadings were of no avail. Grandchemin walked up to the Spanish sentinels, fell on his knees, and begged for his life. And the Spaniards "hacked him to pieces and carried off the dismembered fragments of his body on their spears and pikes" (see page 76).

Le Moyne, who witnessed his friend's end, turned back into the woods. He found Laudonnière and other fugitives, and together they walked onward until they found the French ships.

The two captains—Jacques Ribaut of the *Pearl* and Vivien Maillard of the *Levrière*—were for an immediate return to France. They gave orders to sink the smaller vessels, since there were not enough sailors to navigate them. This done, on September 25 the two larger ships weighed anchor. The *Pearl*, with Le Challeux and other fugitives on board, eventually reached France, while the *Levrière*, with Laudonnière and Le Moyne among the passengers, was swept to England and landed in Swansea Bay in South Wales on the eleventh of October.[46]

45. Jean Ribaut's son, the captain of the *Pearl*.
46. Laudonnière stayed in England until the beginning of the following year. Then he returned to France, presented himself at the Court, and wrote his book.

Ribaut's Fleet Destroyed

The Spaniards who had remained in St. Augustine passed anxious days. There were only a hundred of them—not enough to give battle if Ribaut should attack their fort. They scanned the sea and prayed to the Almighty to keep the French fleet away.

One morning they found a Frenchman wandering on the beach. He told the Spaniards that he was from one of Ribaut's ships and that his vessel had been wrecked in the storm; five of the crew had been drowned, and others clubbed to death by the natives.

The Spaniards sent out a party to float the French boat off the rocks and bring it to St. Augustine. Soon after they returned with the vessel, a Spanish soldier came running into the fort with the news "The French harbor is ours." And in the evening Menéndez himself arrived with fifty of his men. The Spaniards rejoiced. Fort Caroline was theirs; St. Augustine was theirs—and of Ribaut and his fleet there was no sign.

Four days later—on August 28—Indians came to St. Augustine with the report that they had seen a number of French soldiers about six miles from the fort. Menéndez set out immediately with a small force to meet them.

He found 250 Frenchmen trapped on the shores of an inlet; their boat must have been wrecked farther down the shore, and they were marching towards Fort Caroline, but without boats they could not cross the water. When they saw the Spaniards, one of them swam across the lagoon and asked Menéndez for a boat in which they could return to Fort Caroline. Menéndez gave him a short answer. He told the dripping Frenchman that he had captured the fort and killed all its defenders.

With this sad news the sailor swam back to his comrades; soon he returned, asking safe conduct for his captain and other officers who desired to negotiate with the Spanish commander. A boat was sent for them, and when they came, Menéndez repeated that he had taken Fort Caroline and that "all in it are put to the sword." To convince the men that he was speaking the truth, Menéndez showed them the spoils he had taken from the fort and allowed them to speak to his French prisoners, who, in their own language, told their shipwrecked comrades what had happened.

Now that Fort Caroline was in Spanish hands, the French had only one resort; they asked Menéndez to give them a boat so that they could return to France. Menéndez replied that he would gladly have supplied them with a boat if he had had one and if they had been Catholics, but that since he had no ships to spare and they were Lutherans, they would have to give up their arms and banners and surrender.

"All Catholics," he told them, "I will befriend; but as you are of the new sect, I hold you as enemies and wage deadly war against you; this I will do with all cruelty in this country where I command as viceroy and captain-general for my King." Menéndez told them that he had come to Florida to plant the Holy Gospel there and "that the Indians may be enlightened and come to the knowledge of the Holy Catholic faith and of our Lord, Jesus Christ, as the Roman Church teaches it." And he continued "If you will give up your arms and banners and place yourself at my mercy, you may do so, and I will act towards you as our Lord may command me."[47]

The French officers returned to their companions. For two hours they deliberated. Then one of them crossed the lagoon again, saying that they were ready to surrender. He offered Menéndez fifty thousand ducats if he would spare their lives. Menéndez was not in the mood to take a bribe.

What happened after this Menéndez reported to his King in one terse sentence: "They came and surrendered their arms to me, and I had their hands tied behind them, and put them all excepting ten to the knife."

But the Spanish chroniclers—Solis de Merás and Mendoza—had more to tell. From their stories the bloody tale emerges. After the French were ready to surrender, Menéndez ordered them to load their banners, harquebuses, pistols, swords, and powder into a Spanish rowboat. The arms were taken to the shore; then twenty Spanish soldiers rowed the boat back to the trapped Frenchmen. They took ten of them into the boat and rowed them across the lagoon. Then they returned, taking another ten—never more at one time. As each group reached the shore Menéndez spoke to them:

"Gentlemen, I have but a few soldiers with me, and you are many, and it would be an easy matter

47. Menéndez to Philip II, Oct. 15, 1565. See Ruidíaz, *La Florida*, p. 89.

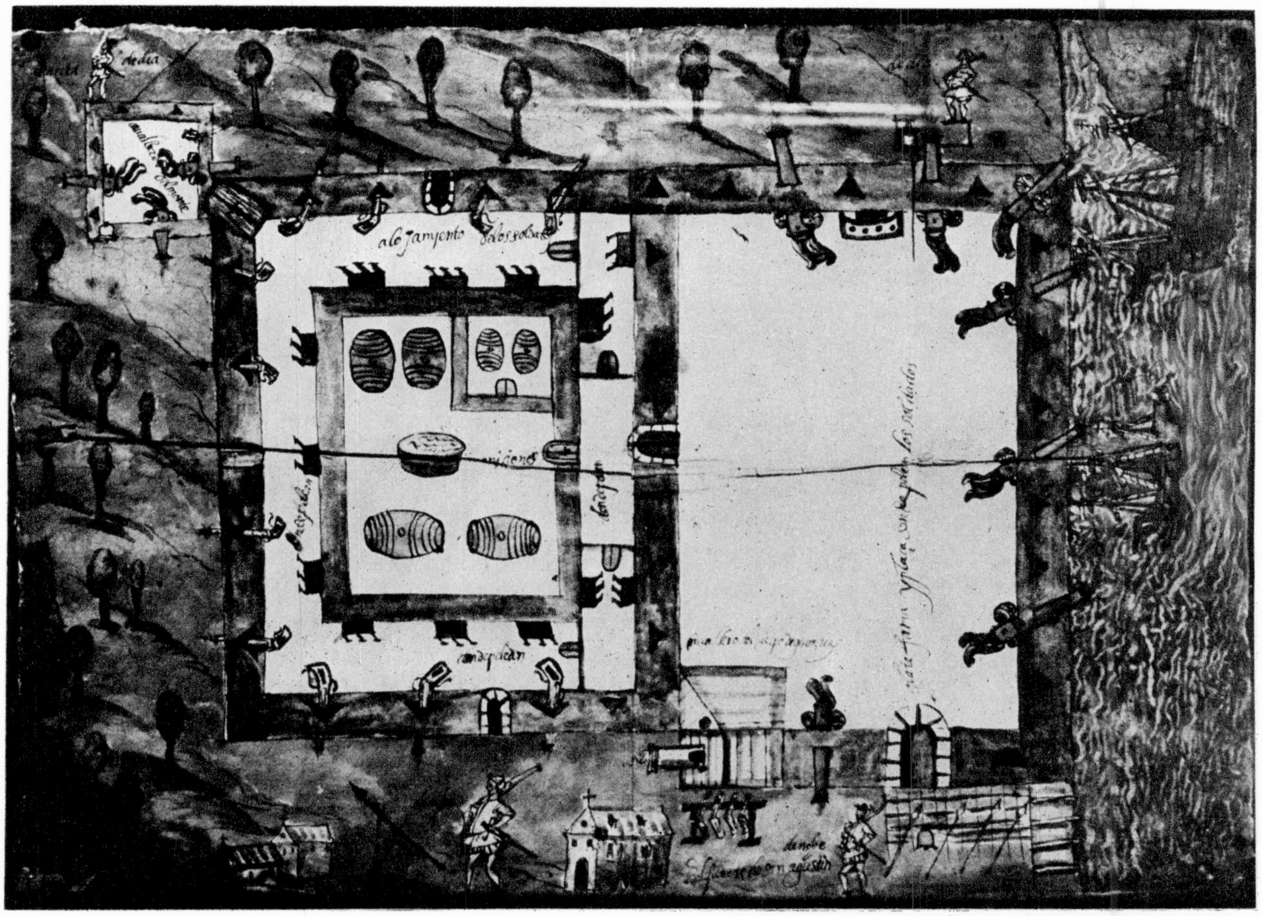

From the *Pageant of America*, Copyright Yale University Press.

THE FORT OF ST. AUGUSTINE

as it appeared in 1593. From the original plan in the *Archives of the Indies,* Seville.

for you to overpower us and avenge yourselves upon us for your people which we killed in the fort; for this reason it is necessary that you should march to my camp four leagues from here with your hands tied behind your backs."

The Frenchmen, trusting the general's words, allowed the Spaniards to tie their hands with the match cords of their harquebuses. They were then led behind a hill. Menéndez walked in front of them, stopping at a lonely spot where he drew a line in the sand with his sword—a fateful line for the French.

The sun had already set. The French soldiers, roped together, marched toward their doom in the twilight. When they reached the line, the Spaniards sprang upon them, and the massacre began. By nightfall, only ten Roman Catholics remained alive; the other two hundred and eight Frenchmen had been killed.[48]

Satisfied with his work, Menéndez and his sixty henchmen returned to St. Augustine. There was still no news of Ribaut.

Twelve more days passed.

Then, on October 10, Indians came to St. Augustine and told of two hundred Frenchmen who were wandering along the shores, looking for food, eating roots and grasses, and drinking the muddy waters.

Menéndez sent out a party of soldiers by land, and he himself followed them by boat. The next morning, when the French were trying to cross the water on a raft, they saw the Spaniards.

A French sailor swam across the inlet. Menéndez told him to return for an officer, with whom he

48. Menéndez said he had killed only one hundred and forty.

would negotiate. Whereupon La Caille came over. Ribaut's sergeant told Menéndez that he, with three hundred and fifty others, had been wrecked when their ship—the *Trinity*—had been dashed upon the rocks farther down the shore,[49] and were now on their way to Fort Caroline. But as the inlet and river cut them off from the mainland, without boats they were trapped. Would, therefore, the Spanish commander be so generous as to lend them boats to cross the lagoon and proceed to their fort?

"Tell your general," said Menéndez, "that I have captured your fort and killed your French there, as well as those who had escaped from the wreck of your fleet."

La Caille rowed back to his comrades. In the afternoon Jean Ribaut himself came over with some of his officers. Menéndez offered them wines and preserves and showed them the corpses of the French who had been massacred twelve days before. "They might have been tricked into believing that the fort was taken," replied Ribaut, unconvinced. Menéndez sent for the French prisoners whom he had captured at Fort Caroline and asked them to tell Ribaut the truth. Now Ribaut was convinced. With the knowledge of doom, his attitude changed. He pleaded with the Spanish commander.

"What has happened to me may happen to you. Since our Kings are brothers and friends, do you also play the part of a friend and give me ships with which to return to France." Menéndez uttered the one word: "Surrender!"

Ribaut returned to his men. They held council. Three hours later the French commander returned and told Menéndez that many of his soldiers hesitated to surrender, since they did not believe in his mercy, but that he was ready to pay the sum of a hundred thousand ducats to Menéndez, if their lives were spared.

"It would much grieve me," replied the Spaniard, "not to accept it, for I have great need of it." Ribaut took his answer as a promise to spare their lives and returned to his men.

It was a fateful night for the French. They had to reach a decision. If they refused to surrender, they faced starvation and death. And if they gave themselves up, they were at the mercy of the Spaniards, and they well knew what this meant.

The next morning Ribaut came to the shore with six of his officers, delivered the royal standard and his seal of office, and reported that two hundred of his men had withdrawn into the woods, but that the other hundred and fifty were ready to give themselves up.[50]

Menéndez sent a boat across the lagoon, and the Frenchmen were ferried across as their comrades had been a fortnight earlier—ten men at a time. On the shore the same scene was repeated. The Frenchmen's hands were tied, and they were asked: "Are you Catholics or Lutherans, and are there any who wish to confess?" Now Ribaut realized that their last hour had come. He answered that they all belonged to the Lutheran religion, recited the Psalm "Domine, memento mei,"[51] and exclaimed: "From earth we come and unto earth must we return. . . . Twenty years more or less can matter little." The Spaniards went to work. They killed all the Frenchmen except the musicians—drummers, fifers, and trumpeters—and four Catholics.[52]

This is how Ribaut died: two Spaniards, San Vincente and Solis de Merás, Menéndez' brother-in-law, asked for his hat. When Ribaut handed it to them, Vincente spoke: "You know how captains must obey their generals and execute their commands. We must bind your hands."

This done, Ribaut was told to walk on. The two Spaniards followed him. They had gone only a few steps, when Vincente sank his dagger into Ribaut and Merás thrust his spike through the Frenchman's breast.

Four days after the massacre Menéndez wrote to Philip II: "I put Jean Ribaut and all the rest of them to the knife, judging it to be necessary to the service of the Lord Our God, and of Your Majesty. And I think it a very great fortune that this man be dead, for the King of France could accomplish more with him and fifty thousand ducats, than with other men and five hundred thousand ducats; and he could do more in one year, than another in ten; for he was the most experienced sailor and corsair known, very skilful in this navigation of the Indies and of the Florida Coast."[53]

49. Between Matanzas Inlet and Cape Canaveral.

50. Menéndez says there were only seventy.

51. There is no Psalm beginning with these words. Perhaps it was "Domine, memento David," Psalm 132 of the King James version.

52. Barrientos says that seventeen men were saved, Merás gives the number as sixteen, while Menéndez asserts that only five were saved.

53. Menéndez to Philip II, Oct. 15, 1565, Ruidíaz, *La Florida*, II, p. 103.

After the Massacre

How did the people of Spain react to Menéndez' horrible deed? Some were shocked, but many thought he had done right; his firmness would teach the French never again to transgress on Spanish territory. And Philip? "This Court," reported the French ambassador, Fourquevaux, to Catherine, "were more gladdened than if it had been a victory over the Turks. For they have also said that Florida was of greater importance to them than Malta. And as a reward for Menéndez' massacre of your poor subjects, the said Florida will be erected into a marquisate, of which he will be appointed the Marquis."[54]

Barrientos, professor at the University of Salamanca, wrote this defense of Menéndez: "He acted as an excellent inquisitor, for when asked if they were Catholics or Lutherans, they dared to proclaim themselves publicly as Lutherans, without fear of God or shame before men; and thus he gave them that death which their insolence deserved. And even in that he was very merciful in granting them a noble and honourable death, by cutting off their heads, when he could legally have burnt them alive. . . . He killed them, I think, rather by divine inspiration, than through any counsel of the human understanding, for he had no wish that his own people, by touching pitch, should be defiled by it."[55]

Philip II, receiving Menéndez' report[56] on the massacre, scribbled on the margin: "As to those he killed, he has done well. And as to those he has saved, they shall be sent to the galleys."

The Spanish King was well satisfied. Menéndez assured him "that in the future Florida will be of little expense, and will pay Your Majesty much money, and will be of more value to Spain than New Spain or even Peru, and it may be said that this country is but a suburb of Spain, for it does not take more than forty days' sailing to come here."

France Is Notified of the Massacre

Weeks passed and France still had no knowledge of what had happened to Ribaut and his men. The news travelled slowly. By December Philip must have known of the massacre—he must have had Menéndez' report, which had been written on October 15th—three days after Ribaut had been murdered. Yet the Spanish King remained silent.

Shortly before Christmas the French envoy in Spain had an interview with the Duke of Alba. Fourquevaux had no inkling of what had happened to Ribaut, and the Duke of Alba was not ready to enlighten him. The Duke told Fourquevaux that Spain would not tolerate French aggression in a region which had belonged to her since the time of Ferdinand, and that she was determined to expel the French from Florida.

Fourquevaux used the same arguments with the Duke that Catherine had used in France with the Spanish envoy. He said that the country to which the French had gone was not Florida, but the Land of the Bretons, marked on all sea charts as the Coste des Bretones and that this land belonged to France by virtue of discovery.

The interview ended without result. Fourquevaux went to see Philip II. He found the King just as tightlipped as the Duke of Alba when it came to discussing the fate of the French troops in Florida. Fourquevaux could not discover from him what had happened to Ribaut and his soldiers.

Philip hesitated to make public too soon the news of the Spanish victory. He feared that the French might still send reinforcements to Florida to fight Menéndez.

But by January he was certain that no relief expedition had left France. And he heard from Menéndez that the Spaniards were the absolute masters of Florida.

Now Philip instructed his ambassador in France to speak firmly to Catherine and to demand from her an end of French sailings to Florida.

Alava saw Catherine on January 15th. At that time the Queen Mother had already been informed of the Spanish attack on Fort Caroline. Jacques Ribaut had arrived in France in the middle of December and had reported the capture of the fort. But he did not know that the French fleet had been shipwrecked and that his father was dead. When the massacre occurred Jacques was already on the high seas.

At the interview the Spanish envoy told Catherine that her actions were not in accordance with the treaty of peace between the two countries. Catherine replied innocently that she believed that the Frenchmen who had gone to the Isle des

54. Fourquevaux to Charles IX, Feb. 11, 1566, *Dèpêches* p. 52; Feb. 18, 1566, *ibid.*, p. 54.

55. "Hechos," in Garcia, *Dos antiquas relaciones de la Florida*, p. 72.

56. Menéndez to Philip, Oct. 12, 1565.

Bretones had already left that country. This infuriated Alava. He had heard enough of the Isle, Coast, and Land of the Bretones.

"I know of no Isle des Bretones," he shouted. "You can baptise the country Isle des Bretones and call Peru the Tierra Firme des Bretones, but I know that in the order which was given to your captain to proceed to New France by way of Florida the name of Florida was expressly used."[57] Catherine embarrassed, tried to change the conversation. She usually acted like this when she was caught unawares and had no answer prepared. Alava persisted. Catherine became impatient; she promised the Spanish envoy that no more vessels would sail for Florida, and with this the interview was over.

In early February the story of the massacre was an open secret at the Spanish court. Fourquevaux heard a detailed account of how Menéndez had killed the French soldiers, and he immediately asked for an official explanation.

Now it was useless to conceal the news any longer. Philip had to notify France. Fourquevaux was summoned to the Duke of Alba and told by him that the French soldiers and sailors had been killed in Florida. Fourquevaux protested indignantly over the Spaniards' cruelty. But Alba gave him a variety of reasons why the Frenchmen had had to be massacred. First, they were not regular soldiers (they were not paid by their King) but pirates, and had been killed as such. Second, they were heretics, preaching evil doctrines; had they not been killed they would have continued to disseminate their ideas, thus causing great harm. Third, there was not enough food in Florida to feed both the Spaniards and the French, and if Menéndez had spared the French the Spaniards would have perished from hunger. Fourth, the number of Frenchmen was larger than that of Spaniards; if they had been taken prisoner, they could easily have overpowered their captors and killed them. Fifth, the Spaniards had not enough ships to send the French home; therefore the Duke of Alba could think of "no man, however pious he might be, who would have resorted to other means and expedients than those followed by Pedro Menéndez."

Fourquevaux was enraged. He told the Duke that in his opinion Menéndez was "a butcher rather than a good soldier" and that he hoped that "God would not leave such an execrable deed unpunished."

Alba made no apologies. On the contrary; it was he who attacked French policy. He blamed Admiral Coligny and the Huguenots for the massacre. He said that it was Coligny who had compelled the Spaniards to resort to such drastic measures. It was Coligny who had sent out troops to Florida to prey upon Spanish shipping. Ribaut himself before he had been killed had confessed—so the Duke told Fourquevaux—that he had sailed to Florida under orders from Coligny, and the letters and papers which the Spaniards had found on his body indicated that he had intended to seize Havana.

Alba therefore demanded the punishment of the guilty man—Coligny. It was like the story of the wolf and the lamb, Alba as the clever wolf who not only devoured the lamb but also tried to forge political capital from it. He attempted to place the blame on Admiral Coligny, making him the scapegoat for the massacre, thus helping the French Catholic party in their fight against the Huguenots.

But for once Catherine was unwavering. She would not blame or punish Coligny, who had acted with her full knowledge. When the Spanish envoy came to see her—on March 16—to notify her officially of the massacre, she exploded: "Neither Turks nor Moors have been guilty of so great a cruelty as the Spaniards have practiced on the subjects of my son."

Alava also raised his voice to repeat the charges against Coligny. Nothing would have happened, said he, if the Admiral had not sent out the troops.

Catherine, greatly agitated, interrupted the ambassador. Tears streamed down her face. She told Alava "that the Admiral was without guilt; that the fleet had been outfitted under her orders and that of her son; that the Admiral had only done what the King commanded him to do . . . therefore he did not deserve punishment." She acted "like a mad woman" reported Alava to Philip. She shouted in the Spanish envoy's face: "It was not for you to punish our subjects, and we will not discuss their religion but the murder you committed." Alava retorted sharply, "Please God that no Huguenots enter the country of the King, my master, or they would be cut to pieces."[58] All these

57. Alava to Philip II, Jan. 6, 1566, M.S. Arch. Nat. Paris, K. 1505 (64).

58. Catherine to Fourquevaux, March 17, 1566.

arguments led nowhere. The Frenchmen had been killed, their fort taken, Florida lost. Catherine ordered Fourquevaux to demand redress from Philip. Fourquevaux wrote back that, "There is no hope that any reparation will be made for the aforesaid massacre." Charles IX again urged his ambassador to renew his complaints, "and insist urgently that for the sake of the union and friendship between the two crowns reparation for the wrong done me and the cruelties committed on my subjects, to which I cannot submit without too great loss of reputation."[59]

During the entire year of 1566 the French diplomatic representations continued. Yet Catherine and her son did not press the matter too strongly. They were careful not to antagonize Philip, since they were moving more and more toward the Catholics, and needed his friendship.

In December the Spanish King gave his answer to the French complaints. It took him almost a year to produce the document, a document only one sentence long. It read:

"To all the articles which treat of the Florida incident there is little new to answer other than what has been previously said, that the Adelantado, Pero Menéndez de Avilés, did not chastise the men he found there as vassals of the Most Christian King, but as pirates and infractors of the public peace, having possessed themselves of that country which so properly and rightly belongs to his Catholic Majesty, as is understood, and therefore there can be no doubt that, given the prudence and sense of justice of the Most Christian King, he will be satisfied once and for all with what is here said, since it is the unvarnished truth."[60]

The Revenge

There is a fitting epilogue—as with Shakespeare—to the struggles of the Spanish and the French over Florida. A new character enters the scene—Dominique de Gourgues, a French Catholic. At one time captured by the Spaniards, who had chained him in the galleys, De Gourgues hated Spain with a bitter, personal, and undying hatred.

The massacre of his compatriots in Florida enraged him, and he swore revenge upon Menéndez for his cruel deeds.

Slowly he prepared for the day of retribution. By August, 1567, he was ready. With three ships and a hundred and eighty men he sailed to Florida, attacked Fort San Mateo,[61] and put to death all its defenders. A few of the Spaniards were saved, only to be hanged on those very trees where Menéndez had hanged the Frenchmen a few years earlier. And just as Menéndez was believed to have placed under their bodies the inscription, "I do this not as to Frenchmen but as to Lutherans," De Gourgues—tasting his vengeance to the full—burned on the trees where the Spanish bodies were swinging in the wind: "I do this, not as to Spaniards or as to Marranos,[62] but as to traitors, robbers, and murderers."

With De Gourgue's attack the struggle between France and Spain for Florida came to an end. Never again did France attack Spanish possessions on the eastern shores of North America.

59. Charles IX to Fourquevaux, May 12, 1566.
60. Réponse du Roi Catholique, Dec. 1566, *Dèpêches,* p. 163.
61. As Fort Caroline was renamed by the Spaniards.
62. When Queen Isabella of Spain expelled the Moors and the Jews from the soil of Spain, she forgave those who were converted. The baptized Moors were called Moriscos; the baptized Jews, Marranos.

NOTES ON LE MOYNE, LE CHALLEUX, DE BRY

The French artist Jacques le Moyne de Morgues came with Laudonnière to Florida in 1564. His job was to map the seacoast and harbors, indicate the position of towns, plot the depth and course of the rivers, and portray the dwellings of the natives and anything else in the country worthy of observation. "All of this I performed to the best of my ability," writes Le Moyne in his narrative.

The colonists landed in June on the coast of present day South Carolina and remained in the New World till the twentieth of September, 1565. On that day Menéndez and his Spanish soldiers captured Fort Caroline and killed most of its defenders. Le Moyne was one of the few who escaped from the fort and found refuge on board the French boat, the *Levrière*. In it he sailed for home. But wind swept the vessel off its course and instead of reaching La Rochelle in France the *Levrière* came to anchor at Swansea Bay in England. From here Le Moyne travelled to London, where he married, and became a "servaunt to Sir Walter Raleigh."

And probably we might never have heard of him again. But twenty-one years later—in 1586—Laudonnière's narratives on the French colonists in Florida were published in Paris. The next year Richard Hakluyt, who encouraged his friend Basanier to edit the French volume, translated it into English. In his introduction to the English edition Hakluyt mentions that the exploits of the French "and divers other things of chiefest importance are lively drawne in colours at your no smal charges by the skillful painter James Morgues, sometime living in the Black-fryers in London."[1]

"The skillful painter James Morgues" was no other than Jacques Le Moyne, who in the meantime—he had had two decades at his disposal—had made a series of paintings of the Huguenot colony in Florida, depicting scenes and episodes he remembered. It is fair to assume that Le Moyne painted these pictures with the idea of engraving and publishing them himself. For he was not only an artist and engraver, but a publisher and a bookseller as well.

Theodore de Bry

Now the Flemish engraver Theodore de Bry enters the scene. De Bry had heard of Le Moyne's pictures, and since he had publishing plans of his own, he journeyed to London during the latter part of 1587 or the beginning of 1588.[2]

De Bry was a goldsmith by profession. He had been forced to leave Liège, the place of his birth, in about the year 1570, when the Duke of Alba and his infamous Council of Blood was enforcing Phillip II's policy of ruthlessness against the protestants of the Netherlands. De Bry fled first to Strasburg, then to Frankfurt in Germany, where he opened a goldsmith's shop. Later he turned to engraving, possibly to supplement his income, though in the sixteenth century and later, it was common for a goldsmith also to practise the profession of engraver.

Of his life we know very little. "I was," De Bry writes in the foreword to one of the books which he published when his fame was well established, "the offspring of parents born to an honourable station, and was in affluent circumstances and in the first rank of the more honoured inhabitants of Liège. But stripped of all these belongings by the accidents, cheats, and ill terms of fortune and by the attacks of robbers, I had to contend against such adverse chance that only by my art could I fend for myself. Art alone remained to me of the ample patrimony left me by my parents. On that neither robbers nor the rapacious hands of thieves could lay hands. Art restored my former wealth and repu-

1. Hakluyt, *Principal Navigations,* (MacLehose edition, N. Y., 1905), VIII, 440.

2. During his stay he began his famous engravings of Sir Phillip Sidney's funeral procession, after Laut's drawings.

tation, and has never failed me, its unwearied devotee."[3]

This is about all we know of Theodore De Bry's early years. While in London, he sought out Le Moyne in an attempt to buy his paintings. He had probably read the narrative of Laudonnière, and having himself suffered under religious persecution, he wanted to acquaint the world with the story of the Huguenots in the New World. And what would have been more appropriate than to illustrate such a work with engravings made after the drawings of an artist who himself had witnessed the events. The trouble was that Le Moyne was not willing to sell.

De Bry returned to Frankfurt, but a few months later he was back again in London, this time to make engravings for "The Mariner's Mirrour," a Dutch book to be printed in England. Since his last visit Le Moyne had died, so De Bry now approached the artist's widow and renewed his offer. She was ready to do business. De Bry bought from her not only the paintings but also Le Moyne's narrative of the French colony.

In his narrative Le Moyne inserted parts from Laudonnière's printed report and parts of the small book which had been published under Le Challeux's name in 1566 and in which Le Challeux related his dramatic escape from Fort Caroline.

De Bry was greatly delighted with his buy and noted that his heart "was filled with joy." He must have talked to his friends of his plans and of his projected publishing venture; one surmises that he spoke to Richard Hakluyt, who at that time was putting the finishing touches to his monumental compendium on *The Principal Navigations . . . of the English Nation*. And again, one surmises that Hakluyt, more interested in the English colonization of America than in the abortive settlements of the French, made the suggestion to De Bry to publish a volume on Virginia (where the English went) first and leave the Florida narrative for afterwards. About the changing of his plans De Bry said in his Foreword to the Virginia volume that he did so "beinge there unto requested of my Friends, by Raeson of the memorye of the fresh and laue [late] performance thereof, albeyt I haue in hand the Historye of Florida which should bee first sett foorthe because yt was discouered by the Frenchmen long before the discoueryе of Virginia, yet I hope shortly also to publish the same a Historye doubtless so Rare, as I thinke the like hath not been heard nor seene."

The book on Virginia came out in 1590 with 23 engravings after John White. Issued in four languages — Latin, English, German, and French — it turned out to be a tremendous publishing success. It was followed by the Florida volume a year later, for which De Bry, his sons, and his assistant Gysbert van Veen made 43 copper-plates patterned after Le Moyne's work.

On the following pages are the printed narratives on the abortive French and English colonies.

Le Moyne's only surviving painting, which the editor of this volume discovered in New York in 1947, is reproduced in full color on the next page. The narratives of Le Moyne and Le Challeux on pages 33-117 are illustrated by De Bry's engravings from his 1591 Florida volume.

3. Foreword to "Icones quinquaginta virorum illustrium" (Frankfort, 1597).

OF JACQUES LE MOYNE'S FORTY-THREE PAINTINGS THIS IS THE ONLY ONE WHICH HAS SURVIVED

FOR over three hundred years Jacques Le Moyne's Florida pictures were known only through the engravings of De Bry. All of his originals seemed to have vanished. In 1901 a member of the Académie des Inscriptions et Belles Lettres spotted a small painting in the library of the Comtesse de Ganay. Mr. Schlumberger showed it to his colleagues at the Académie, and one of them—T. Hamy—identified it as the work of Jacques Le Moyne.[1]

Twenty years ago, when the editor of this volume made a search for this painting, which in the meantime had disappeared again, he could find no trace of it. But after the publication of this volume in 1946 he received an invitation from James Hazen Hyde, and there in Mr. Hyde's New York apartment at the Hotel Savoy Plaza was the long-sought-after Le Moyne painting. Mr. Lorant was given permission to make a color reproduction of the original, and he published it in 1951 with an accompanying text.[2] *Thus for the first time Le Moyne's work was reproduced in its original colors.*

Mr. Lorant urged Mr. Hyde to donate the work to a museum or to some public institution for perpetual safekeeping. The painting was eventually willed to the New York Public Library, which received it after Mr. Hyde's death.

De Bry used this painting as the model for his superb engraving (page 51). On the right is Laudonnière, attired in crimson, yellow, and blue costume, with an Indian chief, probably Saturiba, who is resting his arm on the French commander's shoulder. In the center is Ribaut's column, which is worshipped by kneeling Indians.

1. In the *Bulletin of the Académie des Inscriptions et Belles Lettres* for January–February, 1901, Dr. Hamy wrote an article: "Sur une miniature de Jacques le Moyne de Morgues, représentant une scène du voyage de Laudonnière en Floride (1564)."

2. Stefan Lorant: "The First Painting of America," in *Vogue* Magazine, February 1, 1951.

LE MOYNE

The narrative of Jacques le Moyne de Morgues, an artist who accompanied the French Expedition to Florida under René de Laudonnière in the year 1564.

FROM the small French colony which Jean Ribaut had left in Florida to maintain French dominion there came a cry for help. Admiral de Châtillon[1] reported the colony's desperate need to Charles IX and urged the monarch to send reinforcements. The delay had already been far too great. The King gave immediate orders to fit out a fleet and send relief to the colony. Following the Admiral's recommendation, he appointed René de Laudonnière as leader of the expedition and appropriated 100,000 francs to finance the undertaking.

Admiral Coligny, a virtuous and pious Christian, faithfully devoted to the King, gave his instructions to Laudonnière in person and informed him of his duties. He told Laudonnière how important it was to select the right company for such a voyage and advised him to allow only the best and most God-fearing men to join his ranks and to engage as many skilled mechanics as possible. Laudonnière was given a royal commission, bearing the King's seal, to facilitate his preparations.

As soon as the preliminary arrangements were made, Laudonnière set out for Havre de Grace [Le Havre], where he began to outfit his ships and search the entire kingdom for the best men. And I can safely say that he obtained the services of the most skilful mechanics in the land. He was joined by a number of young noblemen also, who came as volunteers at their own expense, drawn simply by their desire to see the world. The soldiers were picked veterans, each one competent to act as an officer in battle. From Dieppe came the two best navigators of our time, Michael le Vasseur and his brother, Thomas le Vasseur, both of whom had been employed in the King's naval service. I also received orders to join the expedition and to report to M. de Laudonnière.

M. de Laudonnière welcomed everyone cordially and with promises of magnificent

1. One of the high officers of the crown and leader of the Huguenots. His full name and title is Gaspard, Comte de Coligny, Seigneur de Châtillon-sur-Loing, Amiral de France.

LE MOYNE'S MAP

THIS is not an accurate map of the Florida region, though it is correct about the places which the French had visited. But as they had never gone farther up the river than Lake George, the accuracy of the map extends only to a limited region. The other geographical names, the positions of rivers and cities, Le Moyne inserted as he heard about them from the Indians of that region, or they were taken from other equally unreliable sources.

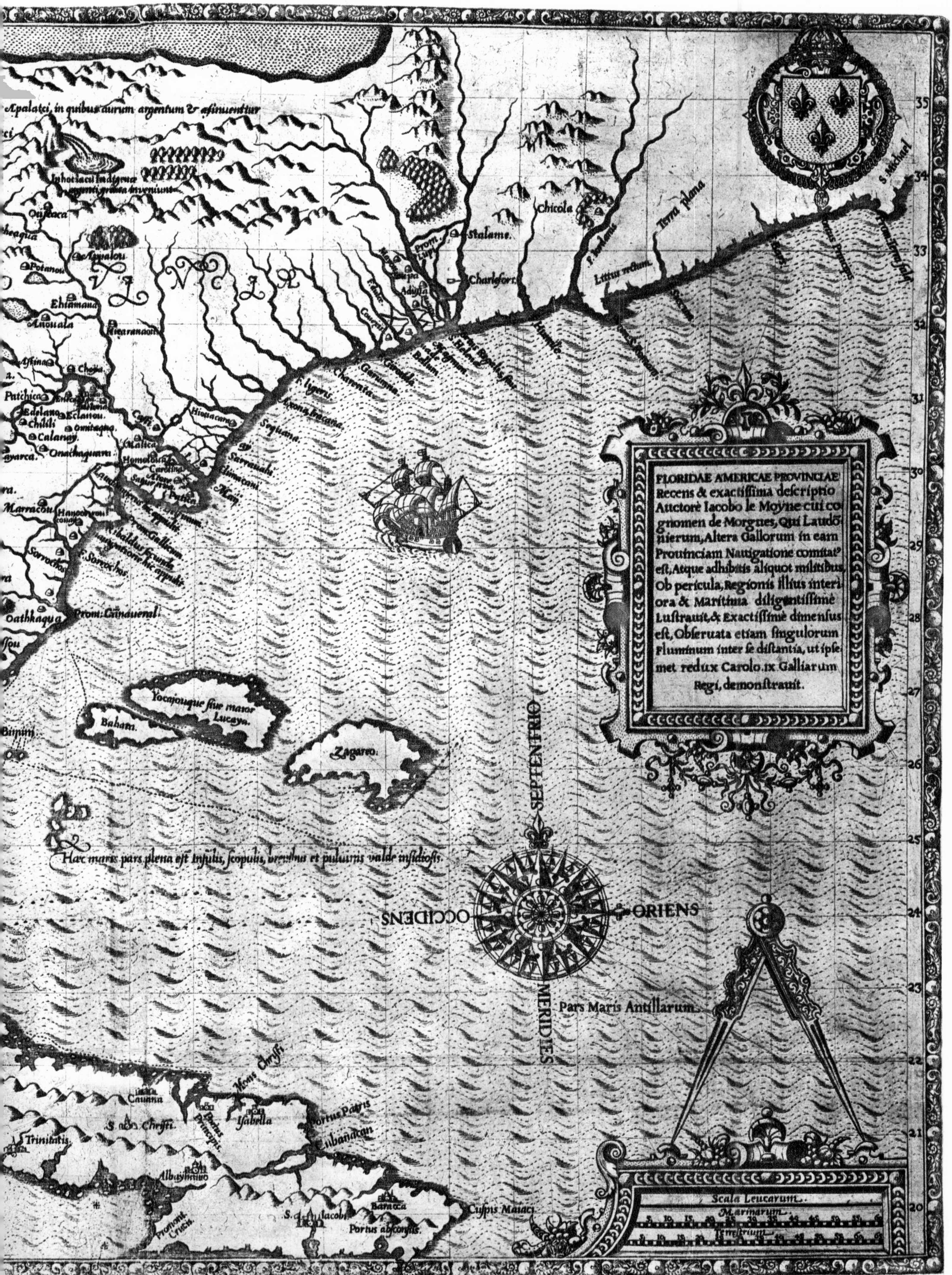

FLORIDAE AMERICAE PROVINCIAE Recens & exactissima descriptio Auctore Iacobo le Moyne cui cognomen de Morgues, Qui Laudonnierum, Altera Gallorum in eam Prouinciam Nauigatione comitat' est, Atque adhibitis aliquot militibus, Ob pericula, Regionis illius interiora & Maritima diligentissimè Lustrauit, & Exactissimè dimensus est, Obseruata etiam singulorum Fluminum inter se distantia, ut ipsemet redux Carolo.IX. Galliarum Regi, demonstrauit.
Apalatci, in quibus aurum argentum & æs inueniuntur
In hoc lacu Indigenæ argenti grana inueniunt
Stalame
Charlefort
Chicola
Terra plana
Littus rectum
S. Michael
Oustaca
Potanou
Ehiamana
Anouala
Patchica
Edelano
Chilili
Calanay
Onathaquara
Homoloa
Saturiona
Marracou
Oathkaqua
Prom: Cañaueral
Yocaiouque siue maior Lucaya
Bahama
Zagareo
Bimini
SEPTENTRIO
OCCIDENS
ORIENS
MERIDIES
Pars Maris Antillarum
Mons Christi
Cauuna
Isabella
Portus Patris
Cubanacan
S. Christi
Trinitatis
Baracoa
S. Iacobi
Portus absconditus
Cuspis Maiaci
Promont. Crucis
Scala Leucarum
Marinarum
Terrestrium
35
34
33
32
31
30
29
28
27
26
25
24
23
22
21
20

benefits which would result from the expedition. As I was aware that gentlemen of the court are in the habit of giving liberal promises, I asked Laudonnière for some more positive statement concerning what he meant to do. I was also curious to know why the King wanted my services. M. de Laudonnière replied that only honorable work would be required of me and that my special duty when we reached the Indies would be to map the seacoast and harbors, indicate the position of towns, plot the depth and course of the rivers. In addition, I was to portray the dwellings of the natives and anything else in the land that was worthy of observation. All this I performed to the best of my ability, as I proved later to His Majesty when I returned to France after escaping from the atrocious cruelties of the perfidious Spaniards.

On April 20, 1564, we left Havre de Grace in three ships and steered directly for the Fortunate Isles, or, as seafaring men call them, the Canaries. From there we proceeded along the Tropic of Cancer to the Antilles. We took on water at Dominica, where we lost two of our men. Making sail again, we reached the coast of Florida, or New France, on Thursday, June 22.

M. de Laudonnière reconnoitered the stream named by Ribaut the River of May [the Saint John's], and found it navigable. As one of its shores offered a suitable site for a fort, he made immediate preparations to erect one. He also decided to send his largest ship, the *Elizabeth of Honfleur,* back to France in charge of Jean Lucas.

Upon our arrival in New France we found the seashore crowded with native men and women, who kept up large fires. At first we thought it necessary to be on guard against them, but very soon we realized that the last thing in their minds was to harm us. On the contrary, they gave numerous proofs of their friendly intentions. They were filled with admiration when they found that our flesh was so much softer and more tender than their own, and they praised our garments, which were so different from theirs. The gifts we received from them were the things they valued most, being useful either for the preservation of their lives or for the protection of their bodies. They brought us grains of roasted maize, ground into flour, or whole ears of it, smoked lizards or other wild animals which they considered great delicacies, and various kinds of roots, some for food, others for medicine. And when they discovered that we were more interested in metals and minerals, they gave us some of these as well. M. de Laudonnière, finding that our men were cheating the Indians, forbade on pain of death any trading for gold, silver, or minerals unless it was put in the common stock for the benefit of all.

Not long after our landing, certain chiefs from the neighborhood visited our commander and told him that they were ruled by King Saturiba, on whose territory we were. They further informed Laudonnière that this chief lived not far away and that he

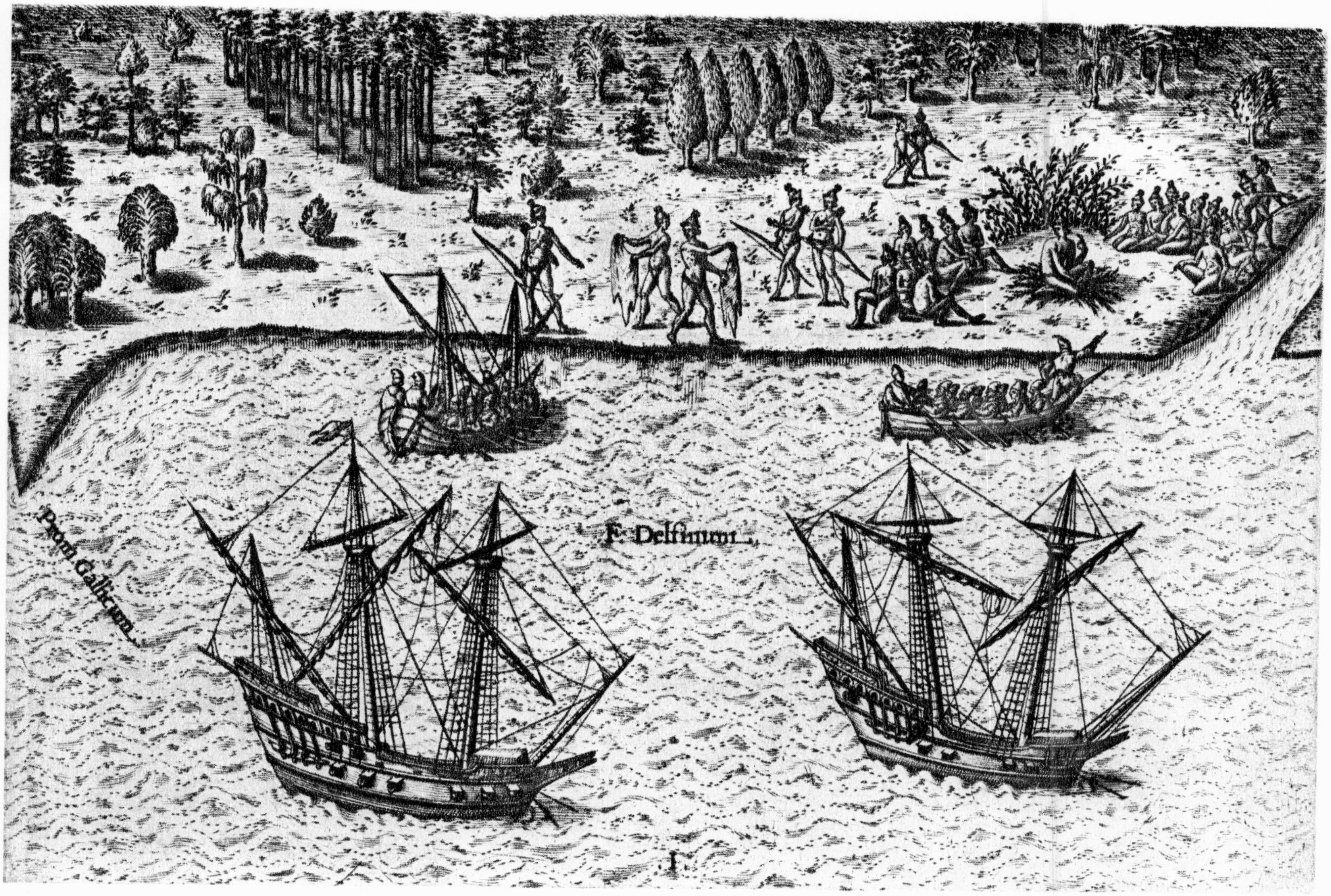

THE FRENCH ARRIVE IN FLORIDA

ON THEIR *first voyage to Florida the French touched at a flat, heavily wooded headland which their commander named Cape François [Promontorium Gallicum] in honor of France. The cape lies about thirty degrees from the equator.*

From there the French sailed northwards along the low, level coast and came to the mouth of a broad and beautiful river, where they cast anchor, since they desired to explore the stream more carefully next day. (When Laudonnière came upon it on his second voyage, he called it the River of Dolphins, because of the many dolphins swimming in it.)*

The French landed on the shore of this river and were met by a number of Indians, who received them with kindness and in the friendliest spirit. The natives were anxious to prove with deeds how well they meant; some of them gave their own garments, made of skins, to the French commander, and they offered to take him to their chief.

When they came before him, the chief was sitting upon boughs of palm and laurel and did not rise; but he presented our commander with a large skin decorated with pictures of wild animals.

*This is a mistake of Le Moyne. Laudonnière landed, not at the River of Dolphins, but at the River of May (the St. John's).

was so powerful he could muster an army many thousand strong. Hearing this, we hurried to finish our fort.

King Saturiba[2] kept our actions under steady observation; he sent out his scouts every day to see what we were doing, and when they reported that we had marked out a triangle by stretching cords and were digging up the earth along these markings, he wished to come and see it for himself.

Some two hours before his arrival, Saturiba sent a chieftain with a hundred and twenty able-bodied men. They were armed with bows and arrows, clubs, and darts, and adorned, after the Indian fashion, with their riches: feathers of different kinds, necklaces of a special sort of shell, bracelets made of fish teeth, belts of silver-colored balls, round and oblong, and pearl anklets. Many of the men wore round, flat plates of gold, silver, or brass, which hung upon their legs, tinkling like little bells.

The chieftain announced the approach of his King and ordered the men to build a shelter for him. Using branches of laurel, mastic, and other sweet-smelling trees, they put up a hut on a nearby knoll. From this vantage point Saturiba could see whatever went on within our lines and examine the tents, supplies, and baggage we had not yet found time to get under cover. Our first concern had been to complete our fort rather than to put up huts, which could easily be built later.

When he received the Indian's message, M. de Laudonnière disposed his force. He was cautious, for he did not wish to be caught unawares. We would have been in a hopeless state if the natives had chosen to attack us, because our ammunition was not yet unloaded. As our commander had once before visited this place with Ribaut, he had already met Saturiba, had learned a few words of the native language, and was familiar with the ceremony with which the chief expected to be received. And as one of the officers, Captain La Caille,[3] had also been with Ribaut and understood the language of the natives, M. de Laudonnière decided it would be best if no one except himself, Ottigny, his second in command, and Captain La Caille approached the King.

Chief Saturiba came with seven or eight hundred handsome, strong, and well-built men, the best-trained and swiftest of his tribe, all armed as if on the warpath. In the van marched fifty youths with javelins and spears; behind these, and next to the chief, came twenty pipers making the wildest kind of noise, without any harmony or rhythm, each

2. Saturiba was the ruler of the territory which lay around the mouth of the St. John's River and extended northward along the coast almost as far as the Savannah. His name is spelled in various ways. The French call him Satouriona, Saturiova, Satirova; the Englishman Hakluyt writes his name as Satourioua; the Spanish narratives refer to him as Sotoriba, Saturibau, and Saturiba.

3. François de la Caille, whom Le Moyne calls Captain, was really the sergeant of Laudonnière; at the time the narrative was written this rank was different from what it is today.

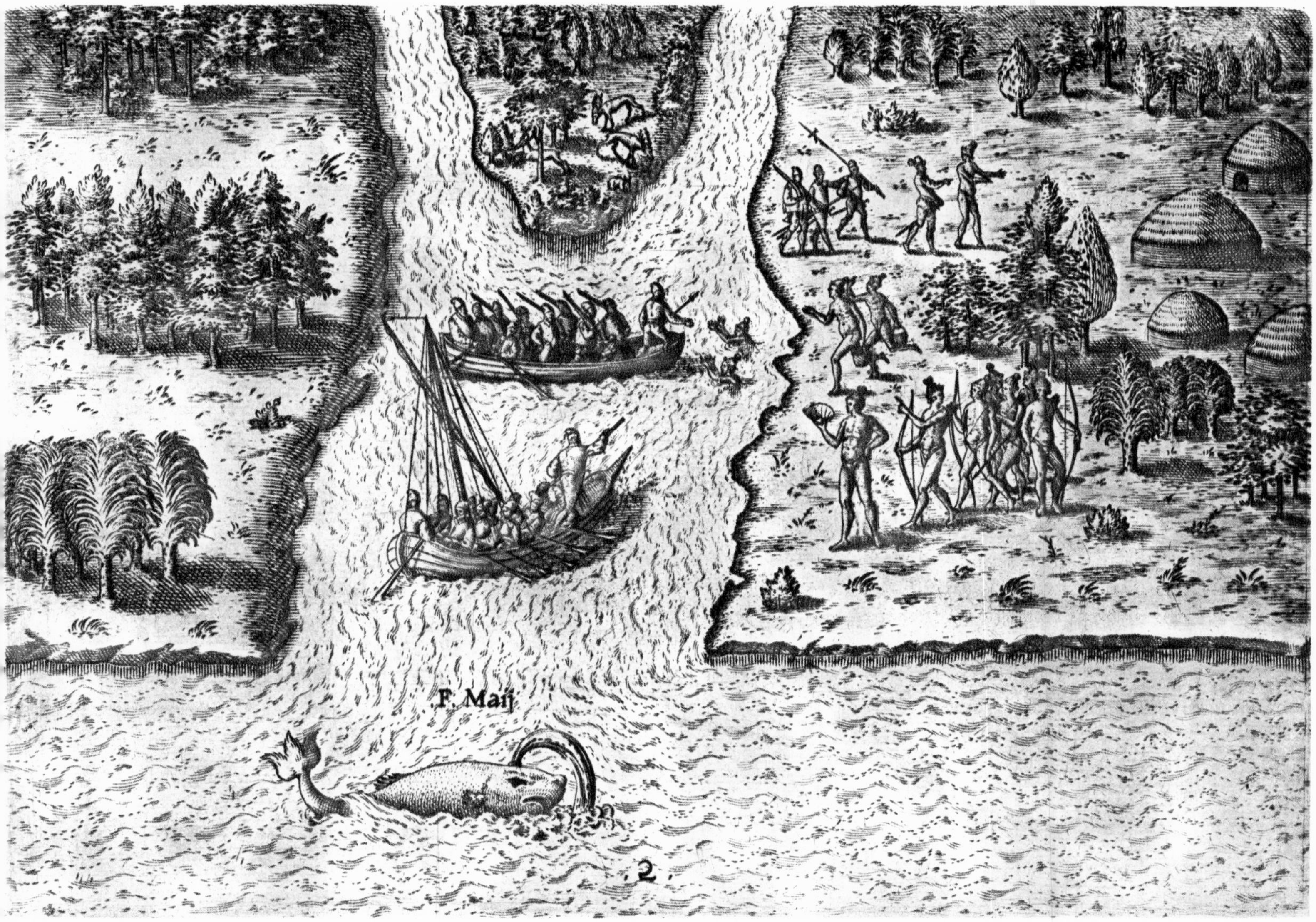

SAILING TO THE RIVER OF MAY

THE French sailed on and made another landing. At this place they were greeted by a crowd of Indians, some of whom waded into the water shoulder high to present the visitors with baskets of maize and red and white mulberries. Others offered to help them to the shore, where they were met by the chief, his two sons, and other warriors, all armed with bows and quivers full of arrows.

After they had exchanged greetings, the French went on into the woods, hoping to discover fresh wonders. But they found nothing except mulberry trees bearing red and white berries and covered with silkworms. They named this river the River of May [the Saint John's], because they sighted it on the first of that month.

blowing with all his might as if to see who could blow the loudest. Their instruments were thick reeds, like organ pipes or whistles, with only two openings. They blew into the top hole, while the sound came out the other end. On the King's right hand limped his soothsayer, and on his left walked his chief counselor; Saturiba never made a decision without asking the opinion of these two.

The chief entered the place especially prepared for him and sat down in the Indian fashion, that is, he squatted on the ground like an ape. Then after a long look around and seeing our little force drawn up in line of battle, he ordered M. de Laudonnière and Ottigny to be invited into his tabernacle, where he delivered a long oration, most of which was unintelligible to them. But they understood enough to know that Saturiba was asking who we were and what our purpose was in landing on his territory.

M. de Laudonnière, using Captain La Caille as his interpreter, replied that he had been sent by a most powerful ruler, called the King of France, to offer a treaty to him by which the King of France would become Saturiba's friend, and the friend of his allies, and an enemy to their enemies. The chief was greatly pleased. After we had exchanged gifts in pledge of our perpetual friendship Saturiba came closer to our forces and was greatly impressed by our arms, particularly by the harquebuses.

When he reached the ditch around our fort, he took all its measurements, both inside and out, and seeing that the earth was being taken from the ditch and formed into a rampart, he asked what our purpose was. He was told that we were making an enclosure large enough to hold us all and that we were going to erect many small houses inside it. Saturiba was filled with admiration and said he hoped to see our work finished as quickly as possible. We asked him for some of his men to help us in the building. He agreed to this and sent us eighty of the strongest; they were of the greatest help to us in completing the fort and the huts.

Every one of us—noblemen, soldiers, workmen, sailors—worked hard to get our post ready to shelter us from the weather and protect us against enemies. And every man was also making sure, through much private trading of gifts, that he would become rich.

Now that the fort, a dwelling for M. de Laudonnière, and a large storehouse for provisions and other necessary military supplies had been finished, our commander began to cut down our allowance of food and drink, until after three weeks only one glass of spirits and water, half-and-half, was given out daily to each man. As for food, which it had been hoped would be so abundant in this new world, none at all was found. If the natives had not supplied us daily from their own stores, some of us certainly would have perished from starvation, especially those who did not know how to use a gun in the hunt.

M. de Laudonnière had ordered his chief carpenter, Jean des Hayes of Dieppe, to

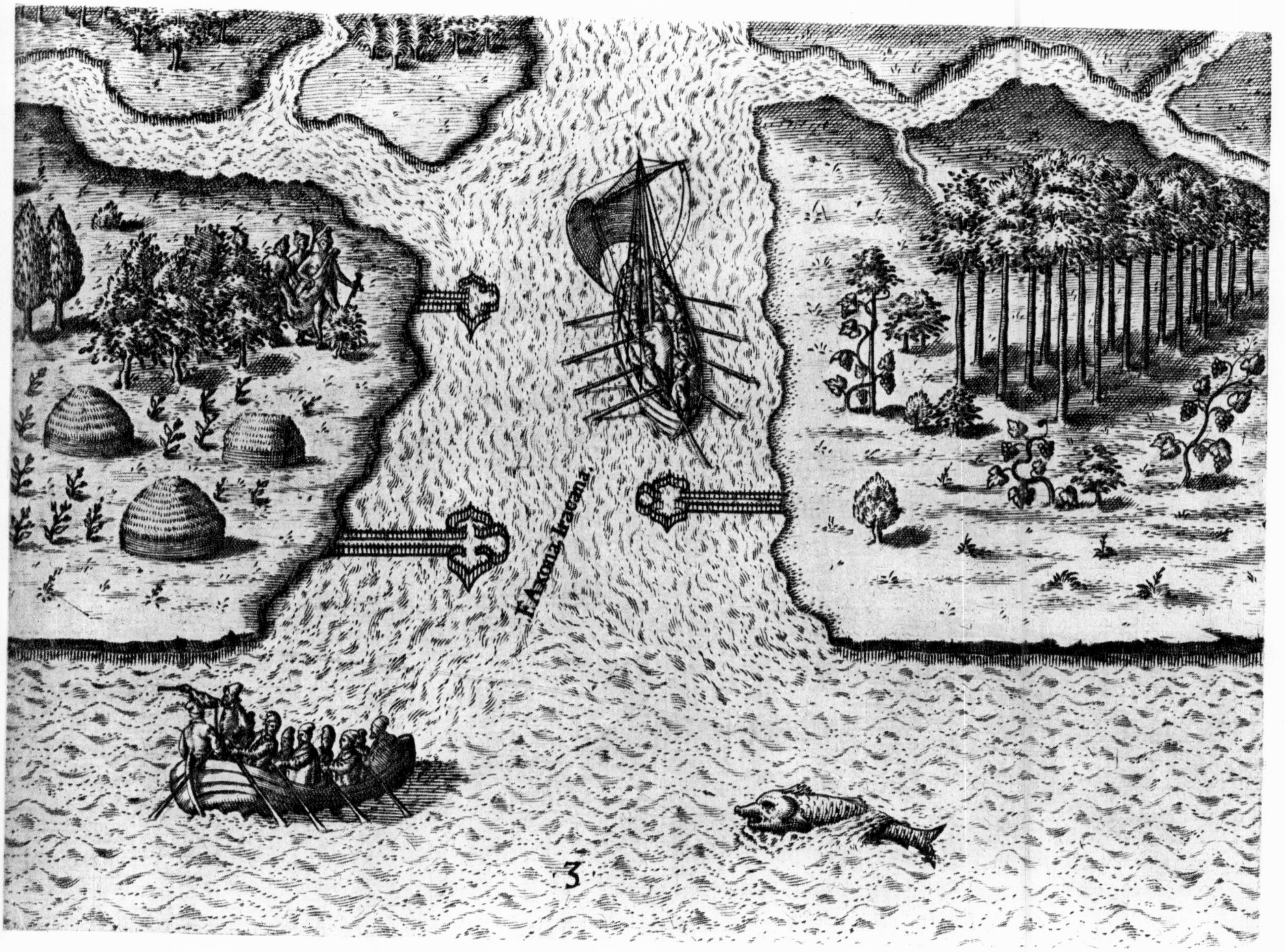

LEAVING THE RIVER OF MAY, THEY DISCOVER TWO OTHER STREAMS

SOME time later the French re-embarked, hoisted anchor, and sailed farther north along the coast. About fourteen leagues from the River of May they reached the mouth of another beautiful stream. This the commander chose to explore himself, accompanied by the chief and some natives of that vicinity. He named it the Seine, because it reminded him of the River Seine in France.

Returning to the ships, they sailed still farther north. They had gone about six miles, when they found another fine river, which they named the Aisne. They sent two boats to explore it. In this stream they discovered an island, whose chief proved no less friendly than the others.

build two shallops, the length of whose keel was to be—if I remember rightly—about thirty-five or forty feet, in order to explore the upper waters of the river and the seacoast. These boats were now nearing completion.

But by this time the noblemen who had come from France began to be dissatisfied at their failure to realize any of those profits which they had expected, and there were daily complaints from many of them. M. de Laudonnière, a man far too easily swayed by others, fell under the influence of three or four of these parasites. He began to treat the soldiers with contempt, though they were just the ones he ought most to have considered. Worse still, many who wished to practice their religion according to the reformed rites, now began to express indignation that they were without a minister to perform their services.

However, let us return to King Saturiba. This Chief sent messages to M. de Laudonnière not only to confirm the treaty which they had made but also to demand the fulfilment of one of its conditions—that of being a friend to his friends and an enemy to his enemies, against whom he was now organizing an expedition. M. de Laudonnière gave an ambiguous answer to these messengers, for meanwhile, during a long voyage up the main channel of the River of May, we had discovered that the Chief of that country was not only an enemy of our ally, but that he was far more powerful than King Saturiba. Besides, his friendship was indispensable to us, since the road to the Apalatcy [Appalachian] Mountains (which we were told was the source of all the gold and silver we had received in trade) lay through his territory. Some of our men had already entered into negotiations with this Chief, whose name was Outina,[4] and they had sent back to the fort much gold and silver. M. de Laudonnière had given orders to make a pact with him.

After Saturiba received our commander's reply, he came to the fort with twelve or fifteen hundred warriors, but found to his surprise that things were now greatly changed. He could no longer get across the ditch, and there was only a single entrance to the fort—a very narrow one. There he met Captain La Caille, who told him that he would only be admitted into the fort without his men, or at least with no more than twenty.

Saturiba was disappointed, but he disguised his feelings well. He selected twenty of his followers, and with these he entered the fort, where he was shown everything. The sound of the drums and trumpets and the reports of the brass cannon, which we fired in his presence, frightened him vastly. When he was told that all his men had run away, he could readily believe it, since he himself would gladly have been somewhere else. This incident, by the way, gave us a great reputation in the whole neighborhood; indeed, after this the natives believed us to be far more powerful than we actually were.

4. He lived on the banks of the St. John's, near the northern shores of Lake George, ruling over forty villages. The region around Cadica (see Le Moyne's map on pp. 34-35) was under his jurisdiction.

THE DISCOVERY OF SIX OTHER RIVERS

*SAILING on, the French discovered six miles farther another river, which they called the Loire, and after this five more, naming them the Charente [Charenta], the Garonne [Garumna], the Gironde [Gironda], the Belle [Bellum], and the Grande [Magnum].**

After they had explored these nine rivers carefully and found many singular things, all within the space of less than sixty miles, they were not yet satisfied. They went still farther north, until they reached the River Jordan, one of the most beautiful rivers of the whole northern region.

*The identity of the rivers is almost impossible to determine, because the names given them by Ribaut "were altered by the Spaniards in their geographical tables," says Lescarbot in his *Histoire de la Nouvelle France* (Paris, 1611), II, 45. But some two hundred and fifty years later Benjamin F. French, in his *Historical Collections of Louisiana and Florida* (New York, 1869), identified the Seine as the St. Marys, the Loire as the Altamaha, the Charente as the Newport, the Garonne as the Ogeechee, the Gironde as the Savannah, and the Grande as the Broad River.

Woodbery Lowery, in *The Spanish Settlements in the United States* (New York, 1905), II, 394-399, lists the findings of the various historians and map makers on the identity of the rivers.

King Saturiba told M. de Laudonnière that, as his own faith was pledged and as his men and supplies were ready and his subordinate chiefs assembled, he could do nothing else but set out on his expedition, even if we would not give him the help he had expected.

While these events were taking place, M. de Laudonnière had decided to send back another ship to France, under the command of Pierre Marchant. It was remarkable how many wished to return home. Among them, one young nobleman, Marillac, was so anxious to go that he promised to reveal to M. de Laudonnière important secret information concerning his life and good name if the commander would send him back to France. He asked only that M. de Laudonnière should not open the papers containing these revelations until his ship had sailed. Too credulously, our commander agreed to this proposal.

On the appointed day, five or six hours before the information was to be put into M. de Laudonnière's hands, another nobleman, named De Gièvre (who was both God-fearing and well-liked) received warning that Marillac was plotting against him and that he would do well to make his escape. He at once took refuge in the forest to be out of the reach of M. de Laudonnière. The papers Marillac handed over to our commander contained some infamous libels, which were supposed to be in Gièvre's handwriting. Their gist was that Laudonnière had misappropriated the 100,000 francs the King had given him for provisions, since he had not brought enough supplies with him, that he had failed to follow the Admiral's order to bring over a minister of the Gospel, and that he encouraged tattlers and gabblers, but despised men of merit, and certain other charges.

Gièvre's departure angered many of the colonists, though at that time they said nothing. But as the days and weeks passed by, discontent grew. Some of the men were dissatisfied with the food; others—particularly the nobles, who considered that they should be treated more respectfully—with the amount and severity of the work. After a period of grumbling, the malcontents got together. At first their group numbered only five or six, but gradually it increased until there were about thirty.

The consultations were begun by the very best of the sailors and noblemen, and they then influenced the others, avoiding those whom they considered unreliable. When the time seemed ripe, they took La Caille into their confidence. The captain had not previously been consulted, since he was known to be a man of the greatest integrity, who would also demand the utmost loyalty from others. They begged him as their senior officer to take up their case, since it concerned the good of all, and they asked him to deliver a written statement of their grievances to M. de Laudonnière. La Caille said that he would try to help them, because he considered their petition to be a just one. He promised to communicate their complaints to M. de Laudonnière, though he was aware that by doing this he was risking his life.

THEY REACH PORT ROYAL

THE French sailed on and came to a river which they called Bellevue [Conspectu Bellum]. When they had gone another three or four miles, they were told that close by there flowed another stream, much bigger and much more beautiful than the others. They found this river so large and magnificent that they named it Port Royal [Portus Regalis]. Here they took in sail and came to anchor in ten fathoms.

The French commander landed with his soldiers in a beautiful country, well wooded with oak, cedar, and various other trees. The woods abounded in turkeys and deer.

The river mouth was three miles wide and divided into two arms, one going west and flowing to the sea, the other turning north and probably connecting with the Jordan. Midway between the two branches lay an island pointing towards the river mouth.

Some time later the French sailed up the northern branch, and after going about twelve miles, they met with a group of Indians. As soon as the natives caught sight of the boats they fled, leaving behind a lynx's whelp which they had been roasting—so the French named the place Lynx Point [Prom. Lupi]. Going still farther, they came to another branch of the river, which joined it coming from an easterly direction. As the commander wanted to explore this, he left the main channel.

Early the next day, Sunday, La Caille went to M. de Laudonnière's house and asked him, in the name of the whole company, to come to the place of public assembly. When all were assembled at the appointed time, M. de Laudonnière appeared with Ottigny, his second in command. After silence had been proclaimed, Captain La Caille made a speech:

"Sir, all of us here agree in recognizing you as the lieutenant of the King, our supreme lord in this province, where our present settlement has been founded in his name," began La Caille. "We will obey your orders on this honorable expedition, even if, for His Majesty's sake, we should have to sacrifice our lives; this you know by experience in the case of most of those present, including many of noble birth who have followed you as volunteers at their own expense.

"Yet we must respectfully remind you that before leaving France we were assured that provisions enough for a full year would be brought over with us and that additional supplies would be on hand before these were exhausted. But far from this being the case, the provisions brought were scarcely enough for one month.

"The Indians, as soon as they found that we had nothing to give in exchange, began to lose interest in bringing supplies, for as you know these savages are not in the habit of giving something for nothing. When they discovered that no more was to be expected from any of us, and when the soldiers began to extort supplies from them by force (as some did to the great concern of the wiser among us), they deserted the neighborhood entirely; thus we lost even those sources of food which we had before. But even if they had continued to supply us with food, it would not have been enough to still our hunger.

"In order to remedy this, we all here most urgently beseech you to repair and refit one of the ships which brought us from France and is now lying in the river. We ask you to send her to nearby New Spain to obtain supplies by purchase or otherwise. We are sure that such a course would relieve us, but if you have any better measures to suggest, we are ready to agree to them."

As soon as La Caille had finished his speech, M. de Laudonnière replied. He said that the soldiers had no right to call him to account for his actions—but he promised to provide supplies for them, as he still had several casks of merchandise. He was ready to put these into the common stock to be traded for provisions with the Indians. And he added that though he would never consent to send a ship to New Spain, he would give permission for the two shallops under construction to be taken on coasting voyages of two or three hundred miles. From such expeditions the colonists should be able to secure provisions in plenty. With this reply he dismissed the assembly.

As I have related, M. de Laudonnière had already sent out an expedition to recon-

THE FRENCH COMMANDER ERECTS A COLUMN BEARING THE ARMS OF THE KING OF FRANCE

After a night spent on board, the commander gave orders that a landmark, carved in the form of a column and bearing the arms of the King of France, be put into one of the boats and set up at some pleasant and well-chosen spot. The French found this at a point about three miles west, where they discovered a small island formed by a creek which left the main stream and a little farther on rejoined it. There, on an open knoll, the commander ordered the column to be erected.

Here they saw two deer, far larger than any they had ever seen before; they could easily have killed them with their harquebuses had not the commander, admiring their size, forbidden it. They named the island Libourne (marked F in the picture). Embarking again, they explored another island close by, where they admired some lofty cedars, much taller than any they had yet seen; therefore they named the island Cedar Island [Cedrorum Insulam].

noiter the distant parts of the country, in particular those in the vicinity of King Outina, our neighbor's enemy. And some of our men had already established trade with Outina, and much gold and silver, pearls, and other valuable articles had been sent to the fort. But as this duty was not given to everybody and as those employed in it were supposed to be growing rich fast, others became envious of them. Discontent spread among the settlers, even though M. de Laudonnière promised to divide the riches equally.

There was one man, called La Roche Ferrière, who, being a great talker and know-all, had gained such influence with M. de Laudonnière as to be considered by him almost an oracle. I do not deny that La Roche Ferrière was a man of ability, that he was useful in initiating this new enterprise, and that it was largely due to his influence with King Outina that we were receiving the gold, silver, and pearls at the fort. He had asked for some soldiers, and five or six harquebusiers were sent to him to be used as he or King Outina might require. In brief, La Roche Ferrière's operations ultimately resulted in Outina's making peace with some of his former enemies near the mountains.

Now, La Roche Ferrière wrote a letter to M. de Laudonnière and asked him to send someone to replace him, since he had much important information to communicate. As soon as M. de Laudonnière received the letter, he sent a man to take La Roche Ferrière's place. La Roche Ferrière returned to the fort and reported that all the gold and silver he obtained for us had come from the Apalatcy Mountains and that the Indians from whom he had received these metals knew of no other place where they could be found. All that they possessed they had secured in wars with three chiefs, named Potanou, Onatheaqua, and Oustaca. These chiefs were keeping Outina out of the mountains. La Roche Ferrière brought with him a piece of rock mined in the Apalatcys containing fair amounts of gold and brass. And he asked M. de Laudonnière to let him undertake the long journey, by which he hoped he could reach the three chiefs and learn more about them. Having received M. de Laudonnière's permission, he set out.

After La Roche Ferrière had gone, the thirty men who had instigated the demonstration and petition threw everything into turmoil in the fort. They were determined to take possession of it and to make a thorough change in the conduct of things. For their leaders they chose De Fourneaux, a great hypocrite and an avaricious person, Stephen of Genoa, an Italian, a third named La Croix, and a Gascon named Seignore, a captain risen from the ranks. All military officers except three were persuaded to join them in the conspiracy. The three left out were Ottigny, the second in command, Arlac,[5] the Swiss ensign, and Captain La Caille. But the rest of the soldiers were so effectively won over that sixty-

5. Though both Le Moyne and Laudonnière spell this name D'Arlac or De Arlac, it is probably an incorrect pronunciation of Erlach, a well-known Swiss family name.

THE FRENCH LEFT IN CHARLESFORT SUFFER FROM LACK OF PROVISIONS

SOON after Ribaut left Florida the men who remained at Charlesfort (erected on an island in a northern branch of Port Royal) found their provisions running low. They held a council and decided that their best plan was to go to Chief Ouadé and his brother Couëxis and ask them for supplies. A few men were sent out in Indian canoes; they journeyed through the inland waters, and about ten miles on they discovered a large and beautiful river of fresh water. The banks of this stream were wooded with lofty cypresses, and in the water were crocodiles much bigger than the crocodiles of the Nile. Chief Ouadé received them in the friendliest manner. When he heard of their plight, he sent to his brother for maize and beans. Couëxis acted quickly, for early next morning Ouadé's envoys returned with the provisions.

Chief Ouadé ordered his men to load the supplies into the canoe. He would not allow the French to depart, but entertained them throughout the day very hospitably. And he showed them his fields of maize the next morning, telling them that as long as that maize was there they should not lack food. After this the Frenchmen went back to Charlesfort.

six of the best veterans joined them. They also tried to corrupt me by revealing the names of my friends who had joined with them and threatening terrible things against those who would not. However, I declared myself against them in this undertaking.

M. de Laudonnière felt that some conspiracy was forming, but did not know who were involved; Ottigny also got wind of it.

On the night appointed by the conspirators for carrying out their plan, I was told by a gentleman, Normans de Pompierre, that they were going to cut the throat of Captain La Caille, with whom I lodged, and he warned me to get out of the way if I valued my life. But as time was too short to make other arrangements, I went home and told La Caille what I had heard. He at once escaped by a back door and hid in the woods, while I decided to trust to Providence and await events.

At midnight De Fourneaux, the chief conspirator, armed with a cuirass and a harquebus and accompanied by twenty harquebusiers, went to M. de Laudonnière's quarters and demanded admittance. Upon entering, he stepped straight to the commander's bedside, put a sword to his throat, and heaped insults upon him. He then seized the keys of the armory and storehouse, from which he removed all the weapons. After this he gave orders that M. de Laudonnière should be put in irons and confined under guard on the ship, which lay in the river opposite the fort.

At the same time the other leader, La Croix, entered Ottigny's lodging with fifteen men. They took away his arms and ordered him not to leave the house before daylight on pain of death, a command that he promised to obey. Stephen, the Genoese, exacted a similar oath from the ensign Arlac.

Captain Seignore, with the rest of the conspirators, came to kill Captain La Caille, as La Caille was in open opposition to their plan. But in this they had no success. Though they searched everywhere, they could find neither La Caille nor his two brothers. They did, however, carry away all their arms, as well as mine, and they decided that I should be taken to the soldiers' quarters as a prisoner. Yet at the request of several gentlemen of high character—who had been persuaded to join the conspiracy without clearly understanding what it was all about—I was allowed to keep my weapons. The only condition was that I should not leave the house until daylight, which I promised. Captain Seignore then visited the quarters of those soldiers who had not joined them and seized their arms. Thus the conspirators secured complete control of affairs.

With M. de Laudonnière in chains, Ottigny and Arlac disarmed and confined to their homes, La Caille a fugitive in the woods, and the rest of the loyal men disarmed, the conspirators proceeded to reverse Laudonnière's orders, using his name and authority to further their aims. One of them, De Fourneaux, drew up an order on parchment in which

THE NATIVES OF FLORIDA WORSHIP THE COLUMN ERECTED BY THE COMMANDER ON HIS FIRST VOYAGE

WHEN the French came to Florida the second time, they were commanded by Laudonnière. Upon their arrival crowds of Indians gathered on the shore to welcome them. They assured Laudonnière that they bore no enmity against him. So he went ashore with twenty harquebusiers where he was met by the chief, Athore. After presents had been exchanged and promises of friendship given, the chief asked the French to go with him. This they agreed to do, though as Athore was accompanied by a great number of men, they acted with great caution.

The chief took them to the island where Ribaut had set up the stone column carved with the arms of the King of France. When the French came closer to the column, they found Indians worshiping the stone as an idol. Athore kissed the stone with the same reverence that his subjects showed him. His men also kissed the column, and they asked us to do likewise. In front of the monument lay offerings of fruits, edible and medicinal roots, jars of perfumed oils, a bow, and arrows; the stone was wreathed with flowers and boughs of the choicest trees.

This Chief Athore was very handsome, wise, honorable, and strong, and at least half a foot taller than the tallest of our men. He was grave and modest, and his bearing was majestic. He had married his own mother and had a number of sons and daughters by her, whom he proudly showed us, striking his thigh as he did so. It is well to remark that after he married his mother, his father, Saturiba, did not live with her any longer.

M. de Laudonnière as lieutenant of the King of France authorized the greater part of his force to proceed to New Spain for provisions and requested all governors, captains, and other Spanish officials to aid them in this undertaking. They then forced M. de Laudonnière to sign this document.

The conspirators had outfitted the two newly built shallops with arms and provisions from the King's stores and had chosen their pilots and crews. Old Michael Vasseur of Dieppe was to be the master of one of the vessels, and the pilot Trenchant of the other. Thus prepared, they set sail from the fort on December 8, calling us cowards and greenhorns and threatening that if, on their return from New Spain with the wealth they proposed to acquire, we refused to admit them into Fort Caroline, they would destroy us.

While these pirates are in pursuit of wealth, let us return to La Roche Ferrière. Having arrived at the mountains, he succeeded by untiring diligence in winning the good will of the three chiefs, who were, as I mentioned before, the most bitter enemies of King Outina. La Roche Ferrière was astonished at their civilization and wealth, and he sent back to M. de Laudonnière at the fort many presents they had given him—round gold and silver plates as large as a medium-sized platter that they wore to protect the back and breast in war, much gold alloyed with brass, and some partly smelted silver. He also sent quivers covered with choice skins and filled with golden-headed arrows, pieces of material made of feathers decorated most skilfully with varicolored rushes, and some green and blue stones in the shape of wedges, which they used instead of axes for cutting wood (we thought they were emeralds and sapphires). In return for these gifts, M. de Laudonnière sent them whatever he had on hand: some thick, rough cloth, a few axes and saws, and other cheap Parisian goods. All these articles delighted the natives.

One result of these dealings was that La Roche Ferrière incurred the intense dislike of King Outina, and even more of his subordinate chiefs. They conceived such hatred for him that they even refused to mention his name; they referred to him simply as "Timogua," which means "Enemy."[6]

As long, however, as La Roche Ferrière kept the friendship of the three chiefs, he could travel to and from the fort. He had only to avoid Outina's tribe, by using some of the many small streams that emptied into the River of May fifteen or sixteen leagues below their territory.

I do not think I shall digress too much if I tell the story of a soldier who tried to emulate La Roche Ferrière and who therefore asked M. de Laudonnière if he could do

6. Timoga (Timoqua, Tymangona, Thimogona, etc.) was one of the villages of the Timuquanan Indians on the right bank of the St. John's. As Chief Outina, one of the headmen of the Timuquanan confederacy, was Saturiba's enemy, Le Moyne thought that the name itself meant "enemy."

A SITE FOR THE FORT IS CHOSEN

MANY rivers were explored before the French decided that the River of May was the best one for a settlement because maize and flour, as well as the gold and silver that they had discovered on their first voyage, were more abundant there. They sailed upstream until they came to the neighborhood of a certain hill, where they chose a spot which seemed to be more suitable for building a fort than any they had so far seen.

Next day, at dawn, they offered prayers to God and gave thanks for their happy arrival; then they all went briskly to work. First they marked out a triangular outline in the ground; then they began to dig the earth, to make fences of brushwood, and to build the wall. Each man was busy with spade, saw, ax, or some other tool, and all toiled so hard that the work progressed rapidly.

some trading on his own account. The commander gave him permission, but warned the man to be careful or he might lose his life—which in fact he did.

This soldier, whose name was Pierre Gambié, a strong and active young fellow who had been brought up in the home of Admiral Coligny, left the fort with nothing more than his harquebus and a parcel of cheap goods. He soon began trading up and down the country. And he was so successful that within a short time he was able to exercise a sort of authority over the natives and use them as messengers in communicating with us. At last he visited Adelano, a certain chieftain who lived on a small island in the river, and here he became such a favorite that the chief gave him his daughter as wife.

When Adelano was absent from his home, he allowed Gambié to represent him. On these occasions his rule was so tyrannical—he demanded that the Indians obtain for him things they were utterly powerless to get—that he was soon hated by all the natives. But since the chief liked him, no one dared to complain. Eventually he asked Adelano's leave to visit the fort, as he had not seen his friends there for twelve months. Adelano allowed him to go so long as he returned in a few days.

Gambié packed all his wealth into a canoe, and, with two Indians to paddle, he said good-bye to Chief Adelano. On the journey to the fort one of these Indians, remembering that he had once been beaten with sticks by Gambié and being tempted also by the boat-load of booty, concluded that such a favorable opportunity for combining revenge and profit was not to be missed. Thus, while Gambié was bending over a fire with no thought of danger, the Indian picked up an ax and cut his head open. Then he and his companion fled, taking with them all the goods.

I now return to M. de Laudonnière, to relate what happened after the men's departure. (They, by the way, had carried off some half-casks of rich Spanish wine, which both M. de Laudonnière and his maidservant declared had been put aside for the use of the sick.) Captain La Caille, still wandering in the woods, used his younger brother as messenger. He brought La Caille such supplies as his friends could send and told him that the men who had threatened his life had departed. Thereupon the captain returned to the fort and encouraged the soldiers to take possession of their arms again. M. de Laudonnière was escorted ashore from the ship, and Lieutenant Ottigny and Ensign Arlac were released from their huts. At roll call all soldiers renewed their oath of allegiance to the King and of resistance to their enemies, among whom they now counted the absent conspirators. Four captains were then appointed, and the whole company was divided into four companies under them. Thus all returned to their regular duties.

About this time, a young gentleman from Poitiers named De Groutaut arrived at the fort. He had been sent by La Roche Ferrière, whose constant companion he had been

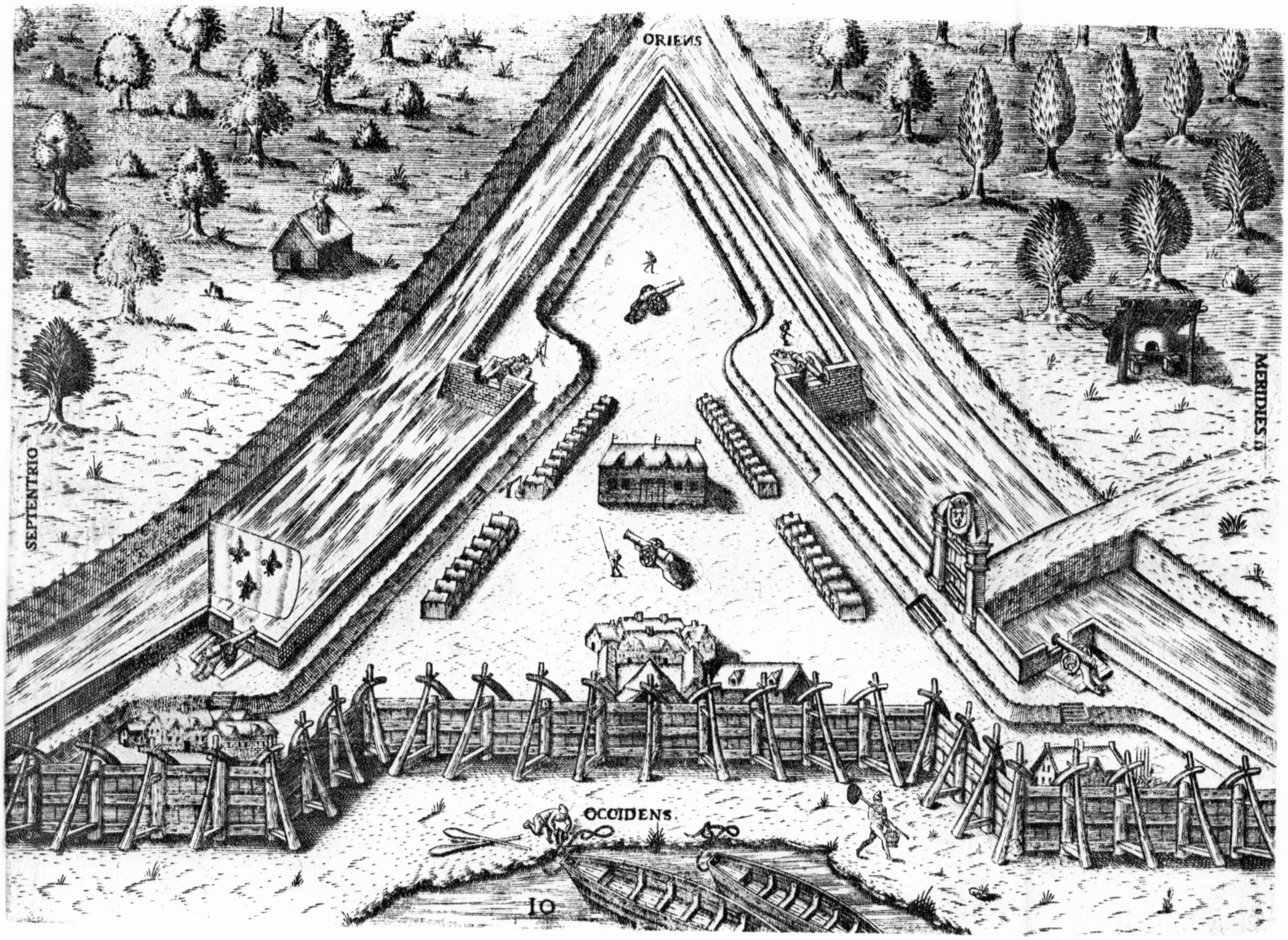

FORT CAROLINE

When the fort was completed, the French named it Fort Caroline. The base of the triangle, facing westward, was defended by a small ditch and a wall of sod nine feet high, while the side near the river was built up with planks and brushwood. On the south side stood a granary, built like a citadel, of earth and brushwood; the upper part of the wall was of sod for two or three feet.

Inside the fort was an open space eighteen yards long and as many wide. Here were the soldiers' quarters and one other building, which had been built too high and soon was blown over by the wind. (Thus we learned from experience that in this country of furious winds the houses had to be low.)

There was another large open space inside the fort, enclosed by the granary on one side and by Laudonnière's house on the other. The commander's house faced the river and had a porch all around it. The front door opened into the fort; the rear door gave upon the stream.

The oven was set at a safe distance so that the houses, thatched with palm branches, should not catch fire.

during his expedition to the three chiefs near the Apalatcy Mountains. He brought word to Laudonnière that one of these chiefs had developed a great affection for the Christians; he was powerful and rich, with a military force of four thousand men. This chief told La Roche Ferrière that he desired to form a perpetual league with Laudonnière. As he understood that we were searching for gold, he was ready to bind himself by any conditions we might make, and if we could provide him with a hundred harquebusiers he promised to make us the victorious masters of the Apalatcy Mountains. La Roche Ferrière, knowing nothing of the trouble at the fort, had undertaken to arrange this, and there is no doubt the league would have been completed had we not been so shamefully deserted by most of our men. But Laudonnière realized that if he sent away a hundred harquebusiers he would not have enough men to defend the fort. He therefore put off the expedition until reinforcements arrived from France. Besides these considerations, he was suspicious of the chief's sudden friendship toward us. He did not have much confidence in the Indians, particularly since the time he had been warned by the Spaniards not to trust the natives. While speaking of this, I shall insert here a passage from the *History of Florida,* written and published by Laudonnière: [7]

"When the Indians visited me," writes Laudonnière, "they always brought some gift or other, such as fish, deer, turkeys, leopards, bear cubs, and other produce of the country, and I on my part rewarded them with hatchets, knives, glass beads, combs, and mirrors. One day two Indians came to greet me in the name of their King, Marracou, who lived about forty leagues south of the fort. They told me that living with King Onatheaqua was a person called The Bearded and there was another with King Mathiaca whose name they did not know; both of these men were strangers. I surmised they might be Christians, and I notified all the chiefs in the vicinity that if they had any Christians in their domain, they would receive a double reward on bringing them to me. With this inducement, both the men were delivered to me at the fort. They were naked, and their hair hung down to their thighs in the Indian fashion. Though they were Spanish by birth, they had become so used to the customs of the natives that at first our ways seemed strange to them. I talked with them, gave them clothes, and ordered their hair to be cut.

"After this was done, they kept their hair, wrapping it in a cotton cloth, saying that they intended to carry it back home with them as proof of the hardships they had endured in India. We found in the hair of one a piece of gold, worth about twenty-five crowns; this he presented to me. When I inquired about their travels and asked them how they had

7. René Goulaine de Laudonnière wrote three long letters describing the French expeditions to Florida. These letters have been translated and printed in English in Richard Hakluyt, *The Principal Navigations Voyages Traffiques and Discoveries of the English Nation* (See Bibliography).

SATURIBA GOES TO WAR

ON THEIR *second voyage the French made a treaty with Saturiba [Saturioua], the great chief of the adjoining country. They had agreed to erect a fort in his territory, to be friends of his friends, and enemies of his enemies. About three months after this pact had been made, Saturiba requested some soldiers, as he was ready to make war. Laudonnière declined to send the harquebusiers, for he hoped to make peace between the chief and his enemies.*

Saturiba was indignant. His preparations for war were far advanced; it was too late now to put off the expedition. He asked the neighboring chiefs for assistance. When they came, the whole force—in war paint and feathers—sat down in a circle, with Saturiba in their midst. A fire was lighted to his left, and two large vessels of water were placed at his right. The chief, rolling his eyes angrily and gesturing with his arms, raised a horrible yell. His men repeated the cry, striking their hips and rattling their weapons. Then Saturiba, taking a wooden bowl full of water, turned toward the sun, worshiped it, and prayed for victory over the enemy. He prayed that their blood might be poured out like the water he was about to scatter from the bowl. He then flung the water into the air and said: "As I have done with this water, so I pray that you may do with the blood of your enemies." After this he poured the water from the other vessel onto the fire, saying: "So may you be able to extinguish your enemies and bring back their scalps."

With this the ceremonies ended. The men rose and set off for war.

come to this province, they replied that about fifteen years before they had been aboard one of three ships which were wrecked near Calos[8] on the rocks called The Martyrs. King Calos had salvaged for himself most of the riches with which these ships were laden, and through his efforts nearly all the crew had been saved. A number of women were also rescued; three or four were married noblewomen accompanied by their children. They were still living with this King Calos.

"When I questioned them further about this King, the men told me that he was the handsomest and biggest Indian of all that region, and an energetic and powerful ruler. He possessed a great store of gold and silver, which he kept in one of his villages, in a pit as deep as a man is tall and as large around as a cask. The men assured me that if I would go there with a hundred soldiers, they could help me to acquire all this wealth, besides whatever else I might obtain from the natives of the country. They also told me that when the women met for dancing, they wore on their belts flat gold plates as large as quoits and so heavy that they interfered with their movements and that the men, too, were similarly loaded. They believed that most of this wealth came from Spanish ships, for many vessels are wrecked in that strait. What they did not obtain from the boats, they gained by trade with the other chiefs in the neighborhood.

"The King was greatly revered by his subjects, since he had convinced them that it was his magic incantations that caused the earth to provide them with the necessities of life. To maintain this belief he shut himself up with two or three confidential companions in a certain building. There he performed these incantations, and anyone who tried to spy on what happened inside this hut was immediately put to death on the King's orders. The men related that every year at harvest time this barbarian sacrificed a victim chosen from among the shipwrecked Spaniards who were his prisoners. One of my informants also told me that he had often been sent as a courier to another chief, named Oathkaqua,[9] who lived four or five days' journey from Calos and who was a faithful ally of its King. Half way through this journey, in a great fresh-water lake called Sarrope [probably Lake Ware in Marion County], was an island five leagues wide and as many long, abounding in a great variety of fruit, especially dates, in which there was a considerable trade. There was a still bigger trade in a certain root used for making flour. From this flour excellent bread could be made, which supplied the country for fifteen leagues around. As a result the islanders were growing rich at the expense of their neighbors, because they sold the root only at a very high price.

"The people on the island were considered to be the bravest tribe in the entire region.

8. Calos is shown on the Le Moyne map, pp. 34-35, on the southern end of the Florida peninsula. On John White's chart, pp. 186-187, it is called Catos.

9. See Le Moyne's map on pp. 34-35.

OUTINA CONSULTS A SORCERER

LAUDONNIÈRE *had some of Chief Outina's soldiers in the fort. They had been made prisoner by Saturiba, and Laudonnière now decided to send these men back to Outina. This deed led to a treaty of friendship between them. The French were glad to make this pact, because the only route to the Appalachian Mountains, where gold and silver were found, passed through Outina's territory. After it was made, Outina asked Laudonnière for harquebusiers to help fight his enemy. Twenty-five men were sent to him under the command of Lieutenant Ottigny.*

As soon as Outina was ready, his army began its march. The first day's journey was easy, but the second led through swamps thickly overgrown with thorns and brambles. It was very hot, and the Indians were forced to carry the Frenchmen on their shoulders, which the harquebusiers found a great relief. At last they reached the enemy's territory. Outina halted his force, summoned a sorcerer, who was more than a hundred and twenty years old, and questioned him about the enemy. The sorcerer prepared a place in the middle of the army and asked Ottigny to allow him to use his shield. He laid the shield on the ground, drawing a circle around it and inscribing it with various signs. Then, kneeling on it, he whispered some unintelligible words and made gestures as if he were engaged in animated conversation. After a quarter of an hour his appearance became so frightful that he looked scarcely human; he twisted his limbs until the bones snapped out of place and did many other unnatural things. Then suddenly he became calm. He stepped out of his circle, saluted the chief, and revealed to him the number of the enemy and the place where they were to fight.

They proved their bravery when they took the daughter of Oathkaqua prisoner after she was betrothed to King Calos, and this is the story:

"Oathkaqua, with a large retinue, was escorting one of his daughters, a maiden of great beauty of face and form, to King Calos, to whom she was to be married. Hearing about this, the people of the island ambushed the cortege, attacked and routed Oathkaqua and his followers, captured the bride and her attendants, and carried them off to their island. This sort of victory is considered a splendid feat by the Indians, who put a high value on wives taken in this way. Their custom is to marry virgins captured in this manner and to love them above all measure.

"King Calos lived near a river forty or fifty leagues southwest of the promontory of Florida, while Oathkaqua's village was just north of the Cape, at a place called Canaveral, twenty-eight degrees north of the equator.

"On about January 25 King Saturiba sent me [Laudonnière] presents by two of his men, wishing me to join forces with him in an attack on Outina, who was a friend of mine. He asked me in particular to recall some of my soldiers who were staying with Outina, on whose account he had refrained from attacking and overthrowing his enemy. During the next month a number of other chiefs sent me messages to the same effect. But I was not inclined to comply with their requests; instead, I did all I could to promote friendliness among them all. They responded to my suggestions in such a manner that I was almost convinced they were ready to agree to anything I proposed.

"However, at this point the two Spaniards, who had had long experience with the native character, warned me not to put any faith in them at all, since they invariably behaved most amiably when they were plotting some treachery, and were by nature utter traitors and deceivers. As time passed I, too, had learned to distrust them, for my own knowledge as well as certain accounts I had read of them had shown me how given to fraud and deception they were.

"The two shallops were now ready, and I gave orders to Vasseur, who was in charge of one of them, to explore the seacoast to the north and go as far as the river in the region where Adusta[10] was king. (He was the chief from whom the French procured supplies in 1562.) I sent him two suits of clothes, some axes, knives, and other goods of little value, as I desired to gain his friendship. I also dispatched with Vasseur a soldier named Aimon. This man had already visited Adusta on a previous expedition, and I hoped that the chief would remember him. Before the men embarked I asked them to make inquiries about the fate of Rouffi, a soldier who stayed behind alone when Nicolas Mallon and the rest of his men returned to France on a vessel under Mallon's command. When our men arrived there,

10. Adusta, or Audusta, was probably the chief of the Edisto Indians.

OUTINA DEFEATS POTANOU

THE sorcerer's report frightened Outina so much that he contemplated marching home again without even giving battle to the enemy. But Ottigny, annoyed at the idea of having made all his sacrifices in vain, accused him of lacking courage and of being a poor leader. These reproaches and threats at last forced Outina to order an attack. He put the French harquebusiers in the front line, where they very willingly bore the brunt of the fighting, killing many of the enemy and routing Chief Potanou's army.

Had it not been for the French, Outina would have been defeated, for the enemy had come in great force. (Thus the report of the sorcerer was proved true; he must certainly have been possessed of a devil.) When Potanou's army fled, Outina ordered his men back and marched home again, to the great wrath of Ottigny, who wished to follow up the victory.

they learned that Rouffi had departed in a ship. Some time later I learned that it was a Spanish vessel on a coasting trip and that Rouffi had been taken to Havana.[11]

"King Adusta sent the shallop back filled with maize and beans and presented me with two deer, two painted skins, and some pearls. (The pearls were of little value, as they had been exposed to fire.) He also offered me land and as much corn as I wanted, if I would settle in his territory.

"When Vasseur returned, I ordered the shallops on another expedition to carry a present to Hiouacara, the widow of a deceased chief, who lived about twelve miles north of us. She received my men kindly and loaded both shallops with maize and nuts, and also added several baskets of *casina* leaves, from which the Indians make a drink. The territory ruled by this widow was exceptionally fertile and produced the best maize along the whole seacoast; the woman herself was said to be of remarkable beauty and so reverenced by the members of her tribe that they would not allow her to walk, but insisted upon carrying her on their shoulders.

"For seven weeks there had been a flight of pigeons in such numbers that we sometimes shot as many as two hundred in one day; with these and my other provisions, I now believed we would have food enough to last until the supply ships arrived from France. As I did not wish to allow my men to be idle, I sent the two shallops on an exploring expedition up the river, which they ascended for thirty miles above Mathiaca.[12] They discovered a lake so wide that its farther shore could not be seen from the top of the tallest tree on this side [Lake George]. For this reason they did not attempt to go any farther, but returned by way of Chilili.[13] Here, in the middle of the river, they found Edelano [Drayton Island], the most delightful island in the world. It is a populous island about three miles square, abounding in fruits. Between the town of Edelano and the riverside there is a walk three hundred yards long and fifteen wide bordered by great trees whose overarching branches form a vaulting that seems to be constructed, not by nature, but by art, and has, perhaps, no equal in the world. On leaving this place our men proceeded to Enecaque, thence to Patchica, and thence to Choya,[14] where they left the shallops with a guard in a small inlet.

"They went to see Outina, who received them hospitably and asked them to stay. Six of the party, including De Groutaut, accepted the invitation, and they remained with the chief for two months. During this time De Groutaut explored the country with

11. Guilluame Rouffi, or as the Spanish called him Guillermo Rufin, was the only Frenchman of the Ribaut colony who did not leave the New World. When Manrique de Rojas came to Florida at the end of May, 1564, he found Rouffi living with the tribe of Chief Audusta. (See Bibliography.)

12. See Le Moyne's map on pp. 34-35. On John White's chart the name is spelled Machiaca.

13. See Le Moyne's map on pp. 34-35.

14. See Le Moyne's map on pp. 34-35.

OUTINA'S ORDER OF MARCH

WHEN Saturiba went to war, his men followed him in whatever order they happened to be. But his enemy Holata Outina (the name means "King of Many Kings"), who was more powerful, both in the number of his men and in wealth, than Saturiba, marched his forces in regular ranks like an organized army.

Outina was painted red, and he walked alone in solitary grandeur in the middle of his warriors. On the flanks of his force were his young men, wearing red war paint; the swifter of them acted as advance guards and scouts. They followed their enemies by scent, as dogs follow wild beasts, and when they found them they immediately returned to the main force with their reports. Instead of using trumpets and drums to give orders, as we do in our armies, they have heralds who direct them by cries when to halt, advance, attack, or perform some other military duty.

They never fight after sunset, but make camp in squads of ten each. When the chief has chosen the camping place, and after he has eaten and gone to rest for the night, the quartermasters post ten squads in a circle around him, containing the bravest men. Ten paces outside this circle they place another line of twenty squads, twenty paces farther another line of forty squads, and so on, the number and distance of these lines increasing according to the size of the army.

another man, whom I had previously sent there for the same purpose. When De Groutaut returned to the fort, he was full of admiration. He said that he had never seen finer country. One of the regions which he described was called Oustaca,[15] ruled by a king who was able to master an army of three or four thousand men. De Groutaut was anxious that I should ally myself to this chief in the belief that between us we could conquer all the adjacent tribes and clear the way to the Apalatcy Mountains, which we wanted to reach. The chief himself sent me a flat piece of brass dug out of the mountains; from their base rises a stream rich in gold, though the Indians believe it to be brass.

"They take gold from the bed of this stream by collecting the sand into reeds and shaking them about, whereby the grains of gold and silver appear. From the number of these grains they can guess whether there is a vein of ore in the mountain. As this region was at least five or six days' journey from our fort, I decided that as soon as reinforcements arrived from France I would move our base of operations to a more northerly river to be nearer these mountains."

Here ends the passage which I quote from Laudonnière's narrative.

Now let us return to those members of the expedition who had gone to New Spain for supplies. Near Cuba they encountered some vessels loaded with cassava, olive oil, Spanish wine, and other supplies. They captured some of these ships and decided to use them instead of their own. Not content with this booty, they raided several places on the island and carried off loot to the extent of two thousand crowns apiece. After a sharp fight, they also took a fast ship which had on board not only a very valuable cargo but also the Governor of the port of Havana and his two children. They decided to hold him and his children for a large ransom, including five or six Saguin monkeys and an equal number of parrots, as well as a large sum in gold. The Governor was to remain their prisoner until their demands were met. He agreed to the terms and suggested that it would be quickest to send one of his sons to his wife with a note. The men examined the letter carefully, and when they found it to be quite innocent they allowed the boy to leave the boat. They thought they had been very clever and cautious.

But the Governor had tricked them. He had whispered entirely different instructions to his son from those he had set forth in his letter. Thus, when his wife received the note and the message, she dispatched riders to every port in the island for help. As a result of her action, the French found themselves trapped early the next morning, with a large man-of-war on each side of their vessels and a third blocking their escape through the narrow entrance to the harbor.

In this hopeless situation twenty-six of the Frenchmen got away in their bark. The

15. See the northern part of Le Moyne's map on pp. 34-35.

HOW OUTINA'S MEN TREATED THE ENEMY DEAD

DURING the time the French were fighting with Outina they never saw a regular battle; all the military operations were either secret forays or light skirmishes, with fresh men constantly replacing the fighters. Whichever side killed the first enemy claimed the victory, even though it had lost the greater number of soldiers.

In their skirmishes anyone who fell was instantly dragged off by men detailed for that duty. They carried slips of reeds, sharper than any steel blade; with these they cut the skin of the head down to the bone from front to back and all the way around and pulled it off while the hair, more than a foot and a half long, was still attached to it. When they had done this, they dug a hole in the ground and made a fire, kindling it with a piece of smoldering ember. (This ember, wrapped in skins, they carry on their belts.) Over the fire they dried the scalps until they looked like parchment.

After the battle they invariably cut off the arms and legs of the fallen warriors with their knives, broke the bare bones with a club, and then laid the bloody bones over the fires to dry. They hung the bones and the scalps at the ends of their spears, carrying them home in triumph.

One of their habits astonished me (for I was one of this party Laudonnière sent out under Ottigny). It was this: after they had mutilated the dead, they always shot an arrow into the corpse. They would never leave the battlefield without doing this.

boat was small and fast, and they were able to flee unharmed. The men cut her cable and fought their way out through the enemy. The rest of the party, who remained on board the other vessel, were either killed in the ensuing fight or captured and kept in prison on the mainland. Some time later a few of them were sold as slaves and taken as far away as Spain and Portugal.

The three chief conspirators—De Fourneaux, Stephen the Genoese, and La Croix—were among those who escaped, together with the pilot, Trenchant, and five or six sailors. Finding that their vessel was without provisions, they made up their minds to sail back to Florida. This decision was reached while the rest of the company was asleep. When the soldiers awoke, they were enraged, as they feared that Laudonnière would punish them. After some argument they all agreed that it would be best to put in at the River of May, get supplies from certain Indians, and set sail again before the garrison at the fort should discover them.

They cast anchor in the mouth of the river and began to look for provisions. Soon an Indian brought the news to Laudonnière. The commander was about to order them to bring their boat up opposite the fort and to present themselves before him, when La Caille dissuaded Laudonnière from doing this. He said that in his opinion the rebels would rather take to flight than obey the order.

"What else do you suggest?" asked Laudonnière.

"Let me have twenty-five harquebusiers," replied La Caille, "and I will hide them in a shallop, covering them with a sail. Then at daybreak I will approach their ship. If the rebels see only two or three of us with a couple of hands to manage the shallop, they will let us come alongside their vessel, and as soon as we are there, we can take them by surprise."

La Caille's plan was accepted. The next morning, when the watch on the boat caught sight of the approaching shallop, he called all hands. But as soon as the rebels recognized La Caille and saw that he was accompanied by only a few others, they allowed his shallop to come alongside their boat. When she was made fast, the soldiers hidden under the sail sprang up and boarded the ship. The surprised mutineers tried to resist, but were quickly disarmed and told that they would be brought before M. de Laudonnière. This news terrified them, as they well understood their peril.

They were taken to the fort, where the three main conspirators were regularly tried, condemned, and executed, while the rest of the men were pardoned. After this there was no more sedition.

Now we began to suffer from an acute shortage of food, for the Indians had changed their attitude and refused to supply us any longer. They complained that they were never given anything in exchange for their provisions and that our men often used violence in

TROPHIES AND CEREMONIES AFTER A VICTORY

RETURNING from their wars, the Indians assemble in a place designated for this purpose. Here they bring the legs, arms, and scalps of the fallen adversaries and with great solemnities attach them to tall poles. Then the men and the women sit down in a circle before the poles, where their sorcerer, holding a small image, begins to curse the enemy, uttering a thousand imprecations in a low voice. While the sorcerer is repeating his curses, three men kneel opposite him. One of them pounds on a flat stone with a club, marking time with the spells; two others rattle pumpkins filled with small stones or seeds and accompany the sorcerer's words with a chant. This is their way of celebrating whenever they win a victory over their enemies.

collecting supplies and had even burned down their houses to force them to give us food. As time passed, our relationship with the natives became more and more difficult. Soon we had to walk three or four leagues before we could find any of them.

It was during this period that we had also to undertake a campaign against the powerful Outina. A description of this fight M. de Laudonnière has included in his account. We suffered terribly from want, and if I had space I could give you a heart-rending description of our miserable condition. After some of us had already died of hunger and the rest were starved until we were nothing but skin and bones, Laudonnière called a general council to discuss means of returning to France. He had now given up hope of receiving the reinforcements for which we had been waiting eighteen months. The general council decided to refit our third ship as well as possible and to build up her sides with planking to increase her capacity. While this work was in progress, a number of French soldiers were sent along the coast to collect supplies.

Just then an English commander named Hawkins arrived at our fort on his way home from a long voyage. Seeing our miserable and half-starved condition, he offered to help us. He sold Laudonnière one of his ships at a low price, along with some casks of flour for biscuits and some of dried beans and peas. For these articles Hawkins accepted a few of our brass cannon as part payment. We were extremely grateful for the Englishman's kindness, for now we had enough provisions for the return voyage and a second ship as well.

The council ruled that our fort was to be destroyed before we left, as the Spaniards were very anxious to establish themselves in the region, and it was feared they might use the fort against us if we ever came back. Yet another reason for demolishing the fort was to prevent Saturiba from occupying it.

After the necessary preparations had been made and the fort had been destroyed, we still could not leave for three weeks because of unfavorable winds. Before we were able to sail, we were surprised and delighted at the arrival of a fleet of seven ships under the famous Jean Ribaut, who had been sent out to succeed M. de Laudonnière. Ribaut landed on the shore with his officers and associates, and we were overjoyed. They were just as happy as we were and thanked God that they had found us alive. Ribaut was very generous in giving us food and other necessities and tried in every way to make our life easier. So after all our afflictions, God sent us happiness, though unfortunately it was to prove short-lived, as we soon discovered.

When Ribaut found that there was too little water for the larger vessels, he ordered only the three smaller ones into the river. One of these, the *Pearl,* was commanded by his son, Jacques Ribaut, with Vallard [Ballaud] of Dieppe as his lieutenant; Captain Maillard, also of Dieppe, commanded the second, and the third was under a man named Machon-

HERMAPHRODITES AS LABORERS

HERMAPHRODITES are common in these parts. They are considered odious, but are used as beasts of burden, since they are strong. Whenever the Indians go to war, it is the hermaphrodites who carry the provisions. And whenever an Indian dies, be it from wounds or from disease, it is the hermaphrodites who carry the dead to the burial ground. They lay the deceased on a woven mat of reeds attached to crosspieces on stout poles. One skin is placed under the head, a second about the body, a third around one thigh, a fourth around one leg. Why this is done I never discovered, but I suppose it is for ornamentation, since sometimes they bind a skin around only one leg. Then the hermaphrodites take thongs of hide, fasten them to the ends of the poles, and rest these upon their heads (which are remarkably hard), and in this way they carry the bodies to the burial ground.

The hermaphrodites also look after those who have contagious diseases; they take the sick on their shoulders to places selected for the purpose and feed and care for them until they are well again.

ville.[16] The four larger ships remained at anchor a mile from shore, as the water was shallow there. They were unloaded by means of canoes and other small boats.

A week or so after Ribaut's arrival, at about four o'clock in the afternoon, when all except a few of the newcomers were on shore and engaged in putting up dwellings and rebuilding the fort, some of the soldiers saw six strange ships sailing toward our four anchored vessels. They immediately sent someone to inform Ribaut, who arrived at the shore some time later. The soldiers told him that when the six strange ships had anchored near ours, the French boats had quickly cut their cables and gone out to sea under full sail. The six strangers weighed anchor and set out in pursuit. Ribaut and the men with him were able to see part of the chase, though our ships were so fast that they were out of sight in a very short time, and the pursuers disappeared about a quarter of an hour later. We were very uneasy, and all the following night we feared the worst. Ribaut ordered that the small craft should be cleared for action, and he stationed five or six hundred harquebusiers on shore, ready to embark if necessary.

Nothing happened that night or the next day until about noon, when we discovered the *Trinity*, the largest of our four ships, coming in our direction. Shortly afterwards the other three vessels came in sight, one by one. They signaled us to come on board, but Ribaut thought that it might be a trap and that the ships might now be in the hands of the enemy, so he would not allow anyone to take the risk and go out to them. As the wind was adverse the ships could not stand in close to shore, and therefore Captain Corsette, who came up with the second boat, called for a volunteer to swim to land with a letter for Ribaut. The man had to swim a long way, and he nearly drowned before we saw him. We sent a boat from shore to pick him up. The report which he handed to Ribaut read:

M. DE RIBAUT: *Yesterday, at four* P.M., *a Spanish fleet of eight ships hove in sight, six of which cast anchor near us. As soon as we saw that they were Spaniards, we cut our cables and stood out to sea. They gave chase immediately, and we were under fire all night. Fortunately, we could outsail them, and at last they gave up the chase and made a landing five or six miles below our position. Here they have put ashore a large number of Negroes with spades and mattocks. Please act on this information as you see fit.*

After Ribaut read this letter, he called a council of his chief subordinates (about thirty military officers in addition to a number of civilians) and asked for their opinions.

16. Ribaut's fleet consisted of six or seven vessels. The flagship was the *Trinity;* then came the *Emérillon,* commanded by Nicholas d'Ornano of Corsica, nicknamed Corsette, and the *Pearl* under Jacques Ribaut's command. The other vessels were: *Levrière* (*levrette,* from which the word *levrière* derives means a female greyhound) Vincent Collas, master; the *Emérillon* (another boat of the same name) under the command of Vivien Maillard, meaning a small bird of prey; the *Shoulder of Mutton,* commanded by Machonville; probably there was a seventh boat, named the *Trout.*

THE WIDOWS APPROACH THE CHIEF

THE wives of the soldiers who have fallen in battle or died of disease assemble before the chief on a certain day. They approach him with loud demonstrations of sorrow. They squat on their heels, hiding their faces in their hands. They beg him to avenge the death of their husbands, to provide for them during their widowhood, and to give them permission to remarry at the end of the period appointed for mourning.

After the chief agrees to their requests, the widows return to their homes, crying and lamenting in loud tones to show how much they loved their husbands. When they have mourned in this way for days, they carry the weapons and drinking cups of their dead to the burying ground.

The more prudent members of this assembly wanted to finish building and arming the fort, while Laudonnière's men, who were familiar with the country, were sent against the Spaniards. This plan, with the help of God, would quickly settle matters.[17]

Ribaut listened attentively to what the men had to say, and when they had finished he spoke: "Gentlemen, having heard your views, I would now like to state my own. But first, let me tell you that just before I left France the Admiral sent me a letter in which he wrote: 'M. Ribaut, we have information that the Spaniards intend to surprise you. You must not yield a particle.' My objection to your suggestions is," continued Ribaut, "that it might allow the Spaniards to escape to their ships before our men could attack them. If this happens, we lose our chance of destroying those who intend to destroy us. It seems a better plan to me to re-embark our soldiers on our four ships and to seize the Spanish boats where they are now anchored. We must do this while the enemy is ashore. If the Spaniards lose their ships, their only defense will be the works which their slaves have been building, and it will be much easier for us to fight them on land."

Laudonnière, whose experience made him familiar with the climate of the region, urged Ribaut to take the weather into consideration before re-embarking his men. At that time of year, he said, a species of typhoon which the sailors called *houragans* [hurricanes] were likely to occur suddenly at any time and cause immense damage along the coast; for this reason Laudonnière agreed with the majority and favored the plan first suggested.

Ribaut, however, rejected this advice. He persisted in following his own plan, which was without doubt the will of God, Who chose this means not only to punish His own children but also to punish the wicked. Ribaut, not satisfied with his own force, had asked Laudonnière for his captains and ensign, who under the circumstances could not be refused him. When Laudonnière's other men saw that their standard-bearer was boarding the vessel, they insisted on going with their officers. I went along too, though I was lame in one leg, nursing the wound which I had received in the campaign against Outina.

After the troops were on board, all we needed was a fair wind for an hour or two so that we could sail towards the enemy, but just as we were about to weigh anchor, the wind changed and blew from the direction of the enemy towards us. This lasted for two whole days and nights. On the third day, with the weather still showing no signs of changing, Ribaut ordered all officers to inspect their men, and when Ottigny found that I had not entirely recovered from my wound, he told me to go ashore. He sent another soldier with me in the small boat, a tailor by trade, who was busy making Ottigny some clothes for his

17. Here Le Moyne inserts a sentence as an explanation. He says that the plan would make for quick success, as the site of the fort was three or four hundred miles from the limits of Spanish jurisdiction. This is a justification of the French claim that they had the right to occupy the country.

THE MOURNING WIDOWS

AT THEIR husbands' graves the women cut off their long hair below the ears and scatter it over the graves, upon which they then place the weapons and drinking cups of the dead as memorials. When these ceremonies are over, the widows return to their homes, but they are not allowed to marry again until their hair has grown long enough to cover their shoulders.

The Indians, men and women alike, allow their fingernails and toenails to grow very long. The men, especially, trim their fingernails at the sides and sharpen them to a point. So, when they capture an enemy, they can dig their nails into the forehead of a prisoner and tear down the skin over his face to wound and blind him.

return to France. Neither the tailor nor I wanted to return to the fort, but we had to obey the orders of our superior officers.

At last Ribaut's fleet weighed anchor and set sail. The boats were scarcely on the move when such a tempest arose that they had to put to sea at once. Otherwise they would have been destroyed. The storm continued with unabated fury. The ships were blown for fifty miles and in the end were driven ashore on the rocks. We lost no men except Captain La Grange, a relative of Admiral Coligny, who was drowned. But the gale destroyed all the Spanish ships.

The Spaniards must have suspected the fate of our fleet. They evolved a plan to seize our fort by a land attack. Though the rain continued to fall in torrents, they sent an expedition against us. Their men marched all the night.

At our fort everyone who could bear arms was on guard. Of the one hundred and fifty people left behind, there were only about twenty fit enough to serve, as Ribaut had taken with him all the soldiers except fourteen or fifteen sick men, many of whom had been wounded in the campaign against Outina. The others in the fort were either servants or mechanics, who had never heard a gun fired, king's commissaries, who were more used to handling pens than swords, or women—wives of Ribaut's soldiers. Laudonnière himself was sick in bed.

When day broke and there was still no sign of the enemy, De la Vigne, the officer of the guard, pitying the drenched and exhausted sentinels who had kept watch all night, allowed them to go to their quarters and get some rest. The sentinels had scarcely put away their arms when the Spaniards, guided by Jean François, a renegade Frenchman, attacked the fort at three points simultaneously. They gained entrance without opposition and assembled their forces on the parade ground. From there they sent out parties to search the soldiers' quarters, killing every man they found. The cries and groans of the victims being slaughtered sounded terrible.

For my own part, I never cease to wonder at the miracle that God, to Whom truly nothing is impossible, accomplished on my behalf. Coming in from my watch, I had laid down my harquebus and, wet as I was, flung myself into my hammock, where I tried to get some sleep. But soon I was awakened by the sound of blows and the screams of the people. I jumped up from the hammock and rushed out to see what had happened. When I passed the doorway two Spaniards came toward me with drawn swords, but they did not attack me. Seeing that the place of arms was in possession of the enemy, I turned back and made for one of the embrasures. Here I found the bodies of five or six of my companions, La Gaule and Jean du Den among them. I jumped down into the ditch and made my way up the slope to a piece of woods. I was running like a man who had lost his senses. But

HOW THEY TREAT THEIR SICK

THEY build a bench long enough and wide enough for the sick person, and he is laid upon it, either on his back or on his stomach. This depends upon the nature of his illness. Then, cutting the skin of his forehead with a sharp shell, they suck the blood with their own mouths, spitting it out into an earthen jar or a gourd. Women who are nursing or are pregnant come and drink this blood, especially if it is that of a strong young man. They believe that drinking it makes their milk better and their children stronger, healthier, and more active.

For the sick, whom they lay face downward, a fire of hot coals is prepared, onto which seeds are thrown. The sick man inhales the smoke through his nose and mouth; this is to act as a purge, expelling the poison from the body and thus curing the disease.

They also have a plant which the Brazilians call petum *and the Spaniards* tapaco. *After carefully drying its leaves, they put them in the bowl of a pipe. They light the pipe, and, holding its other end in their mouths, they inhale the smoke so deeply that it comes out through their mouths and noses; by this means they often cure infections.*

Venereal disease is common among them, and they have several natural remedies for it.

when I reached the top, my head cleared, and I began to pray to the Almighty to guide me in this extremity of peril. At a suggestion from His spirit, I went forward by one of the wood paths, and I had walked only a short while, when, to my great joy, I met four other Frenchmen. We held council and deliberated as to what to do next. One or two of the men suggested that, rather than take the risk of being eaten by wild beasts or dying of hunger, we should wait until the next day and then surrender to the Spaniards, in the hope that by that time their fury would be spent. But the others thought it would be better to make our way to some distant Indian settlement and await there the course of events.

I said to them: "Brothers, I do not like either suggestion. If you will take my advice, we should make for the seashore and try to find the small vessels that Ribaut ordered into the river to unload the provisions brought from France."

My companions were against this, and they set off to find the Indians, leaving me alone. But God in His mercy had sent me another companion in Grandchemin, the tailor who had come ashore in the boat with me. I made the same suggestion—that we try to find one of Ribaut's small boats. Grandchemin agreed, and we set out, walking through the woods all that day to reach the shore. When night fell we came to a swamp overgrown with large reeds; we had to pass through it. By that time we were very nearly exhausted, for the tide had raised the water to the level of our waists, and a steady rain was falling. Yet we kept onward.

Daylight came, and we still could not see the sea. Grandchemin became impatient. He wanted to surrender to the enemy and suggested that we should return. He believed that when the Spaniards discovered that we were artificers, they would spare our lives. And even if they would not, death was better than our present state. I tried to dissuade him, but met with no success. Finally, when I realized he was going to leave me, I agreed to go back with him. We retraced our way through the woods, and some time later we came in sight of the fort. When we heard the sounds of rejoicing and the general uproar of the Spaniards, I stopped and said to my companion: "Friend, let us not go there yet; let us stay away at least for a while; God will open ways of safety for us about which we now know nothing, and will bring us out of danger." But Grandchemin refused; he embraced me and said, "I am going; goodbye."

I was anxious to know what happened to my companion, so I made my way to a place near by from which I could watch him.

As Grandchemin came down the slope, he was discovered by the Spaniards, and a party was sent out to meet him. Grandchemin fell on his knees before the soldiers, begging for his life, but the Spaniards were merciless; they hacked him to pieces and carried off the dismembered fragments of his body on their spears and pikes.

HOW THEY TILL THE SOIL AND PLANT

THE Indians till the soil very diligently, using a kind of hoe made from fish bone fitted to wooden handles. Since the soil is very light, these serve well enough to cultivate it.

After the ground has been well broken up and leveled, the planting is done by the women, some making holes with sticks, into which the others drop the seeds of beans or maize. Then the fields are left alone, for the three winter months, from December 24 to March 15, are extremely cold. During this time the natives seek shelter in the woods, since they go naked. As soon as the cold winter is over, they return to their homes and wait for the crops to ripen. They gather the harvest and store it all for the rest of the year. None of it is used for trade unless they barter a small amount for some household article.

I fled into the woods, and after I had gone about a mile, I met La Crète, a Frenchman from Rouen, with a Belgian named Elie des Planques and Laudonnière's maidservant, who had been wounded in the breast. We set out for the open fields along the seashore, but before we reached there we came upon Laudonnière himself and another man, named Bartholomew, who had a sword wound in the neck. Together we marched on. From time to time we met other fugitives, until in the end there were fourteen or fifteen of us. As one of our number, the carpenter Le Challeux, has written a brief account of our experiences,[18] I will not elaborate upon them. I would like to remark only that for two days and nights we traveled waist-deep in water through swamps and reeds. Laudonnière, who was a good swimmer, and the youth from Rouen swam three large rivers before we caught sight of the vessels. On the third day, by the blessing of God and with the help of the sailors, we got safely aboard.

I have already related that Ribaut had difficulties in anchoring his ships. When he found that the water at the river's mouth was too shallow for his four large vessels, he sent in his three smaller ones, intending to use the small boats to unload the others. His son, Jacques Ribaut, in charge of the largest of the three, took his vessel up the river and anchored it near the fort. He was there while the Spaniards perpetrated their butchery, and, though his vessel was armed with cannon, he did not even try to fire on them. As the wind was adverse on that day, he could not move his ship out of the river.

The Spaniards made him offers of amnesty and promised him generous terms of surrender. But Ribaut was silent; he did not reply to their entreaties. When the Spaniards saw that Ribaut was continuing his efforts to get his ship to sea, they sent out a small boat with a trumpeter and Jean François, the traitor who had guided them to the fort. They asked for a parley to arrange terms. And though this traitor was so reckless as to come aboard ship, Ribaut was so timid and irresolute that he did not seize him. He allowed him to depart unharmed, despite the fact that he had on his ship more than sixty soldiers in addition to the crew. Though the Spaniards had plenty of small boats, they dared not attack.

Next day Jacques Ribaut succeeded in getting his ship to the mouth of the river, where he found the other two small vessels. They were very nearly stripped of their men, most of whom had gone with the elder Ribaut.

M. de Laudonnière, who now took charge, decided to take the armament and crews of the two vessels on one of them. He consulted Jacques Ribaut and suggested that they should search for his father. But Jacques said that he wanted to return to France—and Laudonnière agreed. The next step was to take on supplies, as the only provisions on the smaller vessel were some ship's biscuits. Two days were spent in taking aboard water

18. Le Challeux's account, *Discours de l'histoire de la Floride,* was first published at Dieppe in 1566.

STORING THEIR CROPS IN THE PUBLIC GRANARY

MANY *of the islands produce an abundance of fruits. These are gathered twice a year, carried home in canoes, and stored in low and roomy granaries, built of stones and earth and thickly roofed with palm branches and a kind of soft earth.*

To keep the contents better, the granaries are usually erected near a mountain or in the shade of a river bank, so as to be sheltered from the direct rays of the sun. There the Indians store everything they wish to preserve, and there they go for supplies whenever they need anything—no one fears being cheated. Indeed, it would be good if among Christians there were as little greed to torment men's minds and hearts.

and other necessities. The ships were moored side by side for fear of attack. The Spaniards sent out small reconnaissance boats from time to time, though they never came within gunshot. Since we knew what they had done to our friends, we were resolved to put up a desperate defense.

Before we sailed, M. de Laudonnière asked Jacques Ribaut to lend him one of his four pilots for the voyage, as he had no experienced navigator, but Ribaut refused. Laudonnière then suggested that we should scuttle the abandoned ships so that they would not fall into the hands of the Spaniards. Otherwise they might be used to prevent Jean Ribaut from entering the river if he ever returned. (At that time we did not know that our entire fleet had been wrecked.) Jacques would not agree to this either, and Laudonnière, finding him so obstinate, had to send his own ship's carpenter, who sank all three vessels—the one we had brought from France, the one we had acquired from the English commander, Hawkins, and the smallest one of Jean Ribaut's. This done, we set sail from Florida, insufficiently manned and badly provisioned, but God gave us so fortunate a voyage that, though we suffered a good deal, we finally made land on the coast of Wales.

This concludes my account of what I witnessed on this expedition, an experience that proves to me that victory is not the work of man, but of God, Who does all things righteously and causes everything to happen through His will. For according to all human judgment, fifty of Ribaut's poorest troops could have destroyed the entire Spanish forces, which consisted mostly of beggars and the dregs of humanity, while Ribaut had more than eight hundred superbly equipped veteran harquebusiers. But when such things are God's will, we can only say, "Blessed be His name forever."

As for the fate of Jean Ribaut after his shipwreck, I can only add a short statement of facts as they were related to me by a sailor from Dieppe who escaped from the Spaniards.

This is what the sailor told me:

When Ribaut had called the roll and found that no one was missing except Captain La Grange, but that all the firearms were lost in the wreck, he made a noble speech to his men, saying that it was their duty to bear with fortitude the calamity with which God had afflicted them. After prayers had been offered, it was decided to set out for the fort, about fifty miles away. This journey was an arduous one. The route the men had to travel was intersected by a number of rivers. As no one lived in the territory, the land was not cultivated, and the company had to subsist on roots and herbs. Still, they courageously overcame all obstacles and reached a point estimated by some of Laudonnière's men to be about four or five miles from the fort.

Ribaut now called a council, and it was voted to send out Vasseur, a skilful sailor familiar with all the branches of the River of May, with five or six men to find out what

BRINGING IN WILD ANIMALS, FISH, AND OTHER STORES

EACH *year at a certain time they gather together a store of wild animals, fish, and even crocodiles. These are put into baskets and carried by the curly-haired hermaphrodites to the storehouse. These supplies are not used save in dire necessity. If such occasion arises, everyone shares according to his rank; the chief, however, has the first choice and takes whatever he pleases.*

had happened to the Frenchmen who had remained behind. They descended the river in an Indian canoe and soon reached a point where they could see the fort. When Vasseur and the men found that the Spanish flag was flying over it, they returned and reported to Ribaut without being observed by the Spaniards. The grief of the company on hearing that the fort had been taken by the enemy can well be imagined. Ribaut faced a difficult situation. He knew how cruel the Spaniards were, but he also realized that most of his force was likely to perish in the woods of starvation and exposure. Before making any decision he was determined to send messengers to the encampment. They were to learn about the intentions of the Spaniards and try to find out what they had done with the Frenchmen who had been left there.

Ribaut chose Nicholas Verdier, captain of one of the ships, and La Caille, Laudonnière's sergeant, whom I have mentioned before. The two men departed in a canoe accompanied by five or six soldiers. When the Spaniards saw them, they came out in a boat to parley. The French asked about the fate of their companions who had been left in the fort. The Spaniards answered that their commander, who was a humane and merciful man, had sent them to France in a well-provisioned ship and that the messengers could assure Ribaut that he and his men would be equally well treated.

With this reply the men returned to Captain Ribaut, who was over credulous and too easily believed their story. He summoned another council, at which the soldiers demanded, "Let us go; let us go to them right away. Even if they kill us outright, that is better than to endure our sufferings. Not one of us but has died a thousand deaths on this fearful journey."

There were, however, a few prudent ones among them, who declared they would never trust the Spaniards, if for no other reason than their hatred of our religion.

Ribaut, following the opinion of the majority that the wisest thing was to surrender, sent La Caille to the Spanish commander asking for a safe-conduct and assuring the Spaniard that if he would swear to spare their lives, the French would come to the fort and give themselves up. As soon as La Caille arrived at the fort he was admitted to the commander's presence, threw himself at his feet, and delivered his message. The Spaniard pledged his faith to La Caille with many signs of the cross in the presence of all his men. He repeated his oath in writing and gave the promise under his seal that he would preserve the lives of Ribaut and his men faithfully, without fraud, as an honorable gentleman. La Caille took the document back to the French camp, where some received it joyfully, while others had little confidence in it. In truth, it was worth no more than the paper on which it was written.

Ribaut made a speech, and after all had joined in prayer, he led his people down to the river bank near the fort, where they were ferried across. Ribaut and Ottigny were taken

DRYING MEAT, FISH, AND OTHER FOOD

FOR *drying their provisions, a grating of stakes is built and placed upon four posts. The game is laid on this, and a fire is lighted underneath to cure it in the smoke. The Indians dry the meat very carefully, to make sure it will not spoil.*

This stock is presumably laid in for their own use during the winter months (when they take to the woods), since they would never give us anything from these provisions. The reason their granaries are always built near a cliff on the bank of a stream not far from the forest is that they should be accessible by water. Thus, if they are in need of food in their winter quarters, they are able to get supplies by canoe.

into the fort, the rest of the men being kept outside and tied in groups of four, back to back. They knew now that their lives were lost. Ribaut asked to see the governor to remind him of his promise, but he spoke to deaf ears. Ottigny, when he heard the cries of his men from outside, appealed to the oath that had been made, but he was laughed at.

While Ribaut kept insisting, a Spanish soldier came in and asked in French if he were the commander, Ribaut. He replied, "Yes." "Then," said the man, "do you not expect your soldiers to obey your orders?" When Ribaut again said, "Yes," the Spaniard continued, "I also obey my commander's orders, which are to kill you." Whereupon he thrust a dagger into Ribaut's breast. Ottigny was killed in the same way. Other Spanish soldiers were detailed to slay all the rest of the Frenchmen by beating their heads with clubs and axes, at the same time calling them Lutherans and enemies of God and the Virgin. Thus were they murdered, most brutally and in violation of an oath, all except four; three of these were musicians who were kept alive to play for dancing—a drummer and a fifer from Dieppe, the former named Dronet, and a fiddler named Masselin. The fourth was the sailor who escaped and lived to tell me the story.

He was among those tied up for slaughter and was battered on the head, but when the three to whom he was tied fell on top of him, he was left there for dead. He was not dead, however, only stunned. A wooden pyre was built, on which the Spaniards wanted to burn the victims, yet they put off the burning till the next day. The sailor, coming to his senses in the night, found himself among the dead bodies. He remembered a knife he wore in a wooden sheath, and he managed to twist himself around little by little until he could get the knife out and cut his fetters. He then slipped away, walking throughout the night. As he had long been a sailor, he knew how to tell direction by the sun. Thus he was able to lay his course the next day. He left the fort behind, and in the next three days he covered forty miles. He arrived at the place of a certain Indian chief, and there he stayed.

About eight months after the capture of the fort, the Spaniards discovered that some of the French had escaped and were in hiding somewhere in the surrounding country. Their commander feared that they might organize a conspiracy among the Indians against the Spaniards. He therefore sent threatening messages to the various Indian chiefs, demanding that they surrender any Frenchmen. The chief, who was very friendly to this sailor, asked him to give himself up, fearing that otherwise the Spanish might attack him and destroy his village. The sailor tried to take refuge with some other chiefs, but to no avail. As he could find no hiding place, he set out for the fort, but when he came within two miles of it, his resolution failed, and, overcome by terror and despair, he lay down to die.

After three or four days, one of three Spaniards who were out hunting found the sailor and felt pity for him—an emotion very rare in a Spanish heart—since the man lay at

HUNTING DEER

THE Indians hunt deer in a way we have never seen before. They hide themselves in the skin of a very large deer which they have killed some time before. They place the animal's head upon their own head, looking through the eye holes as through a mask. In this disguise they approach the deer without frightening them. They choose the time when the animals come to drink at the river, shooting them easily with bow and arrow.

To protect their left forearm from the bowstring, they usually wear a strip of bark. And they prepare the deerskins without any iron instruments, using only shells, in a surprisingly expert way. I do not believe any European could do this better.

his feet more dead than alive, and begged for mercy. When he asked him how he came to the place, the sailor told his tale. The Spaniard felt sorry for him and agreed not to take him to the fort, where the sailor would have been killed at once. He promised that he would see the governor and ask him for mercy and that he would soon return with the reply. He was as good as his word.

He went to the governor and received a promise that the sailor would not be killed, but would be made a slave. After this the soldier returned to the wretched sailor and took him to the fort, where he served as a slave for a year, when he was sent to Cuba. In Havana he was chained to another Frenchman, a gentleman named De Pompierre. He was that same De Pompierre (one of Laudonnière's men) who had been carried off by the mutineers against his will. He had been with them on their expedition, which I have previously described, and in the end he had been captured by the Spaniards. He was made a slave, was sold together with the sailor, and put on a ship bound for Portugal. The vessel carrying them fell in with a French ship commanded by a man named Bontemps and was captured after a long fight. The two prisoners were released and taken to France. This story shows how God finds a way to relieve the unfortunate even after they have lost all hope.

So ends the narrative of the sailor, who told it to me himself. For the destruction of Ribaut and his men we should not blame the Spaniards, whom the Lord used as rods to scourge us according to our deserts, but ourselves and our own sins, which were responsible for our misfortunes. And to God omnipotent, and to His Son, Jesus Christ our Lord, and to the Holy Spirit, be honor and glory forever. Amen.

KILLING ALLIGATORS

THIS is how they attack alligators. Near the river they put up a little hut full of cracks and holes. In this hut one of their men keeps watch. From his hiding place he can see and hear the animals, even if they are a long way off. Then the alligators, driven to the shore by hunger, give themselves away by their loud bellowing, which can be heard at a great distance.

The watchman in the hut now calls his companions, who are waiting in readiness, and they set out for the hunt. They take with them a ten-foot pointed pole, and when they come upon the monster—who usually crawls along with open mouth, ready to attack—they push the pole quickly down its throat. The rough tree bark of its sides prevents the pole from slipping out again.

Then the beast is turned over on its back and killed by beating it with clubs and piercing its soft belly with arrows. The alligators are such a menace that a regular watch has to be kept against them day and night. The Indians guard themselves against these animals just as we guard ourselves from our most dangerous enemies.

LE CHALLEUX

Nicolas Le Challeux's narrative of Captain Jean Ribaut's last voyage in 1565, undertaken at the King's command, to an island in the Indies commonly called Florida.[1]

SOME time before the tumults and troubles of civil war broke out in the land, the King, with the princes and nobles of the court, decided to send a large number of men and many ships to one of the countries of India, called *Florida*—a land recently discovered by the French. When the civil war was finally put down, this intention was revived on the authority of His Majesty. And for the organization of the project, Jean Ribaut, a man of courage and wisdom, and well-experienced in navigation, was summoned to the court, where he received the King's commission to outfit seven ships to transport men, food, and arms. Ribaut was at the same time honored with the title of Lieutenant and made commander-in-chief of all such soldiery as he required. He was given authority to impress as many men as he needed for the undertaking. He received express orders not to attempt to land in any other country or island in those parts, especially one that was under the rule of the King of Spain. In sailing the Atlantic he was to keep his course set straight for Florida.

The news of this voyage was quickly spread abroad, and many men were persuaded to serve under the command of this captain and the King's authority. They were moved by various reasons: some enlisted with a sincere desire to know and see the country, hoping that the mission would profit them later. Others wanted with heart and soul to make war, preferring to risk the rage of the waters rather than to remain in their accustomed condition—which was just as precarious.

The rumor spread here was that Florida promised an abundance of all that man might desire in the world. For that country had received a singular favor from heaven; there was neither frost nor snow there, nor any northern cold, and it escaped the burning heat of the South. Without labor and tillage, the ground brought forth enough to sustain the life of the natives, as well as of those who come to dwell there. This would become the

1. The original title page of Le Challeux's book is reproduced on page 278.

FLORIDIANS CROSSING OVER TO AN ISLAND ON A PLEASURE TRIP

THE country has many delightful islands, lying in shallow rivers of clear, pure water, running no more than breast high. When the natives wish to go to one of the islands to enjoy themselves, they swim skilfully across the rivers, or, if they have their young children with them, they wade. The mother takes with her three of her children, the smallest one on her shoulder, while the two others cling to her arms. She also carries fruit and provisions for the trip in a basket.

When there is danger of meeting an enemy, the men take their bows and arrows on the trip. To keep the weapons from getting wet, they attach the quiver to their hair, and they hold the bow and one arrow above the water, ready for use.

most fruitful and richest country within the bounds of the earth—if men would employ their industry and perseverance in clearing the land.

Florida extends in a northerly direction in almost the same longitude as Europe, along a latitude of twenty-three degrees. Sometimes, when the sun's rays are directly overhead, it receives great heat; but the heat is tempered not only by the coolness of the nights and the dew that drops from Heaven, but by the soft rain, which falls in such abundance that the ground is fruitful and the grass grows to a wonderful height.

The country is also rich in gold and in all sorts of animals, both tame and wild, which roam its large, fair fields. There are high hills, pleasant streams and rivers, and various kinds of trees fill the air with sweet scent. With all these natural riches, one should be able to live there in great happiness and unusual satisfaction.

Men were persuaded by these promises, or by covetousness (believing they would be made rich by this voyage because of the gold), and came in legions to the town where the muster for the voyage was held. Here those whom the King's Lieutenant deemed best fitted for such an undertaking were enrolled.

But the plan was not put into effect as quickly as some desired, especially those who had received the soldiers into their inns and houses. These people were weary of keeping men who made merry without paying their bills, even though the soldiers promised their hosts that they would shortly be paid and fully contented.

They were four months or more in this town before they set forth. In the end, they were bound by oath to behave themselves faithfully in the King's service and received six months' wages. But still not everyone was pleased, for about the month of May, 1565, when the order came for the men to embark, some of those who had been paid were seized with anxiety at the prospect of so long a voyage. Frightened by the angry seas, they changed their minds and deserted secretly without waiting any longer. Now, to make haste, lest their number should daily diminish, the muster was again called. The men were commanded to go aboard ship at that very hour. This was the tenth day of May.

We remained in the harbor until May 22, waiting for certain animals and grain. The number of persons for the voyage was three hundred, besides the craftsmen and their families. And while we awaited the convenience and orders of our Lieutenant—as well as a favorable wind—on Tuesday, the 22d, a great tempest arose. The wind blew from every quarter, and the waves struck with such violence that our sailors were frightened. They could do nothing but cut our cables and let the anchors go, delivering us to the wind's pleasure. A violent north wind drove us swiftly to New Haven [Le Havre]. There we remained three days, waiting for news from Dieppe, whither we had dispatched a brigantine to get our orders. On May 26 we prepared to leave.

PREPARING FOR A FEAST

THERE is a time of the year when the natives feast each other. For this purpose they choose special cooks. These cooks take a great round earthenware pot (which they bake so well that water can be boiled therein as easily as in our own kettles) and put it over a large wood fire. The place where the cooking is done swarms with activity. The head cook empties the raw food into the large pot; another keeps the fire going with a small hand fan; still others pour water into a hole in the ground; women bring water in large vessels; herbs to be used for seasoning are ground on a stone.

Although they give big feasts, they never overeat, and therefore usually live to a great age. One of their chiefs swore that he was three hundred years old and that his father, whom he pointed out to me, was fifty years older than himself—and indeed he looked to be nothing but skin and bones. Such facts might well make us Christians ashamed, for we are so immoderate in both our eating and our drinking habits that we shorten our lives thereby. We might easily learn sobriety and wisdom from these men whom we consider only as savages and beasts.

No sooner were we on our right course than an unfavorable wind took hold of us and forced us to anchor at the Isle of Wight, one of the possessions of England. Here the English asked about our enterprise, and when we had told them of it, they offered us hospitality. We had arrived there May 28 and rode at anchor until June 14; on that day the wind changed to the northeast and was as fair as we could wish.

We hoisted our sails and steered a straight course for Florida, which we longed to see. We were on the great Western Sea two whole months before we had sight of that land. We did see an island, which the natives called *Yocajouque*. Some of our men wanted to name it *Catherine* for the Queen, the mother of the King. They said it was on the twenty-seventh parallel. We also saw a ship two hundred leagues farther to seaward, but we did not come nearer than two or three leagues of it.

On August 14 we arrived off the coast of Florida and saw fires that the Indians had made to greet us. We sent a brigantine to explore a little river. There we found a few natives, who bartered silver for the merchandise we had brought; they said they had got this silver from a ship that had been wrecked coming from the Antilles.

We met a Spaniard who had been shipwrecked twenty years before. When we took him into our brigantine and inquired about the Frenchmen who were living in Florida, he said that while he knew nothing about them himself, the savages had told him that they were encamped fifty leagues or more to the north.

Accordingly we set sail and followed the coast, along a sandy land of stunted trees. The rivers that flow from the southwest are very small there, as are those from the north-northeast. Midway on our trip we explored a river which our men had earlier named the River of May. Because of the shallowness of the water we could see the anchor holds that had been used before. The water was six or seven fathoms, or thereabouts, when we were within three or four leagues of land.

I remember also that between the River of May and another named Aye, we found still a further stream on the north side, about two leagues distant from the River of May; and there we cast anchor, overtaken by night in eight fathoms of water. In some places the bottom was sandy, in others gravelly, and often of clay. We sounded the River of Dolphins, and at its bar found a depth of two fathoms. At high tide there are two and three-quarters fathoms. After we had followed the coast a long time in search of another landing place, we cast our anchors, on August 27, in the roadstead of the River of May. We lay in seven fathoms of water, about two leagues from land.

On Wednesday, the 29th, we took three boats and rowed up the river straight to the settlement established by our men. It had been set up some time before as a place of safety and rest. It is a commodious spot, even though it has the river on one side and a wood on

A COUNCIL OF STATE

ON CERTAIN days in the year the chief meets with his principal men to discuss important affairs. They assemble early in the morning. When the chief has taken his place, his councillors approach. They are led by the oldest member, and they salute him in the order of their age, raising their hands twice to the height of their heads and saying: "Ha, he, ya, ha, ha;" to which the others reply: "Ha, ha." After this salute they all take their seats on the bench, and the chief calls upon his iaruas* *(that is, his priests) and his elders, always one at a time, and asks them for their advice.*

While the men are considering the case, the chief orders the women to boil some casina, *a drink prepared from the leaves of a certain root. One of the councillors stands up and, spreading out his hands, invokes a blessing upon the chief and the assembly. After this the cupbearer brings the hot drink in a large shell, offering it first to the chief and then to the others, according to their rank.*

The casina *is so highly valued that no one who has not proved himself a brave warrior is allowed to drink it in council. And its effect is so strong that the drinkers are immediately thrown into a sweat. For this reason no one is considered fit to be sent on a difficult mission or given any military responsibility who cannot keep the* casina *down. For they often have to go three or four days without food, but those who drink it can easily hold out for twenty-four hours afterwards without eating or drinking. On their military expeditions the only supplies (carried by the hermaphrodites) are gourds filled with* casina, *because it strengthens and nourishes the body, but does not go to the head.*

*Father Pareja, who lived with the Timuquanan Indians half a century later, translates this word as "sorcerer."

the other, not more than a quarter of a mile from the fort. Fair fields lay between. On another side is a pleasant open space covered with grass and various kinds of plants growing luxuriantly. There is no way into the wood except a narrow path made by the men in going to a spring a short distance in among the trees.

When we were near the fort our Lieutenant gave orders to unload the provisions and munitions and carry them to the stronghold. He also ordered that we workmen, with our wives and children, should go there. We were led by the gentlemen of the house of Ully [Pierre Aligre d'Ully, who was in charge of the supplies], and by de Beauhaire, and others, to whose care he also gave the most valuable part of his baggage.

The soldiers at the fort had long been waiting for us and were overjoyed at our coming. They had been troubled at being so long without any news from France. And to add to their distress, they were without food and had had to accustom themselves to what the natives produced for them. And even from the savages they were able to get nothing except by force and violence, as I shall later relate in more detail.

When we were settled there, I studied the form of the natives of the land. The men are straight and well proportioned, of a somewhat ruddy color. To me they seemed kind and gentle. I learned that in every village they have a king. What little clothing they wear is of leather, strangely decorated. Neither the men nor the women dress in any other garb, but the women are girdled with a little fringe or apron, made from the skin of some animal, to cover their shame. They are neither flat-nosed nor big-lipped, but their faces are round and full, their eyes clear and timid. Their hair is very long, and they bind it very neatly around their heads. This trussing of their hair serves as a quiver to carry their arrows when they go to war. It is marvellous to see how swiftly they can take the arrows into their hands and shoot them unbelievably straight and far.

As for their manners, they are dissolute. They do not instruct or correct their children. They will steal without conscience, and all that they can take secretly they count as their own. Every one has his own wife, and they keep the marriage bond with all rigor. They make war against adjacent countries, each of which has a different language. Their weapons are bows and arrows. Their houses are round, much like dove-cotes with foundations and structures of large trees, roofed over with palm leaves.

They have no fear of wind or tempest. Little flies, which they call *maringons,* annoy them often; to get rid of these vermin, they make small fires in their houses—especially under the beds. They say these flies sting cruelly, and those parts that are stung look like the flesh of lepers.

Among these savages nothing is so rich and fair as the feathers of birds, which are of various colors. They also prize little counters, made from the bones of certain fish and from

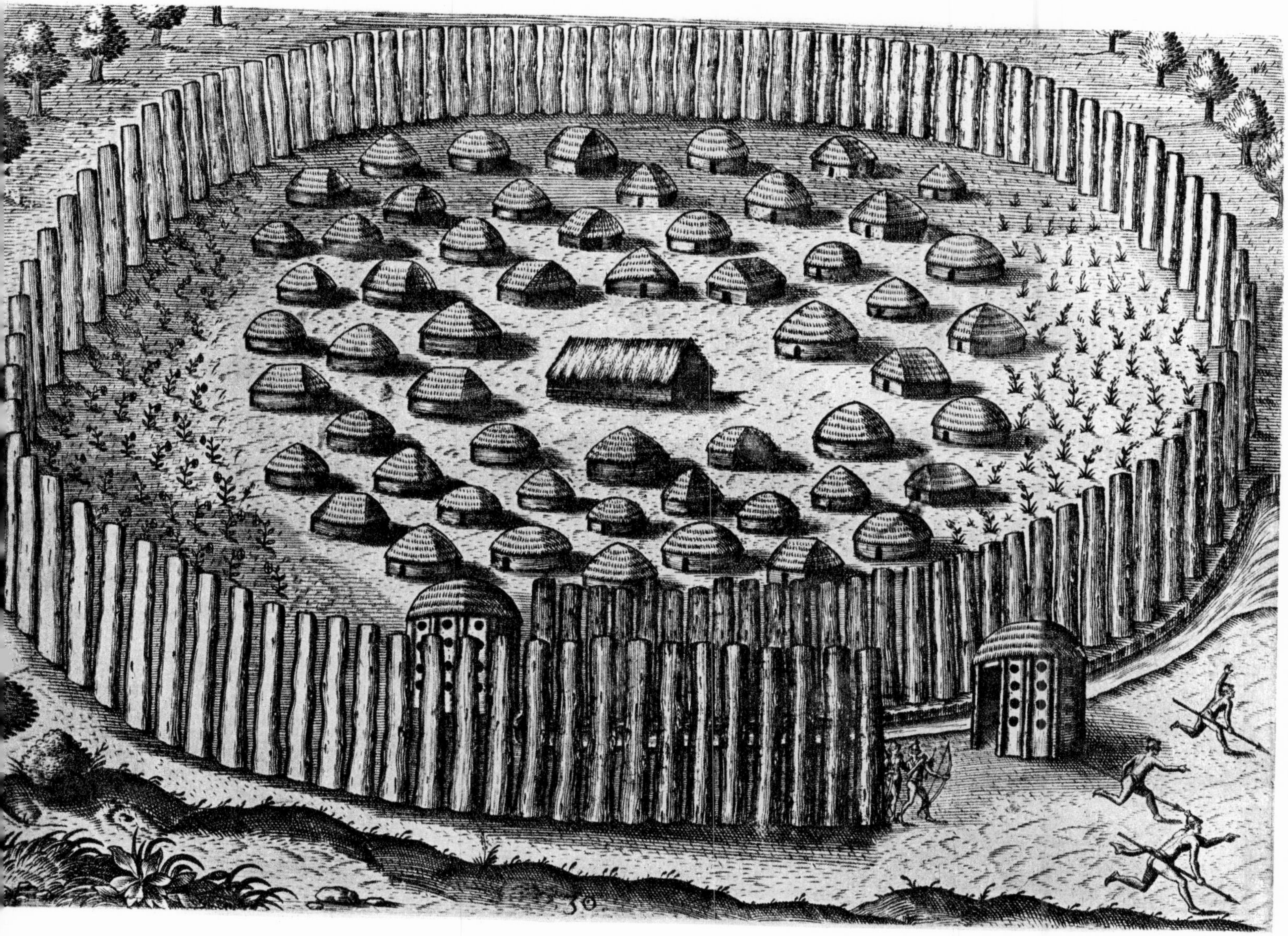

A FORTIFIED VILLAGE

THE Indians build their fortified villages in this way: they choose a site near the channel of a swift stream, which they level as evenly as possible. Then they dig a circular ditch around it, into which they drive thick, round palings, placed close together, to a height twice that of a man. This fencing is carried to a point beyond its beginning, spiralwise, making a narrow entrance and admitting not more than two persons at a time. The course of the stream is diverted towards this entrance, and at each end of it a small guardhouse is built.

The sentinels in these guardhouses have a highly developed sense of smell. They can detect enemies at a great distance. As soon as they smell them, they follow the scent, and when they discover the disturbers of their peace, they set up a clamor, thus summoning warriors from the town, armed with bows, arrows, and clubs.

The chief's house stands in the center of the enclosure and is somewhat sunken into the ground to avoid the heat of the sun. It is surrounded by those of the principal men. The roofs of these huts are only lightly thatched with palm branches, since they are occupied for not more than nine months in the year, the other three winter months—as I have already said—being spent in the forests. When they return from the woods, they go back to their old homes—if the enemy has not burnt them down while they were away. When this happens, they erect new huts, using the same kind of materials.

green and red stones. They eat roots, fruit, herbs, and fish of various kinds. Their fish are very fat, and they cut out the fat to use instead of butter and sauce. They hang and dry the fish, which they called *boquarie* in their language.

They have no wheat, but they have an abundance of a certain seed, which grows seven feet high. The stalk is thick like a cane, and the grain is as large as peas. The ear is a foot long, the color of natural wax. The way they use it is first to bruise and pound it to meal. Then it is mixed and made into *mygan,* which is like the rice we have in this country. It must be eaten as soon as it is made, because it cannot be kept and will quickly spoil.

In some parts of this country many bastard vines grow around the trees, but the natives do not press out the wine. Their drink, which they call *cassinet* [casina] is made from mixed herbs and looks like the ale of our country in color. I have tasted it, and it did not seem strange to me. The countryside is hilly and thickly forested. This may be the reason for the abundance of wild animals, which they say will injure those who do not take great heed. I will not write much about those beasts I know of only by hearsay. There is enough for me to say of the things I have seen that I think worthy to be noted for posterity.

There are the crocodiles, especially, which are often seen coming up on the sand in search of prey. We have observed many—a dead one in particular, which we ate. The meat was tender, white as veal, and had almost the same taste. It was killed by a gunshot, struck between two scales. Otherwise the crocodile is strong enough for any hits. His mouth is extremely large, and his teeth straight, like the teeth of a comb. His body is twelve or thirteen feet long. His legs are short in proportion to his body, the claws strange and cruel. His tail is long and strong. His life depends upon his tail, for it is his principal means of defense. In the mouth I found no signs of a tongue. The lower jaw protrudes over the upper jaw, a monstrous thing; the mere sight of it strikes a man with fear.

I also saw a dead serpent in the woods, killed by one of our men. It had wings with which it might, at times, fly up from the ground. The savages cut off its head and carried it away with great diligence and care. I could not learn the reason. Some of our men thought that the savages did so because of some superstition. As far as I could see, they are not without some idea of Divinity. I conjecture that under certain circumstances they might easily become civilized and made honest. They could also be converted to holiness and sound religion—if God in His mercy should so ordain it. For as soon as the bell rang for prayers at our fort, they would be there, stretching up their hands to Heaven as we did, even with reverence and attentive ear.

Our Governor discharged his duties faithfully. He gave orders that ramparts should be built and the fort supplied so that if the natives should raise an insurrection and overrun us, we should be prepared.

SETTING AN ENEMY'S TOWN ON FIRE

SOMETIMES *revengeful enemies creep up to a village in the middle of the night. If they find the watch asleep and the town quiet, they approach it in dead silence. They shoot burning moss, fastened to their arrow heads, onto the roofs of the houses. Since the roofs are made of palm branches, thoroughly dried by the summer sun, they burn readily.*

As soon as the attackers perceive that the roofs are aflame, they flee. It is very seldom that they are caught, for the people of the village have no time to pursue them; they are all occupied with fighting the flames. However, the damage done by the fires is small; it costs no more than the labor necessary for erecting new huts.

On Monday, September 3, a fleet of five Spanish ships sailed in close to our vessels. The flagship was about four hundred tons, and the bark a hundred and fifty tons. Following these were three pinnaces. All cast anchor near our ships, about nine o'clock in the evening. When we asked them why they had searched us out, they answered that they were enemies and that war had been declared.

Then our men, recognizing with envy the strength of the Spaniards and their evil intent, weighed anchor and hoisted sail. The enemy chased after us, but we escaped. When they saw that they could not overtake us, they sailed into the River of Dolphins, and they landed on its shores.

After they had conspired our ruin with the savages (as the results of their enterprise showed in the end) they sent as many companies of their soldiers from the river as they thought necessary to carry out their plans. We later learned from the savages that the Spaniards had five hundred men under arms. Not long afterwards, three of our ships came into the harbor again (the *Trinity,* our flagship, having no anchor hold, had been carried down the river). Captain Jean Ribaut decided to pursue the Spanish fleet with these ships. He conferred with his men about this plan, telling them that it was necessary to show their force on the water or else risk the loss of our vessels, for the soldiers on land could not defend those left on the ships as they were but a small number in comparison with the enemy. And the loss of our ships would be insufferable, particularly as we could then send no word to France to inform the King of our situation.

Accordingly, on Monday, September 10, Captain Ribaut, Lieutenant of the King, summoned his men three hours before noon, and after he had exhorted them to do well in the King's name, he set sail with them, taking for his defense not only the soldiers newly brought over, but also the best of those that had been at the settlement before we arrived. He took the chief ensign of Captain Laudonnière as well.

Laudonnière, wearied at not hearing news from France and displeased at being deprived of food, had planned to return home a little before we arrived. He did not mind if his soldiers treated the natives so badly that they turned against the French. He had allowed his men to carry them as prisoners to the fort, taking by force their grain and other things required by necessity, which knows no law.

But since a desire for vengeance is planted in man's heart by nature and as the common instinct of all animals is to defend life and limb and to avoid those things which promise hurt, there is no doubt the savages conspired to free themselves from us. They had been troubled and pained, not only in body but in goods as well.

On Tuesday, September 11, at about eight o'clock in the morning, when our Captain was very near to the Spaniards, there arose a great wind, and it continued for a long time.

HOW SENTINELS ARE PUNISHED FOR SLEEPING AT THEIR POSTS

WHEN a town has been burned because of a sentinel's carelessness, he is brought before the chief to receive punishment. The chief sits alone, his principal men placed on a long, semi-circular bench near by. The executioner orders the sentinel to kneel down before the chief. When this has been done, he sets his left foot on the offender's back, and with a sharp-edged club made of ebony or some other hard wood, he strikes him a blow on the head hard enough to split open the skull.

The same penalty is used for other crimes; while we were there, two men were thus punished.

Heavy showers of rain fell, the noise of the thunder was deafening, and the lightning at times made the air like fire. As both sides feared the rage of the weather, the fleets separated. Our three ships waited out the storm; the Spaniards ran before the wind. The rage of the elements lasted until September 23.

Meanwhile, the Spaniards had disembarked and had leisure enough to seek out a way into our fort and invent means of entrapping us. They knew that our commander was at sea with most of our force, waiting for fair weather, and of those that remained in the fort, part were sick—being affected by the smell of the sea—and part were craftsmen with women and children. In all there were two hundred and forty souls. They were under the command of Captain Laudonnière, who did not foresee that the enemy would come by land to entrap him.

Our captain arose early in the morning to refresh himself after the bad weather of the night before. He opened the gate of the fort an hour before sunrise, while most of us were sound asleep in our beds. By then the Spaniards had crossed the woods, ditches, and rivers, guided by the natives. Early on this day—Monday, September 20, a cloudy and rainy morning—they entered the fort with no resistance. They made a horrible, tragic slaughter of our forces, so great was the anger and hatred they had for our nation. They vied with one another to see who could best cut the throats of our people—healthy and sick, women and children. It was a pitiful, grievous sight.

Some of the nimblest of our men hurried out of their beds and fled to the ships that were in the river. (These had been left by Ribaut in charge of his son Jacques, captain of the *Pearl,* and under Louis Ballaud, his lieutenant.) Others, being almost trapped, leaped over the wall of the fort. Captain Laudonnière saved himself by this means; so did his chambermaid.

The Spaniards nearly captured me while I was on my way to work, tools in hand. They met me as I came out of my cabin. I could think of no way of escaping but to turn tail and run as fast as I was able. A pikeman chased me, but by the grace of God my strength was doubled—poor old man that I am, and gray-headed. I leaped over the rampart, which I could not have done if I had thought about it, for it was eight or nine feet high. Once over, I raced toward the forest.

When I was about a bow-shot from the woods, I turned my face toward the fort and waited a little, emboldened because no one was following me. From where I stood I saw the fort. I heard the horrible sound of the slaughter and perceived the three standards which our enemy had planted upon the ramparts.

Having now abandoned all hope of meeting my friends again, I put my trust in God and plunged into the heart of the wood, for I felt that I could find no greater cruelty

HOW THEY DECLARE WAR

A CHIEF who wants to declare war against his enemy does not send a herald to announce it. He simply gives orders that locks of hair should be fastened to the notches of arrows and be stuck up along the public ways. This custom we observed when we took Chief Outina prisoner and carried him through his villages, forcing his people to give us provisions.

among the wild beasts. My misery and suffering made me sigh and weep. I saw on earth no other hope than that the Lord God in His special grace might deliver me beyond man's hope. In a voice of sorrow, I prayed unto God, saying, "O God of our fathers and Lord of all consolation, Who has commanded us to call upon Thee even from the lake of Hell and the pangs of death, promising Thy swift aid, show unto me, for the hope that I have in Thee, what path I might take to come to the end of this miserable age, plunged in the gulf of sorrow and bitterness. Give me, feeling the effect of Thy mercy, the assurance that I have conceived in my heart of Thy promises. Let it not be taken away by the cruelty and furious rage of the wild beasts on the one side, and of Thy enemies and ours on the other. For the enemy seeks our death more because Thy Holy Name is called upon among us than for any other thing. Help me, O God; assist me, as I am so afflicted that I can call no more."

While making this discourse, I was struggling through a thicket of briars and thorns under the high trees, for there was neither road nor path. I had been traveling not more than half an hour when I heard a noise like the weeping and complaining of men. Nevertheless I went forward in the name of God, having confidence in His help, and discovered one of our company, a man named De la Blonderie. Behind him was another, Master Robert, known to all of us because it was his duty to say the service in our fort. Shortly after, we were joined by the servants of Pierre d'Ully, La Beau [the treasurer], Master James Teuse [Jacques Tauzé], and others. After finding each other, we commiserated and then considered what we should do to save our lives.

One among us who knew the Scriptures began, saying: "Brethren, you see in what extremities we are. Wherever we turn our eyes, we see nothing but barbarousness. The heavens, the earth, the sea, the woods, the men—in short, nothing favors us. How do we know that if we yield ourselves to the mercy of the Spaniards they will not show us mercy? Even though they kill us, we shall suffer only for a time. For they are men, and it may be that once their fury is appeased they will compromise with us. Otherwise what should we do? Is it not better for us to fall into the hands of human beings than into the mouths of wild beasts, or to die of hunger in a strange land?"

After he had said these words, most of our company agreed with him and praised his counsel. In spite of this, I pointed out the bloody cruelty of our enemy, and that it was not only for one cause and human difference that they had attacked us with such fury, but it was mainly because they had learned that we are of those who have returned to the preaching of the Gospel.

"Let us not be so willful," I said, "as to trust in man more than in God, Who maketh those that are His to live, yea, even in the midst of death; and Who giveth always his help when man's hope fails."

THE SACRIFICE OF FIRST-BORN CHILDREN

T*HEY offer their first-born son to the chief. On the day of the sacrifice, the chief goes to the place dedicated to that purpose. There he takes his seat on a bench. Not far off is a tree stump about two feet high and as many thick, in front of which the mother of the first-born son squats on her heels, her face covered with her hands in sorrow. One of her women friends or relatives then offers the child to the chief in worship. After the offering is made the women who have accompanied the mother dance in a circle around the stump with great demonstrations of joy. In their midst, singing the chief's praises, dances the woman who holds the child.*

Near by stands a group of six Indians. They surround a magnificently decorated man holding a club. It is he who will perform the sacrifice. When the dance ends, he takes the infant and kills it on the wooden stump in honor of the chief. I saw this ritual performed once while I was there.

I referred to certain examples from Holy Scripture to the purpose, particularly those of Joseph, Daniel, Elijah, and other prophets. I reminded them of the Apostles, especially St. Peter and St. Paul. All of these were saved from affliction by extraordinary means, strange to the sense and reason of man.

"His arm," I said, "is never weakened; His arm is always steadfast. Do you not remember," I went on, "how the children of Israel fled from Pharoah? What hope had these people to escape this mighty, cruel tyrant? He pursued them, hard on their heels. Before them lay the Red Sea; on both sides lofty hills. What then? The Lord opened the sea to make a path for His people and afterwards swallowed up the enemy in the same waters. Might He not in like manner guide us through the woods and fields of this strange country?"

But for all I could say, six of our company followed the first proposal and left us, making their way to the enemy and hoping to find grace and favor with them. They should have known by experience what folly it is to trust more in men than in the promises of our Lord. Once they emerged from the woods, they were taken by the Spaniards and killed. Their bodies were dragged to the river. And the corpses of our comrades slain in the fort had been piled in heaps.

Let me relate an example of extreme cruelty. Jacques Ribaut, captain of the *Pearl,* rode at anchor in his ship about a hundred paces from the fort. He had taken on board many of those who had escaped the slaughter. The Spaniards, drunk with victory, were bent on dispatching the rest of the Frenchmen. They trained their cannon upon the ships and small boats, but the rainy weather put their guns out of commission; they could do no harm to our soldiers. They sent a trumpeter to summon the men to yield. When they found that this accomplished nothing, they dispatched a messenger to our ships; he showed an order from Don Pedro Maluendo [?Menendez], their commander, offering to make terms. The lives of the French would be spared if they would abandon their ships and make their way, with their luggage, in small boats to the other ships that were lower in the mouth of the river, about two leagues distant from the fort.

To this our men answered that no war had existed between our countries when, six months previously, they had received orders from the King to make this voyage. Therefore we had done no wrong and made no demands on anyone. Further, it had been expressly forbidden by His Majesty, and also by the Admiral, that we should land in any part of Spain, or even go near any territory of hers for fear of giving offense.

"We have kept the King's command inviolate," they said, "so you cannot assert that we are the cause of the slaughter you have made, a slaughter against all the rules of warfare—for which our hearts bleed. In another time and place you may suffer for this deed.

OFFERING THE SKIN OF A STAG TO THE SUN

EVERY year, just before spring, Chief Outina's subjects take the skin of the largest stag, with its horns still on, and stuff it with the choicest roots that grow there. On its horns, neck, and body they hang long garlands of the best fruits. Thus decorated, it is carried with music and song to an open, level place and hung on a high tree with its head and breast towards the sunrise.

They then pray to the sun that such good things as these offered may grow on their lands. The chief, with his sorcerer, stands near the tree and offers the prayer, while the common people, some distance away, make the responses. After the prayer they salute the sun and depart, leaving the deer's hide on the tree until the next year.

As for giving up our ship, as you demand, you could more easily take our lives. And if you think to constrain us, we will employ the means that God and nature have given us to defend ourselves."

The Spaniards returned and reported to their Commander that the French feared nothing and wanted to fight. When the Spanish soldiers learnt of this, they vented their anger and bloody hate on the dead and showed the corpses to our soldiers in the ships—seeking to break their spirits, since they could not fight them otherwise. They plucked out the eyes from the dead bodies, stuck them on their dagger points, and with exclamations, taunts, and mocking, they threw them at the boats.

As for those of us who remained in the woods, we kept on moving, following a path we thought was the right course to the sea. And since it pleased God to direct our steps, by and by we came to the brow of a hill, and from this we saw the sea. There was still a great distance to go, and worse, the way seemed marvellously strange and hard. First, the mountain we had to descend was so steep and so high that it was difficult for any man to go down on his feet. None of us would have dared to do it save that we hoped to help ourselves by holding to shrubs and small trees which grew on the hillside.

We managed to climb down, though not without pain. For the briars scratched and tore our hands and legs; even our bodies were covered with blood. When we reached the foot of the mountain we lost sight of the sea; a small forest stood in our way. To get to the wood, we had to cross a wide field of marshy ground, with many wild roses and strange plants. Their stalks and leaves were hard as wood and cut our feet and legs enough to make them bleed. We were always in water up to our knees. And our misery was increased by the heavy rain; we were caught between two seas. The more we progressed, the deeper we waded in the water. Now we were convinced that we had come to the end of our lives. We embraced one another, and with a common love we began to sigh and cry unto the Lord God, accusing our sins and remembering the rigor of His judgments.

"Alas, O Lord," we said, "what are we but poor worms of the earth. Our souls, altered by sorrow and grief, do yield themselves unto Thy hands. O Father, full of mercy, and God of charity, deliver us out of this place of death. Or if thou willest that in this desert we make end of our lives, assist us, O Lord, that when death, most terrible of all things, cometh to take hold of us, that we fear him not. Let us, O Lord, remain firm in mind, sure of Thy favor and good will, which we have so many times tasted of and approved through Thy Son, Jesus Christ. Let us not give way to the spirit of Satan, the spirit of despair and defiance. If it be that we must die, we proclaim now, before Thy Majesty, that we die unto Thee. But if we live, it shall be to tell of Thy marvellous works in the midst of the congregation of Thy Saints."

EXERCISES OF THE YOUTHS

THE *young men are trained to run races, and a prize is given to the one who shows the greatest endurance in the contest. They also practice a great deal with bow and arrow.*

They play a game in which they cast a ball at a square target placed on the top of a high tree, and they take great pleasure in hunting and fishing.

Our prayers ended, we went on with great pain toward the forest. We arrived at a large river running through the middle of the marsh. Though the stream was not wide, it was very deep and swift in current, since the marsh was not far from the sea. This river added to our troubles, for there was not one of us who dared to swim across it.

While we were worrying about how to cross the stream, I remembered the forest we had left behind us. I exhorted my brethren to have patience and to hope for God's mercy. I traced my way back to the woods, and with the head of an axe that I had had in my hand at the time the fort was taken I cut a long branch. Then I returned to the others, who were waiting in great perplexity. "Now brethren," I said, "let us see if God will favor us and help us bring our journey to an end with this staff."

And so we laid the staff upon the water. Each man in turn took hold of it, and pushing it with all his strength, managed to struggle across to the reeds on the other side. Thus we all got over, but not without great danger. We swallowed so much salt water that we were half-drowned, and our hearts failed us.

After we had come to ourselves and gathered courage, we moved on toward the forest that lay before the sea. And soon we had to use the staff again to cross another arm of water. This gave us no less difficulty than the one before. But, thanks be to God, we crossed it. And towards nightfall we entered the woods, where we remained all night, in great depression and fear, standing upright with our backs to the trees. In spite of our travail and journeying, we had no mind to sleep. For what rest could the spirit have, being in such fear? About daybreak we saw a huge beast, like a stag, within fifty paces of us. Her head was big, her ears hanging, her enormous eyes were monstrous and seemed to blaze fire. However, she did not come near enough to harm us.

When day dawned, we emerged from the woods, and then we saw the sea for which we had wished so much, and which, next to God, was the only means of saving our lives. But we were again troubled, for in front of us lay a marsh ground full of water and covered with briars and wild roses, like the swamp we had traversed the day before.

We waded through these marshes, where we saw, among the wild roses, a company of men whom we thought at first were our enemies come to cut us off. But when we came closer, we perceived they were as desolate and naked as we. Then we knew they were our countrymen seeking safety.

Among them were Captain Laudonnière, his chambermaid, James Morgens of Dieppe [Le Moyne], François Duval of Rouen, and many others—to the number of twenty-six persons. They were all contemplating what should be done. One of the men climbed a high tree; he recognized one of our ships, which was under the command of Captain Mailarde [Vivien Maillard]. We signalled our distress, and the captain sent a boat for us.

THE QUEEN-ELECT IS BROUGHT TO THE KING

WHEN the king is ready to take a wife, he gives orders that from among the daughters of his principal men the tallest and most beautiful shall be chosen. The newly selected queen is brought to him on a litter covered with the skin of some rare animal and fitted with a canopy of boughs to shade her head.

Four strong men carry her on their shoulders, each of them holding a forked wooden stick on which he rests the poles when they halt. Two more walk at the sides, shielding her from the sun with large round fans. Before the queen march the trumpeters, blowing on horns made of bark, large at the far end and small at the other, and hung with small oval balls of gold, silver, and brass, which tinkle as they march. Behind the queen are the most beautiful girls that can be found, clad in skirts made of pendant Spanish moss, their necks and arms decorated with necklaces and bracelets of pearls, each carrying a basket of choice fruits. At the end of the procession are the bodyguards.

To reach the beach we had to pass through the wild roses and two little rivers similar to the ones we had crossed previously. For this purpose the staff I had cut the day before was necessary again, as well as two others which Captain Laudonnière provided.

Thus we got near enough to the boat, but our hearts failed us, what with so much hunger and travail, and we would have had to stay there had not the mariners come to our aid, proving themselves great rescuers. They carried us, one by one, into their boat and ferried us to the ship, where we were well and cheerfully received.

They gave us bread and water and after we had eaten, we began little by little to regain our strength, a certain token of the mercy of God, who had saved us from the infinite dangers of death all around us that we might render unto Him most hearty thanks and praise forever.

We passed the night talking of the miraculous works of God, and comforting one another in remembrance of our delivery. On the next day, Jacques Ribaut, Captain of the *Pearl,* boarded the ship to confer with us on what we had best do to save the rest of our men and vessels. We learned from him that food was scarce.

Our strength was broken, our munitions of war were in the hands of the enemy, and what had happened to our Governor we did not know. We had no knowledge of where the tempest's rage had driven him. We concluded, therefore, that we could do no better than try to return to France.

Most of our company thought that we should separate those who escaped from the fort into two parties, some to go in the *Pearl,* the others to go with Captain Maillard [master of the *Levrière.*] So on Thursday, September 25, we left the coast with a favorable north wind, meaning to sail for France. Yet on that very day our ships were separated, and we did not meet again upon the seas.

We sailed five hundred leagues happily. Then one morning, before sunrise, we were attacked by a Spanish ship, which we got into our power. We fired so much gunshot into her that she yielded, while blood ran out of the scupper holes. No man was seen above hatch. We could not board her because of the weather, for fear of damaging our ship. The Spaniards were content to let us go, and so we left them, thanks be to God, joyful that none of us was hurt or killed in the fight except our cook.

On the rest of our voyage we did not have any further meeting with our enemies; but we were sorely weather-beaten and almost driven onto the Spanish coast. This we feared most—and if it had happened it would have increased our sorrows. We also endured many privations on the seas, besides cold and hunger. For you will understand that we had escaped from *Terra Florida* with no apparel for night or day but one poor shirt and another thin garment over it. This was very poor defense against the injury of the weather. What

THE KING RECEIVES THE QUEEN

THUS arrayed, the queen is brought to the king. He is waiting for her, sitting on a large platform of round logs especially erected for the purpose. His principal men sit below him on long benches on both sides of the platform. When the queen arrives, she takes her seat at the king's left. He congratulates her and tells her why she was chosen.

Then a dance is performed before them by young girls, dressed for the occasion, their hair tied at the back of the head and flowing down over their shoulders; below the navel they wear a broad girdle with something like a purse hanging down in front to cover them. All around this girdle are hung little balls of gold and silver that dangle down upon their thighs and tinkle when they dance. They chant the praises of the king and his bride, raising and lowering their hands in unison.

All the men and women have their ears pierced and wear in them small oblong fish bladders, which shine like pearls when inflated and when dyed red look like light-colored rubies. It is remarkable that these savages should be able to produce such tasteful ornaments.

was worse, the bread we ate was mouldy, and the fresh water stank—and all we could have of it was one small cup a day.

This rotten nourishment is the reason that we have fallen into so many kinds of diseases, which have caused a great many of our company to die since we landed. At the end of this perilous and lamentable voyage, we were driven onto the coast of La Rochelle, where we were gently received by the inhabitants of the country and those of the town, who gave us as much of their goods as necessity required. Being assisted by their good will, we had sufficient for everyone to return home.

The Second Book

You have heard how Captain Jean Ribaut took shipping with the soldiers to seek out the Spaniards. After five days of fruitless searching, he met the flagship of his fleet, the *Trinity*. He did not know what had happened at the fort and decided to protect the coast against a Spanish attack. The weather was troublesome. The wind blew hard, and it rained continually. On the fifth day the tempest increased to such strength that the sailors were not able to resist it, but were driven by force to the shore about fifty leagues from the River of May. There the ships foundered, and the munitions were lost.

Nevertheless, the men reached safety, except for Captain La Grange, who threw himself onto a mast and was drowned. His death was much lamented among the others, for he was always a good counselor and an amiable companion.

Although they had been saved from the rage of the waves, the soldiers found themselves with a new trouble. The hunger that assailed them could only be stilled by eating the produce of the earth—herbs, roots, and such like. These had to satisfy their craving stomachs. Nor was there anything to quench their thirst but old pools of muddy water. One look at the scum which floated on it was enough to make a well man sick. But the rage of their extreme hunger and thirst forced them to consume these unwholesome meats and drinks. In this way they lived for eight days.

On the ninth day, by luck, they found a small boat. This was some comfort to them, for they hoped it would enable them to reach the fort with news of their shipwreck. The stronghold lay twelve leagues distant by land and fifty by water, and between them and the fort was the River of Dolphins. As this stream was very deep and a quarter of a mile broad, the men could not have crossed it without some vessel.

They caulked the boat, using their shirts instead of oakum. Captain Ribaut, with his grace and accustomed modesty, called the men to his counsel and said, "Companions and Friends, we cannot continue living in such misery and calamity. It were better to wish for death than to live in such affliction, unless God in His grace has given us faith in his provi-

.39.

THE KING AND THE QUEEN TAKE A WALK

WHILE hunting with some of my comrades in the forest, I once saw Chief Saturiba and his queen taking an evening walk. He was clad in a deerskin so exquisitely prepared and painted with so many colors that I have never seen anything more lovely. Two young men walked by his side carrying fans, while a third one, with little gold and silver balls hanging at his belt, followed close behind him holding up his train. The queen and her maidens were adorned with belts worn either at the shoulder or at the waist, made of a kind of moss that grows on the trees. This moss is woven into slender threads of a bluish-green color and is so delicate in texture as to be mistaken for filaments of silk. The trees laden with this moss hanging from the highest branches down to the ground are beautiful to see.

All these chiefs and their wives paint the skin around their mouths blue and are tattooed on the arms and thighs with a certain herb which leaves an indelible color. This process is so severe that it sometimes makes them sick for seven or eight days. For greater adornment and magnificence they allow the nails on their fingers and toes to grow long and file the fingernails at the sides with a shell, so that they become very sharp.

dence and taught us to look for succor, such as it shall please Him to send. And in the meantime, let us plan how we can end our troubles. I think some of us should go to the fort in this boat and let our friends know our extreme need, so that they can rescue us."

The French threw themselves on their knees and began tearfully to call upon the name of God. Their prayers finished, they looked about them to select the men best fitted for the journey. They named Thomas LeVasseur of Dieppe as leader, and Captain Jean Ribaut charged him to let those at the fort know of their distress as soon as he could. With him went Vincent Simon, Michel Gonnor, and others to the number of sixteen.

As I said before, our men were on the far side of the fort, and the River of Dolphins was between them and the stronghold. On the very first day, while they were marching forward on land, they saw a company of armed men on the other side of the river, with their standards flying. When they realized that they were Spaniards, they were perplexed in their hearts; they did not know what to do. The best they could think of was to send some of their company swimming over the river to offer to yield if their lives would be spared.

The swimmers were received courteously. The captain of this Spanish company was named Vallemande, and he swore by his faith as a gentleman and a Christian knight to use his good will in the interests of the Frenchmen. He said that it was the order which the Spaniards always practiced in war—that after being victorious they were content not to struggle further. He showed them by signs that they might not find any violations here with which nations hereafter might quarrel.

Immediately he caused a barge to be made ready and commanded five Spaniards to board her and ferry the French over. When the boats came side by side, a Spaniard spoke in the name of Vallemande. Captain Jean Ribaut went aboard, as did others to the number of thirty. The Captain was gently received by Vallemande; but the men were carried away and all bound, two and two together, their hands behind their backs.

All of our men were taken prisoner, thirty at a time, while Vallemande entertained our good Captain with fair, flattering words. Ribaut placed trust in the faithful promises of Vallemande, to whom he had yielded.

Now the men were bound two and two as they stepped out of the boat, Frenchmen and Spaniards marched toward the fort. But Captain Ribaut and others (especially the Sieur D'Ottigny) changed countenance when they saw their men coupled together. Again they solicited the favor of Vallemande, who reassured them that those bonds were only to get them to the fort in safety. He said he would fulfil all that he had promised once he arrived there.

When the men reached the stronghold, they were asked to tell which among them were mariners, ship's carpenters, gunners, and other seamen. There were thirty of them in

BURIAL CEREMONIES FOR A CHIEF OR A PRIEST

When a chief dies, he is buried with great solemnities; his drinking cup is placed upon the grave, and arrows are planted in the ground around it. His subjects mourn for him for three whole days and nights without eating anything. The other chiefs and his friends do likewise, and both men and women cut off half their long tresses in token of their love for him. The household goods belonging to the dead chief are put in his house, and the house is set on fire. For six months after his death certain chosen women mourn for him three times a day—at dawn, noon, and twilight—with a great howling.

When a priest dies, he is buried in his own house, and the whole is then burned, dwelling, furniture, body, and all.

all. Not long after a company of Spaniards came from the fort, and our men were made to trail behind Vallemande and his soldiers, like a herd of beasts being led to the slaughter.

Then, in a din of drums, flutes, and trumpets the Spaniards spent their courage wildly upon the poor Frenchmen—still bound. They vied with one another to see who could strike best with pike, halberd, and sword. This contest of might continued for half an hour, until they won the field (and the name of this glorious victory), most cruelly killing there those who had surrendered and whom they had received in faith and honor.

In the horror, Captain Ribaut begged Vallemande to save his life, and the Sieur of Ottigny, on his knees, recalled his solemn promise—but all to no avail. Turning his back, Vallemande stood off a short distance while one of his murderers came from behind and struck Captain Ribaut to the ground with a dagger. Then he was stabbed until there was no life left in him. In such a way were our men handled, men who had yielded in the shadow of Spanish assurances.

To show even greater cruelty, the Spaniards in spite cut off the beard of the King's Lieutenant as proof of their prowess and sent it to Seville. As some of our sailors, whose lives had been spared were also sent to Seville, they told us of this. One of them was Christophe le Breton, who escaped and fled from Seville to the town of Bordeaux and thence by ship to Dieppe. It was he who related what had happened to that faithful servant of the King, Jean Ribaut. As a memorial of their victory, the Spaniards quartered his body and his head, which they stuck at the four corners of the fort.

Here hast thou, Gentle Reader, seen the discourse of two sorts of people; and in this thou mayest calmly judge and see what covetousness causeth. Both parties were desirous of gain, and on one part there was monstrous cruelty. But history suffices in itself. God is a righteous judge, who sees the acts of all humankind, and He shall reward everyone according to his deserts. God keep us from murder and bloodshed and give us grace to fear Him and honor His Holy Name aright.

AMEN.

HOW THE NATIVES COLLECT GOLD IN THE STREAMS

A LONG way from our fort are the Appalachian Mountains. There, as can be seen on the map, three great rivers rise, and in the sands of these a great deal of gold, silver, and brass is found. The natives dig ditches in these streams, into which the sand brought by the current falls because of its weight. Little by little they collect the precious metals and bring them in canoes down the River of May, which empties into the sea. The Spaniards use the wealth thus obtained to great advantage.

TIMETABLE

OF THE FOUR FRENCH EXPEDITIONS TO FLORIDA

Ribaut's first expedition

Ribaut leaves Le Havre. . . . . . . 18 February 1562
Ribaut reaches the Florida coast. . . . . 30 April
He finds the entrance of the
River of May (the St. John's). . . . . 1 May
Discovery of the Seine, Somme, Loire,
Charente, Garonne, Gironde,
Belle, Grande. . . . . first two weeks of May
Building of Charlesfort. . . . . 15-20 May
Ribaut explores the countryside. . . . . . 20-25 May
Ribaut sails for France. . . . . 11 June
Ribaut arrives in Dieppe. . . . . 20 July
Famine at Charlesfort. . . . . . . January-May 1563
Ribaut's book on Florida
is published in England. . . . . May

Laudonnière's expedition

Laudonnière leaves Le Havre. . . . . 20 April 1564
He arrives at the coast of Florida. . . . . 22 June
He reaches the River of May. . . . . 23 June
He meets Saturiba. . . . . 24 June
At the River of Seine. . . . . 26 June
At the River of Somme. . . . . 27 June
The founding of Fort Caroline. . . . . 1 June
Saturiba's visit to the fort. . . . . June
Ottigny with the Timuquanan Indians. . . . . June
Vasseur and La Caille with Molloua. . . . . . . July
A storm devastates Saturiba's village. . . 29 August
Captain Bourdet arrives from France. 4 September
Vasseur and Arlac escort Saturiba's
two prisoners back to Outina. . . . 10 September
Thirteen men desert the colony. . . . 20 September
Ottigny goes to Outina's aid. . . . . October
Departure of Captain Bourdet. . . . . 10 November
Departure of the conspirators
for New Spain . . . . 8 December
Good relations with Hiouacara,
widow of Indian chief. . . . . January 1565
Famine at Fort Caroline. . . . . April
Capture of Outina. April
Return of the conspirators. . . . . 25 May
Landing of Sir John Hawkins. . . . . 4 August
Hawkins leaves Florida. . . . . 7 August

Ribaut's second expedition

Menéndez' asiento with Phillip II
to conquer Florida. . . . . 20 March 1565
Ribaut leaves Dieppe. . . . . 10 May
He arrives at Le Havre. . . . . 23 May
Ribaut at the Isle of Wight. 26 May-14-June
Menéndez leaves Cadiz but has to turn
back because of a tempest. . . . . 29 June
A tempest rages in the Atlantic. . . . . . . 20-21 July
Menéndez lands at Porto Rico
for repairs . . . . 9 August
Ribaut reaches the Florida coast. . . . . . 13 August
Menéndez leaves Porto Rico
with five vessels. . . . . 15 August
Menéndez in sight of Florida. . . . . 25 August
Ribaut lands with reinforcements. . . . . 28 August
Three French ships enter the river. . . . 29 August
Spanish sails sighted. . . . . 3 September
Menéndez discovers Ribaut's ships. . 4 September
Menéndez returns to San Augustine. 7 September
He takes possession of the country. . . 9 September
Ribaut's fleet sets out. . . . . 10 September
Storm destroys the French ships. 10-23 September
Menéndez begins his march against
Fort Caroline . . . . 17 September
The Spanish capture Fort Caroline. 20 September
The Pearl and the Levrière
leave for France. . . . . 25 September
The first massacre. . . . . 29 September
Menéndez hears of Ribaut's
shipwreck . . . . 10 October
The second massacre; Ribaut slain. . . . 12 October
Laudonnière arrives in England. . . . . . 11 October

De Gourgues' expedition

De Gourgues leaves Bordeaux but
has to return. . . . . 2 August 1567
Fresh departure . . . . 22 August
De Gourgues lands in Florida. . . . . April 1568
He takes the two Spanish forts. . . . . 24 April
Captures Fort Caroline. . . . . 27 April
Massacre of the Spaniards. . . . . 27-28 April
De Gourgues leaves Florida. . . . . 3 May
Arrives in France. 6 June

MURDER OF THE FRENCHMAN PIERRE GAMBIÉ

IN MY narrative I spoke of Pierre Gambié, a Frenchman who obtained a trading license from Laudonnière for that province and not only succeeded in acquiring considerable wealth but also married the daughter of a local chief. As he wished to visit his friends at the fort, he was permitted to go, on condition that he would return within a certain time. He was given a canoe with two Indians to paddle it, and the wealth he had acquired was stowed in the boat. On the journey, however, while the Frenchman was bending over to make a fire, his Indian companions murdered him. They might have done this out of revenge, since once when the chief was absent and Gambié had taken his place, he had beaten one of them; or they might have killed him because of the riches he had with him in the canoe. The Indians fled with the goods, and nothing was known of the crime for a long while afterwards.

This picture is put at the end so as not to interrupt the series. It would not have been included at all had the author not suddenly remembered the episode.

THE GREAT WEROANCA OF ENGLAND:
QUEEN ELIZABETH (1533-1603)

Engraving by Crispin van de Passe, after a drawing by Isaac Oliver.

NOTES ON THE ENGLISH SETTLEMENTS IN VIRGINIA

1585—1590

The French Huguenot settlements in Florida made English adventurers, merchants, and speculators realize suddenly that there existed a great continent with tremendous resources, in whose treasures they were not participating.

Jean Ribaut came to London in 1563, and in the spring of that year his book appeared, describing in vivid colors the fabulous riches of Florida. At that time Ribaut believed that his men were still holding out at Charlesfort, and he made every effort to organize a relief expedition to bring supplies to them. He talked to Queen Elizabeth and joined Thomas Stukeley in his venture of outfitting a fleet to sail to Florida. In the notes on the French settlements (see p. 10) I have described how this undertaking came to nothing. Ribaut was already a prisoner in the Tower of London when his soldiers, after a crazy crossing of the Atlantic (see pp. 8-9), were found by an English vessel and brought to London. They were fêted like heroes; they were received by the Queen and were the center of attention. Juicy roast beefs and English ale made them quickly forget their privations. Now they remembered only the treasures of Florida and not that they had nearly starved to death there. They spun tales of jewel mines which could be approached only by night, for by day the flashing light of the precious stones would strike men blind. They talked of gold and silver, pearls and silks, and their tales made that far-away land appear so enticing that a regular Florida fever infected the English. The adventurers, merchants, and speculators, the young men who hoped to get rich quickly, all planned journeys to Florida.

Till then—the date is 1563—no other power thought of challenging the supremacy of Spain in her overseas possessions. Pope Alexander VI had issued his famous Bull in 1493—a year after Columbus landed at San Salvador—dividing by a stroke of the pen the still unexplored and heathen world between Spain and Portugal. For many decades to come neither France nor England was strong enough to question openly the validity of the Pope's division. During that time Spain and Portugal consolidated and strengthened their hold in their newly discovered possessions—Portugal in West Africa and Brazil, Spain in Mexico, Peru, and Central America—building up a commercial and colonial monopoly, and forbidding other nations to trade or settle in those areas.

But with the death of Mary Tudor in 1558, and with Elizabeth's ascent to the throne, the political situation in England had altered. "Bloody Mary," the devoted wife of Philip II, in the last years of her reign, made the country a vassal of the great Spanish monarchy. England had to fight a war against France as Spain's ally and lost Calais, her last stronghold on the continent. But with Elizabeth a different era began. The friendship with Spain turned gradually to enmity. The political and economic life of the English Isles underwent radical changes. The national will, embodied in Crown and Parliament, triumphed. Mediaeval society belonged to the past.

A new class emerged, a class of merchants eager for business opportunities, searching for new markets, looking for cheaper and more abundant sources of material. Home industries flourished, aided by the refugee craftsmen who had fled from the Netherlands to escape the cruelty of the Spanish Inquisition.

In agriculture the farmers with small holdings were replaced by yeomen who tilled a hundred acres or more. This more intensive and effective farming produced a surplus, and the surplus increased the national wealth, stimulating home and foreign trade. The yeomen had enough butter, cheese, and meat to sell in the nearby towns. They made more money. They began to buy small luxuries. Pewter, tapestries, silk hangings, carpets, and fine napery found a place in their homes. The expanding cloth trade made sheep raising extremely profitable, thus lands were turned into sheep pastures, the enclosed holdings increased, and the former tenants found themselves without work.

The unemployed flocked to the towns, searching for jobs; they swelled the ranks of the highwaymen; they roamed the seas as pirates.

England had to expand; she looked for foreign trade, she looked for a place in the world where her unemployed could find work and food. (It is strange to think that England with a population of only four million was unable to feed and provide jobs for all her subjects.) She looked with envious eyes at Spain's overseas possessions and at the treasures which Philip was wresting from the New World. Englishmen felt that the foundation of Philip II's power was based on the gold and silver which the Spanish treasure ships brought from America. It was these treasures which paid for Spain's wars in the Old World and financed her struggle against the reformation. Raleigh wrote: "It is his [Spain's] Indian gold that endangereth and disturbeth all the nations of Europe."

Now that she had a navy England wanted foreign markets. Spain stood in her way; not only excluding all foreigners from her overseas possessions, but forbidding all foreign trade with them. It was this monopoly which England wanted to break.

The first Englishman to challenge it was John Hawkins. In October, 1562, he set out with three small ships to establish a slave trade with the Indies. He captured a number of natives in Africa and sailed with them to Hispanola, where he sold them as slaves. A year later—it was when the English had already caught the Florida fever—Hawkins arrived in England with rich returns in pearls, gold, silver, hides, and sugar. The results of this voyage were so encouraging that soon Hawkins organized a new expedition and sailed this time with a fleet of five vessels, among them the *Jesus of Lubeck*—a ship of the Royal Navy, loaned to him by the Queen. Again Hawkins kidnapped some natives down the African coast and brought them to the ports of the Spanish Main, where he disposed of his living cargo at great profit. On the return voyage he visited Laudonnière's colony at Fort Caroline (see p. 16). The trade in slaves turned out to be a lucrative business. Many adventurers, merchants, noblemen, and even Queen Elizabeth herself, invested in it. In 1567 Hawkins set out again, but now Spain was on the alert. All ports in the Indies were warned not to trade with the foreigner. Driven by a storm into the harbor of San Juan de Ulloa, Hawkins was attacked by the Spaniards. With this encounter began the twenty years of piratical fighting on England's part, which culminated in the battle against the Spanish Armada.

At San Juan de Ulloa a twenty-two-year-old seaman fought with Hawkins—Francis Drake. He never forgot that fight and how the Spaniards had betrayed them. From then on this bold and sagacious sea captain, who more than anyone else was responsible for making England mistress of the seas, set out to plunder Spanish galleons, and prey upon Spanish treasure.

While Hawkins, Drake, Frobisher, and Davis were out after Spanish gold, Sir Humphrey Gilbert and his half-brother, Walter Raleigh, thought of the vast lands in the New World not only as suppliers of gold but as a country where one day English would be spoken, where one day an English community could be established whose imports and exports might benefit the Mother Country. Even after his many unsuccessful ventures to colonize Virginia, Raleigh was convinced that "I shall yet live to see an English nation."

In 1574 Gilbert wrote in his *Discourse to Prove a Passage by the Northwest to Cathaia and the East Indies* that there were "divers very rich countries, both civil and others, . . . where there is to be found great abundance of gold, silver, precious stones, cloth of gold, silks, all manner of spices, grocery wares, and other kinds of merchandise of an inestimable price, which both the Spaniard and Portugal, through the length of their journeys, cannot well attain unto." Therefore he suggested that "we might inhabit some part of those countries, and settle there such needy people of our country, which now trouble the commonwealth, and through want here at home are forced to commit outrageous offences, whereby they are daily consumed with the gallows."

In June, 1578, Gilbert obtained a patent from Queen Elizabeth "to inhabit and possess at his choice all remote and heathen lands not in actual possession of any Christian Prince." The grant was limited to six years and was to expire on June 11, 1584, if in the meantime no settlement had been made or colony founded. All of Gilbert's attempts ended in failure. Though in 1583 he took formal possession of Newfoundland, on the return voyage he, with all his men, perished in a storm.

After Gilbert's death, Walter Raleigh continued his half-brother's work. He obtained another patent with similar rights, privileges and limitations to that of Gilbert's. It was dated March 25, 1584, and it left the whole unoccupied coast of the New World to Raleigh's selection. The patent was limited to six years.

A month after Raleigh had received his patent, he sent two ships under Philip Amadas and Arthur Barlowe to explore the coast of North America. When the two captains returned to England, they gave a glowing report on Virginia (see Barlowe's narrative on p. 125).

Raleigh now organized an expedition and dispatched a colony to settle in Virginia. Sir Richard Grenville (the hero of "The Revenge") was in command of the fleet and took a colony to Roanoke Island. The settlers stayed in the New World from August 17, 1585, to June 18, 1586. What they did in Virginia can be read in the narrative written by their Governor, Ralph Lane (see p. 135). They spent most of their time in search of gold. They behaved badly toward the natives and drove them into hostility. Their food gone, they prayed for Sir Richard Grenville's return, since he had promised to come back with supplies. But Summer came, and there was no sign of Grenville. In June, Sir Francis Drake visited the colony. He was on his return voyage to England after "singeing King Philip's beard" and plundering Cartagena, San Domingo, and St. Augustine. The colonists sailed home with him.

A fortnight after their departure, Sir Richard Grenville arrived at Roanoke. As he could not find the settlers, he left fifteen men behind to hold the country for England (see anonymous narrative on p. 151).

A year later—in May, 1587—Raleigh sent a second colony to Virginia under the governorship of John White. A few weeks after their arrival, White sailed back to England for supplies. (see White's narrative on p. 155). But war with Spain was imminent and White could not return to Roanoke until 1590. By then the colony had disappeared. John White describes his search after the "lost colonie" in his report to Richard Hakluyt (see White's letter on p. 167).

With Raleigh's second settlement English efforts to colonize America ceased. Not until two decades later—in 1607—was England able to plant a permanent colony on American soil—Jamestown.

SIR WALTER RALEIGH (*ca.* 1552-1618)

Queen Elizabeth granted a patent to Raleigh on March 25, 1584, "for the discovering and planting of new lands and Countries." A month later he sent two sea captains, Amadas and Barlow, to the New World.

Contemporary portrait in the collection of Mr. Preston Davie, New York. Courtesy Frick Art Reference Library.

BARLOWE

Captain Arthur Barlowe's narrative of the first voyage made to the coasts of America by two ships. They were commanded by Philip Amadas and Arthur Barlowe, who, in the year 1584, discovered the part of the country now called Virginia. This account is addressed to Sir Walter Raleigh, who financed the expedition.

ON April 27, 1584, we set out from the West of England in two ships fully manned and provisioned, having received your final orders in writing, in which you confirmed the instructions given by you in person when we left the River Thames. Since it contributes nothing to the knowledge of the country we visited, I will omit the tedious tale of the daily happenings of the voyage there and back. I will make only this brief report, so that you may judge how profitable this land will be to yourself (on whose account the expedition was made), to Her Majesty, and to the Commonwealth. We hope that it will justify your undertaking, for we have brought to light as much as could be expected from the few supplies and small number of men we had.

On May 10 we arrived at the Canary Islands, and on June 10 sighted the islands of the West Indies. We kept our course farther to the southeast than was necessary, because we feared that the current in the Bay of Mexico, swerving away between the Cape of Florida and Havana, was stronger than we later found it to be. The air of the West Indies was very unwholesome, and most of our men became ill. For this reason, after taking on fresh water and foodstuffs, we departed twelve days later. I will not trouble you with the description of these islands and their vicinity, since they are well known to you.

On the second of July we came into shallow water, and the air smelt as sweet and strong as if we were in a fragrant flower garden. From this we knew that land could not be far off. Keeping careful watch, with sails slack, we came in sight of the coast on the fourth of the month. We thought that we had reached the mainland of the continent, and we sailed along it for a hundred and twenty miles before we found an entrance. We entered the first inlet, though not without difficulty, and cast anchor a distance of three harquebus shots within the harbor mouth.[1] After giving thanks to God for our safe arrival, we manned the boats and rowed to land, taking possession of it in the name of the Queen's Most Excellent Majesty. We proclaimed her rightful queen and ruler and then delivered it to your use according to Her Majesty's grant and letters patent under Her Highness's great seal.[2] When these ceremonies were over, we surveyed the land and found the shores sandy and low toward the water's edge and so overgrown with grapes that the surging waves flowed over them. The grapes grew everywhere, on the sand, on the green soil of the hills, over the plains, climbing on every little shrub and toward the tops of high cedars. I do not think such plenty could be found in any other place in the world—and I have seen those parts of Europe where grapes grow most abundantly. The difference was so great that one could scarcely believe it.

We walked away from the shore toward the nearby hilltops; from this spot we could view the sea on both sides, to the north and to the south, as far as eye could reach. The land stretched to the west, and we found later that it was an island only twenty miles long and not more than six miles wide.[3] Beyond the hills we saw the valleys thick with fine cedar trees. We fired a harquebus, and the sound disturbed a great flock of cranes, mostly white, which arose below us. Their cries were multiplied by many echoes; they made a noise as if an army had shouted all together.

The island has many large forests overrun with deer, rabbits, hares, and woodfowl in great abundance, even in midsummer. The woods are not barren and fruitless like those in Bohemia, Moscovia, or Hercynia,[4] but are thick with the highest and reddest cedars in the world, far better than the cedars of the Azores, of the Indies, or of Lebanon. Pine, cypress, sassafras, and the lentisk, or gum tree, all grow there, as well as the tree whose bark is black cinnamon, which Master Winter[5] brought back from the Straits of Magellan; and there are many other trees of excellent quality and fine fragrance.

Two days passed without sight of any inhabitants, but on the third day we perceived a small boat with three persons in it. They rowed toward us, and when they were about four gunshots from our ships, one of its occupants got out of the boat. He walked along

1. It is not possible to identify the harbor. In four hundred years many changes have occurred. The inlets in the sandy barrier of North Carolina are not in the same places they were when Amadas and Barlowe visited the coast.

2. Hakluyt wrote on the margin opposite this passage: "July 13, possession taken."

3. Hakluyt noted: "The isle of Wokokon"—one of the more southerly islands enclosing Pamlico Sound. See De Bry's map on pp. 274-275.

4. Moscovia, an ancient name for Russia; Hercynia, the land of the forest-covered German mountains, including the Thüringerwald and the Schwarzwald. Caesar's *Hercynia silva* in Germany was sixty day's journey in length and nine in breadth.

5. John Winter was one of Drake's companions in his voyage around the world.

the shore to a point opposite us. Simon Ferdinando,[6] the master and pilot of the flagship, Captain Philip Amadas, myself, and others rowed to shore, where the man waited for us with no sign of fear. We understood nothing of his speech, but since he made no objection, we took him aboard our ship. There we gave him a shirt, a hat, and other gifts, and then made him taste our meat and our wine, which he seemed to like very well. After we had shown him over both our ships, he was taken back to shore.

He returned to his own boat and began to fish. In less than half an hour's time he had laden his boat to the scuppers and returned to the shore, where he divided his catch into two parts, indicating with signs that one half was meant for each of our ships; this was his way of repaying our hospitality.

The next day several boats came to our anchorage, one bringing the King's brother accompanied by forty or fifty handsome men. The natives' behavior was as civil and mannerly as that of any European. The name of the King's brother was Granganimeo, the King was called Wingina, and the country Wingandacoa,[7] now named Virginia by Her Majesty.[8] The natives left their boats some distance from our ships, just as our visitor of the day before had done. Then the King's brother came with some forty followers to the shore opposite us. There his men spread a long mat on the ground, on which he seated himself. At the other end of the mat his four companions took their seats, while the rest of his men stood nearby. When we came ashore, fully armed, the King's brother did not seem to be afraid or distrustful. Nor did he or his four companions move from their places upon the mat. He beckoned and invited us to sit by him, which we did. When we were seated, he made signs of joy and welcome, first striking his own head and breast and then ours, smiling and trying to show that we were all brothers, all made of the same flesh. He then delivered a long speech, and we presented him with gifts, which he received with pleasure and thanks. None of his companions dared to speak a word during all this time except the four men sitting at the other end of the mat, who whispered among themselves.

The King is strictly obeyed in this land, and his brothers and children are held in great reverence. King Wingina himself had been seriously wounded in a fight with the chief of the neighboring country. He had been shot through the body in two places, and though one arrow had passed clean through his thigh, he recovered. But as he lay some six

6. Ferdinando played a villainous part in the Roanoke Colony when he was sent there in 1587.

7. This was a misunderstanding. When the English asked the name of the country, one of the savages, who did not understand the question, replied, "Win-gan-da-coa," which means, "You wear fine clothes." As the Englishmen were no better linguists than the natives, they reported this as the name of the country. Winsor, *Narrative and Critical History of America*, III, 109.

8. The Queen, not less delighted than Raleigh, named the newly discovered country Virginia in commemoration of her maiden life and conferred upon Raleigh the honor of knighthood.

day's journey from our harbor, in the main village of this country, we could not see him.

After we had presented Granganimeo with some gifts we thought he might like, we made a few presents to his companions sitting with him on the mat. But the King's brother arose at once, took the presents away, and stowed them all in his own basket. He made signs to us that everything should be given to him, as the others were only his servants.

A day or two later we began to trade with the natives, exchanging our goods for chamois, buff, and deer skins. When we showed Granganimeo our merchandise, the thing that pleased him most was a bright tin dish. He grabbed this, clapped it to his breast, and after making a hole in the edge he hung it around his neck, declaring with signs that this would shield him against his enemies' arrows. For these savages carry on a constant deadly warfare with the chief and the people of the adjoining country.

We exchanged our tin dish for twenty skins, worth twenty crowns, and a copper kettle for fifty skins, worth fifty crowns. We made good bargains for hatchets, axes, and knives; they would have given us anything for a sword, but we would not part with one.

After two or three days had passed, the King's brother visited us aboard our ships and dined with us. He greatly enjoyed our meat, bread, and wine. Some time later he returned, accompanied by his wife, his daughter, and two or three of his younger children. His wife was very beautiful, small in stature, and shy. She wore a long cloak of leather, the fur side next to her body. Her forehead was adorned by a band of white coral, just as her husband's was. Her earrings of pearls as big as peas, hung down to her waist. The other women had pendants of copper in their ears, so had the children of Granganimeo and of the other nobles, five or six in each ear. The King's brother wore a broad plate of gold about his head. As the metal was unpolished, we could not determine if it was really gold or copper, since he would not allow it to be taken from him. But when we felt it, it bent easily.

Granganimeo was dressed much like his wife. The only difference in the appearance of men and women being, that the women wore their hair long on both sides, while the men only on one. The color of their skin is yellowish, and their hair is generally black, although we saw some children with very fine auburn and chestnut-colored hair.[9]

After these women had visited us, a great many people from all parts of the country came down to the ships, bringing coral, leather, and several kinds of fine dyes to do some trading. But when Granganimeo was present, no one else dared to trade but himself or those men who wore red pieces of copper on their heads. These copper beads were a sign of noble birth; people without them were of the ordinary sort.

We had noticed, just as I am certain you must have seen for yourself in the men we

9. These were the descendants of the white people who were shipwrecked on the coast of America and lived with the savages for several weeks before they could outfit their boats and leave.

brought home with us, that no people in the world have more respect for their King, their nobles, and their governors than these savages. When Granganimeo's wife came to see us, as she did many times, she was always accompanied by forty or fifty women. But when she came aboard our ship, she left them behind on land; only her daughters, her nurse, and one or two others were allowed to come with her. And when the King's brother visited us, he always ordered his followers to build a fire on the shore, one fire for each boatload of men so that we should always know the number of warriors he was bringing with him.

Their boats were made of a pine or a pitch tree, a wood which is not commonly known to us and not grown in England. The savages have no sharp-edged tools to use in making boats, except a very few which came into their possession twenty years ago, when a ship was wrecked on their coast. From this ship's sides they drew the nails and spikes, and with these they made some of their best instruments.

They build their boats in the following manner: first, they burn down a large tree, or take one blown down by the wind. Then they put pitch on one side of this tree and set fire to it; when it is burnt hollow, they scrape away the burnt part with shells. If they want to burn it deeper or wider, they put some resin into it which, when lighted, burns away the timber. Thus they make very fine boats, large enough to carry twenty men. Their oars are like scoops, but when the water is shallow they use long poles.

Granganimeo took a great liking to our armor, a sword, and several other things, and he offered to give us a large box of pearls in exchange for them. For the time being we refused this bargain, as we did not want him to know how highly we valued his pearls until we learned exactly what parts of the country they came from. (This Your Worship will well understand.) He was very fair in keeping his promises. On many occasions we had given him merchandise on the strength of his word, and each time he brought what he had promised on the following morning. He sent us a pair or two of fat bucks, rabbits, hares, and the best fish in the world every day. And he presented us with different kinds of fruits, melons, walnuts, cucumbers, squash, peas, and several root vegetables, all very good. The corn he gave us was white, tempting, and of excellent flavor; it is harvested three times in five months, for the savages sow it first in May for a July crop, then in June for an August crop, and finally in July for a September crop. They cast the corn into the ground after breaking a little of the soft turf with a wooden pick. We tested the soil by putting in some of our peas, and in ten days they were up fourteen inches. The beans which grow there in great abundance are of various colors, some wild, some cultivated in their gardens; they also have wheat and oats.

The soil is deep, sweet, healthy, and the most fruitful in the world. We saw at least fourteen different sweet-smelling timber trees, and the greater part of the underbrush is bay and growths of that nature. They have the same oaks that we have in England, but far larger and better.

After the natives had been aboard our ships several times, I went with seven others of our company on a trip up into the river that flows toward the city of Skicoak,[10] which they call Occam.[11] The next evening we arrived at an island called Roanoke,[12] about seven leagues from our harbor. At the northern end of the island we found a village of nine houses, built of cedar, standing near the water's edge. It was fortified with a palisade of sharpened trees to keep out enemies. The entrance was very cleverly contrived, being like a turnpike. Granganimeo was not at home, but his wife came running toward us in a cheerful and friendly fashion. She ordered some of her men to draw our boat up onto the shore, where the beating waves could not reach it. Others were to carry us on their backs to dry ground, and she saw to it that our oars were brought into her house in order that they should not be stolen. When we came into her lodging, a house of five rooms, she asked us to take our seats by a huge fire, made in one of the rooms. We had removed our clothes, and she had them washed and dried. While some of the women took off our stockings and washed them, others bathed our feet in warm water. She was greatly concerned about our comfort, and she herself saw to it that meat should speedily be prepared for us.

When we were warm and dry, Granganimeo's wife led us into an inner room, where she placed some food on a huge board standing along the wall. There we found boiled wheat pudding, venison, both boiled and roasted, fish, boiled and roasted, raw and boiled melons, and several kinds of root vegetables and fruits. Although ordinarily the savages drink water, they have wine when the grapes are ripe. Only they have no casks to keep it in; therefore when the season for grapes is over, they must drink water for the rest of the year. Their water is boiled with ginger, black cinnamon, sassafras, and other wholesome medicinal herbs.

We were entertained with kindness and friendship and were given everything they could provide. We found these people gentle, loving, and faithful, lacking all guile and trickery. It was as if they lived in a golden age of their own. Their only care is how to protect themselves from the cold of their short winter and to obtain their food. The meat they eat is boiled thoroughly, and they make very sweet and well-seasoned soups. Their cooking vessels are clean, white, large earthen pots, and their dishes are platters made of sweet wood. Beyond the room in which they ate was another where they slept, and farther on still another, which held the idol they worship. Of this idol they tell most incredible tales.

10. See De Bry's map on pp. 274-275. Skicoak was situated where Portsmouth, Virginia is today.

11. Perhaps the northern part of Pamlico Sound and Currituck Sound.

12. Probably a corruption of the Indian name Ohanoak.

While we were having dinner, two or three men came through the gate, home from hunting. Glancing at the armed natives, we immediately reached for our weapons. Granganimeo's wife was very much upset when she saw this and told her men to take the hunters' bows and arrows and break them. She further ordered that the poor fellows should be beaten and driven out of the gate.

We decided to leave before nightfall. This made Granganimeo's wife sorry. She was grieved that we did not wish to stay longer. She gave us a supper, half-prepared, in the cooking pots, so that we could take the food with us to our boat. We thought it best to spend the night aboard, and therefore we rowed the boat a good distance from the shore. When she realized our distrust, she was hurt and sent some thirty men and women to sit up the whole night on the bank near our boat. She also sent five mats to protect us from the rain and continued to entreat us to spend the night in the shelter of her house. But as there were only a few of us and we feared that if anything should happen the voyage would be endangered, we refused. We did not dare to take the slightest risk, though in our minds we had no doubts of them, for we have never in the world so far encountered a more kind and loving people.

Beyond the Island of Roanoke is the mainland, opposite which empties the great river, called Occam by the inhabitants. Here, on the shore of the Occam, lies the town of Pomeiock,[13] and six days' journey from Pomeiock is the town of Skicoak, which the people say is very large, though none of the savages have seen it. But they have heard about the great size of the city from their fathers, who reported that it takes about an hour to journey all around it.

Into the Occam empties another large river, called Cipo,[14] and this river has an abundance of mussels containing pearls. Upon the banks of another river, the Nomopana,[15] which also flows into the Occam, stands the great town of Chawanook, and the name of the chief of that town and country is Pooneno. This Pooneno is not a subject of the King of Wingandacoa, but is an independent chief. Beyond his country there is another king whom they call Menatonon, and these three kings are in league with each other.

Four days' journey toward the southwest lies the town of Secota, the southernmost town of Wingandacoa. Near this town a ship was lost twenty-six years ago, and some of its survivors were saved by the natives. At first they spent ten days on an uninhabited outlying island called Wokokon,[16] but later, with the help of the men of Secotan, they set to work and fastened two native boats together, fitted them with masts, and made sails of

13. Pomeiock was west of the present site of Engelhard, N. C.
14. Perhaps the Alligator River.
15. The Chowan.
16. Probably one of the more southerly of the islands enclosing Pamlico Sound.

their shirts. When these boats were ready, they took on such food as the country provided, and three weeks after their rescue they sailed away. Later their ships were found cast up on a neighboring island. These were the only white men ever known to come to this part of the world, the only ones before us who wore clothing, and they were seen only by the inhabitants of Secotan. As the savages had never met white men, they were astonished at the sight of us; they admired the whiteness of our skins and wanted constantly to touch our chests. They marvelled at our ships also, and everything we possessed seemed strange and wonderful to them.

Whenever we fired a gun, even if it was only a harquebus, they trembled with fear at the sound, for the weapons they use are bows and arrows; and though the arrows are only made of small canes, headed with a sharp shell or the tooth of a fish, yet they are strong enough to kill a naked man. Their swords are of hardened wood, and they use breastplates of wood for defense against enemy arrows. Besides these weapons they carry a kind of club with the sharp horns of a stag, or some other animal, fastened to its end. When they go to war, they take their idol with them and ask counsel of it just as the Romans used to consult the Oracle of Apollo. They do not march to battle to the sound of drum and trumpet, but sing songs as they go. They have bloody and cruel wars, and since there have been too many in late years, a great number of the people have been killed, and parts of the country left desolate.

Adjoining Secotan is the country of Pomooik,[17] belonging to a king called Piemacum. This king is in league with his neighbor to the west, through whose country, called Newsiok, the River Neuse flows. These chiefs carry on a bitter warfare with Wingina, the King of Wingandacoa. Although some two years ago peace was made between King Piemacum and the King of Secotan (this was told us by the natives we brought to England), there remained undying hatred in the Secotans' hearts for the many injuries and the slaughter done to them by Piemacum. They did not forget how Piemacum and his tribe had invited them to come to a feast in his town. They accepted the invitation and came with about thirty of their handsomest women. While they were all sitting happily together and praying before their idol (which is nothing other than the image of the devil), the chief of the town fell upon them, slew all the men, and carried off the women and children.

Our friends have often urged us to attack Piemacum's town to get the rich stores he has there. But whether they urge us because they want revenge on their enemies or because they wish us well, only time will tell.

Beyond Roanoke Island are other large islands, all very fruitful and rich, and there

17. This name is given on the De Bry map of Virginia as Panauuaioc. See pp. 274-275.

are many towns and villages along the mainland, some situated on the shores near the islands, some farther inland.

When we first saw this country, we thought it to be a continent, but after we reached the harbor, we perceived another mighty sea before us. For a string of islands lay along the coast for a distance of some two hundred miles, and there were not more than two or three entrances to the inner water between the islands. Only after we had entered this water, did we realize that beyond these narrow islands (most of them not more than six miles wide) emerged another great sea, twenty to fifty miles broad, before the mainland could be reached. And in this enclosed sea there were about a hundred islands of varying sizes.

We visited one of these isles. It was about sixteen miles long, and we found it pleasant and fertile, thick with fine cedar trees and other sweet woods; there currants flourished, and flax, and other valuable crops which at that time we had no leisure to examine. Besides this island there are many others, as I have said, some two, three, four, or five miles long, some more, some less, but most of them beautiful to behold and rich in deer, rabbits, hares, and other animals. Here the best fish in the world are to be caught in great abundance.

Thus, Sir, we have acquainted you with the particulars of the explorations we made on this present voyage, as far as the shortness of time allowed us to investigate. We were satisfied with what we had achieved, and with the hope that at some later time we could enlarge our discoveries if granted further assistance and opportunities, we left Virginia. We set sail for home and arrived in the West of England in mid-September.

As we have described to you above, we took possession of the country and dedicated it to Her Majesty's use and, through Her Majesty's grant, to yours. As proof, we thought it best to record the names of the particular gentlemen and responsible persons who were present as witnesses. Thus all occasion for argument over the title to the country may be prevented in Her Majesty's behalf; without this precaution, those who are displeased by our success might make some claim to the land. The names of our witnesses are:

CAPTAINS

Master Philip Amadas
Master Arthur Barlowe

CREW

William Greenevile
John Wood
James Browewich
Henry Greene
Benjamin Wood
Simon Ferdinando
Nicholas Petman
John Hewes

We also brought home two savages, named Wanchese and Manteo, choosing them for their strength and endurance.

SIR FRANCIS DRAKE (*ca.* 1540-1596)

He found Raleigh's first colonists at Roanoke Island, and took them back to England.

An enlarged replica of a Hilliard miniature painted in 1581, in the Imperial Gallery of Vienna.

LANE

Ralph Lane's report to Sir Walter Raleigh concerning the English Colony which had been left in Virginia by Sir Richard Grenville. The Colony was governed by Ralph Lane from August 17, 1585, to June 18, 1586 when the settlers left for home.

IN order to make a clear and orderly report, I think it best to divide this account into two parts. The first will be a detailed description of such portions of the mainland as we could explore with the small number of men and the limited supplies at our disposal. The second part will give the reasons for leaving so hurriedly with General Sir Francis Drake when the ships he had given us and the men he had brought to stay and strengthen our Colony were carried away in a storm. In this part I will also tell how Pemisapan and the savages conspired against us.

The First Part

DESCRIBING THE PARTICULARS OF VIRGINIA

We established our settlement on the Island of Roanoke, and from here we set out for explorations to the north, northwest, south, and west.

The limit of our penetration to the south was Secota, about eighty miles from Roanoke. To reach it we had to pass through a broad sound lying along the mainland. From this body of water we saw no sight of the land, although the sea was full of shoals and sandbars. We could not use our pinnace,[1] as the water was too shallow to float it, even if it could have been rowed. Only our four-oared boat could navigate the sound, and this carried not more than fifteen men with their equipment and food for seven days. For these and other reasons—one being that winter would soon come—we decided to abandon further explorations of these territories until we had more men and supplies.

To the north our farthest discovery was the country of the Chesepians, about a hundred and thirty miles from Roanoke. The way led through the wide and shallow sound and was full of danger; we dared not venture far from land, because if we had had an accident

1. A small armed vessel under sail; also a ship's boat which could be hoisted aboard.

there, no one could have rescued us. We found the country very beautiful, with fertile soil and a mild climate; the nearby sea provided the inhabitants with an abundance of fish. This territory, lying fifteen miles off shore, contained numerous bears (an excellent food) and was thickly forested with sassafras and walnut trees. Many other fertile provinces border the Chesepians, whose inhabitants, the Mandoages, Tripanicks, and Opossians, all came to visit the English Colony. These natives are ruled by kings, whom they call *Weroans*.

To the northwest we went as far as Chawanook, about a hundred and thirty miles from Roanoke. Our way there lay through a broad sound,[2] this one of fresh water. The channel was deep enough to permit heavy shipping, though there were shallow reaches on both sides.

The towns of Passaquenoke called the Women's Town, Chepanoc, Weapomeiok, Muscamunge, and Metackwem[3] lay along the shores we passed. They are all under the jurisdiction of the King of Weapomeiok, whose name is Okisko. At Muscamunge we entered a river and came into the country of Chawanook. As we progressed, the river became narrower, until at Chawanook it was no wider than the Thames between Westminster and Lambeth. The land beyond the left bank between Muscamunge and Chawanook is fairly high, and on the high bank is a town called the Blind Town, which the savages call Ohanoak.[4] It has fine grain fields and is subject to Chawanook.

Chawanook is the largest province on the river and can muster a great fighting force. The town of that name alone can put seven hundred men into the field. Its King, Menatonon, although he suffers from lameness, is, for a savage, unusually grave and wise. He spoke with much knowledge of conditions in his own country and the surrounding lands, explaining the commodities of each territory to me. When I took him prisoner, in March, 1586, during the two days he was with me he taught me more about his land than I had been able to learn from any other savages or from our own discoveries. Among other things Menatonon told me about the territory of a certain King which lay three days' journey by canoe up the Chawanook River, then four days' journey overland to the northeast. This country lies upon the sea, but its chief center is on an island,[5] surrounded by very deep water in a bay. Out of this bay the King received a huge quantity of pearls so easily obtained that there were enough to adorn not only his own skin garments but also those of his followers. He used these pearls to decorate his houses and even his beds; this he did with such profusion that it was wonderful to see.

2. Albemarle Sound.

3. These towns are marked as Chepanuu, Weapemeoc, Mascoming, and Metpquuem on De Bry's map on pp. 274-275. On John White's chart, pp. 186-187, Weapemeoc is on the spot where Edenton stands today.

4. Marked Ohaunoock on De Bry's map.

5. Probably Craney Island, in Chesapeake Bay.

Menatonon related that when this King had paid him a visit at Chawanook two years earlier he had brought some pearls with him. Although they were of the poorest kind, he had purchased them, giving the King some copper in exchange. Now he presented me with a rope of these same pearls, but they were black and not worth much. Yet some were very large, and a few of them were round and lustrous. By ill fortune I lost the rope, together with other of my belongings, when I went aboard Sir Francis Drake's ship. Menatonon also revealed that this King possessed many fine pearls that were white, large, and round and that his men customarily found the black pearls in shallow water, while they found the white pearls in very deep water.

I learned from him that the King of the pearl country traded the white pearls only with white men who wore clothing, while the black pearls he exchanged with his own people. Menatonon promised to give me guides who would lead me overland into that King's country whenever I wanted to go. But he advised me to take a large company of men with me, well supplied with food, because the King did not like to see any strangers within the borders of his territory, nor would he allow anyone to interfere with the pearl fishing. A strong fighting force of his highly able warriors was ready to enforce his commands.

After I heard all this I made up my mind that if the supplies you were to send arrived before the end of April, and if I had a sufficient number of boats or shipwrights to make them, with enough men and food to keep us until the new grain was harvested, I would dispatch a small bark[6] and two pinnaces to the bay which Menatonon had described. The men would make soundings for sandbars and then lie over in the bay near the island, while I, led by the guides, would go with all my small boats and two hundred men to the headwaters of the Chawanook River. Only one thing troubled me. I needed the assurance that the guides given me by Menatonon were really reliable, and to make certain of this I decided to take the King's best-loved son, whom I held prisoner, as hostage with me on the voyage.

I planned to build a bulwark with a small trench and a palisade at the headwaters of the river, where the boats would be left. There I would leave twenty-five or thirty men to guard the boats. The rest of my force would come with me, bringing picks, spades, axes, and as much food as each man could carry. I intended to raise another small fort at the end of two days' march, and there again I would leave fifteen or twenty men. This fort would be built near grain fields, so that the men could find their own food.

In this manner I planned to proceed, building forts two days' march apart until I arrived at the bay of pearls. If upon my arrival I found that the bay and its harbor seemed worth taking, I would there raise the main fort for the defense of the harbor and of our

6. The general name for a small ship.

ships. I would then move our colony from Roanoke and from its harbor, which had proved not to be of much value, to the new fort.

The place where I had left my boats moored below the small fort was four days' journey away, near the largest and best-known river in that part of the country, the Moratoc.[7] This stream flows from the west into the broad sound of Weapomeiok.[8] And while neither the Chawanook River nor the other sounds and bays, whether salt or fresh, show any current in calm weather—although they are influenced by the wind—the Moratoc has such a violent one flowing from the west and southwest that I doubted if we could navigate it by rowing. The river is full of twists and turns and receives the waters of many creeks; for thirty miles or more it is as wide as the Thames between Greenwich and the Isle of Dogs, sometimes even wider, and in the upper reaches the current is as strong as that at London Bridge in the spates of spring.

Menatonon and the savages of Moratoc tell strange tales about the source of this stream. They say it is thirty days' journey from the town of Moratoc, the largest city on the river, and they assure us that the water springs from a huge rock in such torrents that it at once becomes a violent stream. This rock is so near the sea that if the wind blows onshore during a storm, the sea waves beat into the fresh waters of the stream, making them salt and brackish for a time.

I freed Menatonon when I had received the ransom agreed upon, but I did not release his son, whom I sent to Roanoke in the pinnace. After that I set out in two double rowboats, taking about forty men with me—we had no room to carry food for more—and I was resolved to row up the river until we met some of the Moratocs or the Mangoaks, the tribes living west of the stream. As it happened, we travelled much farther than our food supplies allowed, and as our hopes of obtaining supplies from the savages were not realized, we almost starved to death.

We did not meet with any savages on our way, for Pemisapan (who had changed his name to Wingina after his brother, Granganimeo, had died) had warned both the Mangoaks and the Choanists to be on the alert. He knew my intentions toward them, since I had been forced to confide my plans to him when I had asked him to give me a guide to lead me to the Mangoak country. Pemisapan had never stopped urging me to march against them, telling me that Menatonon had assembled all his chiefs and allies at Chawanook and that three thousand men with bows and arrows were making preparations to surprise us at Roanoke. He informed me that the Mangoaks were also in this plot; thus, the number of warriors against us was doubled.

Arriving at Chawanook, I found that Pemisapan had not lied. There a meeting was

7. Roanoke River.

8. Albemarle Sound.

being held, and plans against us were being discussed. But our sudden and unexpected appearance so took the savages by surprise that we were able to get the upper hand and defeat them. Now I found out that Pemisapan had played a double game. Menatonon confessed that the whole conspiracy had been arranged by Pemisapan himself. It was he who had sent messages to the Mangoaks and Choanists saying that our only purpose was to destroy them, while at the same time he had told me that the Mangoaks and Choanists were prepared to attack us.

Pemisapan not only had sent word to the Mangoaks that I intended to go up their river and fight them but had also informed the Moratocs that I was marching against them. Although we were the declared allies of this tribe and had always kept friendly relations, now they withdrew into the mainland, taking away both their women and their grain supplies. As a result we journeyed up the river for three days without coming upon a single native or finding any food in the abandoned towns. At this time we were a hundred and sixty miles from home and had food for only two more days. If a storm or unfavorable winds blew up, we would take much longer than that to get back to our base.

I suspected disloyalty and thought that our savages had informed the river natives of our approach. Actually we had no evil intentions toward them; all we wanted was to trade and to exchange our copper for their grain. That night, as we were settling our camp, I told the company how low our food supply was and gave them my opinion that we had been betrayed by our own savages. They had led us forward in the knowledge that we would not be able to get food from the natives, and now starvation faced us. Therefore I suggested that we turn back while we still had food for two days. In that time we could reach the far side of Weapomeiok Sound, where we could get food from the fish-traps of either Chipanum or the Women's Town, even if the inhabitants had left these towns.

I asked the men to vote whether we should continue our exploration of the river as long as our food lasted with the hope of finding something we could eat on the way, or whether we should return to our base. And I advised the company to think the matter over carefully during the night and to decide by the next morning.

The next morning the majority of the men voted to go on as long as there was half a pint of grain apiece, and they suggested that after our food was gone we could make a soup from the meat of our two large hounds and flavor it with sassafras leaves. This would sustain us for yet two more days, and by the end of that time we would have been carried down to the river mouth by the current. And once we had reached the river mouth we could cross the sound and row to the fish-traps. During these two days we would fast. The men said they would rather accept this plan than retreat, because they wished to meet the Mangoaks, whether as friends or foes.

I was much pleased with their decision; yet I pretended to be in favor of returning for fear of what might afterwards happen to us. My reason for wanting to meet the Mangoaks, and either take some of them prisoner or be friendly with them, was because they knew of a land farther up the Moratoc River with whose people they traded and where a strange and marvelous metal was to be found. The mine was well known, not only to the Chawanooks and to all the savages dwelling on the river banks, but to the natives living to the west and those of all the mainland as well. It was in the country named Chawnis Temoatan.

The natives call the mineral *wassador,* which is copper, but they also give this name *wassador* to any other metal. They say it is the same color as our copper, though our copper is better than theirs, of a deeper red in color and harder. We were told that they find the metal in the shallow water of a river which falls very swiftly from the high rocks and the hills. Taking a huge bowl, about the size of a shield, they wrap a skin over the top, but leave an opening. Then they watch the current coming down the river, and when the water changes color, they dip the bowl into it with a sudden chopping motion so that it is filled with ore. This ore, when melted in a fire, yields two parts of metal to three parts of slag. According to the tales of their neighbors, the Mangoaks have so much of this metal that they beautify their houses with huge plates of it. Everyone told me that this was true, and I have it also from young Skiko, the son of the King of Chawanook, my prisoner, who at one time had been a captive of the Mangoaks. Though Skiko had not himself been in Chawnis Temoatan, he knew that it was a journey of not more than twenty days overland from the Mangoaks and that several other territories had to be crossed before the country of the mineral could be reached.

When I heard all this, I became even more anxious to reach the Mangoaks. I had asked questions of all the savages I met in these parts, and had inquired in particular of Menatonon what he knew of that country. He gave me information in great detail and promised me guides from among his own men to accompany me there.

The overland journey from Chawanook to the Mangoak people can be made in one day from sunrise to sunset, but by water the journey requires seven days at the least.

As I say, all these tales of the precious metal increased my anxiety to meet the Mangoaks and obtain some of their copper for testing, and for this reason I willingly accepted the men's decision.

What happened after we proceeded on our journey was contrary to all our expectations. We travelled for two days, and though all our food was gone, we had not caught sight of a single native. Lying on the shore that night, we saw the fires of the savages in the regions we should reach the following day. On the afternoon of the next day, at about three o'clock, we heard their voices and thought they were calling Manteo, who was with me in the boat. At this we were all very glad, for we hoped to have a friendly talk with them. We made Manteo answer their cries, and they began to sing what sounded like a song of welcome. But Manteo snatched up his arms and told us that the song was their war song and that they meant to fight us. He had scarcely spoken before a volley of arrows fell among the men in the small boat.

Nobody was hurt, God be thanked, and the other boat made ready to scour the shore with their shot so that our spearmen could land. We made the landing, although the bank was very steep. When the savages saw this, they fled inland. Our other men now reached the shore and pursued them without much difficulty until they took cover in the woods. As the sun began to set, we decided to give up the chase. We knew that even if we could catch them, they would not give us food. So we spent the night at a sheltered place, chose a strong guard, and sent out trustworthy sentinels. I had made up my mind to begin the return journey the next morning before the sun rose and to try to reach the mouth of the river and get into the sound in one day. The entire company agreed to this suggestion. They were tired and hungry; the dogs had already been killed, stewed, and eaten.

We made rapid progress. By the end of the next day we had come within four or five miles of the river mouth, having rowed downstream in one day as far as we had done against the current in four. That night we spent on an island, with nothing to eat but a soup made of sassafras leaves, a food which nobody had ever tried before. The next day we had nothing to eat. We wanted to cross the broad sound, but the wind blew so strong and the waves were so high that we could not do it without losing the boats. This was on Easter eve, and we truly fasted.

The next morning, Easter Sunday, the wind fell and we entered the sound. We arrived at Chipanum by four o'clock in the afternoon, but found no one there. All the savages had fled from the village. However, we discovered some fish in their weirs. Many of our men in the small boats were exhausted, yet it was God's will that we should be saved. The following day we reached our home at Roanoke.

I have reported this journey in some detail so that you may see how much every man, from the greatest to the least among us, wished to discover the mine. For nothing but the discovery of a rich mine or of a passage to the South Sea will make our countrymen settle in Virginia. If either of these could be found, the merits of this country, with its healthy climate and fertile soil, would be recognized. And if trade were established, such roots as sassafras and the gums and resins found here would make excellent merchandise to fill out cargoes; otherwise they would not be worth fetching.

A better harbor would have to be found than exists at present. If there is one, it must lie to the north, and I intended to spend this summer looking for it and also searching for the mine of Chawnis Temoatan. I should have succeeded in finding a harbor if the boats Sir Francis Drake so kindly and courteously gave us had not been lost in the storm. And I am certain I should have discovered the mine if I had received additional men and the necessary supplies from you.

The Moratoc River promises great things, and in the opinion of Master Thomas Hariot it has its source either in the Bay of Mexico, which opens out into the South Sea, or very close to it. Concerning the mineral, Mr. Youghan testifies that even if it is not gold, but copper, it must be one of the richest minerals in the world, since the savages are able to melt it.

The exploration of the most promising parts of the mainland could be carried out without difficulty if careful preparations were made. First a good harbor must be found to the northward; then forts must be raised to protect the overland journey to the Choanoak and Moratoc rivers. Here, also, we would have to build forts to protect the boats. If this were done, one could safely travel two hundred miles into the mainland in four days and so more easily make important explorations in the mine country.

Thus, Sir, I have written down for you simply, yet truly, what we have been able to discover for you. My labor, and that of the rest of the gentlemen and crew, was accomplished with great pain and peril (though God in His mercy saved us from the worst). We might have done better if the Lord had been pleased to see that the supplies and men you provided for us had been landed with us in the beginning, or if He had not, in His eternal providence, allowed them to be lost. Everything we needed to complete our explorations was most courteously supplied by Sir Francis Drake, but as I have related, all the provisions, the ships, the captain, and the crew were carried away in an unexpected storm, together with some of my own men. The loss of our supplies was the will of God, for what good purpose I shall never know, since no mortal can understand His infinite wisdom.

The Second Part

CONCERNING THE CONSPIRACY OF PEMISAPAN AND HOW WE DISCOVERED IT, CONCLUDING WITH OUR REQUEST TO BE TAKEN BACK TO ENGLAND WITH SIR FRANCIS DRAKE

Ensenore, the father of Pemisapan, was our only friend in that tribe who had any influence with the Chief. It was our great misfortune that he died on April 20, 1586. Since Granganimeo's death, the savages had been unfriendly and had plotted against us in many ways. Ensenore alone had opposed them. During his lifetime, by the providence of God, he not only guarded us from harm but even saved our lives many times when the savages conspired against us. He always worked for our good and was of the greatest aid—especially in this conspiracy.

King Pemisapan and his followers set out to destroy us in the month of March, 1586. They had planned to desert the neighborhood before their fields were planted. Had they done so, we should certainly have starved if God had not shown us His mercy. For at that time we had no weirs for trapping fish and did not know how to make them, nor had we so much as a single seed to put into the ground.

While we were away against the Chaonists and Mangoaks, it was rumored among the savages at Roanoke that these tribes had slain me and many of my men and that the rest of our company had starved to death. Even though these stories were false, they had their effect on Pemisapan and his tribesmen. They began to treat us with contempt, and also to blaspheme against our God. During the early days of our stay at Roanoke they had shown great reverence for the Almighty God and Jesus Christ, Whom we serve and worship, and had acknowledged Him as the only true God. But now they declared that our Lord was not God, since He had allowed us to go hungry and to be killed by the Renapoaks (this name they give to all the inhabitants of the mainland, no matter to what tribe they belong). Neither old Ensenore nor any of his followers were able to help us, and matters had gone so far that Pemisapan had decided to leave Roanoke.

Not long after these reports about us had begun to circulate, we returned to Roanoke, and Pemisapan saw that the tales were untrue. I and my whole company were safe, and the three savages who were with us and who belonged to his own tribe, Tetepano, Eracano, the chief's brother-in-law, and Cossine, as well as Manteo, told him that the Chaonists and Mangoaks, despite their great reputation for valor, had fled before us. Furthermore, they reported that we had killed the savages who fought us and that we had taken Menatonon prisoner and brought back his best-loved son, Manteo, as our captive.

The truth did much to stop their plotting and to bring Ensenore's opinions back once more into favor with the natives. For he had continually repeated to the King and his followers that we were the servants of God and that therefore they could not hurt us, but that those who sought our harm would be themselves destroyed. He told them that if we were dead, we could do them more harm than if we were alive, and this belief continued to be held by their oldest and wisest men. They believed that our dead had killed some of theirs, for the killings had happened at night when the savages were more than a hundred miles away from us.

Many of them think that we are dead men who have returned to the world, and they believe that when we die we remain dead only for a certain time, after which we return to the earth. All these ideas were again accepted when Pemisapan and his people saw our safe return from the territories of the enemies they feared most.

Our difficulties with Pemisapan ended, at least temporarily, by accident, or, rather, I should say, by the grace of the Almighty. This is what happened: shortly after my return a messenger from Menatonon arrived to see the chief's son, who was my prisoner. He brought me a present of some pearls, which Pemisapan told me was intended as ransom for the youth. I refused to accept the pearls. But more important than the ransom, Menatonon sent word that he had commanded Okisko, King of Weapomeiok, to give homage to the great Weroanza of England[9] and to Sir Walter Raleigh. To confirm Okisko's surrender, he sent twenty-four of his chieftains to Pemisapan at Roanoke. These chiefs assured me that from now on Okisko and his successors would acknowledge Her Majesty as their only sovereign and Sir Walter Raleigh as her representative. This was the incident—taking place in the presence of Pemisapan, Ensenore, and all the savages—which changed their attitude toward us.

Pemisapan promised that he would order his men to build fish-traps for us at once, and he gave us some fields to sow for ourselves. By the end of April we had sown enough grain fields to give us food for a year, if God blessed the growth. Our most difficult time would be from April until the beginning of July, when the first harvest came in. If we could manage to exist until then, we would have plenty of food from our own crops, if not from new supplies arrived from England. But we had still to live through these two months, and unless the savages helped us with gifts of cassava[10] and other food, we might starve. We would be like the horse in the fable who perished in his stable for want of the grass which was growing outside. This fate we escaped only because God in His mercy was pleased to preserve us.

A few days after our return, as I have already related, our friend Ensenore died, and no sooner was he dead than those men close to Pemisapan who hated us bitterly, Osacan, Tanaquiny, and Wanchese[11] in particular, began to work against us. By this time it was too late to prevent the planting, for already the fields of Roanoke Island as well as those on the mainland opposite at Dasamonquepeio had been planted. But there was plenty of other mischief they could do us, and this they did.

First they tried to win over Okisko, King of Weapomeiok, and the Mangoaks. In order to do this they presented them with great quantities of copper, and for this bribe Okisko and the Mangoaks were to bring seven or eight hundred bows against us. Then they invited

9. Queen Elizabeth.
10. A tuber yielding a starch-like flour.
11. One of the two savages who had been taken to England the year before by Amadas and Barlow.

the braves of Weapomeiok to the month-long memorial ceremonies for Ensenore, which were customary after one of their great men had died. During these celebrations the Chesepians and the Mangoaks, a force seven hundred strong, were to be encamped on the mainland opposite our island. Pemisapan's plan was to kill me and my principal officers and afterwards to light fires to signal to the savages on the mainland that this had been accomplished. They in return would light fires and attack the rest of our company, hoping to take us by surprise while we were scattered over the island hunting crabs and fish.

I found out later the details of the scheme: Tarraquine and Andacon, two of Pemisapan's best and strongest chieftains, were to lead twenty men against my house, setting fire to its roof in the dead of night, expecting (as would have been very likely) that I would run out, caught by surprise, unclothed and unarmed. In that moment they would have killed me, knocking out my brains. In the same way all the other leaders in our company, including Master Hariot,[12] were to be slain; the savages were to set fire at the same moment to all our houses, both those in the fort and those in the town.

As they wanted to be certain that we would be dispersed over the island rather than together (the savages could more easily deal with us separately, since ten of us armed would be a match for a hundred of their best men), they agreed—and put into immediate effect—not to sell us any more food. Further, they intended to rob the weirs at night and break them. And once broken, they would not be repaired. Thus, so they believed, we would be obliged to disband in search of food. Some of our men would be forced to go to places where they could live on shellfish, just as the savages do before their crops are ripe, while others would have to obtain food by hunting and fishing at Hatorask, Croatoan,[13] or at some other place.

Everything went according to Pemisapan's plan. We were faced with famine, and our weirs failed us. I had to send Captain Stafford and twenty men to Croatoan to forage for food and keep watch for ships coming from England. He was to give us news directly they sighted the vessels. I sent Pridiox in the pinnace to Hatorask, with ten men and the provost marshal, to live there and wait for ships. And every week I sent fifteen or twenty men to the mainland to feed themselves on cassava and oysters.

Meanwhile Pemisapan went to Dasamonquepeio for three purposes. First, he wanted to see his second crop of grain sown; secondly, he was anxious to leave my neighborhood and so avoid my daily requests for food, because he was afraid to deny me outright. For the time being I could do nothing but accept his excuses and bear with my wrongs, mean-

12. Thomas Hariot, the eminent mathematician and astronomer.

13. See De Bry's map on pp. 274-275. Hatorask may have been where New Inlet is today, while the Island of Croatoan was situated between Cape Hatteras and the present Hatteras Inlet.

ing to settle with him in due course. I thought to ally myself with Menatonon and the Chaonists, who were strong in number, valiant fighters, and more trustworthy than Pemisapan's tribe. Since my journey to their country I had received many signs of their desire to be our allies. Moreover, they were embittered against Pemisapan and Weapomeiok for the lies they had told about us.

Pemisapan's third purpose in going to Dasamonquepeio was to send messengers to Weapomeiok and the Mangoaks with bribes of copper and promises of great spoil. Within a few days he received his answer from Weapomeiok. Okisko refused to be involved in the conspiracy and retired with his closest followers to the mainland. But the rest of the savages of Weapomeiok and the Mangoaks accepted the copper and promised to come to the funeral ceremonies for Ensenore on June 10.

The whole plot was discovered by Skiko, Menatonon's son, whom I still held prisoner. Skiko had once attempted to escape, and I had been forced to confine him in shackles and to threaten to cut off his head. At Pemisapan's request I had reprieved him, but after this Pemisapan was certain that Skiko would be our enemy. So Pemisapan, counting on Skiko's enmity against us, gave him food and took him into his confidence. However, the youth, who had always been well treated by me and respected by my men, revealed Pemisapan's conspiracy to me out of gratitude. I had the story also from one of Pemisapan's own followers, who told me of the plot the night before he was slain.

There was not much time to take measures against the conspiracy and to save my scattered men. Somehow I had to gain time; I therefore sent a message to Pemisapan to allay his suspicions, telling him that I was going to Croatoan because our fleet had arrived there (in truth I did not even dare to hope that such a thing could happen). I asked him to lend me some of his men to fish and hunt for my colony at Croatoan, and I also inquired if he would sell me provisions sufficient for the four-day journey.

Pemisapan sent word to me that he himself would come over to Roanoke, but he put it off from day to day. It was clear that he was waiting for the Weapomeioks and the Mangoaks, who were to arrive in about a week. On the last day of May, 1586, his followers began to gather at Roanoke just as he had commanded them to do. Now I decided not to wait for him any longer (since he meant to bring so many men with him), but to rally my followers and attack him the next day. My plan was to surprise the savages on the island by night and to seize all their canoes so that they would not be able to warn Pemisapan.

But unfortunately the alarm had been given before I was ready to strike. I had sent the captain of the light boat and a few men to gather up all the canoes at sunset and to prevent any savages from going to the mainland, although he was to allow them to land on the island. When the captain came upon one canoe making ready to depart from the island, he overturned it and killed two of the occupants, cutting off their heads. Though this was done secretly, one of Pemisapan's men saw the incident from the shore and gave warning. At once the savages took to their bows, we to our arms, and after a brief skirmish, in which we killed three or four of their men, the rest fled into the woods.

The next morning I took twenty-five men and two of the Chesepians in the boats to Dasamonquepeio. When we landed we met one of Pemisapan's followers. I asked the savage to go to his chief and deliver a message, that I was going to Croatoan and that I desired to see him, as I wished to complain to him about Osacan, who had tried to steal my prisoner, Manteo, the night before. Pemisapan, with a group of seven or eight of his chiefs and their followers, came down to the shore, and as soon as they arrived I gave the word agreed upon (which was "Christ, our victory"). At this we began to fire.

One of the Chesepians shot Pemisapan with a pistol, and he lay on the ground as if dead. I was busy trying to save Manteo's friends, and the rest of my men were making sure that none of the savages should escape. In the confusion, Pemisapan suddenly got up and fled. He was running so fast that we could not catch him. But an Irish boy in my company shot him in the back with my petronel.[14] Then Nugent, another Irishman serving with me, followed after him with one companion, and they eventually caught him in the woods. I had already given up hope of seeing Nugent alive and Pemisapan captured, when Nugent returned, carrying Pemisapan's head in his hands. All this happened on June 1, 1586.

On June 8 Captain Stafford, who was lying off Croatoan Island, sent word that he had sighted a great fleet of twenty-three ships, but it was still too soon to say whether they were English or if they belonged to the enemy. He advised me to keep careful guard. The next day he arrived in person, having travelled all day and all night. It must be said for Captain Stafford that, from beginning to end, he never spared himself any danger on land or on sea, in fair weather or in foul, but always performed whatever services were asked of him. He brought me a letter from General Sir Francis Drake with the best news I could hope for.

The General offered to give me all I needed for carrying out my plans. He was ready to give me not only food, munitions, and clothing, but also barks, pinnaces, and rowboats, as fully manned and provisioned as I wished. The next day he himself came to anchor in our harbor, and I found him ready to grant everything he had promised so generously in his letter. Sir Francis Drake had already taken the matter up with all the captains of his fleet, and they were in full agreement with him. I expressed my thanks both to the General and to his captains for their consideration of us and our mission in Virginia, and having decided beforehand what I would ask for, requested him to take those of my men who were weak and no longer fit for action back to England and to replace them with some badly

14. A large pistol.

needed craftsmen and oarsmen. I asked for enough provisions and shipping to see us through the month of August and to get us back to England, for I hoped that by that time I would have finished what I expected to do. I wanted him to give us enough captains not only to get my whole company home but also to search for some better harbor and to help us out with small boats and oarsmen. And I asked for muskets, hand weapons, matches, lead, tools, clothing, and the like.

The General, I was told, received my requests in his usual pleasant manner and called his captains into council. My master of provisions, my storekeeper, and my vice-treasurer were all invited to meet him aboard his ship, bringing with them their notes of their wants.

The *Francis*, a fine bark of seventy tons, was allotted to me, and she was immediately provisioned with enough food to last a hundred men four months and stocked with whatever else I had asked for. Two pinnaces and four small boats were assigned to me as well. But the greatest token of the General's liberality was that he had got the full consent of two of his most experienced sea captains to serve with me. Their names were Abraham Kendall and Griffith Herne, and they were to come to me with their full crews, ready to assist me in any way I wished for the whole term of our proposed stay in Virginia.

By June 12 the provisions had been transferred to the *Francis*, and she lay with the two captains and my own officers aboard. But on the 13th a mighty storm arose and continued for four days. Had it not been for the intervention of God and the foresight of the General, the entire fleet would have been driven ashore. Many of the ships were blown out to sea. The *Francis* was buffeted about in the treacherous harbor, but at last she too was able to set safely forth.

After the storm, which lasted from June 13 to June 16, had abated, the General came ashore with a new offer. I was to have a ship of a hundred and seventy tons, the bark *Bonner*, with a captain and pilot and with sufficient provisions to last us until we could get back to England. He did not wish to have her brought into our harbor, however, but to keep her riding off shore. All else he left to me, and he asked me to send my requests in writing if I or my company wanted anything. He promised that he and his captains would do their utmost to help me.

I called my captains and the other gentlemen of my company together, all of whom were grateful for the General's offer. We took stock of our situation. Our company was weak; only a small number of men remained. Our newly gained ship was lost, together with the two captains and the most important part of our stores. It seemed as if the hand of God had turned against us. Furthermore, although Drake's second offer was very generous and honorable, the bark was not of much value to us unless we could bring her into our harbor. There was not much hope either that Sir Richard Grenville, who should have arrived by Easter at the latest, would relieve us. Since England was to help the Dutch against Spain and to provide for other American ventures, it was unlikely that he would come at all.

For these reasons we decided to ask the General to give us immediate passage back to England in his ships. I delivered the request to him myself, and he readily agreed. He sent his pinnaces to Roanoke to take on our baggage and the few men who remained there. The weather was boisterous, and the pinnaces often ran aground; the sailors, whose patience was already exhausted with their stay in those dangerous waters, threw most of our possessions, including our charts, books, and writings, overboard to lighten their journey.

When we were all aboard, the General weighed anchor with a prayer to Almighty God. In that terrible storm he had undergone more dangers from shipwreck in his desire to bring aid to us than in all his previous engagements with the Spaniards.

Giving thanks to God for all our blessings, we set sail on June 19, 1586, and arrived in Portsmouth on July 27 of the same year.

SIR RICHARD GRENVILLE (*ca.* 1541-1591)

He landed Raleigh's first colonists at Roanoke Island in 1585, went back to England for supplies, and returned to Virginia again in the summer of 1586. But he was two weeks too late; the colonists had already left in Drake's ships. Unwilling to lose the land that Englishmen had so long held, Grenville put fifteen men ashore on the island of Roanoke, furnished them with provisions, and then departed for England.

Engraving in Henry Holland: Herwologia Anglica (London, 1620).

GRENVILLE

An anonymous report on Sir Richard Grenville's voyage to relieve the Virginia Colony in the year of our Lord 1586.

IN the year of our Lord 1586 Sir Walter Raleigh, at his own expense, loaded a ship of a hundred tons with a large cargo of provisions to supply and relieve his Virginia Colony. But Easter had gone by before she could set sail from England, and by that time the colonists had given up hope that any relief would come. They had therefore made their own preparations and, resigned to spending the rest of their lives in Virginia, thought no more of returning to England. They had sown and planted enough to provide themselves with food for the next two years. While they waited for their own harvest, they managed to pass the early summer until the tenth of June, when only two weeks remained before their first reaping.

At this time Sir Francis Drake, returning home from plundering Santo Domingo, Cartagena, and St. Augustine, decided to visit his countrymen, the English Colony in Virginia. He sailed along the coast of Florida and came to those parts of the country which the Englishmen had settled. There he sighted the colonists, anchored, and went ashore to learn how things had gone with them. They told him that, while all of them were still alive, they had suffered from scarcity of food and had no way of knowing whether the relief from England would be forthcoming. They therefore asked him to leave them two or three of his own ships so that if after a reasonable time they had heard nothing from England, they could return home. This Drake agreed to do.

The colonists at once began to write letters, which Sir Francis Drake was prepared to carry to England for them. While they were thus engaged in making the reports of their travels a great storm suddenly arose and drove most of the fleet from its anchorage, carrying out to sea with it the chief persons of the English Colony. When those who had remained on land saw what had happened, they hastened to board the three ships which had just been granted them. For fear they would be left behind, they abandoned all their goods in the greatest confusion and raced to the boats as if a mighty army were on their heels. And indeed they were put to flight by a mighty power, for God Himself stretched out His hand against them because of the cruelties and outrages they had committed against the natives.

Immediately after the Colony had left this paradise of the world, the long-awaited supply ship sent by Sir Walter Raleigh reached Hatorask.[1] Her sailors spent a long time searching for the colonists, and when they did not find them, returned to England, carrying back all the provisions.

Fourteen or fifteen days later, Sir Richard Grenville, Governor-General of Virginia, arrived with three vessels laden with provisions. He found neither the supply ship nor the colony which he had left there in 1585 in charge of Ralph Lane, his deputy. He made various trips into the mainland to explore and seek news of the lost men, and though much

1. Situated where New Inlet is today. See De Bry's map on pp. 274-275.

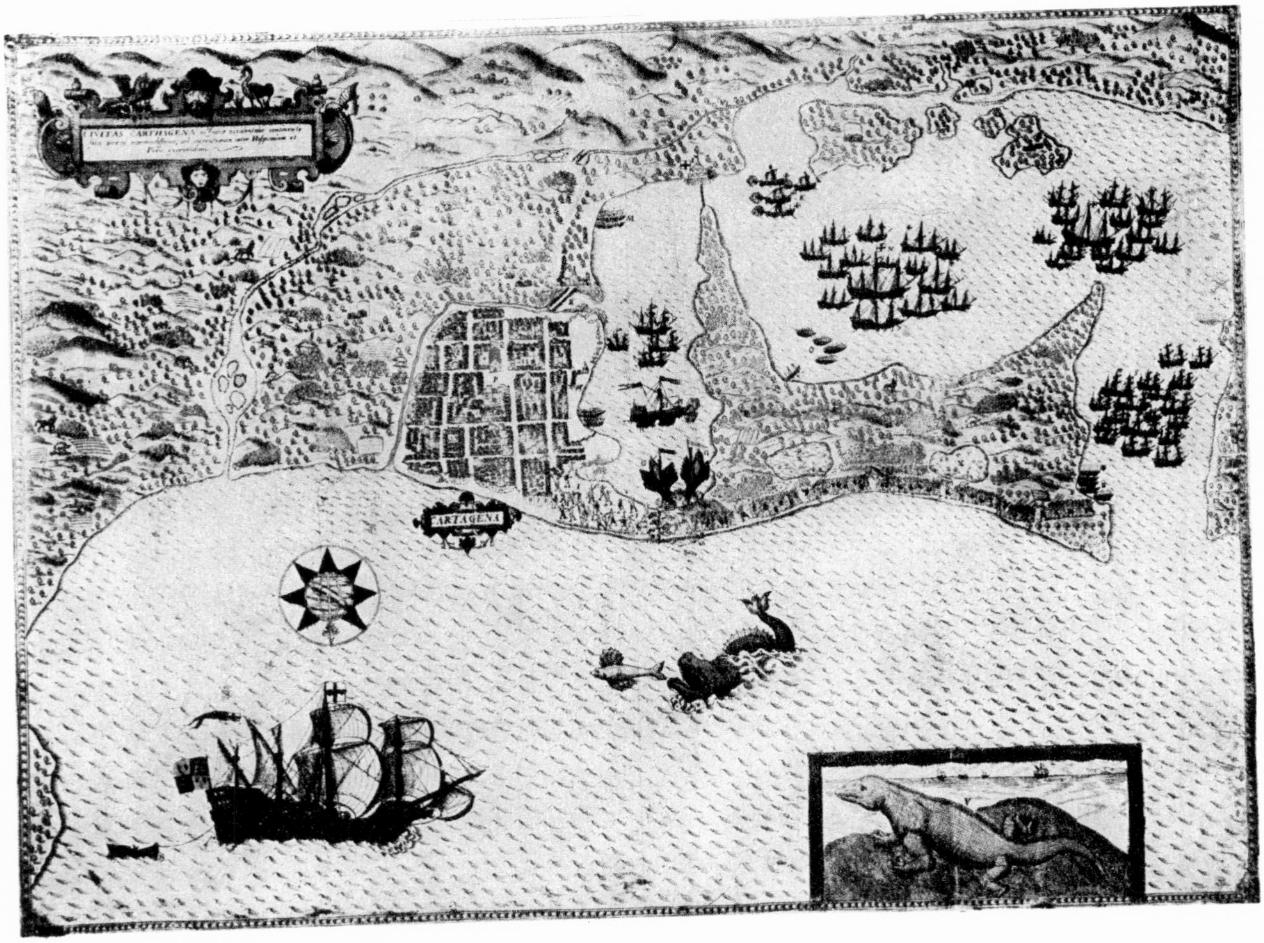

From "Expeditio Francisci Draki" (Leyden, 1588)

DRAKE AT CARTAGENA

In 1585, when the rivalry between Spain and England broke into open hostilities, Sir Francis Drake sailed into the heavily fortified harbor of Santo Domingo. After he had plundered and burnt the town, he sailed for Cartagena. He captured and held it until a ransom of 110,000 ducats was paid.

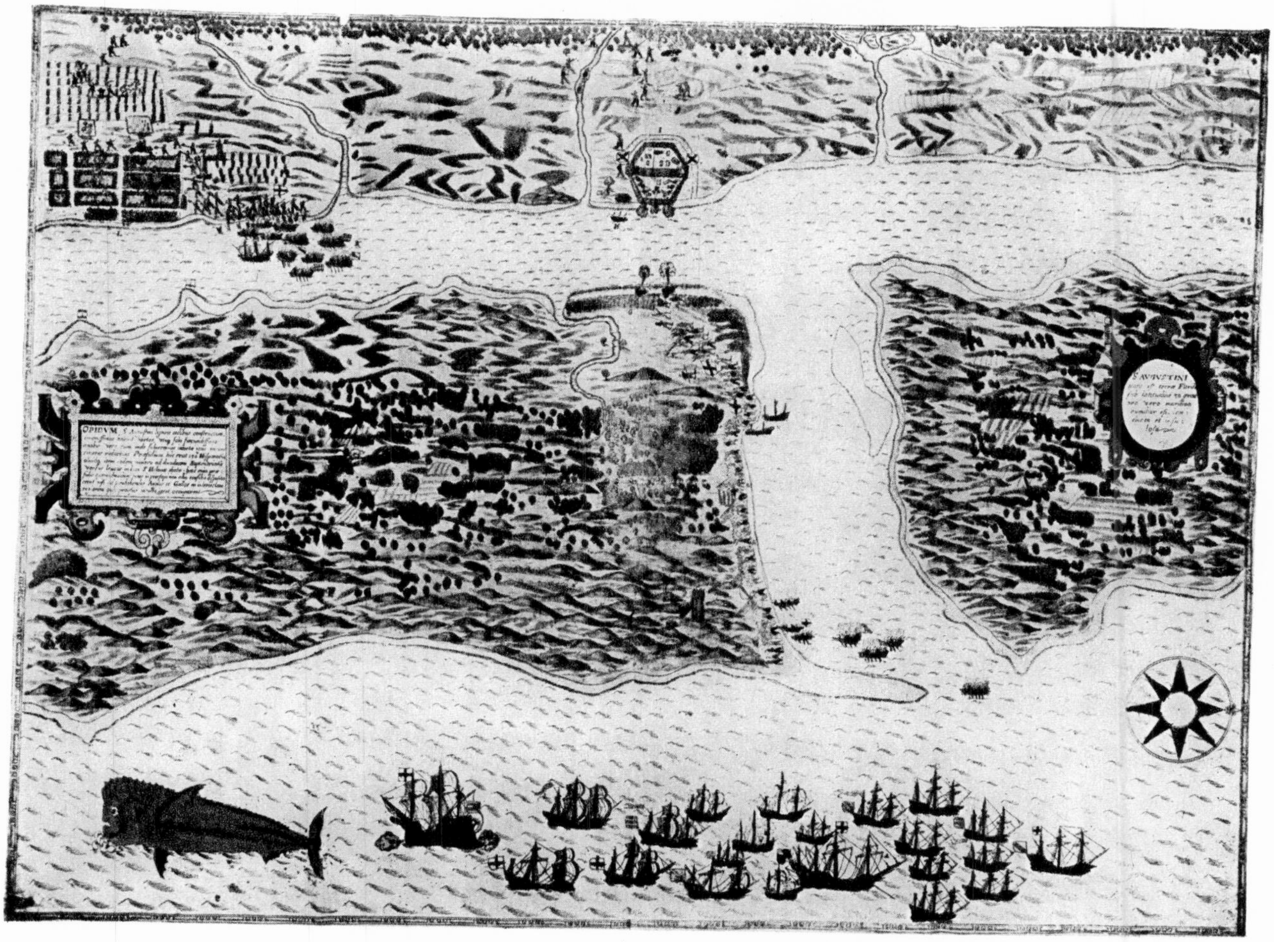

From "Expeditio Francisci Draki" (Leyden, 1588)

DRAKE DESTROYS ST. AUGUSTINE

From Cartagena the English ships made for St. Augustine, the Spanish stronghold in Florida. Drake gave orders to set the town afire and when this had been done he sailed along the coast to visit the English settlers in Virginia. On June 10, 1586, he found Raleigh's Colony at Roanoke Island. The colonists were almost without food. They were discouraged because the relief ship from England, which they expected by Easter, had not yet arrived. At first they asked Drake only for supplies, as they planned to hold out longer, but after a violent storm they changed their minds. They left in Drake's ships two weeks before Sir Richard Grenville landed in Virginia with supplies and fresh colonists.

time was spent in the search, no sign of the colonists was found. The places where they had been were desolate.

Yet, unwilling to lose the land that Englishmen had so long held, Grenville determined to leave some of his men behind to retain possession of the country. He therefore put fifteen ashore on the island of Roanoke, furnished them with provisions enough to last two years, and then departed for England.

On his homeward voyage he came in sight of the Islands of the Azores. Here he cast anchor, went ashore, and plundered the towns of everything worth carrying off. With this and many other exploits to his credit, he finally returned to England.

THOMAS HARIOT (1560-1621)

He came with Raleigh's first colony to the New World, and spent almost a year there. He was a friend of Raleigh's, an outstanding mathematician, astronomer, and writer. His "Briefe and True Report of the New Found Land of Virginia" (see p. 227) was first published in 1588.

Portrait in Trinity College, Oxford, England.

WHITE

John White's Journal of his voyage to Virginia in 1587, with three ships carrying the second colony to the New World.

IN the year of Our Lord 1587 Sir Walter Raleigh, who was determined to plant a colony in Virginia, assembled together a new group of a hundred and fifty men to be sent there under the charge of John White. Sir Walter Raleigh appointed John White as governor of the colony and he appointed twelve assistants who were to serve under him. They were given a charter and were incorporated under the name of Governor and Assistants of the City of Raleigh in Virginia.

APRIL. Our fleet consisted of three ships, the admiral,[1] a ship of a hundred and twenty tons, a flyboat,[2] and a pinnace. We left Portsmouth on April 26 and laid anchor that day at Cowes, in the Isle of Wight, where we stayed eight days.

MAY. On May 5, at nine o'clock at night, we arrived at Plymouth, and we remained there for two days. On the 8th we weighed anchor and left for Virginia. On the 16th Simon Ferdinando, master of the flagship, shamefully abandoned the flyboat, leaving her in distress in the Bay of Portugal.

JUNE. On the 19th we came in sight of Dominica, and the same evening we sailed between it and Guadaloupe. On the 21st the flyboat also sighted Dominica.

On the 22d we laid anchor at an island called Santa Cruz,[3] where all the planters were set ashore. There we stayed until the 25th. As soon as we landed on this island some of our men and women were made ill by eating small fruits that looked like green apples. Their mouths began to burn, and their tongues swelled to such a size that many of them could not speak. Even a child nursing at the breast of one of these women was affected, its mouth so painfully burned that it was pitiful to see the infant's sufferings. But after twenty-four hours, the discomforts of the sickness disappeared.

1. In Elizabethan times, the flagship, which carried the commander, was called the admiral.
2. A small sailing vessel; also, a ship's boat.
3. St. Croix, in the Virgin Islands.

The first night we were on the island we caught five giant tortoises, some of them so large that sixteen of our strongest men were exhausted by carrying one the short distance from the shore to our cabins. We found no watering place on the island save only a stagnant pond. The water was so evil that many of our company fell sick from drinking it. Others, who merely washed their faces there in the early morning, before the sun had purified the water, suffered from such a burning and swelling that their eyes closed up and they could not see for five or six days—many for even longer.

On the second day we sent some of the men to search the island for fresh water, three going one way, two the other. The Governor, with six men, climbed to the top of a high hill to get a good view of the island. They saw no sign of man or beast or anything of value. But they found some parrots and the resinous trees of lignum vitae. We returned to our cabins by another way and while descending a hill discovered pottery fragments made out of the clay of that island; whereupon we judged that the island was inhabited (though Ferdinando had told us that it was not). That evening those who had gone in search of water rejoined the Governor. One group reported that they had seen eleven savages and a cluster of houses in the valley about a half a mile from the top of the hill where they were. The other group had found a fine spring of fresh water flowing from a high rock. They had brought three bottles back with them, so that from that time on we no longer had to drink the foul water of the pond.

On the night of the second day Captain Stafford left in the pinnace for an island called Beake,[4] which lay near San Juan.[5] He was directed there by Ferdinando, who assured him he would find sheep in great plenty. On the following night our planters left the island of Santa Cruz to come aboard, for on the next morning, June 25, we weighed anchor and sailed on. The 27th we arrived at Cottea,[6] where we found the pinnace riding at anchor awaiting us.

On the 28th we left Cottea and soon landed at Mosquitoes Bay, where we spent three unprofitable days in taking on fresh water. During this time we drank more beer than the amount of water we gained.

JULY. On the first day of July we weighed anchor at Mosquitoes Bay, leaving two Irishmen there, Darby Glaven and Dennis Carroll. We sailed along the coast of St. John and came to Ross Bay as evening fell.

Ferdinando had assured us that we could take on salt at this place, and we had provided ourselves with as many sacks as possible for that purpose. The Governor, who had

4. Vieques, a small island near Puerto Rico.
5. San Juan is an abbreviation for San Juan de Porto Rico: Puerto Rico.
6. A small island near Puerto Rico.

been told that there was a town at the end of the bay, not far from the salt hills, had appointed thirty of the company armed with guns, ten pike-men, and ten with shields to go ashore for the salt. When Ferdinando saw that they were ready, he sent a message to the Governor to persuade him not to take on salt there, saying that he was not sure whether this was the place or not. He insisted that if the pinnace went into the bay, she could not return without great danger before the next evening, and if a storm should in the meantime arise, the flagship would very likely be blown away. While he was trying to convince the Governor, he caused the lead to be cast and craftily brought the ship into shallow water. At three fathoms and a half he suddenly began to swear by all the parts of God's body. He screamed that we were in great danger, and cried out to the helmsman, "Bear up hard, bear up hard!" So we sailed away, cheated of our salt because of his meanness.

The next day, while we were sailing along the west end of St. John, the Governor determined to go ashore in San German Bay to gather young plants of orange, pine,[7] mammee,[8] and plantain[9] to transplant in Virginia. We could easily get them, because they grew near the shore, and the Governor and some of the other planters knew the places well. But Simon Ferdinando denied this, saying it would be better to land at Hispaniola,[10] where the Governor and some of the Assistants could go ashore with him in the pinnace. He wanted to talk with his friend Alanson, who would supply him—so he hoped—with cattle and all the other things we needed. Simon Ferdinando always made great promises, but some time afterwards we found out that he meant nothing he said.

On the next day, July 3, we saw Hispaniola and sailed along its coast all day, expecting that the pinnace would make the landing where Ferdinando's friend Alanson lived. But the hours went by without any signs of preparation for going ashore.

On July 4 and until the following day at noon we continued to sail along the coast of Hispaniola. Then we knew that we had passed the place where Alanson lived and had reached Isabella.[11] The Governor asked Ferdinando if he were going to talk with Alanson about our taking on cattle and other things we needed, as he had promised. Ferdinando replied that we were now past the place, and it was to no purpose to touch there on this voyage. And he said that even though Sir Walter Raleigh and the French ambassador had told him that the King of Spain had sent for Alanson, he himself believed Alanson to be dead.

The next day we lost sight of Hispaniola and sailed away for Virginia at about four o'clock in the afternoon. On July 6 we came to the island of Caycos,[12] where Ferdinando said there were two salt ponds, which—if they were dry—would give us enough salt to last

7. Pineapple.
8. Tree with large, yellow-pulped fruit.
9. Fruit similar to the banana.
10. Haiti.
11. On the north side of the island.
12. One of the Turk's Island group.

until our next supply arrived. But this proved to be no truer than his promise to get us sheep at Beake. Here, while Ferdinando enjoyed himself on shore with a companion, the men spent the afternoon in other parts of the island, some shooting birds, some hunting swans (of which they caught many), and some looking for the salt ponds. Early the next morning we weighed anchor, leaving Caycos with high hopes that the first land we saw thereafter would be Virginia.

On about July 16 we sighted the mainland of Virginia and what Simon Ferdinando thought to be the island of Croatoan. There we rode at anchor for two or three days, but, as so often before, Ferdinando was wrong again. When he discovered his mistake, he sailed along the coast and in the night came near to foundering on Cape Fear. Had it not been for Captain Stafford, who had kept more careful watch than Simon Ferdinando, we would have been wrecked, for we came within two cables' length of the Cape. Such was the ignorance and carelessness of our captain.

On July 22 we arrived safely at Hatorask, where our ship and the pinnace came to anchor. The Governor went aboard the pinnace, accompanied by forty of his best men. He intended to set out immediately for Roanoke, where he hoped to find the fifteen Englishmen Sir Richard Grenville had left the year before; he wanted to hear their reports about the state of the country and the disposition of the savages. After doing so, he meant to return to his ships and sail to Chesapeake Bay; there according to the written orders of Sir Walter Raleigh, we were to make our base and fort.

But as soon as we had left the ship for the pinnace, one of Ferdinando's followers, who was anxious to return to England, talked to our sailors and persuaded them to prevent the planters from boarding the ship again. Only the Governor with two or three men of whom he approved should be allowed to return to the boat, while the others would be left on the island. He said that as the summer was so far spent he did not want to carry the planters farther. Since Ferdinando had influenced all the sailors, in both the pinnace and the ship, to agree to this, it did the Governor no good to argue with them.

At sunset we went ashore on Roanoke island, where the fifteen Englishmen had been left the year before. We found none of them, nor any sign that they had been there. We discovered, however, the bones of one of the colonists, who had long before been slain by the savages. On July 23 the Governor and a party of his men went to the north end of the island, where Master Ralph Lane had built his fort and several dwellings the year before. There we hoped to find some clue that might lead us to the discovery of the small colony. When we reached the place we found the fort torn down, but all the houses standing, still undamaged. The fort was overgrown with melons, and inside were deer feeding upon them. There was nothing to do but to return and give up hope of ever seeing the fifteen men alive again. On the same day the order was given for every man to work at repairing the dwellings which were still standing and to build as many new houses as we should need.

The flyboat arrived at Hatorask with the rest of our planters on the 25th, to the great joy and comfort of everyone. Only Ferdinando, the master of the flagship, was put out at their safe arrival, for he had purposely left them behind in the Bay of Portugal, sailing away quietly at night with the hope that Edward Spicer, the flyboat's captain, who had never before been in Virginia, would not be able to find the place. Ferdinando thought that the boat would be captured by the men-of-war and that the crew would be slain. But God worked against his evil schemes.

On July 28 George Howe, one of the twelve Assistants, was killed by the savages who came over to Roanoke. We did not know whether they came to find out who we were and what we were doing in this country or merely to hunt the deer that were so plentiful on the island. The savages, hidden in the high reeds where they often find the wild deer sleeping, espied Howe wading in the water. He was alone, almost naked, and without any arms save a small forked stick with which he was trying to catch crabs. They wounded him with sixteen arrowshots. Then they killed him with their wooden swords, beat his head to pieces, and escaped over the water to the mainland.

On July 30 Captain Stafford sailed to the island of Croatoan with twenty men and Manteo. Manteo's mother and many of his relatives lived on the island, and we hoped that they would be able to supply us with news of the fifteen men. We also wanted to test their feelings towards us and to renew our old friendship with them. At first, when we landed on the island, it seemed as if they would fight us, but when they realized that we were prepared to use our guns against them, they ran away. Manteo called to them. As soon as they heard their own language, they returned, throwing away their bows and arrows. They embraced us and entertained us in the friendliest manner. They begged us not to gather or destroy any of their grain, because they had only a little. We promised them we would not touch their corn or any of their possessions and that we had come only to renew our old friendship and to live among them as brothers.

The savages were much pleased with our answer and invited us to go to their village, where they gave us a feast and urged us to give them some token by which they might be known as our friends when we met them in any strange place. They told us that for want of some such token a few of them had been hurt the year before when they had been away from the island and had met with Ralph Lane and his company. They showed us one of their men who had been wounded at that time; he was lame and would never recover from the wound. The savages said they now bore no ill will that the English had shot at them, for they knew they had been mistaken for Wingina's men.

AUGUST. The next day we talked with them about the people of Secota, Aquascogoc, and Pomeiock. We asked the Croatoans to tell the people of those towns that if they would accept our friendship we would deal with them again, forgiving and forgetting all the unfriendly happenings of the past. The chiefs of Croatoan answered that they would do their best and would try to bring either the chiefs of those towns or their answer to our Governor at Roanoke within seven days.

The savages revealed that George Howe had been slain by some of Wingina's men dwelling then at Dasamonquepeio, with whom Wanchese[13] lived. They further told us how the fifteen Englishmen left at Roanoke the year before by Sir Richard Grenville had suddenly been attacked by thirty warriors from Secota, Aquascogoc, and Dasamonquepeio.

The savages had hidden behind trees near the houses where our people lived without suspecting any trouble. When they saw only eleven Englishmen, two of them stepped forward, signifying that they wanted to speak to two of our leaders. As the natives seemed unarmed and friendly, the English were glad to meet them. But while one of the savages embraced one of our men, the other brought out his heavy wooden sword, which he had hidden under his cape, struck him on the head, and killed him. At this moment the rest of the savages appeared. The other Englishman ran back to his companions, and they fled. They were pursued by the savages, who shot their arrows so close that the English were forced to take refuge in the building where they kept most of their food and weapons. The natives set the house on fire, and our men were forced to pick up such weapons as came first to hand. They left the house and fought the attackers for about an hour. In this fight one of the colonists was shot in the mouth with an arrow and died, while one of the savages was killed with a fire arrow.

The spot where the skirmish took place was of great advantage to the savages, because they were able to hide themselves behind the thickly growing trees. From there they shot their arrows with such good aim that our men had to retire to the water's edge. Here they took to their boats and fled to Hatorask. They had rowed no more than a quarter of a mile, when they saw the other four belonging to their company, who had been gathering oysters in a near-by creek. They took them aboard, and the boat left Roanoke. The men landed on a little island near the entrance of Hatorask harbor. Here they remained for the time being, but later departed; where they went we could not discover.

As we had now finished our business at Croatoan, we took friendly leave of the natives and returned to the ships at Hatorask.

13. Wanchese was one of the Indians taken to England by Amadas and Barlowe in 1584. After he returned to Virginia, he was bitterly hostile to everything English.

On August 8, when our Governor realized that the chiefs of Pomeiock, Aquascogoc, Secota, and Dasamonquepeio, who had promised to come to us within seven days or send their answers by the men of Croatoan, had neither appeared nor been heard of, and, as he had also learned from the Croatoans that the remnants of Wingina's men living at Dasamonquepeio were the same who had slain George Howe and driven our eleven colonists from Roanoke, he now decided to defer his revenge no longer.

Therefore, at about midnight, we crossed the water and reached the mainland with Captain Stafford and twenty-four soldiers. To guide us to the place where the savages were, we decided to take Manteo with us, who during our whole expedition proved as loyal to us as the most faithful Englishman of our company.

The next day, August 9, we landed near our enemies' dwelling place so early in the morning that it was still dark and passed through the woods until we had their houses between us and the water. We saw the flames of their fire and the savages sitting around it. We attacked them at once, taking the miserable souls by surprise. They ran into a place where reeds grew very thickly. There we found them, killing one with a bullet. The others fled into the reeds, with us hard on their heels, hoping to make them pay for all their evil deeds against us.

But now we realized our mistake. For these savages were not our enemies but our friends. They had come from Croatoan to gather fruits and harvest grain. They had heard that our enemies fled after they had killed George Howe, leaving in such haste that all their grain, tobacco, and pumpkins were abandoned in the fields. So they had come to take in the harvest, which otherwise would have been lost to the birds and the deer. In the darkness we took them all to be men, for the men and women were dressed alike. We almost killed the wife of one of the chieftains, but in the last moment we realized that she was carrying a child on her back. The fight ended when one of the savages who knew Captain Stafford ran up to him calling him by name.

We gathered all the ripe grain, peas, pumpkins, and tobacco and left the rest to grow. After this we returned to Roanoke, taking Menatonon's wife and her young child and the other savages with us. Manteo was grieved by our mistake, but he blamed the savages for their misfortune. He told them that if their chiefs had kept their promise and come to the Governor by the appointed day, the fight would never have taken place.

On August 13 our savage friend Manteo was christened in Roanoke by the command of Sir Walter Raleigh. He received the name Lord of Roanoke and of Dasamonquepeio in recognition of his faithful service.

On August 18 a daughter was born to Elinor,[14] daughter of the Governor and wife

14. "Elyoner" Dare was John White's daughter.

of Ananias Dare, one of the Assistants. The child was christened on the following Sunday and was named Virginia because she was the first Christian born in Virginia.

By this time our ships had unloaded the provisions and goods of the planters, and now they began to take on wood and fresh water and to be caulked and trimmed ready for the voyage home. The colonists prepared their letters and their gifts to send to England.

Our two ships, the *Lion* and the flyboat, were almost ready to sail, when, on August 21, a great tempest blew out of the northeast. The flagship, lying outside the harbor, was forced to weigh anchor and put to sea. We feared she would be wrecked, the more so as most of her good sailors were on land at the time the storm struck. For six days the ship beat on and off shore before she could come in again.

About this time there was some argument between the Governor and the Assistants over which of the twelve Assistants should return to England to act as our agents. Only one of them wished to go, the others refusing to depart. At length, as we thought at least two men should leave, our Governor persuaded Christopher Cooper. But the next day, at the persuasion of his intimate friends, he changed his mind, and again the matter stood as before.

The next morning, August 22, the Assistants and the planters came in a group to request the Governor himself to return to England so that they would receive the supplies and necessities as soon as possible. The Governor refused to oblige them and gave several good reasons why he did not wish to go. For one thing, he could not return so soon without being discredited for abandoning the expedition, many of whose members he had himself persuaded to leave their native country and undertake the voyage. For another, his enemies would slander both the expedition and him by saying that he went to Virginia for expediency only, to lead the company into a country where he never meant to stay himself and leave them there. Again, he pointed out that since the colony planned to go some fifty miles farther up into the mainland, his own possessions would be ruined or stolen while being transported in his absence. Then, when he returned he would have to provide himself with new equipment or go without while he was in Virginia. And he spoke from experience, since when he had been away for three days such losses had occurred. Therefore, he concluded, he would not go himself.

The next day not only the Assistants but also many of the other colonists, both men and women, renewed their requests to the Governor to return to England for supplies and the speedy accomplishment of the things that had to be done there. They pledged him in writing, signed and sealed by them all, that his possessions would be kept safely until his return to Virginia and that if any part of them were spoiled or lost they would restore it to him, or whomever he should designate, at such time as it might be missed and demanded. This bond was made out and delivered into his hand.

I thought it well to set down a copy of this testimony: "May it please you, Her Majesty of England's subjects, we, your friends and countrymen, the planters of Virginia, do by these presents give all of you to understand that for the immediate supply of certain of our apparent needs, requisite for our successful planting in Virginia, we have unanimously and earnestly entreated, with incessant requests, John White, Governor of the planters in Virginia, to sail to England speedily to obtain the help and supplies aforesaid. We are sure that he can best perform this labor and will take the utmost pains for our sakes. Not once, but often, he has refused to do so, bearing in mind our safety and the reputation and success of the expedition. But at last we have importuned him much against his will to leave his government, as well as all his personal property, in our hands and return to England in our behalf. Of his wisdom and fidelity in handling this matter, as in all else, we do assure ourselves by these presents and beg you to concur this twenty-fifth day of August, 1587."

At last the Governor accepted the colonists' demand that he return to England. Only half a day remained to prepare himself for his departure. He left Roanoke on August 27 and on the same day, about midnight, went aboard the flyboat, which had already weighed anchor and rode outside the bar. The flagship was there also, as she had returned that morning. Both ships set sail for England, but in weighing anchor, twelve men at the capstan of the flyboat were thrown from it. One of the capstan bars had been broken, and in whirling about, the other two bars struck the men and hurt them so badly that some of them have never recovered. After this mishap the men tried to weigh anchor again, but weakened by their first effort, they were not able to do so; they were thrown down and hurt for the second time. Since there were only fifteen men on board, and most of them bruised and hurt in this accident, they were forced to cut the cable and let the anchor go. They kept up with the flagship, however, until September 17, when Cuervo was sighted and then Flores.[15]

SEPTEMBER. On the eighteenth of this month, of the fifteen men in the flyboat there remained only five who could work, the others all having been hurt in the accident. The flagship stayed near the island of Terceira to seek profitable adventure before returning to England. The flyboat set sail for England alone, carrying letters. The men hoped to arrive there shortly, with God's help. For twenty days the homeward course was followed with very little wind blowing. As the casks had leaked, the fresh water was almost gone. A northeasterly storm arose. The wind blew so strongly for six days that we were driven farther off our course than we could make up in thirteen days. Most of our sailors fell sick, and two of them died. The weather continued close, and our captain saw neither sun nor

15. Two islands of the Azores.

star for as much as four days running. Our beverage was foul water, dregs of beer, and the three gallons of wine which were left. We expected to perish of starvation.

OCTOBER. On the 16th we saw land, but had no knowledge of what country it might be. At about sunset we put into a harbor where we found a large ship from Dublin and a pinnace from Southampton at anchor. We still did not know where we were, as we had no boat in which to go ashore. Finally the pinnace sent a boat to us with six or eight men, and they told us we were in Smerwick, in the western part of Ireland. They gave us water, wine, and other fresh provisions.

On the 18th the Governor and the captain went to Dingen,[16] about five miles away, to order provisions for the flyboat and medicines to relieve our sick and injured men. Four days afterwards the boatswain, the steward, and the boatswain's mate all died aboard ship, and on the 28th the first mate and two of the chief sailors were taken to Dingen ill.

NOVEMBER. On the first of the month the Governor shipped for England in a vessel called the *Monkey*, which was ready to sail from Dingen, leaving the flyboat and its crew in Ireland. On the same day we set sail, and three days later we sighted the north side of Land's End, where we were swept toward the Severn, but the next day we rounded Land's End and set a course for Mount's Bay.[17]

On November 5 the Governor landed in England at Martasew,[18] near Saint Michael's Mount in Cornwall.

We reached Hampton[19] on the 8th, where we learned that our flagship had arrived in Portsmouth three weeks before. We heard also that Captain Ferdinando and all his men had come home not only without the cargo he meant to win but also with a sick and exhausted crew. Some of the best men had died, and the others were so weak that they could not bring their ship into harbor, but were forced to let the anchor go outside. They were not strong enough to weigh the anchor again. There they might all have perished had not a small ship sailed by and given them help. The names of the chief men who died are Roger Large, John Mathew, and Thomas Smith. Some other sailors died as well, but I do not know their names.

In the year of our Lord, 1587.

16. Dingle, on Ireland's southwestern coast.
17. The bay between Land's End and the Lizard.
18. A village on Mount's Bay.
19. Southampton.

The names of all the men, women, and children who arrived safely in Virginia and stayed there to live, 1587, in the twenty-ninth year of the reign of Queen Elizabeth:

MEN

John White
Roger Baily
Ananias Dare
Christopher Cooper
Thomas Stevens
John Sampson
Dyonis Harvie
Roger Prat
George How
Simon Fernando
Nicholas Johnson
Thomas Warner
Anthony Cage
John Jones
William Willes
John Brooke
Cutbert White
John Bright
Clement Tayler
William Sole
John Cotsmur
Humfrey Newton
Thomas Colman
Thomas Gramme
Marke Bennet
John Gibbes
John Stilman
Robert Wilkinson
John Tydway
Ambrose Viccars
Edmond English
Thomas Topan
Henry Berry
Richard Berry
John Spendlove
John Hemmington
Thomas Butler
Edward Powell
John Burden
James Hynde
Thomas Ellis
William Browne
Michael Myllet
Thomas Smith
Richard Kemme
Thomas Harris
Richard Taverner
John Earnest
Henry Johnson
John Starte
Richard Darige
William Lucas
Arnold Archard
John Wright
William Dutton
Mauris Allen
William Waters
Richard Arthur
John Chapman
William Clement
Robert Little
Hugh Taylor
Richard Wildye
Lewes Wotton
Michael Bishop
Henry Browne
Henry Rufoote
Richard Tomkins
Henry Dorrell
Charles Florrie
Henry Mylton
Henry Paine
Thomas Harris
William Nichols
Thomas Phevens
John Borden
Thomas Scot
Peter Little
John Wyles
Brian Wyles
George Martyn
Hugh Pattenson
Martin Sutton
John Farre
John Bridger
Griffen Jones
Richard Shabedge
James Lasie
John Cheven
Thomas Hewet
William Berde

WOMEN

Elyoner Dare
Margery Harvie
Agnes Wood
Wenefrid Powell
Joyce Archard
Jane Jones
Elizabeth Glane
Jane Pierce
Audry Tappan
Alis Chapman
Emme Merrimoth
Colman
Margaret Lawrence
Joan Warren
Jane Mannering
Rose Payne
Elizabeth Viccars

BOYS AND CHILDREN

John Sampson
Robert Ellis
Ambrose Viccars
Thomas Archard
Thomas Humfrey
Thomas Smart
George How
John Prat
William Wythers

CHILDREN BORN IN VIRGINIA

Virginia Dare
Harvie

SAVAGES WHO HAD BEEN IN ENGLAND AND RETURNED HOME TO VIRGINIA

Manteo
Towaye

WHITE

John White's letter to the worshipful Richard Hakluyt, his very good friend, written on February 4, 1593.

SIR, to satisfy your earnest request and fulfill my promise to you made when I was in England with you last, I have sent you a true account (although the style may be too homely to content the delicate ear) of my last voyage to the West Indies and those parts of America called Virginia, which was undertaken at the end of February, in the year of our Lord, 1590. And what events occurred on our journey you shall see plainly in the following discourse.

At that time there were three ships commissioned to go to the West Indies at the special orders of John Wattes,[1] *a London merchant. But when they were fully loaded and ready to take their departure, a general order was issued, forbidding all ships to leave the ports of England. As soon as I heard of it I thought it necessary to acquaint Sir Walter Raleigh with the news. I begged him to try to get an immediate release for the three ships so that they could proceed with their voyage as planned. I have many times before been an expense and a trouble to him in my pleas for the supplying and relief of the planters in Virginia, but he could now be rid of my importunities, and the people in Virginia (if it were God's pleasure) could speedily receive comfort and relief and be no longer a responsibility to him.*

Sir Walter Raleigh obtained a license from Her Majesty, the Queen, and an order that the owner of the three ships was to put up a bond of three thousand pounds, payable to him or his assignees. In consideration of their release, the three ships were to transport a convenient number of passengers, with their goods and equipment, to Virginia. Nevertheless, the order was not followed, nor was the bond furnished. The owner and the captains of the ships refused to carry any passengers and goods except myself and my chest. I was not permitted to take even a boy to attend me, although I earnestly begged them to be allowed to do so. I was much put out by this unkind dealing, but because of the shortness

1. Probably Sir John Watts, later Lord Mayor of London.

of time I had no opportunity to complain to Sir Walter Raleigh, for the ships were ready to go to sea and would have departed before I could return.

The leaders, captains, and sailors showed very small regard for the welfare of their countrymen in Virginia. There was nothing they wanted less than to touch in those parts. Their whole desire was to plunder Spanish ships and take prizes, and they spent so much time doing this that summer was over before we arrived in Virginia. And when we did get there, the weather was so foul and unseasonable that we were forced to leave the coast without seeing any of our planters. In addition, we lost one of our small boats and seven of our best men, as well as three anchors and most of our casks of fresh water, which had to be abandoned on shore.

All of these unfortunate events, harmful to the planters in Virginia as well as to the expedition itself, would not have occurred if the order set down by Sir Walter Raleigh had been observed, or if my own continued daily petitions for its observance had been heeded.

Thus, you can easily judge the success of my fifth and last voyage to Virginia, no less unfortunately ended than rashly begun, as luckless to many as it was evil to myself. But I would to God it had been as prosperous to everyone as it proved poisonous to the planters and as joyful to me as it was useless to them. Yet, seeing that it was not my first unsuccessful voyage, I must rest content. And without having obtained my wishes, I leave off attempting that in which I would to God my wealth could support my will. Thus I commit the relief of my uneasy company of planters in Virginia to the merciful help of the Almighty, whom I most humbly beseech to help and comfort them, according to His most holy will and their good desire, and so take my leave.

From my house at Newtown in Kilmore, February 4, 1593.

Your most well-wishing friend,

JOHN WHITE

JOHN WHITE'S REPORT

of his last voyage to Virginia, in the year 1590, which he sent with his letter to Richard Hakluyt.

ON March 20 the three ships *Hopewell, John Evangelist,* and *Little John* put to sea from Plymouth, towing two small sloops. At midnight of the 25th the sloops sank, through the negligence of the boatswains. On the 30th we saw, far ahead of us, the coast of Barbary lying east of Cape Cantyn and the Bay of Asaphi.[1] The next day we came to the Isle of Mogador, and as we passed by we sighted the *Moonshine,* a pinnace[2] from London.

APRIL. On April 1 we anchored at Santa Cruz,[3] where we found two large ships from London loading sugar. We obtained two small boats from them to take the place of the sloops we had lost. On the 2d we set sail, and on Saturday, the 4th, we reached Alegranza, the easternmost island of the Canaries.

On Sunday, April 5, we gave chase to a large flyboat, fought and took her, killing three of her men and wounding another. On Monday, the 6th, we saw the Grand Canary Island and on the next day landed on the south side to take on fresh water. We left the Grand Canary on the 9th and set our course for Dominica. On the last day of April we sighted Dominica and the same night dropped anchor on the south side of the island.

MAY. On the morning of May 1 some of the savages came aboard our ships in their canoes to trade with us. Later we went ashore and visited their town. We returned to our ship without any resistance from the savages, nor did we do them any harm.

On May 2d our flagship, the *Hopewell,* and the pinnace sailed from Dominica, while the *John* lurked near the island, hoping to capture some of the Spanish ships outward bound to the Indies. The same night we sighted a group of three small islands called Los Santos.[4] We left them and Guadaloupe on our starboard.

On May 3d we came to St. Christopher's Island, lying east-northeast of us. On the 4th we sailed by the Virgin Islands, a group of several broken islands lying at the east end

1. On the African coast.
2. A small man-of-war, under sail.
3. Now called Agadir, in Morocco.
4. Northwest of Guadeloupe.

of St. John.[5] The same evening we landed on one of them, called Blanca,[6] where we killed an incredible number of fowl. After we had stayed three hours on Blanca we headed northwest along the shore. Towards nightfall we sailed through an opening called the Passage, lying between the Virgins and the east end of St. John. Here the pinnace left us to sail along the south side of St. John.

On the 5th and 6th the flagship continued up the north side of St. John; we were so close to the shore that the Spaniards recognized our ship as a man-of-war. They built fires along the coast as we sailed by, for that is their custom when they see a warship off their coasts.

On the 7th we landed on the northwest end of St. John, where we took on a supply of water from the Yaguana River. That night we captured a frigate of ten tons, coming from Guatemala with a cargo of hides and ginger. At this place a mulatto named Pedro, who knew everything about our condition, deserted to the Spaniards. On the 9th we left the Yaguana.

On the 13th we landed on Mona Island, where we found ten or twelve houses inhabited by Spaniards. These we burned, and we sank a pinnace which they had drawn into shallow water. The Spaniards had taken all her sails, masts, and rudders into the woods so that we could not get them. We chased the men all over the island, but they hid in caves, hollow rocks, and bushes, and we could find none of them.

On the 14th we departed from Mona and the day after came to the island of Saona,[7] about five leagues from Mona, lying near the east end of Hispaniola. We sailed between these two islands and waited there for four or five days, still hoping to capture some of the Domingo fleet which was coming towards the shores of Hispaniola, as this was a shorter route to Spain than the way around Cape Tiburon[8] or Cape Antonio.[9]

On Thursday, the 19th, our second flagship, which we had left at Dominica, joined us at Saona. We left a Spanish frigate with them and asked them to keep watch for the Domingo fleet for five more days between Saona and Mona. Then we sailed for Cape Tiburon, where I learned from our men on the second flagship that they had taken two prisoners in Dominica, sons of the chiefs of that country, but that the savages had run away at Santa Cruz Island when the ship landed to take on ballast.

On the 21st the flagship reached Cape Tiburon, and there we found our pinnace, the *John Evangelist,* awaiting us. We took two Spaniards aboard who had almost starved on the shore. They had made a fire to attract our notice as we passed by. Those places for

5. San Juan de Porto Rico—Puerto Rico.
6. Probably Culebra, one of the Virgin Islands.
7. Off San Domingo.
8. On Haiti.
9. On Cuba.

a hundred miles along shore are a desolate wilderness without any human habitation, full of wild bulls, boars, and great serpents.

On the 22d our pinnace also came to anchor at Aligato Bay, Cape Tiburon, where we learned from Captain Lane[10] that she had been set upon by one of the King's galleys belonging to Santo Domingo. The Spanish ship was manned by four hundred men, and after a fight which lasted three or four hours without any great harm done on either side, she fled.

On the 26th the *John,* our second flagship, joined us at Cape Tiburon with the frigate we had left at Saona. This was the appointed place where we were to wait for the Santo Domingo fleet.

Whitsunday evening we spent at Cape Tiburon, and one of our boys ran away from us. But ten days later he returned to the ship, half starved. It was in this part of the Cape that we found human bones and carcasses, the remains of men who had probably been set out there by some warship and had died of starvation.

JUNE. On the 14th, as we lay in the bay of Cape Tiburon, we took a small Spanish frigate which came upon us so suddenly that it had no time to escape. This frigate came from Santo Domingo and had only three men aboard; one was an expert pilot, another a mountaineer, and the third a vintner. They had broken out of the prison at Santo Domingo, and they intended to flee to Yaguana, a town in the west of Hispaniola where many fugitive Spaniards live.

On Wednesday, the 17th, Captain William Lane was sent to Yaguana with the pinnace and a frigate to capture a ship which the old pilot (whom we had taken on board three days before) told us was taking on freight there. On the 24th the frigate returned to Cape Tiburon, bringing us word from Captain Lane that he had taken the ship with many passengers and Negroes. This was not so rich a prize as we had hoped for, because a French man-of-war had taken and plundered her before we came. Nevertheless, her cargo of hides, ginger, canafistula,[11] copper, and cassava was worth a thousand or thirteen hundred pounds.

JULY. On the 2d, Edward Spicer, whom we had left in England, joined us at Cape Tiburon with a small pinnace, of which a Captain Harps was master. The same day we caught sight of a fleet of fourteen sails from Santo Domingo. We immediately gave chase, but as soon as they saw us they fled, separating and scattering here and there. We, too, divided and made after them until twelve o'clock at night. Then, because of the darkness,

10. Not Ralph, but William Lane.

11. A purgative.

we lost sight of each other. Yet, in the end our flagship and the *Moonlight* were together when they caught up with the second flagship of the Spanish fleet. The next morning we fought and captured her, losing only one of our men with two others wounded, while the Spaniards lost four men with six wounded. But we were ignorant of what had become of our fleet. We did not know the whereabouts of our second flagship, nor did we know what had happened to our pinnace, the prize we had taken earlier, or the two frigates.

The 3d of July we spent in rifling and rummaging our newly taken prize and fitting it to sail with us. On the 6th of July we saw Jamaica and left it behind on the larboard side, keeping Cuba in sight on our starboard. On July 8 we reached the Isle of Pines, on the south side of Cuba near Cape San Antonio. That very day we gave chase to a frigate, but lost sight of her at night; our flagship was far too slow, and we had neither the *Moonlight* nor our pinnace with us.

On the 11th we came to Cape San Antonio, where we met the *Moonlight* and the pinnace. The men from these ships told us that the day before some twenty-two boats had passed them, some of them as large as three hundred and four hundred tons. They belonged to the King of Spain's treasure fleet coming from a port on the Spanish Main, and were bound for Havana. From this day until the 22d the weather was calm. There was little wind, and we suffered from the heat. The Spaniards whom we had taken on board caused us such annoyance that we were forced to put them ashore. We landed them—all but three—at a place which they themselves chose on the south side of Cuba.

On the 23d we came in sight of the Cape of Florida and saw its broken islands, called the Martyrs.[12] On the morning of the 25th, St. James's day, we approached the Matanzas, a headland eight leagues east of Havana. We planned to stay there two or three days and take on fresh water.

On Sunday, July 26, we were plying to and fro between the Matanzas and Havana when we saw three small pinnaces from St. John de Ullua bound for Havana with exceedingly rich cargoes. They sailed very boldly up to us, until they were within musket shot. We supposed them to be Captain Harps's pinnace and the two small frigates he had taken, and so showed our flag. But as soon as they saw it they turned about and made all the sail they could away from us. They kept close to the shore, in such shallow water that we could not follow them. We had to give up the chase, having spent our shot and powder to no purpose. But if we had not so rashly run up our flag we could have taken all three vessels, for they would not have recognized us before they were in our hands. While chasing these ships, we came as far to leeward as Havana.

As we found none of our other boats at the Matanzas, we set a course for the Cape of

12. The Florida Keys.

Florida again, and from there we sailed through the Bahama channel. On the 28th the Cape of Florida lay to the west of us, but on the 30th we lost sight of it and stood out to sea to make use of the current,[13] which runs much swifter far out than it does near the coast. For between the Cape of Florida and Virginia, all along the shore, there are none but eddy currents, flowing to the south and southwest. On the 31st all three of our ships were in the open sea, the flagship, the *Moonlight,* and our large prize. This last vessel left us without taking leave of the flagship or the escort and sailed directly for England.

AUGUST. On the 1st, a wind came up and from that time we had very foul weather with much rain, thunder, and great waterspouts which fell all around our vessels, threatening our safety.

On the 3d we stood in for shore, and at midday we looked at the sun to determine the position of the land. We found it to be thirty-four degrees of latitude. When night came we were within three leagues of the low sandy islands west of Wokokon. But the weather continued to be so bad that we could not come to anchor near the coast. We stood off to sea again until Monday, August 9.

On Monday the storm ceased, and we had promise of fair weather. Making for land again, we came to anchor in eleven fathoms of water, latitude thirty-five degrees, within a mile of the shore, and landed on a narrow sandy island, one of those west of Wokokon. Here we took on some fresh water and caught a good supply of fish. As the island was only a mile from the mainland, the water was very shallow; in most places not more than three or four feet deep.

On the morning of the 12th we left, and toward night we came to anchor at the northeast end of the island of Croatoan, where we found a breach in the reefs which extended two or three leagues out into the sea. Here we rode at anchor all night.

The next morning we sent the boats to take soundings over the breach. Our ships were riding on the side of the breach in five fathoms of water, and a ship's length from us we found only four and a quarter fathoms, deepening and shallowing for a distance of two miles. At times we measured five fathoms, then seven, and within two casts of the lead nine, then eight, next cast five, then six, then four, then nine again, and deeper. The last sounding showed three fathoms, two leagues off shore. This breach is in thirty-five and a half degrees of latitude and lies at the very northeast point of Croatoan, but a bar runs from the ocean into the inner waters separating the islands from the mainland.

Towards evening on August 15 we came to anchor at Hatorask, in thirty-six and a third degrees of latitude, five fathoms of water, three leagues from the shore. As soon as

13. The Gulf Stream.

we reached this place we saw a great column of smoke rising from Roanoke Island, near the spot where I had left our colony in the year 1587. The smoke gave us good hope that some of the colony were still there, awaiting my return from England.

The next morning, the 16th, our two boats were rowed ashore. I took Captain Cooke, Captain Spicer, and their men with me; we meant to go to the place at Roanoke where our countrymen had been left. As we pushed off from the ship we told the master gunner to load two minions and a falcon[14] and to fire them at short intervals. We hoped that the reports would be heard by our people if they lived. In the admiral's boat we took soundings all the way and found nine, eight, and seven fathoms of water from our ship to within a mile of the shore.

Before we had gone half-way between our ships and the shore we saw another column of smoke to the southwest of Kindriker's Mountains. We decided to go there first, however the smoke proved to be much farther from the harbor than we had supposed. When we reached the spot, we were sorely tired. But what grieved us more was that we found no one, nor any sign that men had been there lately. We returned to our boats, worn out with exhaustion and very thirsty. During our entire march we had nothing to drink. While we were away our men had brought the cask ashore for fresh water, and we put off going to Roanoke until the next morning. The sailors dug in the sandy hills for water and found plenty. We boarded our ship that night with our whole company in safety.

The next morning, August 17, we were prepared to go up to Roanoke, but as Captain Spicer had sent his boat ashore for fresh water it was ten o'clock before we could leave the ships, which were then at anchor two miles from the shore. The flagship's boat had already covered half way toward the shore and passed the breach before Captain Spicer put off from his ship. We nearly sank while getting through, for a great sea broke into the boat and filled us half-full of water, though by the will of God and the careful steering of Captain Cooke we got safely ashore. But much of our equipment, food, matches, and powder was wet and spoiled.

The wind was blowing a great gale from the northeast into the harbor. The breakers were very high on the bar, and the tide pulled strongly at the entrance. By the time we had carried our boat to shore and taken out most of our things to dry, Captain Spicer had reached the entrance of the breach. His mast was up, and he was half-way through when the rash steering of Ralph Skinner, the master's mate, let a huge sea break into the boat and capsize it. The men stayed with the boat, some in it, others clinging to it. But the next sea grounded the vessel, and the waves beat against it so that some of the men were forced to let go their hold and try to wade ashore. The sea beat them down again and again. They

14. Small cannon.

could neither stand nor swim, and the boat was turned keel upward two or three times.

Captains Spicer and Skinner hung on until they sank and were seen no more. Four of the men who could swim a little kept themselves in deeper water and were saved by Captain Cooke. As soon as he saw their boat capsize, he took off his clothes and, with four others who could swim very well, rowed out as fast as possible and saved the four of them. There had been eleven men in the boat, and seven of the best were drowned. Their names were Edward Spicer, Ralph Skinner, Edward Kelly, Thomas Bevins, Hance, the surgeon, Edward Kelborne, and Robert Coleman.

This accident so upset the sailors that they were all of one mind not to go any farther to search for the planters. But later they got ready the boats, moved by the commands and persuasion of Captain Cooke and myself, and seeing how resolute the captain and I were, they became much more willing.

When our boats were again fitted, we put off from Hatorask with nineteen men in the two vessels. Before we could reach the place where the planters had been left, it was so dark that we missed it by a quarter of a mile. At the north end of the island we espied the light of a great fire through the woods. We rowed towards it, and when we were opposite the place we let fall our grappling anchor near the shore, sounded a trumpet call, and then played the tunes of many familiar English songs. We hailed the shore with friendly greetings, but got no answer. At daybreak we landed, and when we approached the fire we found the grass and some rotten trees burning. From there we went through the woods to the part of the island opposite Dasamonquepeio. We proceeded to walk along the shore, rounding the north point of the island, until we came to the place where I had left our colony in the year 1586. During the walk we saw in the sand the prints of the feet of two or three savages which must have been made during the night. As we went inshore up the sandy bank we saw a tree on the brow of the cliff curiously carved with the clear Roman letters C R O.

We knew at once that these letters indicated the place to which the planters had gone. Before I left them we had agreed upon a secret token. They were to write or carve on trees or doorposts the name of the place where they had settled, for at the time when I departed for England in 1587 the men were ready to move from Roanoke fifty miles up into the mainland. And we had agreed that they should carve a cross over the letters or name if they had trouble in any of these places. We looked everywhere, but found no such sign of distress. So we went to the place where they had been left.

We discovered that their dwellings had been torn down and that a strong enclosure with a high palisade of huge trees, with connecting walls and flankers like a fort, had been built. One of the trees at the right side of the entrance had had the bark stripped off, and five feet above the ground in clear capital letters was carved CROATOAN, without a cross or sign of distress. We entered the palisade, where we found two bars of pig-lead, some iron bars, four iron fowling guns, iron cannon shot, and other heavy things, overgrown with grass and weeds. From there we went to the beach and then towards the point of the creek, hoping to come upon some of the settlers, or their boats or pinnaces. But there was no sign of them or of any of the small cannon which were left with them when I departed.

When we came back from the creeks, some of our sailors reported the discovery of a spot where several chests had been hidden, but dug up again and opened. Much of the goods in them had been spoiled and scattered about, and nothing the savages knew the use of had been left unbroken. Captain Cooke and I immediately went to the place, which was at the end of an old trench made two years before by Captain Amadas. There we saw five chests that had been carefully hidden by the planters. Three of them were my own, and these lay open. My things were spoiled, my books were torn from the covers, the frames of my pictures and maps were rotted and broken by rain, and my armor was almost eaten through with rust. This could only have been the deed of our enemies, the savages of Dasamonquepeio, who must have watched the departure of our men for Croatoan and as soon as they had gone, must have dug up every place they suspected anything was buried in. Though it grieved me much to see my goods spoiled, yet on the other hand I was deeply joyful for the certain token of their safe arrival at Croatoan, where the savages of the island were our friends, and where Manteo was born.

When we had thoroughly searched the place, we returned to our boats and went back to the ships as speedily as we could, for the sky had become overcast, and it was very likely that a foul and stormy night would follow. The same evening, after much danger and labor, we got ourselves on board. By that time the wind and the seas had risen so high that we doubted the cables and anchors would hold until morning. Therefore the captain commanded the boat to be manned by five strong sailors who could all swim well, and he sent them to the little island on the right side of the harbor, where six others remained to fill the casks with fresh water. The boat returned the same night with the men, but they had been forced to leave behind all the casks, ready filled, because the night proved to be very stormy and foul. They could not get them aboard without the danger of losing both men and boats.

The next morning the captain and I agreed, with the master and others, to weigh anchor and go to the place at Croatoan where we thought to find the planters. The wind was favorable. We left the casks of fresh water on the island to await our return. Then the cable was hauled to the capstan, but when the ship was over the anchor the cable broke and we lost the second anchor. At this we drove so fast inshore that we were forced to let a third anchor go, which fell so rapidly that the ship was almost aground at Kindriker's Mountains. We had to let the cable slip to the limit, and if we had not reached a channel of deeper water closer to the shore than we thought possible, we could never have got clear of the point that lies to the south of Kindriker's Mountains. We had thus avoided some of the dangers and come into deeper water, but not without some loss.

Now we had left only one cable and anchor out of four. The weather grew fouler and fouler. Our food supply was diminishing, and we had lost our cask of fresh water. We therefore decided to go to St. John, or some other island to the south, for fresh water and to stay at Hispaniola, St. John, or Trinidad all the following winter, if we could only get some food and other necessities. We hoped to make two rich voyages in one and visit our countrymen in Virginia on the return trip. The captain and crew of the flagship, with my earnest petitions, agreed to this plan, but we had to obtain the consent of the men on the *Moonlight.* When we asked her crew to accompany us in our new undertaking, the men said that they did not think their weak and leaky ship could survive it. So we parted that same night, leaving the *Moonlight* to sail directly for England, while we set our course for Trinidad.

We kept on our course for two days. On the 28th the wind changed, and foul weather set in again. The storm brought the wind from the west and northwest, and it blew so strongly that we could carry no sail but the foresail at half-mast. So we were forced to run before the wind on the exact course for England. We had to change our plan. Instead of going to Trinidad, we headed towards the Azores, where we thought to take in fresh water and hoped to meet some English men-of-war who would give us supplies.

Thus we continued on our way to the Azores, sometimes becalmed and sometimes with very little wind.

SEPTEMBER. On the 15th the wind blew south-southeast so strongly that we were forced to heave to all that day. At this time we thought we were about twenty leagues west of the islands of Cuervo and Flores.[15] At night the storm ceased and fair weather followed.

On Thursday, the 17th, we saw Cuervo and Flores, but could not come to anchor because the wind shifted. The next morning, heading for Cuervo, we discovered a sail ahead of us and gave chase. Coming close, we saw it was a Spaniard, and we hoped to take it. But when we hailed it we found it was already a prize, one of the Domingo fleet taken by the *John,* our consort, in the Indies. We learned that our second flagship and the pinnace had fought with the rest of the Domingo fleet and forced them to flee to Jamaica and

15. The islands of Gratiosa, St. George, Cuervo, Flores, Fayal, and Pico belong to the group of the Azores.

take refuge under the fort there. Some of the ships ran aground, and one of these was taken by our ships, while the others were plundered as thoroughly as time would allow.

Later, when our second flagship was sailing back from Jamaica, she met with two ships near the Organs at Cape San Antonio. They had come from Mexico and were bound for Havana. In the ensuing fight the lieutenant of our second flagship was slain, and the captain's right arm was struck off; four others of his men were killed, and sixteen wounded. But in the end the Spanish ship was taken, though so badly riddled by our shot below the water line that it sank before our men could take out the treasure. Thus we lost thirteen tubes of silver, which sank with her, besides much other rich merchandise. In the confusion the other Spanish ship, pierced by nine shots under the water, got away. Our second flagship intended to pursue her, but the men aloft saw some rocks above the water near the shore which they took to be galleons coming from Havana to rescue the two ships. Therefore they gave up the chase and sailed for England. This intelligence was given us by the men on our prize.

On Saturday, September 19, we came to anchor near a small village on the north side of the island of Flores, where we found five English men-of-war. We learned from them that our second flagship and our prize had gone to England. One of the five vessels was the *Moonlight,* our consort; but as soon as she saw us coming into Flores she set sail and left for home without even taking leave of us.

On Sunday, the 20th, the *Mary Rose,* flagship of the Queen's fleet, carrying General Sir John Hawkins, came into Flores. And there were many others of the Queen's ships, namely, the *Hope,* the *Nonpareilia,* the *Rainbow,* the *Swift-sure,* and the *Foresight.* There were also many good merchant ships-of-war, the *Edward Bonaventure,* the *Merchant Royal,* the *Amity,* the *Eagle,* the *Dainty* of Sir John Hawkins, and other good ships and pinnaces, all waiting to meet the King of Spain's fleet coming from Terra Firme in the West Indies.

On September 22 we went aboard the *Rainbow,* and towards nightfall we spoke with the *Swift-sure,* to whom we gave three cannon. The captains, bound for Fayal with ten other ships, desired our company, and we willingly went along. The General, with the rest of the fleet, was separated from us, making two fleets, one of which was sure to come up with the Spanish fleet.

On Wednesday, the 23d, we saw the island of Gratiosa, where the flagship met with the rest of the Queen's fleet. Here a council was held, and it was determined that all vessels should sail towards the mainland and spread out along the coasts of Spain and Portugal to make sure of meeting with the Spanish fleet in those waters.

On the 26th we came to Fayal. There the flagship was anchored with some of the rest of the fleet, while others plied up and down between there and the island of Pico until midnight. Then the *Anthony* shot off a cannon and weighed anchor, showing a light. After that the whole fleet followed her eastward, the wind blowing northeast-by-east.

On Sunday, the 27th, towards evening, we took our leave of the flagship and the whole fleet, as they headed out to the east. But our ship, accompanied by a flyboat, sailed in for St. George, where we planned to take on more fresh water and food.

On Wednesday, the 30th of September, seeing that the wind stayed so northerly, we knew that we could not reach the island of St. George, and we gave up our purpose of getting water there. The next day we set a due course for England.

OCTOBER. On the morning of the 2d we saw St. Michael's Island on our starboard quarter. On the 23d, at ten o'clock in the morning, we saw Ushant in Brittany. On Saturday, the 24th of October, we came in safety, God be thanked, to an anchorage in Plymouth.

NOTES ON JOHN WHITE

THEODORE DE BRY, the Flemish engraver, was not content to be only an artist; he also wanted to publish books, presumably to earn more money and to better his lot. His enterprising zeal bore fruit when in 1590 he issued the first volume of a series of illustrated voyages — and what a magnificent series it became — that kept his name green for centuries to come. For his first volume on Virginia, as the vast territory on the Atlantic seaboard from Florida to Newfoundland was then called, De Bry used the narrative of Thomas Hariot that had been printed in London two years earlier. But even more impressive than the text were the twenty-three engravings based on originals "diligentlye collected and drawne by John White, who was sent thiter [to America] speciallye and for the same purpose by the said SIR WALTER RALEIGH. . . ." These illustrations presented the first authentic pictorial representations of life in the New World.

Who was this John White who made these drawings in America less than a century after Columbus set foot in this Hemisphere? Little is known of him.

The historian Randolph G. Adams, who spent considerable time in search of White's identity, summed up his life in these sentences: "He appears in the pageant of American history about the year 1584, slips off the stage nine years later, apparently vanishes. Whence he came, where he went, and where he died still seem to baffle the investigator."[1]

To fill in the empty spaces of White's life all we can do is to speculate. He may have been with Frobisher in 1577 searching for a northwest passage, as a drawing that has come down to us shows a skirmish with the Eskimos on Baffin Island which may have been done by him. He may have been a member of the Painters-Stainers' Company while learning his craft, as a John White is listed among its members in 1580. And he may have been with Amadas and Barlowe on their exploratory expedition to America, as White speaks in his 1593 letter to Hakluyt of having made five voyages to Virginia. As we know of four of his other voyages, it is probable that the first one was made with Amadas and Barlowe in 1584. So far the speculation.

But we do know that he was one of the 107 men whom Sir Richard Grenville left on Roanoke Island in the summer of 1585. Incidents of that voyage — like taking in salt near Cape Rojo on May 26 — can be traced through his drawings. At Roanoke White made sketches of the area: of the plants, fish, and birds; of the Indians; and of their villages of Pomeiooc, Aquascogoc, and Secoton, working hand in hand with Thomas Hariot, the scientist of the expedition.[2]

That first colony stayed in the New World over the winter months, sailing back to England the following spring. On this voyage White probably took with him his sketches and drafts, from which he then made his final watercolors.

A year later — in 1587 — he was on the way to America once more, this time as governor of a colony of 113 men, women, and children, among them his daughter Elinor and her husband Ananias Dare. When difficulties arose, he sailed home for supplies, only a few days after the birth of his granddaughter Virginia, the first white child born to English parents on this Continent.

In England he reported the troubles to Raleigh and made preparations for his return. But he could not reach America until the early part of 1590. Arriving at the spot where he had left his colony in the middle of August, he found no living soul, only the word CROATOAN carved on a tree. As there was no cross behind it—the sign of distress — he may have thought that the colonists had moved voluntarily and were safe at Croatoan.

The search for them was hampered by foul weather. White's ships lost their cables. He decided to sail southward toward Hispaniola or Trinidad to take in fresh water and supplies, then return and make a fresh attempt to find the colony. But the elements were against him; his ship had to run before the wind and was blown to England, reaching Plymouth in the last week of October.

1. Randolph G. Adams, "An Effort to Identify John White," *The American Historical Review* (October, 1935).

2. Hariot wrote that they had "taken, eaten & haue the pictures as they were there drawne" of several birds.

On February 4, 1593 from his home in Ireland he wrote a report to his "worshipful friend" Richard Hakluyt in which he described his search for the lost colony. (Why he waited for more than two years and why he did not return to America to find the colony remains a mystery.) This report turned out to be his swan song — we never hear from him again. He disappears from history, leaving no trace.

For a century and more White's memory lived mainly in the engravings of De Bry, though here and there one of his sketches found its way into the work of others and his name was mentioned by them. Thus in the various manuscript versions of John Mountgomery's *A treatise concerning the navie of England*, originally written in 1570 but enlarged upon by the author in 1588 and 1589, we can find his turtle, his flying fish, and his dolphin, all of them placed in seascapes. In John Gerard's celebrated *Herbal* published in 1597 one of the illustrations — the milkweed — was made after a White drawing. And Dr. Thomas Penny in the manuscript of his "*Insectorum . . . Theatrum*" noted that the picture of the common American tiger swallow-tailed butterfly was given to him by White, who brought it from Virginia in 1587. ("Hanc è Virginia Americanâ Candidus ad me Pictor detulit. 1587.") When after Dr. Penny's death his friend Thomas Moffet completed and published the book in 1634, White's butterfly appeared on page 98. Moffet referred to White as a "pictore peritissimo," and a "pictor non incelebris."

But what happened to the large body of his original drawings? Did he give them to De Bry, who engraved them for the Virginia volume? And if he did, are they the same watercolors which have come down to us? Or did White give De Bry only copies of his work? And if so, what happened to them? Were they lost, as were the copper plates of De Bry?

For a century and a quarter there is no record of the whereabouts of the drawings. Then, in 1709 the English doctor Hans Sloane, a passionate bibliophile, came upon a volume in the possession of the White family which he believed contained White's originals. A notation on the flyleaf read: "this Lent to my son Whit, 11 April 1673," an indication that the descendants had owned the book all along. Dr. Sloane eventually acquired the book, which passed under his will to the British Museum in 1753, where it has been ever since.[3]

Another 112 years went by before it was ascertained that the drawings were not White's originals but copies of them. This happened in 1865, when a volume with 75 watercolors was offered for sale in London by the famous auction house of Sotheby's. A comparison of the drawings with those in the Sloane volume clearly proved that the book at Sotheby's contained White's originals.

Why the drawings were bound in such a volume we do not know. White may have wanted to present them to some high personage, but who that personage was we do not know. What we know is that the first Earl of Charlemont (James Caufeild) acquired the volume in 1788, as correspondence about that purchase has been preserved.[4]

It was on March 12, 1788 that Edward Malone, the London drama critic, who was helping Charlemont to build up his library in Dublin, wrote to his Lordship:

"In Payne's catalogue[5] just published is a book I thought you would like, but the price being fourteen guineas, I would not venture on it without your knowledge. I enclose the title. The drawings are finely executed, many of them whole-length figures of the savage persons discovered in the voyage, and the whole in fine preservation. Payne promised to keep it unsold till I could get your answer; let me know therefore by return of post."

The item from the catalogue, which Malone enclosed, read:

"284. The pictures of sundry things collected and counterfeited according to the truth, in the voyage made by Sir W. Raleigh, knight, for the discovery of La Virginea, in the 27th year of the most happie reigne of our sovereigne lady Queene Elizabeth. Seventy-five drawings coloured, in the original binding. Folio. —Fourteen guineas."

Lord Charlemont's answer came posthaste. He wrote to his friend:

"The book of which you sent the title must be worth the money if the drawings be well executed. If you think them so, by all means purchase it for me."

Malone thought it so and bought the book, which remained in the Charlemont library for seventy-seven years.

This was the very volume offered for sale by Sotheby's in August 1865 with other books from the library of the third Earl of Charlemont (James

3. The volume contains 113 leaves of drawings; of these we have White's originals on 27 Indian, Eskimo, and natural history subjects. Some of the other drawings are probably copies from White of which the originals have been lost. However, the remaining 57 pages of flower renditions in the volume have no relation to White's work.

4. Historical Manuscripts Commission, 13th Report, Part 8.

5. Thomas Payne, the Elder, was a London bookseller.

Molyneux) and which was bought by the American bibliophile Henry Stevens of Vermont, for £125 — over eight times more than its purchase price in 1788.

That the volume survived was a miracle. On June 30, 1865 a fire broke out at the warehouse of Sotheby's. Many books perished in the flames, but the volume with White's drawings suffered no more damage than some slight charring on the page edges and some running of the colors. However, as its pages were saturated with water, the pressure on them created copies on the intervening leaves. Thus seventy-two of the volume's seventy-five drawings left an imprint, creating fairly good reproductions of the drawings.

After Stevens gained possession of his purchase, he separated the originals from the copies, which he called "off-tracts," and asked the bookbinder F. Bedford to make up two volumes, both in red morocco, one with the originals, the other with the copies. And when the books were ready he offered them to leading American collectors. But when neither James Lenox nor William Smith was willing to buy them, Stevens tried his luck on the other side of the water. He approached Anthony Panizzi, the principal librarian of the British Museum. On March 24, 1866, Panizzi received authorization from the trustees for the purchase of the volumes at the price of 225 guineas — 200 for the one with the originals and 25 for the one with the off-tracts.[6]

The two books were "placed for sentimental reasons, next to the copy of De Bry's America in the Grenville Library, and they disappeared from sight since no one would look for drawings among printed books; and in fact, when the late Mr. Thomas Seccombe wrote the life of White for the *Dictionary of National Biography* in 1900 he was unaware of their existence."[7]

For the next forty years the drawings remained on the shelves of the library gathering dust.[8] Early in 1906 they were transferred to the Department of Prints and Drawings and were described in the Museum's newly issued Catalogue published in the following year.

In 1934, the British Museum issued six colored postcards reproducing White's originals and making them available to the public.

Two years later, in 1936, exactly seventy years after the drawings were purchased by the museum, the first serious attempt was made for the publication of the entire set of White's works. With the financial aid of the Pilgrim Trust, a prospectus was issued asking subscriptions for a volume of the seventy-five drawings to be ready in 1938 for the price of fifteen guineas.[9]

Although, as Professor Samuel Eliot Morison later pointed out, "it seemed reasonable to suppose that enough libraries, museums of fine arts, and collectors of Americana would be willing to pay that sum for competent renderings of the first paintings ever made of the Indians, fish, flora and scenery of the United States" so few subscriptions were received that the project was abandoned.[10]

In America J. Franklin Jameson of the Library of Congress and George Watson Coe of the Huntington Library "spent years hammering on the superlative importance of these pictures, and they were never able to make Americans understand why they were important."[11] Only Randolph G. Adams, the head of the William L. Clements Library at Ann Arbor, would not give up. By 1942 it seemed as though he would be successful where everyone else had failed. In that year, supported by Archibald MacLeish, then Librarian of Congress, Adams made arrangements with the British Museum for the publication of the drawings. On the other side of the ocean he had the enthusiastic support of Laurence Binyon, the poet and orientalist, who was with the British Museum. So at last the project got off the ground. But when Binyon died in 1943 and MacLeish left the Library the following year to take a new post in the State Department, once again the publication was shelved.

It was during these years that the editor of this volume was doing research at the William L. Clements Library for a work on the early French and English colonies that he planned to illustrate with the engravings of De Bry. Adams strongly urged him to include not only De Bry's engravings but White's originals pertaining to North America and to reproduce them in color. The obvious obstacle to such a suggestion was the almost prohibitive cost of color printing. As the book was intended for the

6. Henry Stevens, *Bibliotheca Historica*, p. 225 (1870).

7. Laurence Binyon, *The Walpole Society Transactions*, XIII, pp. 19-20 (1925).

8. The American writer Edward Eggleston was aware of their existence—the first reproductions of White's Indian figures and his maps were done in black and white by the *Century Magazine* in 1882 and 1883 illustrating three historical articles by Eggleston.

9. Prospectus of the British Museum (1936).

10. Samuel E. Morison, *The William and Mary Quarterly*, (January, 1947).

11. Letter of Randolph G. Adams to the editor of this volume (September 22, 1941).

JOHN WHITE'S FIGURE DRAWINGS

These watercolors have no connection with the English settlements in the New World; they are printed here only to have all of John White's work (75 drawings) complete within the covers of this volume.

TURKISH WOMEN, BOTH VEILED

MALE AND FEMALE ESKIMO

PICTISH MEN AND WOMAN; THE FIRST TWO HAVE BEEN ENGRAVED BY DE BRY

ANCIENT BRITONS
Both have been engraved by De Bry

TURKISH MAN AND WOMAN
The woman may be a Greek

TARTAR
or perhaps Usbek

De Bry engraved the Picts and early Britons for his first book "to showe how that the Inhabitants of the great Bretannie haue bin in times past as sauuage as those of Virginia"—an amusing editorial license.

general public, the price had to be within the range of the average book buyer. However, when Charles H. Duell and Samuel Sloan, the enterprising heads of the publishing house Duell, Sloan and Pearce, were approached, they were willing to risk the additional investment and add forty color pages to the volume.

Before going ahead with the plans, another difficulty had to be overcome. Because of the war, White's originals were hidden in the English countryside to be safe from German bombs. Adams suggested reproducing them from the hand-colored photographic copies which Mrs. Sonia Tregaskis had made for him at the British Museum. He pointed out that even if the originals were in their proper place they could not be taken out for reproduction because of Museum's regulations. Thus whoever would want to reproduce them would have to do so through copies.[12]

Adams' suggestion was taken. And so it came about that 361 years after John White made his sketches in early America, his completed watercolors relating to the New World were printed for the first time in their original colors in this book.

The publication of the volume in 1946 revived interest in John White's work. In 1947, the British Museum, prodded by American scholars, began to take steps to issue the White drawings in their original sizes. Money was collected from the Old Dominion Foundation, the Pilgrim Trust and the Wellcome Trust, while the British Parliament voted a sizable amount for the printing. A reliable estimate put the collected funds in excess of a quarter of a million dollars.

In 1964—ninety-nine years after the acquisition of the drawings and eighteen years after they appeared in this book—the British Museum finally issued its two-volume set of the White drawings in a limited edition of 600 copies for $225 the set.[13]

As the 300 copies of the edition allocated to the United States were quickly taken up, the publication was almost immediately out of print.

Thus once more this volume remains the only one in print which contains John White's watercolors of early America in their entirety and in their original colors.

12. To the editor of this volume Adams wrote on September 22, 1941: "So in 1934, when I happened to be in London and was impressed with the imminence of bomb raids, which have since occurred, I determined to get at least one complete set of color facsimiles. I wanted to have these in America before Hitler's destruction started. So with the photographer at the Museum, we devised a technique for making very faint photostats on drawing paper. We then hired a brilliant young artist-copyist [Mrs. Sonia C. Tregaskis] who painted remarkably faithful facsimiles which, because of the underlying photostats, are extremely accurate.

"Each of these pictures was approved by Mr. Hind, the curator of prints at the Museum, before we paid the final bill. . . ."

That Adams was right about the reproduction process was patently proven when in 1964 the British Museum issued its limited edition of John White's drawings. In the Preface to that work the Keeper of Prints and Drawings of the Museum explained: "Under the Statutes of the British Museum, White's drawings could not be taken out of the building so that models had to be made from which the craftsmen concerned produced their colour plates. These models, consisting of lightly printed monochrome collotypes, were coloured and patinated by hand direct from the originals . . ." If one translates the jargon into plain English, one realizes that the Museum's edition of the White drawings was reproduced from hand-colored photographic copies — the very way they were reproduced in this book.

That there can be no doubt about this is clearly admitted by the British Museum's officials. On page xiii of Volume I it is acknowledged that the "important work" of copying of the White originals "has been carried out by Mrs. P. D. H. Page, who was responsible for the majority of the models, and Mrs. Jeanne Holgate, who copied most of the Indian subjects."

Now, if one wishes to argue about this matter, it can only be whether the coloring of Mrs. Tregaskis in this volume or that of Mrs. Page and Mrs. Holgate in the British Museum volume is more faithful to the originals. However, as all three ladies applied their colors over photographs, with the original watercolors before them for comparison, one cannot see how there could be a substantial difference.

This is only mentioned here because an American librarian tried to make an issue of this in a professional magazine.

13. In volume II of *The American Drawings of John White* the pictures are exquisitely reproduced; unfortunately the editorial notes of volume I are pedestrian and pedantic, at times bordering on the ridiculous, as when a printer's error of omitting the letter "n" from "contemporary" in Sotheby's catalogue is bracketed (see page 28), or when the narratives of Elizabethan sea captains, whose works were printed by Richard Hakluyt in his classic *Voyages* (1598–1600), are credited not to Hakluyt but to a 1955 reprint by one of the editors. Curiously, in the two-volume set not a single footnote carries the name of Richard Hakluyt, even though the two editors refer to themselves and to their meager output no less than 636 (six hundred and thirty-six) times — a probable record for professional narcissism.

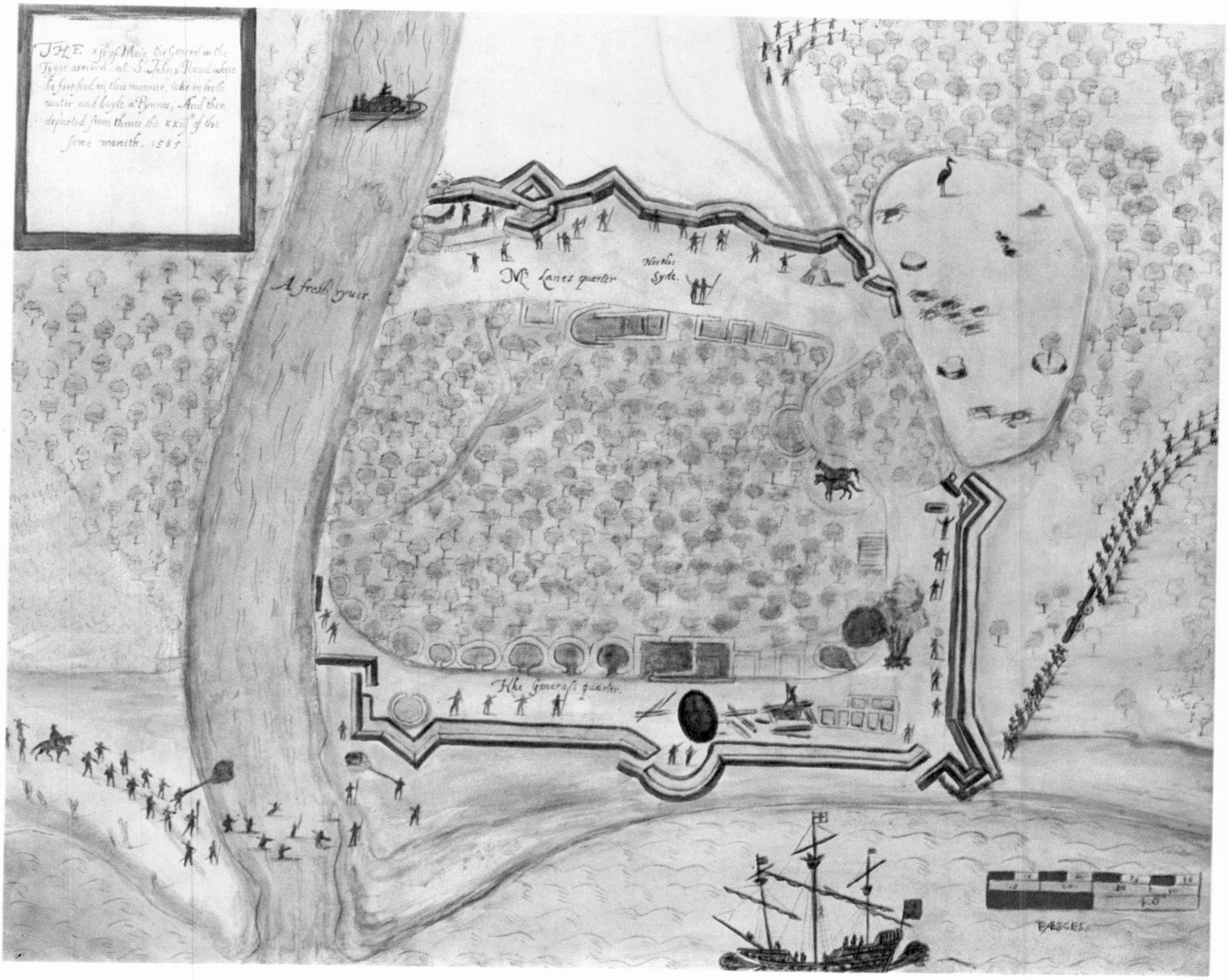

14¼" x 17½"

THE CAMP OF THE ENGLISHMEN ON ST. JOHN'S ISLAND

On May 11 (or 12), 1585, Sir Richard Grenville's *Tiger* anchored at Mosquetal (Tallaboa) Bay on the southwestern coast of Puerto Rico. As soon as the men disembarked they started to build an entrenchment. The drawing of John White depicts their fortifications. Governor Ralph Lane's quarters (in the upper center) are guarded by a line of soldiers. Near the sea (at the bottom) four soldiers keep watch before the dwelling of Sir Richard Grenville, who is riding towards the river (on the left).

Outside the fort (on the right) a long line of men drag a tree trunk towards the enclosure. In the pond (at top right) land crabs and water fowl are basking in the sun.

In the panel (top left) the legend reads: "The XIth of Maie the Generall in the Tyger arriued at St. Johns Iland where he fortified in this manner, toke in fresh water, and buylt a Pynnes, And then departed from thence the XXIIIth of the same moneth. 1585."

JOHN WHITE'S WATERCOLORS

ORIGINALLY DRAWN BETWEEN 1585 AND 1587 IN AMERICA ARE HERE REPRODUCED FOR THE FIRST TIME IN THEIR ENTIRETY

JOHN WHITE'S CHART OF THE EAST COAST

from Florida to Chesapeake Bay, with the arms and crest of Sir Walter Raleigh. Six three-masted ships are sailing in the sea which abounds in whales and dolphins.

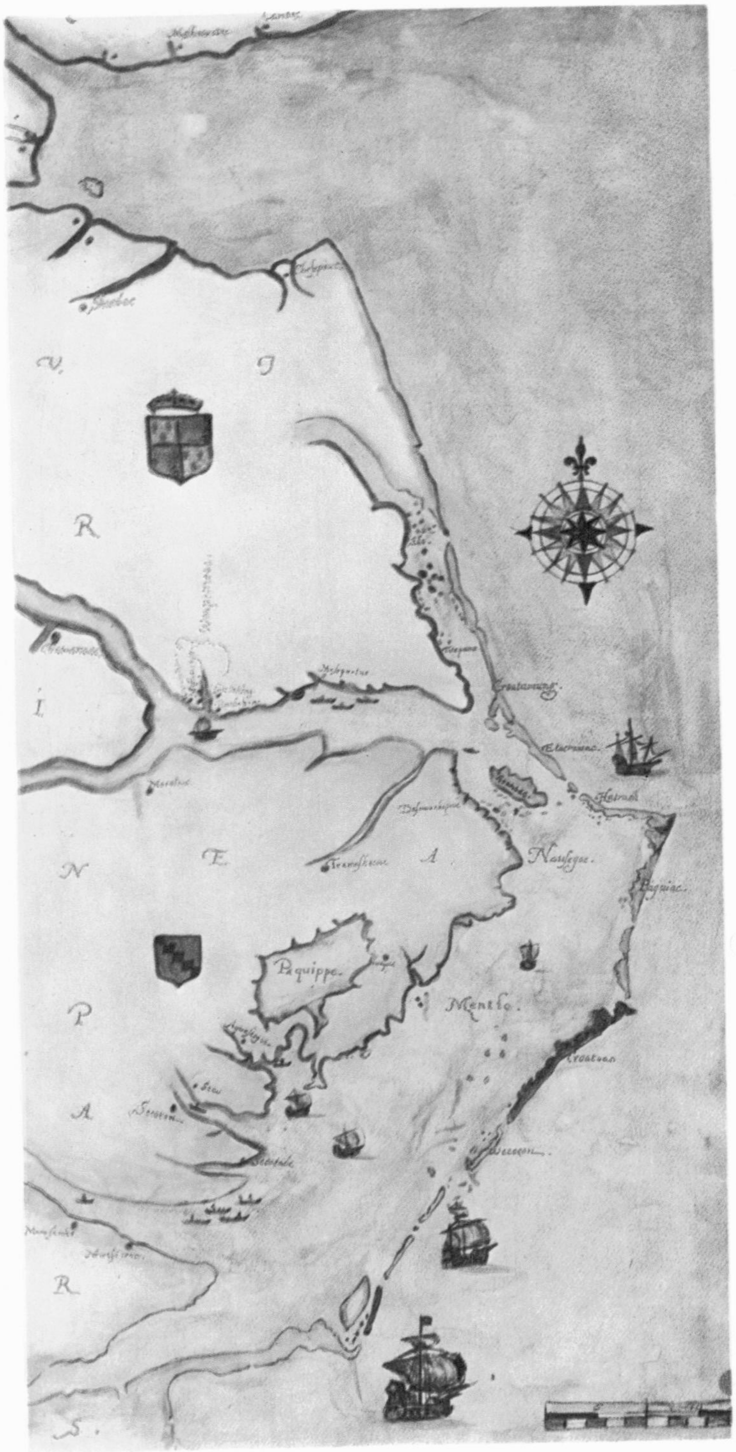

18⅞" x 9¼"

THE COAST FROM CAPE LOOKOUT TO CHESAPEAKE BAY

Red dots mark the places visited by the settlers.

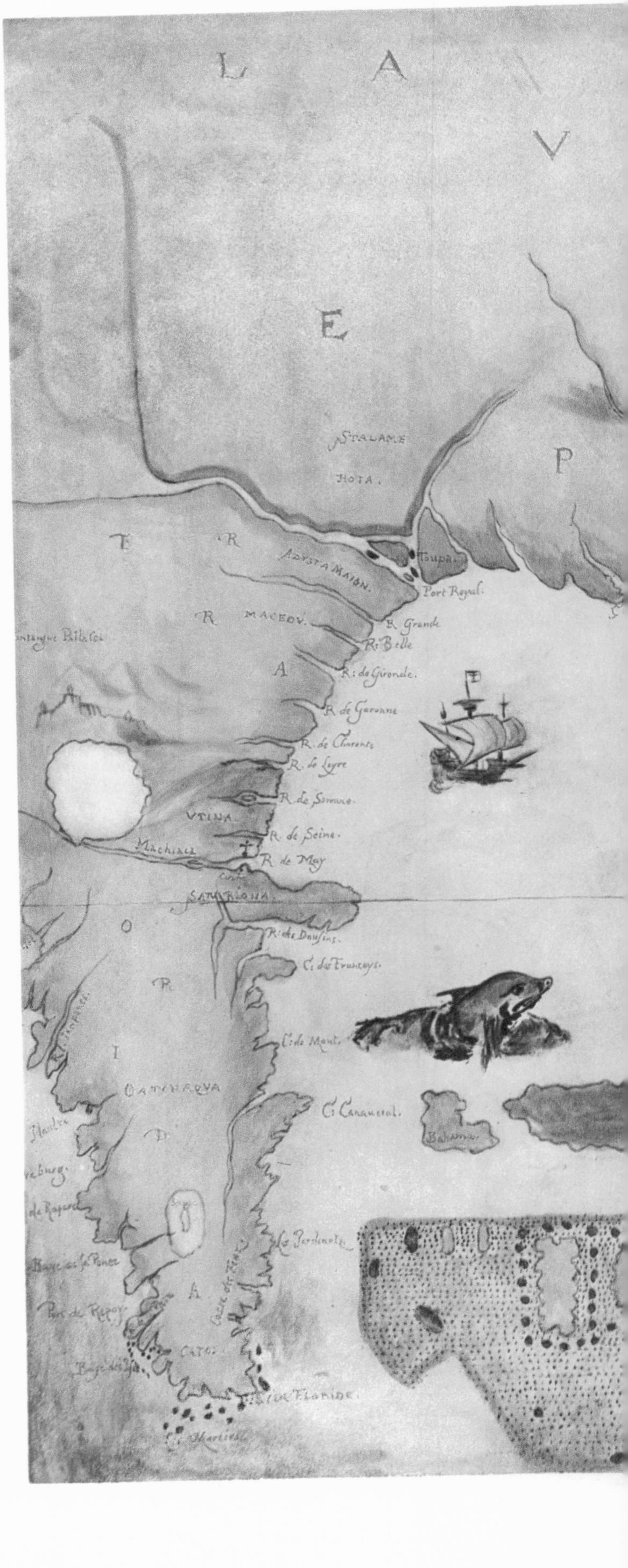

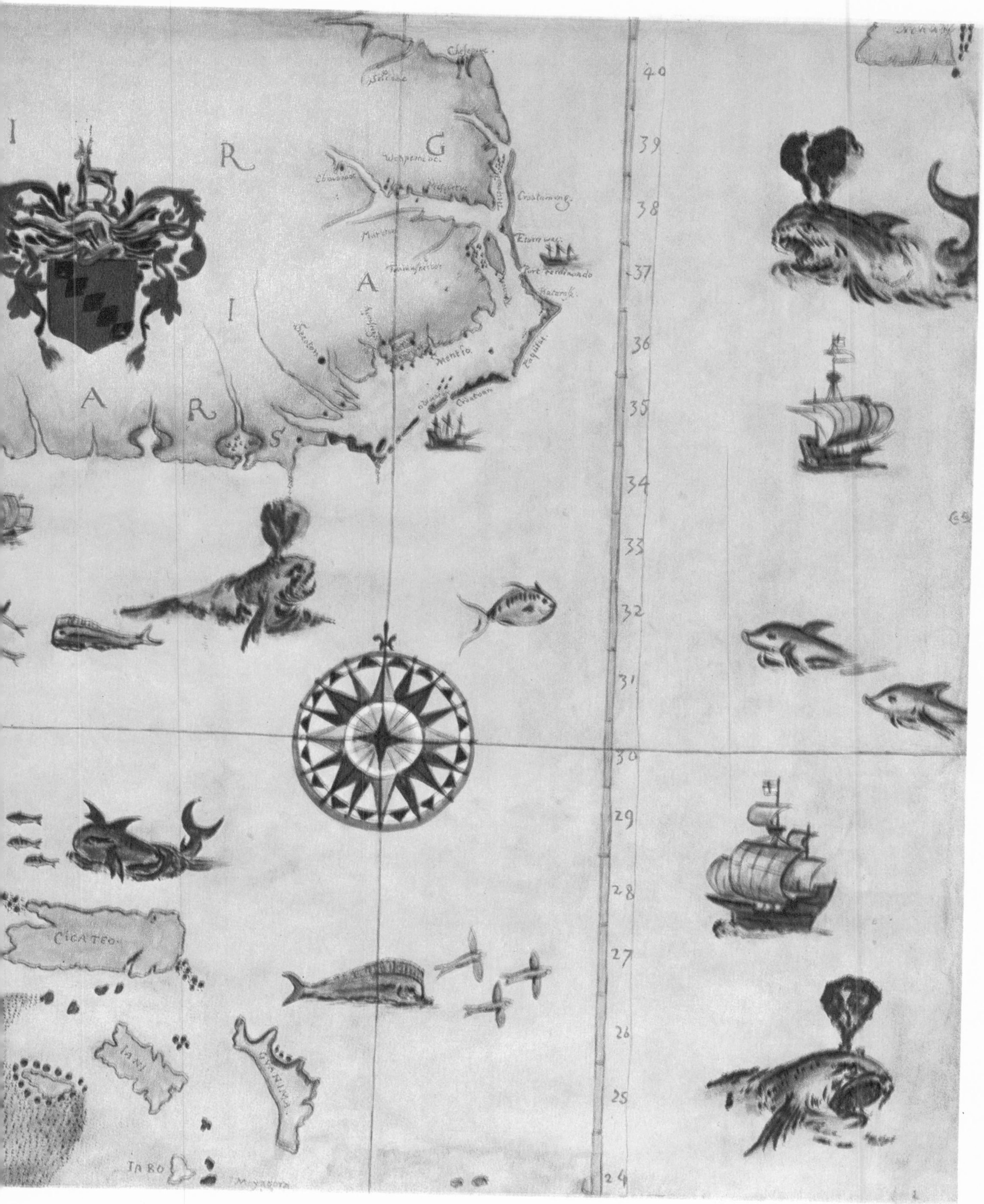
R
G
A
I
A
R
S
CICATEO
IANI
GVANIMA
IABO
Port Ferdinando
Menteo
Croatoan
Chesepeac
40
39
38
37
36
35
34
33
32
31
30
29
28
27
26
25
24

14½" x 18½"

The forme of a fort wch was made by Mr
Ralfe Lane in a parte of St Johns Ilande
neere Capross where we toke in salt
the xxvjth of May. 1585.

12⅜" x 8¾"

RALPH LANE'S MEN TAKE IN SALT NEAR CAPE ROJO, PUERTO RICO, ON MAY 26, 1585.

Picture slightly cropped 13⅞" x 9¼"

INDIANS FISHING. (See Theodore De Bry's engraving of this watercolor on page 251.)

The towne of Pomeiock and true forme of their howses, couered
and enclosed some wth matts, and some wth barcks of trees, All compassed
abowt wth ſmale poles ſtock thick together in stedd of a wall.

8¾″ x 8½″

THE VILLAGE OF POMEIOCK

near the mouth of Gibbs Creek (in the present Hyde County, N.C.). There are eighteen structures inside the circular palisade. In the center a group of Indians crowd around the fire. Others go about their work; one man is splitting a log, another carries wood. In the left background a man walks his dog. (De Bry engraved this picture; see pages 263 and 293.)

THE VILLAGE OF SECOTON

was situated on the south side of the Pamlico River (near the present Bonnerton, N.C.). Thomas Hariot wrote that this particular village of thirteen dwellings lacked a palisade.

In the center of the picture three villagers are eating food placed on a mat in large bowls while another man, a bow in his hand, watches them. On the right above the dancing group are corn fields with three stages of maize. The Indians planted three crops, one in May, another in June, still another in July. They were harvested in July, August, and September. (De Bry's engraving of this picture is on page 265.)

12¾" x 7¾"

8⅝″ x 8″

SITTING AROUND THE FIRE

The singing of the Indians—six men and four women—is accompanied by rattles made of gourds or pumpkins filled with pebbles or fruit stones. Hariot thought that the scene represented a ceremony in which the natives were offering thanks for their safe return from war or for their escape from perils on land or sea.

The manner of their attire and
painting them selves when
they goe to their generall
huntings, or at theire
Solemne feasts.

THEIR ATTIRE

The apron is made of deerskin; the tail may be that of a puma. Three feathers adorn the head. From the ears hang bone ornaments with shining metal balls. A six-strand necklace of dark beads or pearls is around the neck; two bracelets dangle on the right wrist. The face, chest, arms, and legs are painted in reddish brown and white colors. The upper part of the body shows a painted necklace with circular plaques as additional ornaments.

(De Bry engraved this Indian fighter, changing its position and adding a background to it; see page 231.)

10⅜" x 5⅞"

8¼" x 8½"

A MEAL

The man and woman are eating grains of food from "woodden platters of sweete timber"—the regular dish of the Indians. (Theodore De Bry engraved this scene with additions; see page 257.)

★

right:

THE WIFE AND DAUGHTER OF A CHIEF

The little girl is holding a doll which she probably received from the Colonists as a gift. (The picture was engraved by De Bry, with an added background; see page 241.)

A cheife Herowans wyfe of Pomeoc.
and her daughter of the age of .8. or.
.10. yeares.

10⅜" x 5⅞"

A RELIGIOUS DANCE

Seventeen Indians—of whom seven are women—are dancing around seven posts, the tops of which are carved in the form of human heads. Hariot wrote that at certain times of the year a dance was held by the villagers at night to which visitors came from the neighboring towns. The place of the dance was probably Secoton.
(Engraved by De Bry; pages 260–261.)

10¾″ x 14″

9¾″ x 6″

The flyer.

THE CONJUROR

(Engraved by Gysbert van Veen, with additional background, see page 247.)

5¾″ x 6¾″

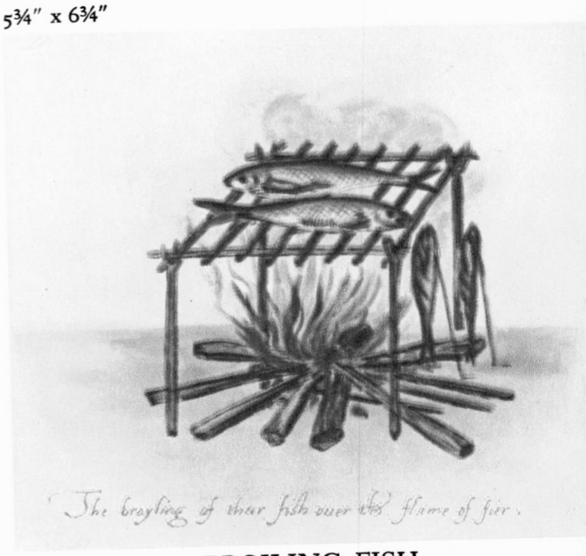
The broyling of their fish over the flame of fier.

BROILING FISH

Engraved by De Bry, who added a man at each side of the grill (see page 253).

One of their Religious men.

10¼″ x 5⅞″

★

A PRIEST

(Engraved by van Veen, with additional landscape; see page 235.)

5⅞″ x 7⅝″

COOKING IN A POT

Engraved by De Bry, who added a man and a woman next the vessel (see page 255).

9¼″ x 5¼″

10⅜″ x 5¾″

A ROANOKE CHIEFTAIN

Engraved by De Bry, with another view of the same figure (see page 239).

★

ONE OF THE WIVES OF WINGINA

(Engraved by van Veen, with another view of the same figure; see page 237.)

10⅛" x 5⅛"

INDIAN WOMAN
OF SECOTON

(Engraved by De Bry, with another view of the same figure and a landscape background; see page 233.)

10⅛" x 5⅝"

A POMEIOCK CHIEFTAIN'S
WIFE AND CHILD

(Engraved by De Bry, with an additional front view and an elaborate landscape background; see page 245.)

★

10¼" x 5⅞"

AN OLD MAN OF POMEIOCK

(Engraved by De Bry; see page 243.)

11⅝" x 8"

The Tombe of their Cherounes or cheife personages, their flesh clene taken of from the bones saue
the skynn and heare of theire heads wch flesh is dried and enfolded in matts laide at theire
feete, their bones also beeing made dry or couered wth deare skynns not altering
their forme or proportion. With theire Kywash, which is an
Image of woode keeping the deade.

BURIAL HOUSE OF THE VIRGINIA ALGONKIANS. (De Bry engraved this picture; see page 269.)

10¼" x 5⅜"

A WOMAN
OF FLORIDA

It is doubtful whether this picture was made from a model. Probably White copied it from a drawing of Le Moyne.

(De Bry engraved this figure; see pages 74 and 113.)

A WARRIOR
OF FLORIDA

This watercolor, like the one on the opposite page, seems to be a copy from a Le Moyne original. It shows a Timucua Indian who lived in the northeastern part of Florida near the mouth of the St. John's River.

(De Bry engraved similar figures for his Florida volume; see pages 51, 63, 71, and 105.)

14″ x 8¼″

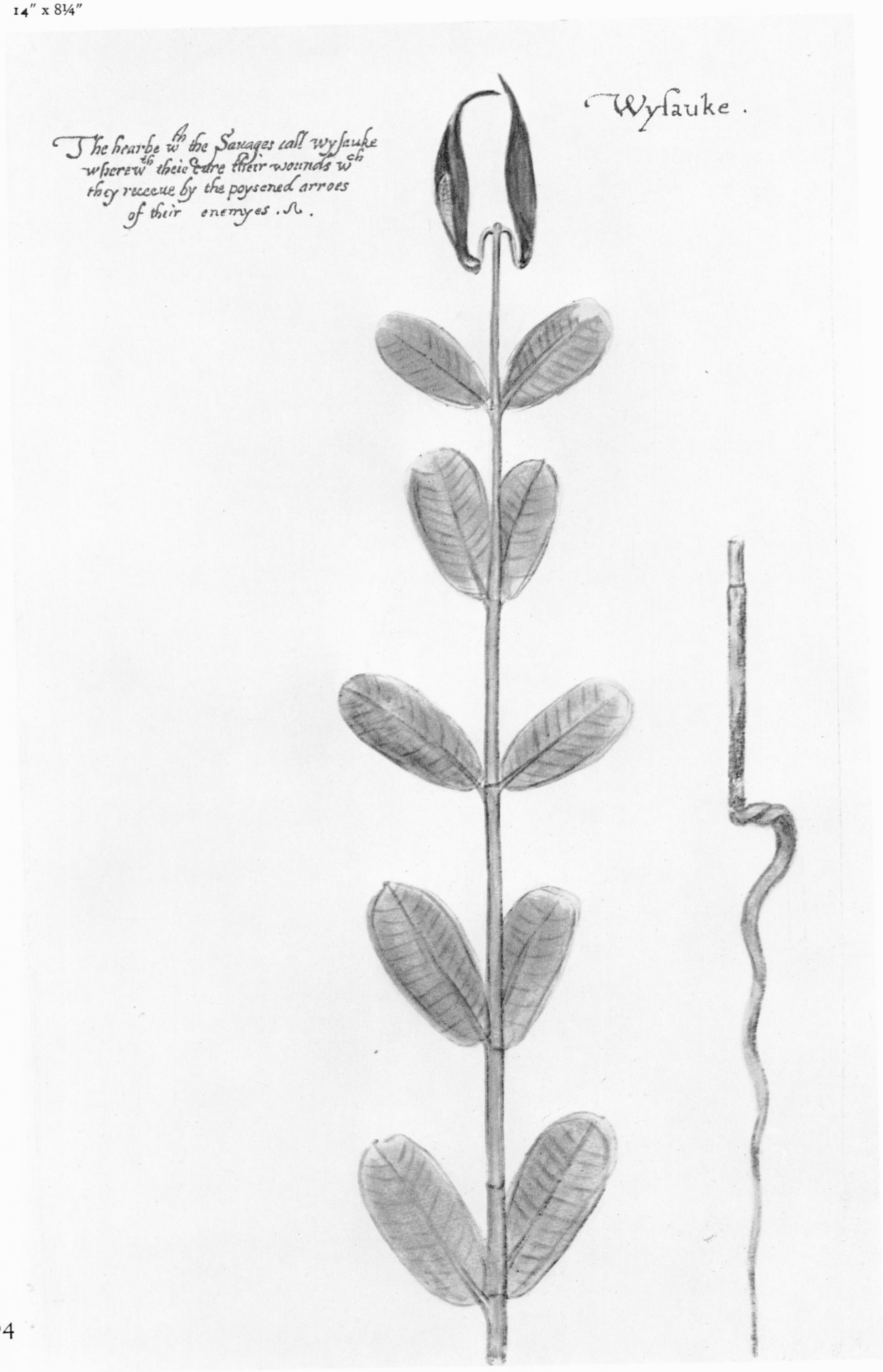
Wysauke.
The hearbe wch the Savages call wysauke
wherewth theie cure their wounds wch
they receaue by the poysened arroes
of their enemyes.

MILKWEED

Asclepias syriaca

White drew this plant in two parts: one shows the stalks with leaves and fruit, the other (on the right) the roots and part of the stalk.

12¾" x 8¾"

HORN
.ANTAIN

a paradisiaca

wing of the
fruit is on the
ing page.

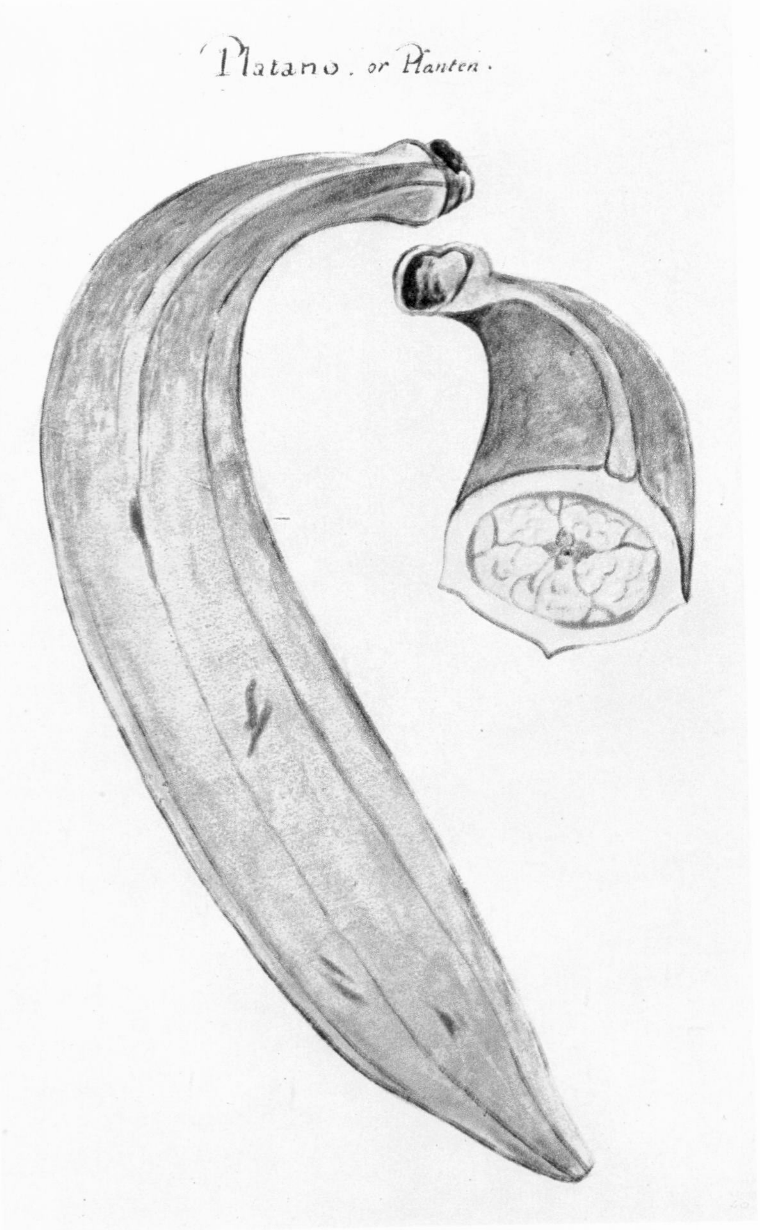

11½" x 7"

HORN PLANTAIN

Musa paradisiaca

8¼" x 7¼"

MAMMEE APPLE

Mammea americana

10⅛" x 5½"

PINEAPPLE

Ananas comosus

13¾" x 7"

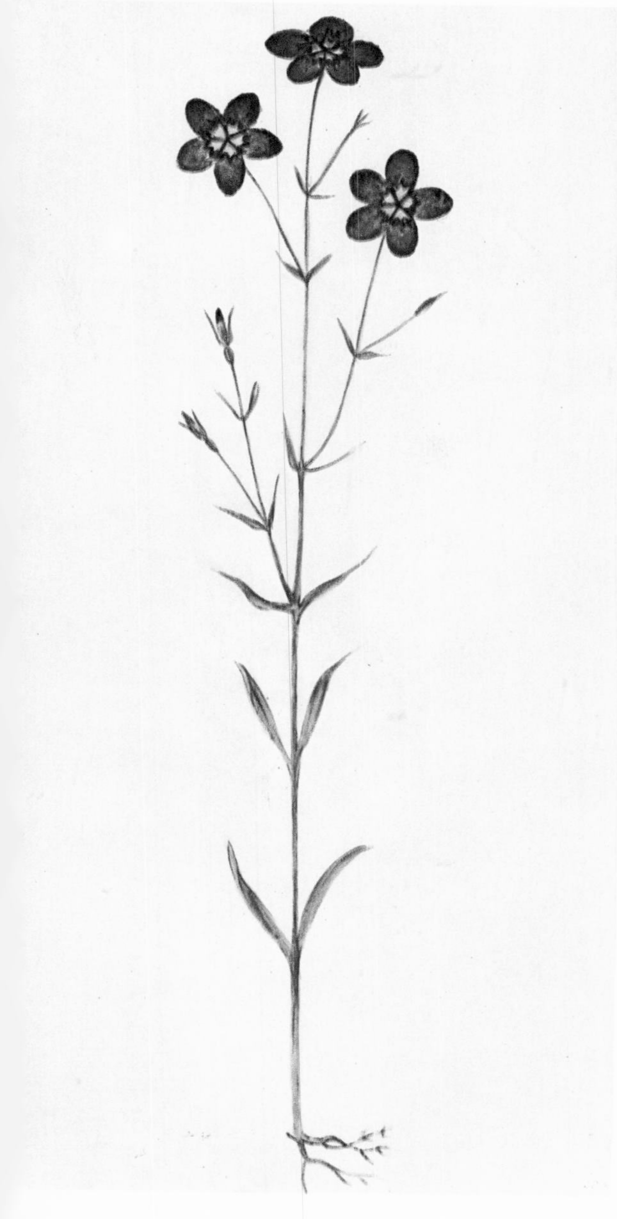

SABATIA

Sabatia stellaris

known as rose gentian, a flower which grows along the Atlantic seaboard.

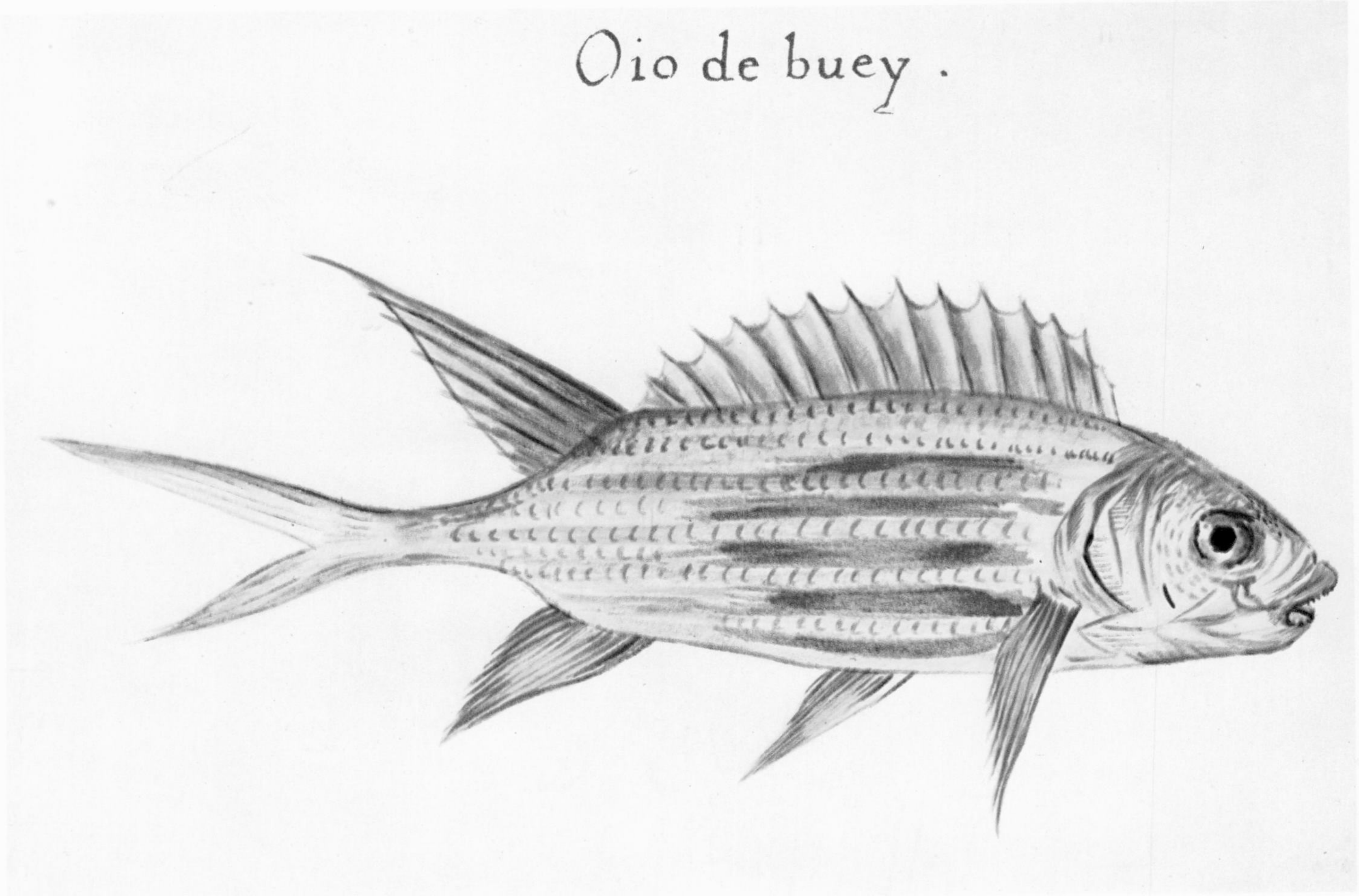

5⅛" x 7¾"

SOLDIER OR SQUIRREL FISH

Holocentrus ascensionis

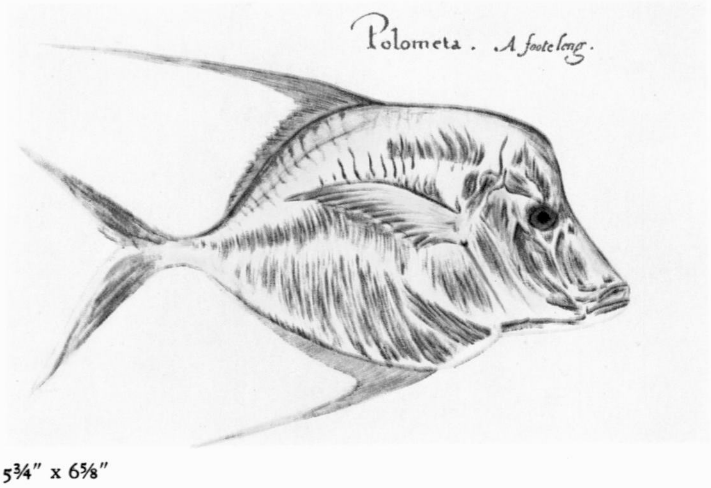

5¾" x 6⅝"

LOOKDOWN OR MOONFISH

Selene vomer

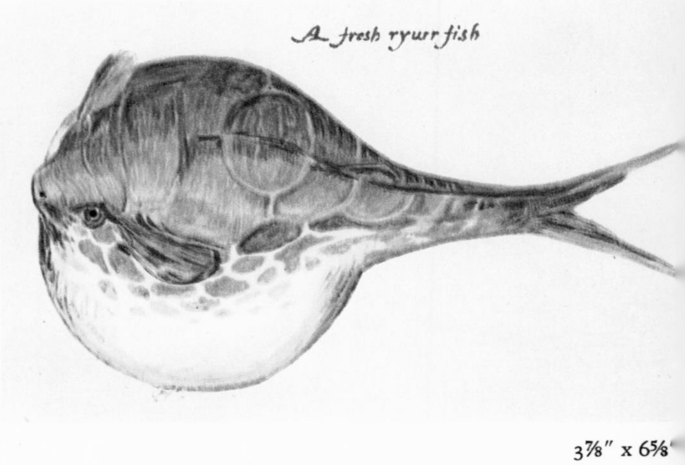

3⅞" x 6⅝"

PUFFER

Lagocenphalus laevigatus, probably the Smooth Puffer

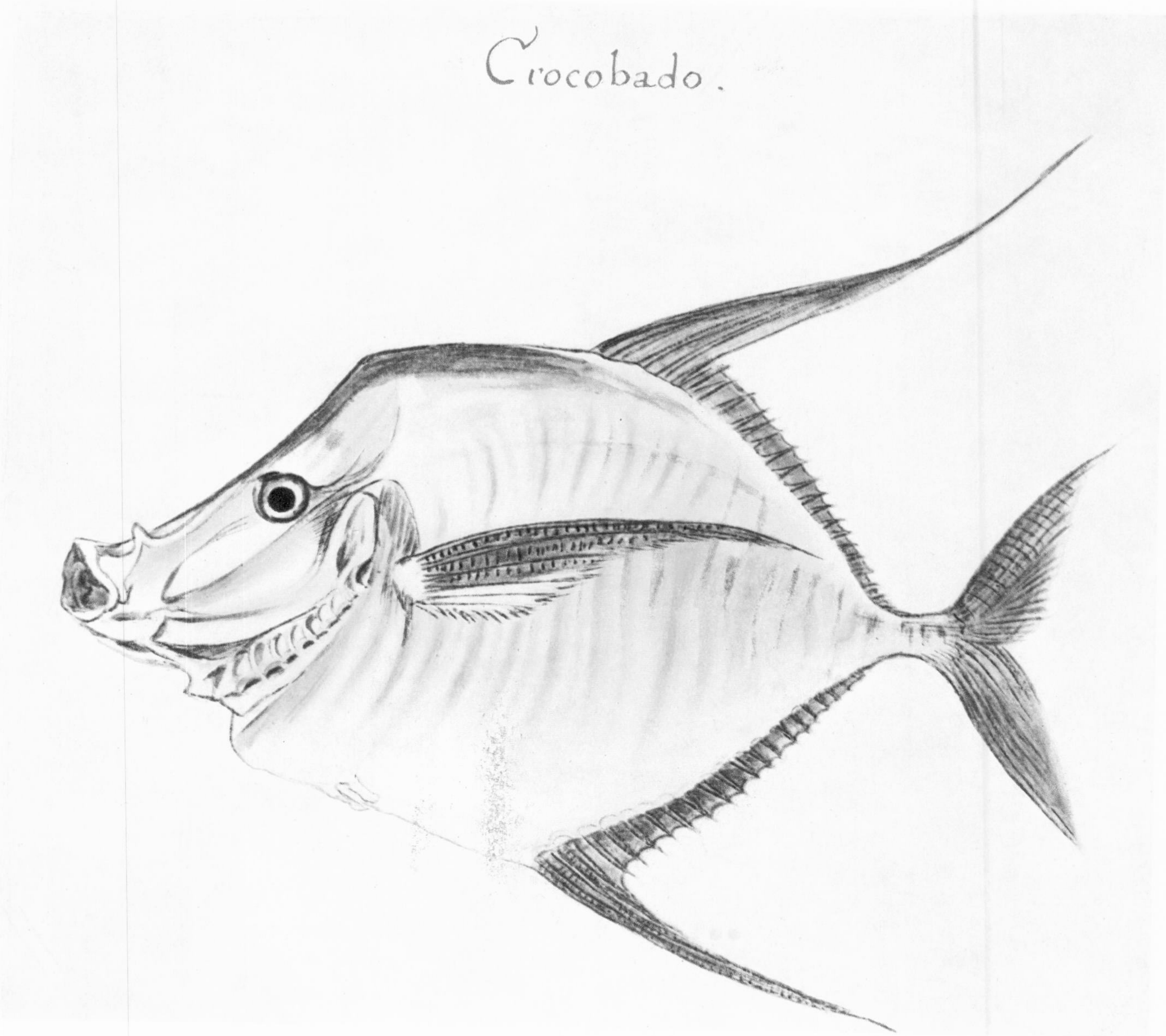

LOOKDOWN OR MOONFISH

Selene vomer

7½" x 8¼"

GROUPER

Epinephelus ascensionis

3⅝" x 8⅝"

DOLPHIN

Coryphaena hippurus

5" x 9"

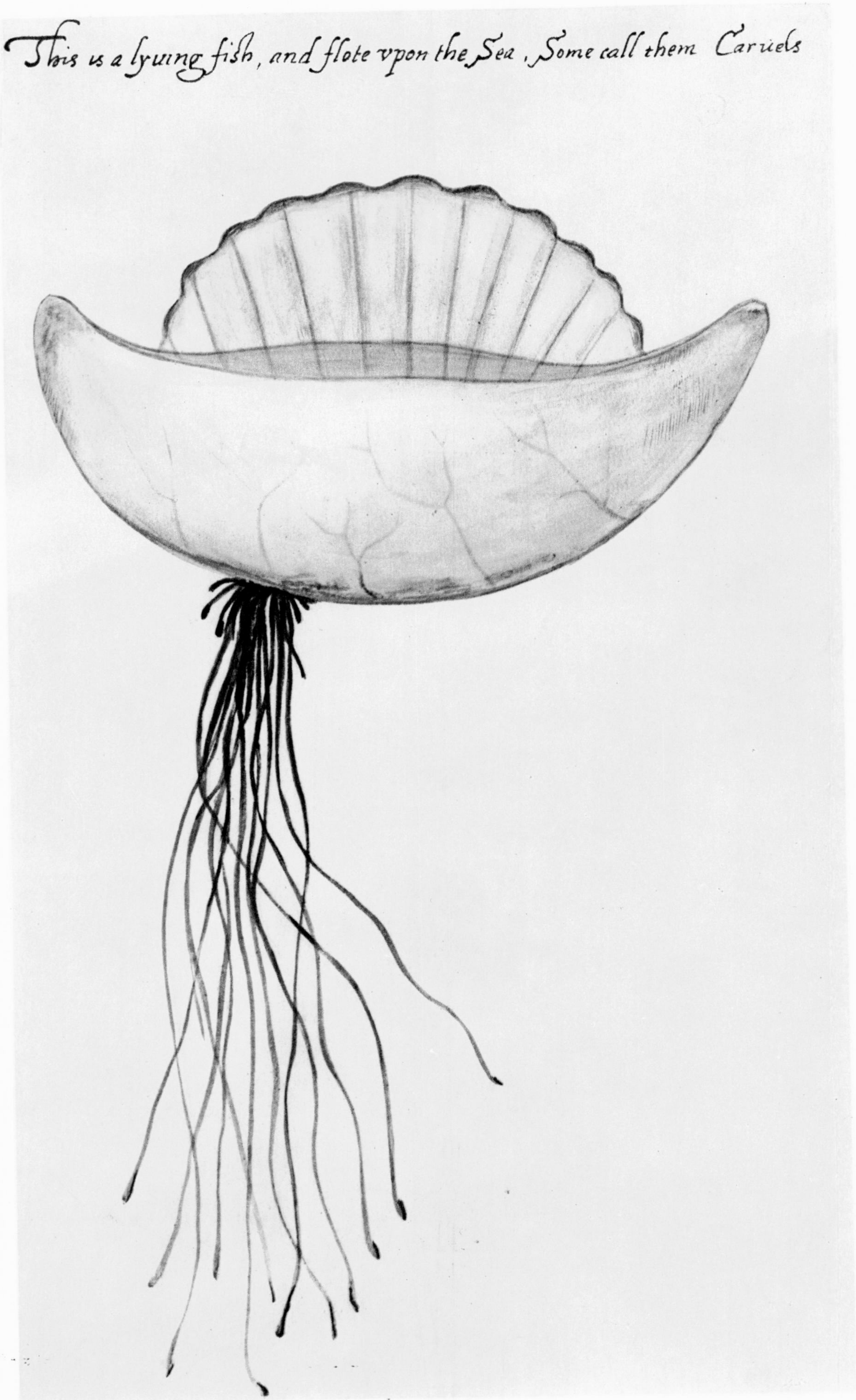
This is a lyuing fish, and flote vpon the Sea, Some call them Carvels

PORTUGUESE MAN-O'-WAR

Physalia physalis

12" x 6⅞"

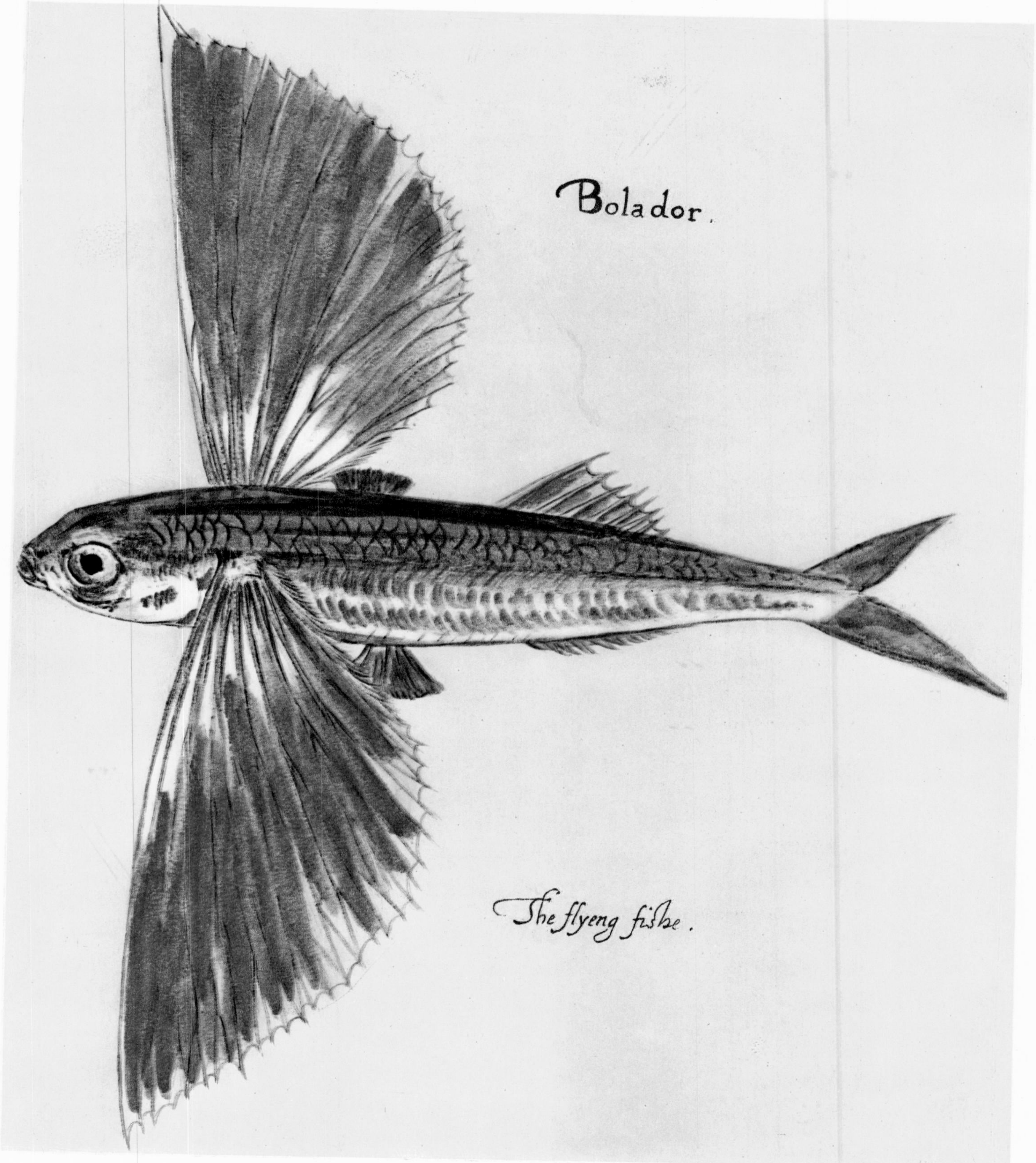

10⅞″ x 9⅛″

FLYING-FISH

Exocoetus volitans

Pese porco . Of this , some are . 2 . fote in length

5⅝″ x 8¾″

TRIGGER-FISH
Balistes vetula

REMORA
ventral view
probably *Remora remora*

4¾″ x 6⅛″

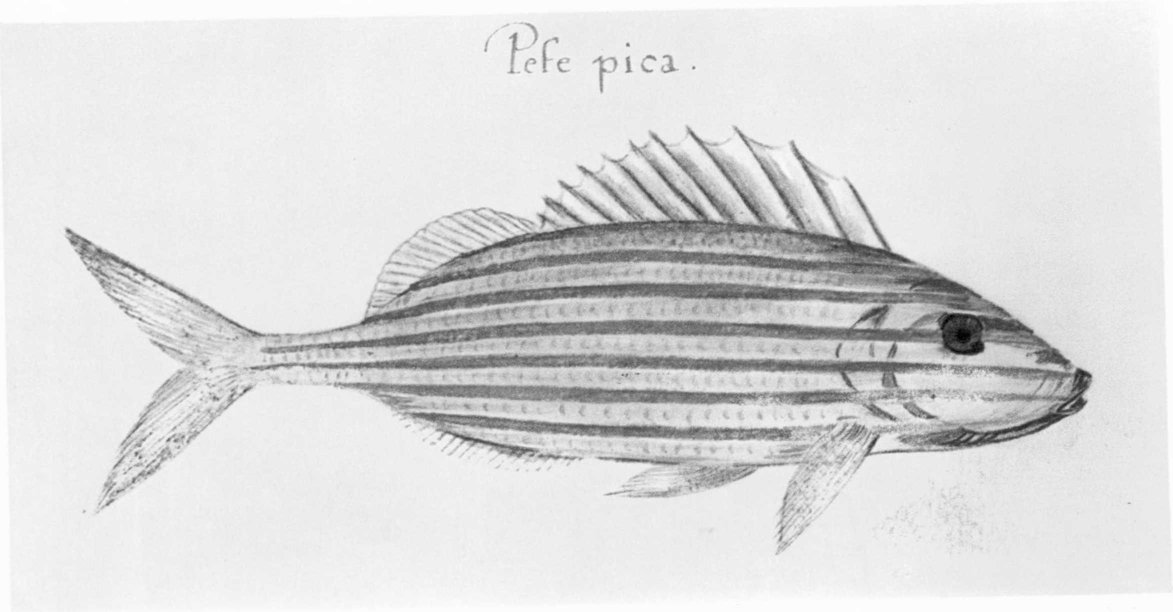

GRUNT
blue-striped
Haemulon sciurus

4⅜″ x 8⅜″

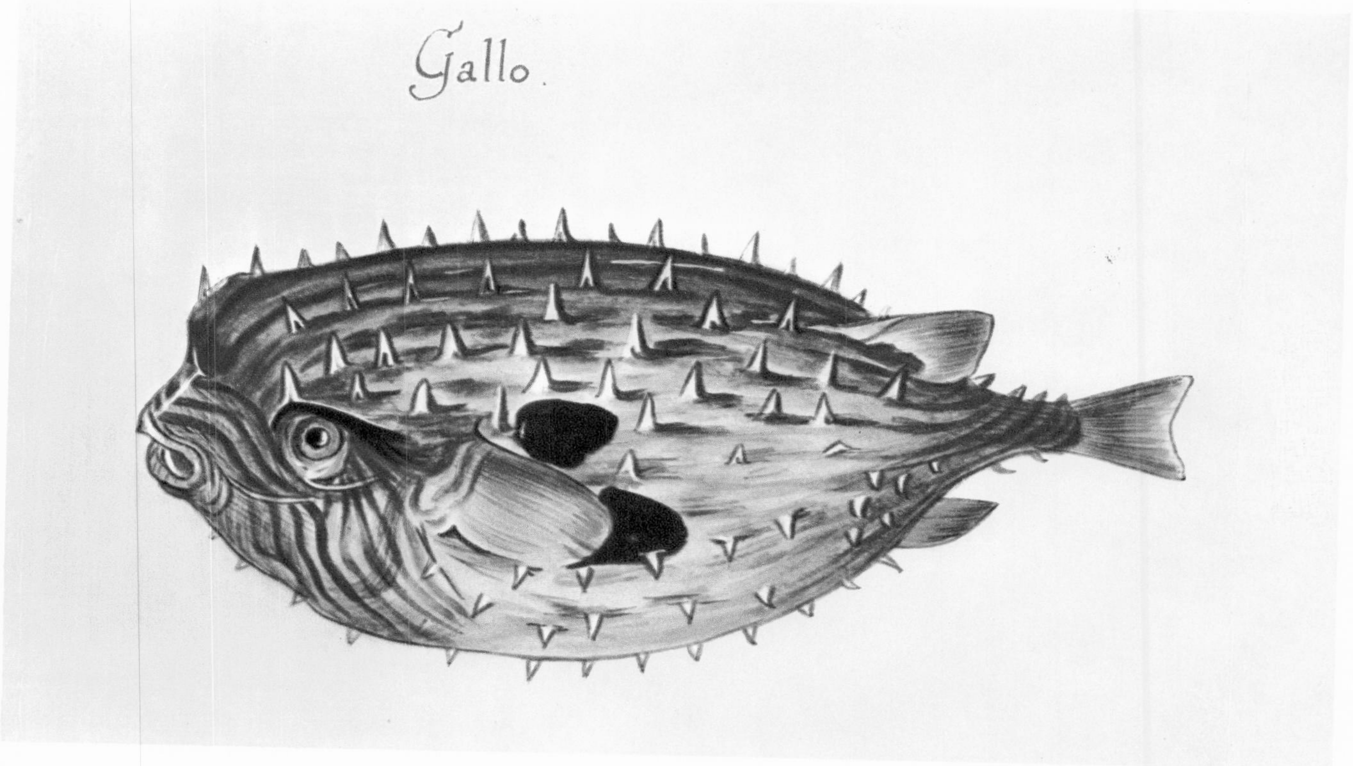

5⅛" x 8"

SPINY BOX-FISH
Chilomycterus schoepfi

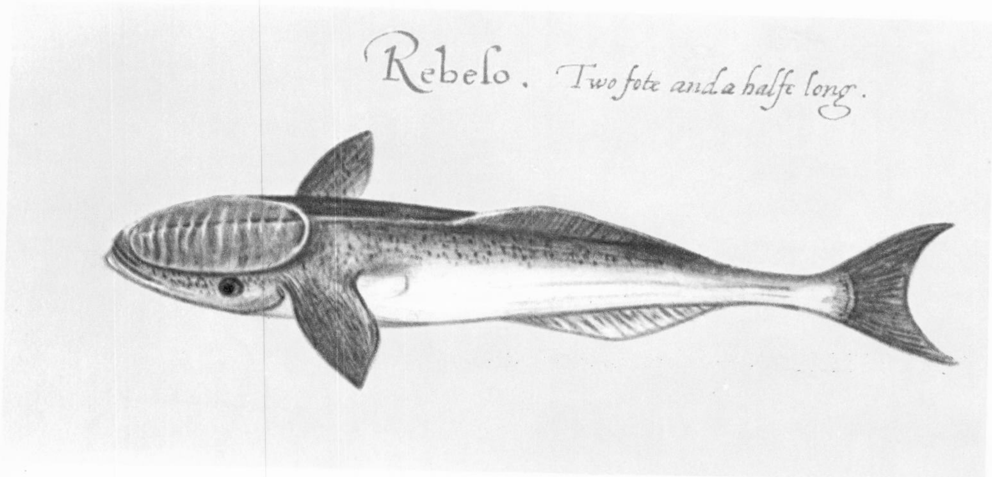

6" x 7¾"

REMORA
dorsal view
probably *Remora remora*

GROUPER
probably Yellow-fin Grouper
Mycteroperca venenosa

5⅛" x 8⅜"

Alcatrassa. This fowle is of the greatnes of a Swanne.
and of the same forme sauing the heade wch is in length 16 ynches
Tanhoril

HEAD OF A BROWN PELICAN—*Pelecanus occidentalis occidentalis*

7¼" x 8¾"

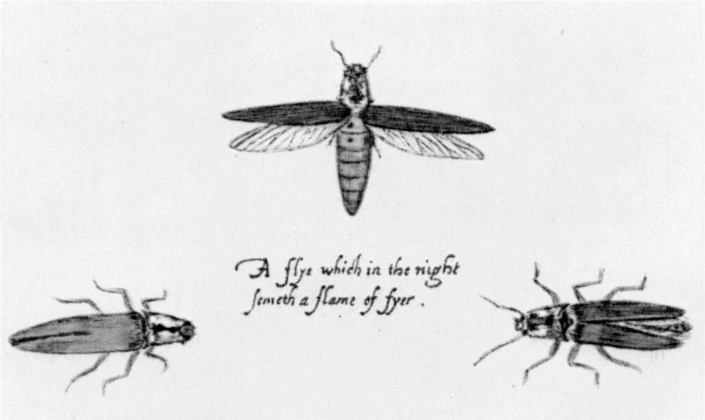
A flye which in the night semeth a flame of fyer.
A dangerous byting flye.

7⅞" x 7⅜"

FIREFLIES AND GADFLY

Three studies of a firefly (*Pyrophorus noctilucus*), a West Indian variety, and one gadfly (*Tabanus* sp.), which might be either from the West Indies or from North Carolina.

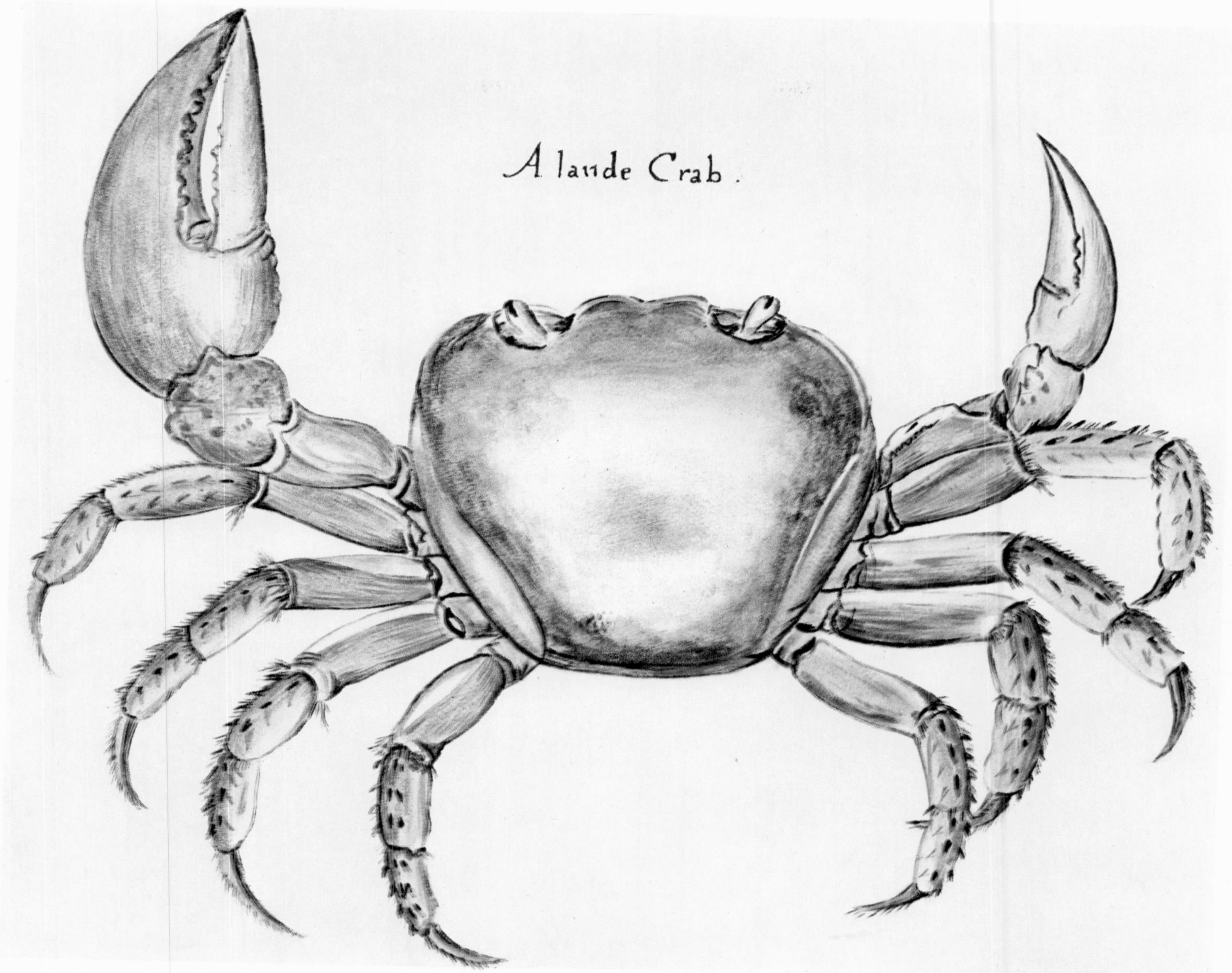

LAND CRAB, probably *Cardisoma guanhumi*

9⅛" x 10⅞"

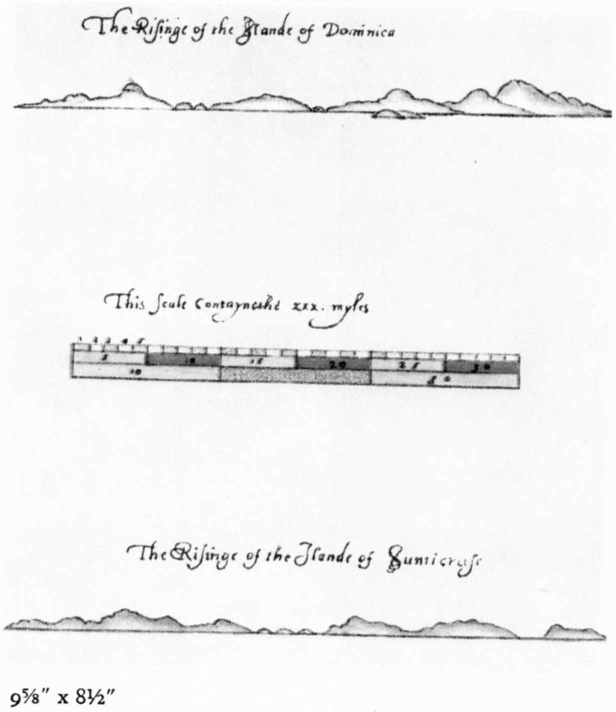

THE ISLANDS OF DOMINICA AND SANTA CRUZ

At the top, a coastal view of Dominica; at the bottom Santa Cruz (St. Croix of the Virgin Islands). Center: a scale of miles.

9⅝" x 8½"

 11⅝" x 7¾"

FLAMINGO

Phoenicopterus ruber

NODDY TERN 6⅛" x 9¼"

Anoüs stolidus stolidus

EUROPEAN COMMON ROLLER 6¼" x 8⅞"

Coracias garrulus; this drawing and the one on the following page depict European birds.

6⅞" x 8¾"

HOOPOE

Upopa epops; another European bird drawing by John White

5⅛" x 9⅛"

BROWN BOOBY

Sula leucogaster leucogaster

FRIGATE BIRD

Fregata magnificens Rothschildi

5⅜″ x 8¾″

6⅜″ x 8″

TROPIC BIRD

Phaeton aethereus mesonauta

5½" x 7¾"

SWALLOW-TAIL BUTTERFLY

Papilio glaucus

7⅜" x 6⅛"

LAND HERMIT CRABS

Coenobeta clypeatus

The shells are *Turritella variegata* (top) and *Natica canrena* (bottom).

4⅝" x 1⅞"

FIREFLIES

In the Sloane volume and in the manuscript of Thomas Moffet's *Insectorum . . . Theatrum* one can find almost identical representations of these flies.

A land Tort wch the Sauages esteeme aboue all other Torts

BOX TORTOISE

Terrapene Carolina Carolina

5⅝″ x 7¾″

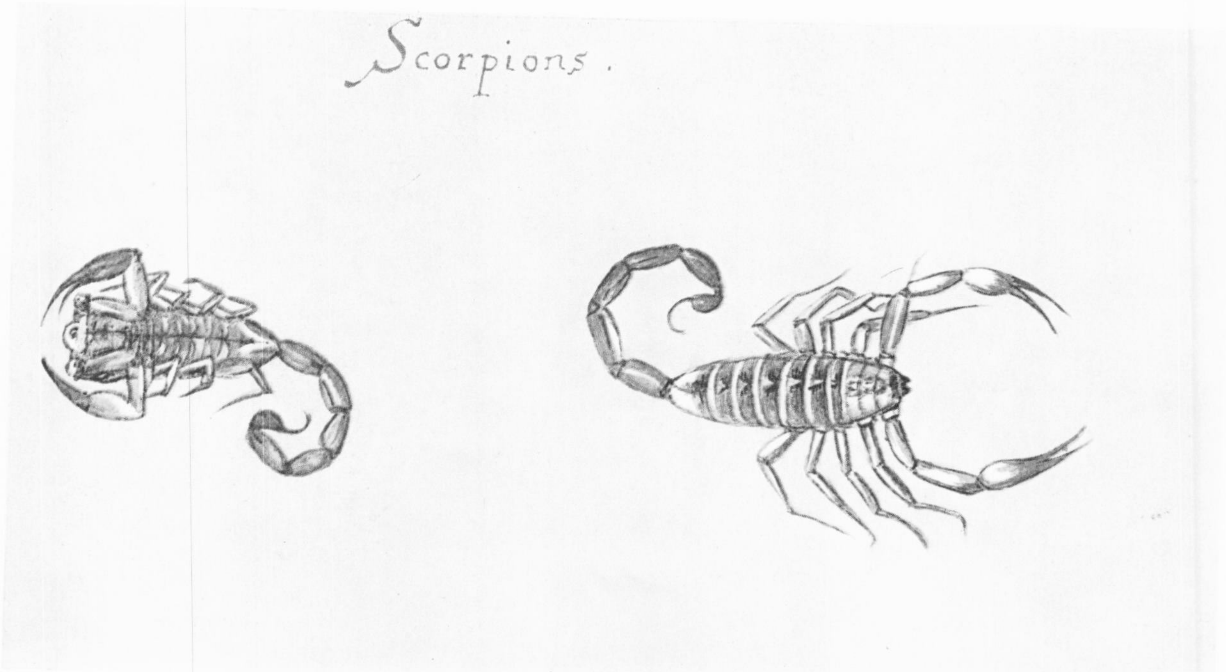
Scorpions.

STUDIES OF SCORPIONS

possibly *Tityus* genus, from the West Indies

4⅛″ x 7¼″

6⅞" x 10"

DIAMOND-BACK TERRAPIN

Malaclemys terrapin

Igwano . Some of thes are .3. fote in length. and lyue on land.

IGUANA 5⅝″ x 8¼″

probably *Cyclura* species of the West Indies

Allagatto . This being but one moneth old was .3. foote 4. ynches in length . and lyue in water .

ALLIGATOR OR CROCODILE 4⅜″ x 9⅛″

Crocodylus acutus or *Alligator Mississipiensis*

LOGGERHEAD TURTLE

Caretta caretta caretta

7⅜" x 10¼"

NOTES ON HARIOT

THE details of Hariot's life are lost in the mists of the past. Here and there an episode stands out clearly and sharply like a tree suddenly hit by the rays of the sun; yet, an instant later the clouds thicken, the sunshine departs, and the view is lost in darkness.

This we know. He was a friend of Raleigh. He was a protégé of Henry Percy, the ninth earl of Northumberland. He corresponded with Kepler, the great astronomer. He was a philosopher, a mathematician, and one of the foremost scholars of his age.

Born at Oxford in 1560, he studied in the town of his birth and was graduated from the University in 1580. Some time later Hariot met Sir Walter Raleigh and became his tutor in mathematics. And for nearly four decades, until that October day in 1618 when Raleigh's head rolled from the scaffold, the two remained close and devoted friends.

It was Raleigh who sent the twenty-five-year-old Hariot to Virginia in 1585 as surveyor and historian to the first English colony. Hariot stayed for a year in the New World investigating and exploring the land and making notes on the commodities and products of the country. He left Virginia the following spring when Sir Francis Drake called at Roanoke Island and took the exhausted colonists on board his ships. Hariot carried with him his notes and two strange plants, one of which later became known as *tobacco*, the other as the *potato*. Reaching England, he delivered the plants to Raleigh and his manuscript to the printer.

In 1588 Hariot's book was published under a long and tedious title (see original title page on p. 278). Yet what he wrote was vivid, crisp, and concise. It was an honest and trustworthy narrative of the English settlement at Roanoke Island, the first authentic eyewitness account of Raleigh's colony and a description of the *New found land of Virginia*.

It was not a large book, only a quarto in size, and it was printed in a small edition. It sold for a testone or two (about twenty-five cents). Today a copy of the first edition—if it should ever come to light—would be worth more than $10,000; the last recorded sale, in 1930, was made for $7,300.

Hariot's "True Report" was included in the first folio edition of Hakluyt's *Principal Navigations* and republished by De Bry in 1590 with engravings from John White's watercolors.

After Hariot's return to England, he was introduced by Raleigh to the Earl of Northumberland. They became friends, and Henry Percy gave the young scientist a life pension of one hundred and twenty pounds a year. Later, when Henry and Raleigh were in the Tower of London, accused of high treason, it was Hariot who brought the prisoners information and scientific data. It was he who collected material for Raleigh's *History of the World*, written during those long years of captivity, and supplied the Earl of Northumberland with news on mathematical problems. He was the prisoners' book of reference, their teacher, and their contact with the world outside.

In 1607 Henry Percy, while still in the Tower, assigned Thomas Hariot a residence at Sion House near Isleworth. Here Hariot settled down, studied, and worked until his death. Here he used a telescope at about the same time as Galileo. From here he sent letters to Kepler, complaining of his sickness and of his inability to write or even to think accurately upon any subject. Then, from 1615 on, a cancerous ulcer of the nose caused him great suffering. He died in July 1621 and was buried in the old St. Christopher's Church in London.

THEODORE DE BRY (*ca.* 1528-1598)

The engraver and publisher of the first pictures of America was born in Liège and took refuge from the religious persecutions in Frankfurt, Germany, where, in 1590, he began the publication of his "Grands et petits voyages." This portrait, engraved by the artist himself, shows De Bry a year before his death.

HARIOT

Thomas Hariot's *A Brief and True Report of the New Found Land of Virginia,* directed to the investors, farmers, and well-wishers of the project of colonizing and planting there. Imprinted at London in 1588.[1]

INTRODUCTION BY THEODORE DE BRY, THE PUBLISHER

ALTHOUGH, Dear Reader, on account of Adam's disobedience man was deprived of those good gifts with which he was endowed at the Creation, yet, as will be seen in the following account of the life of savage tribes, he still retained wit to provide for himself and to make whatever was necessary for his life and health—except in the matter of his soul's health. For although these savages have no knowledge of the true God or of His holy word and are without any learning, yet they surpass us in many things. Their way of eating is far more wise and moderate than ours, and they show the greatest ingenuity in making, without the aid of any metal tool, such fine and delicate articles as could hardly be believed if the Englishmen had not brought back the proofs from their travels in that country.

Admiring, as I did, the paintings made of these people, I wished to offer them to the public. This I have been able to do by the help of Master Richard Hakluyt of Oxford, a minister of God's word, who first encouraged me to publish the work. I copied exactly from the originals themselves, which were made by Master John White, an English painter who was sent to the New World by Her Majesty the Queen especially to make exact drawings of the country and its inhabitants, their way of dressing, their manner of living, and their several habits. This he did under the direction of Sir Walter Raleigh, the worthy knight who from 1584 to the end of 1588 spent large sums of money in the discovery and exploration of that country.

At the request of my friends, and because the memory of that recent feat is so fresh, I am publishing first the account of that part of the New World which the English call Virginia. If I were to regard the order of events, the history of Florida (which I already

1. The original title page of Hariot's book is reproduced on p. 278.

have in hand) should have first been published, since the French discovered and conquered that land in a notable victory long before the discovery of Virginia. However, I hope shortly to publish this work also. I obtained both of them in London and brought them here to Frankfurt, where I and my sons have taken the most earnest pains in engraving them carefully on copper, since the subject is one of great importance. I have had the text of both narratives translated into excellent French and Latin by a very learned friend of mine. In conclusion, I ask most earnestly that if anyone else should be found attempting to pirate this book of mine (for nowadays there are many dishonest people who try to get the benefit of another's work), that no credit should be given to the counterfeit copy, for I have put many secret marks in my drawings which will certainly cause confusion if they are omitted.

FOREWORD BY GOVERNOR RALPH LANE

GENTLE READER, *the truth of the reports contained in this treatise can little be furthered by the testimony of one like myself, judged to be partial, though without desert, because of my affection for the land. Nevertheless, at the request of some of my particular friends, who conceive more rightly of me, I have decided to write freely what I know of it. I do this not only to satisfy them but also for the true information of anyone else who comes without a prejudiced mind to its reading. This much upon my reputation I do affirm, that everything is truly set down in this treatise by its author, a member of the Colony and a man no less commended for his honesty than for his learning. I dare boldly avouch its truth will compare favorably with that of even the most true relations of this age. For my own part, I give my word it is true, assured of its certainty by my own experience, and I make this assertion publicly. Farewell in the Lord.*

THE ENGLISHMEN'S ARRIVAL IN VIRGINIA

BECAUSE of the many islands on the seacoast of Virginia it was difficult to discover an entry to the mainland. We found a number of large river mouths, yet, they proved to be so shallow and full of dangerous sandbanks that we could not follow them up into the interior. Before we came upon an entrance we made many attempts at different places and had sailed only a short way when we reached a broad river that descended in waterfalls into the sound opposite the islands. The shallows prevented us from going far up this stream; for the mouth of the river was choked with the sands that the tide drove in. Sailing farther, we reached a large island.

As soon as the inhabitants of this island caught sight of us, they set up a loud and terrible outcry, as if they had never before seen men dressed as we were, and they ran off screaming like beasts and yelling like madmen. But we called them gently back and offered them presents such as glass, knives, dolls, and other trifles which we thought would please them. Convinced of our good intentions and kindness, they slowly approached and made us welcome. They took us to their island village, called Roanoke, and to their Weroans, or chiefs, who entertained us courteously in spite of their astonishment at our appearance. Thus we reached the part of the world called Virginia.

On the following pages I will give you an exact account of the inhabitants of this country, their manners and customs, their dress, and their way of living.

HARIOT'S REPORT

TO THE INVESTORS, WELL-WISHERS, AND FRIENDS OF THE SETTLING AND PLANTING OF VIRGINIA

SINCE Sir Walter Raleigh first undertook the exploration of the country now known as *Virginia,* many voyages have been made there at different times at his expense. The first was in the year 1584; others followed in 1585 and 1586 and more recently, last year, in 1587. A number of reports about this land, some of them slanderous and shameful, were put in circulation by travellers who returned. These rumors were spread in particular about the voyage of 1585, when Sir Richard Grenville established a Colony in the New World. This was the most important of the enterprises, because the Colony stayed in Virginia a whole year, whereas the first settlers remained there only six weeks; all the later trips were made only for purposes of carrying supplies, and on these voyages nothing more was discovered.

These reports about Virginia have done much harm to many people who might otherwise have favored and invested in the project, thus honoring and benefiting the nation, besides making financial profit for themselves. I hope future events will bring shame to these tellers of tales; they will if you, the supporters and friends of the enterprise, increase in number, overcome any doubts you may have had, and renew your interest in the undertaking. I well understand that the various rumors have unsettled the minds of many among you concerning the worthiness of the Virginia enterprise, even of some of those most well disposed toward it.

Since I have been active in the discovery, had much experience in dealing with the native inhabitants and have therefore seen and known more than others, I thought it a good thing to acquaint you publicly with the fruits of our labors that you may see how wrongfully the enterprise has been slandered. I have two reasons for doing so: first, that those of you who are still ignorant or doubtful of conditions in Virginia may know that Sir Walter Raleigh, with the favor of Her Majesty, has seen good cause to proceed with the settlement. Not only has he sent ships there again and replanted the Colony during this last year, but also he is ready to continue further as means afford.

My second reason is that you may get a general idea of what the country is and of

A WEROANS, OR CHIEFTAIN, OF VIRGINIA

THE chieftains of Virginia wear their hair long, tied in a knot close to the ears. Their hair is cut from the top of the head down to the neck in the form of a coxcomb. One long bird's feather is stuck into the crest on their foreheads and a short one above each ear. They hang large pearls in their ears, or whatever else takes their fancy, such as a bird's claw. Their foreheads, cheeks, chins, bodies, arms, and legs are painted, but in a different manner from that of the inhabitants of Florida. Around their necks they have a chain of pearls or copper beads—which they consider of great value—and upon their arms they wear bracelets.

Their chests and stomachs are covered with spots where they have been bled when they were sick. They are dressed in cloaks made of finely cured skins, with the tail of the animal hanging down at their backs. Always ready to defend themselves, they carry a quiver made of rushes and in one hand hold a bow, in the other an arrow. So attired they go to war or attend their solemn feasts.

They love to hunt the deer, for the country abounds in such game; it is fruitful, pleasant, fertile, and thickly wooded. It has also many rivers filled with various kinds of fish.

When the chiefs go to battle they paint their bodies in the most hideous ways they can think of.

how you can profit from supporting it, either by settling there and planting or by furthering it in other ways.

Lest you should doubt the substance of my report, since it will differ from others, I will first say why it is different.

Of our company that returned from Virginia, some were deservedly punished there for dishonesty and bad behavior. In their ill nature they have spoken maliciously not only of their governors but also of the country itself, and they have been borne out in their tales by their companions.

Some of them were ignorant of the country. When they returned to their friends and acquaintances, they pretended to know more than other men, especially when there was no one in the gathering who could disprove them. They made themselves out to have suffered greater hardships than anyone ever suffered before. They put such great value on their reputations that they would have thought themselves disgraced if, after living in Virginia a year, they had not had a great deal to say, true or false. Some of them spun tales of things they never saw. Others shamefully denied happenings which they did not see, but which nevertheless were known to have occurred. Still others made difficulties of simple things because they did not understand them.

The cause of their ignorance was mainly that they never left the island where we had our settlement, at least not to go far from it, during the whole time we were there and therefore had seen little. Or they had lost interest when they did not immediately find gold and silver and spent their time in pampering their bellies. And there were others who had not much understanding, less discretion, and more tongue than was necessary.

Some of them had been nicely brought up, living in cities or towns, and had never seen the world before. Because they could not find in Virginia any English cities, or fine houses, or their accustomed dainty food, or any soft beds of down or feathers the country was to them miserable, and they reported accordingly.

My purpose in these remarks is merely to give a brief explanation of the opinions of these men. I do not mean to trouble you with details of these judgments and their envious, malicious, and slanderous reports; they are trifles not worthy of consideration. But I shall pass to a description of the marketable commodities of the country, which are the subjects of this discussion.

I will divide my treatise on the commodities into three separate parts, so that it may be easily read and understood. In the first I will enumerate commodities already found there, or which could be raised there to serve the ordinary needs of you who will be the planters and inhabitants of that country. A surplus of these can be provided by experienced men for trade and exchange with our own nation of England. It will enrich you, the providers,

ONE OF THE CHIEF LADIES OF SECOTA

THE women of Secota are clad in exquisitely dressed deerskins, which hang from the navel to the thighs and cover their buttocks—the rest of the body is naked. Their hair is cut short in front, somewhat longer at the back, and falls softly to their shoulders. Upon their heads they wear wreaths. Their foreheads, cheeks, chins, arms, and legs are chalked, and the pattern of a chain is pricked or painted around their necks. They have small eyes, plain, flat noses, narrow foreheads, and large mouths. In their ears they wear chains of long pearls or polished bones. They do not allow their nails to grow long, as the women of Florida do.

They love to walk in the fields and along the rivers, watching the deer-hunting and the fishing.

and those who will deal with you and will greatly profit our own countrymen by supplying them with many things which they have had to procure in the past either from strangers or from our enemies. These commodities, for distinction's sake, I call *marketable.*

In the second, I will set down all the goods that we know grow naturally there for food and sustenance of life, such as were commonly eaten by the inhabitants of the country as well as by us while we were in Virginia.

In the last part I will list such other general commodities as I am able to remember. Here I shall also give a brief description of the nature and manners of its inhabitants.

The First Part

CONCERNING MARKETABLE COMMODITIES

Grass silk. There is a kind of grass in the country which has a thin, glistening skin. When this is stripped off, it makes very good silk. The grass grows two feet and a half high or even more, while the blades are about two feet long and half an inch broad. A similar kind can be found in Persia, which has the same climate as Virginia. If one cultivated the grass as the Persians do, it could quickly become a profitable business, because silk is widely used and sold both in our country and elsewhere. And when the grass is planted in good ground, it will grow larger, better, and more plentiful, although there is even now a great abundance of it growing wild in many parts of the country. We tested this grass on our return to England, by making a piece of grosgrain silk, and found it of excellent quality.

Worm silk. In many of our journeys we came across fine, large silkworms, as big as walnuts. Although we did not find them in such abundance as we heard that they existed in other parts of the country, yet since they grow so naturally there, a successful industry could be established. If mulberry and other trees which feed and nourish the silkworms were planted in spacious places, and if they were carefully gathered and husbanded with expert skill, the industry would in time yield as great a profit to the Virginians as it does now to the Persians, Turks, Italians, and Spaniards.

Flax and hemp. The truth is that there is not a great supply of flax and hemp growing in any one place, because it is not planted, but grows wild. Although the leaf and stem, or stalk, differ from ours, those men who know assert that the product is of about the same quality. And if future trials should confirm this, we now have enough experience with the soil to believe that our variety will grow there excellently and, if planted, will yield a plentiful crop. There is so much land that some of it may well be applied to such purposes. The benefits from cordage and linens anyone can easily understand.

ONE OF THE PRIESTS OF SECOTA

THE priests of the town of Secota are well advanced in years and have greater experience than the ordinary natives. Their hair is cut in a crest on the top of their heads; the rest of it is short and falls over their foreheads like a fringe. Earrings adorn their ears. They wear a short cloak made of fine rabbit skins, quilted and with the hair side outward; the rest of their bodies is bare.

These men are well-known sorcerers. Their pleasure is to hunt with bow and arrow the wild ducks, swans, and other waterfowl along the rivers.

Alum. There is a vein of earth running along the seacoast for forty or fifty miles, and in the judgment of those who have tested it here in England good alum could be made from it, of the kind known as *rock alum.* The same earth also yields *white copperas, niter,* and *feather alum,* but not so plentifully as the common *alum,* which is more profitable.

Wapeih. This is the name given by the natives to a kind of earth very like *terra sigillata.* Having been refined, it has been found by some of our physicians and surgeons to be of the same virtue and even more effective than *Lemnian earth.* The inhabitants use it a good deal to cure sores and wounds. It is found in great abundance in many places and is sometimes blue in color.

Pitch, tar, resin, and turpentine. The kinds of trees which yield these products grow abundantly. The island where we lived—fifteen miles long and five or six miles wide—was full of them. There were scarcely any other trees.

Sassafras. The inhabitants call it *winauk,* a wood of the most pleasant and sweet smell and of rare virtues in medicine for the cure of many diseases. It is far better and has more uses than the wood which is called *Guaiacum,* or *lignum vitae.* For the description, manner of using, and manifold virtues of it, I refer you to the book of Monardus, translated and entitled in English, *The Joyful News from the West Indies.*

Cedar. A very sweet wood which makes fine timber. Chests of drawers, fair and fine bedsteads, tables, desks, lutes, virginals, and many other things (which we have already made) could be fashioned from it and shipped to make up freight with other principal commodities that would yield profit.

Wine. There are two kinds of grapes that grow wild there. One is sour and the size of the ordinary English grape; the other is lusciously sweet and much larger. When they are planted and husbanded as they should be, an important commodity in wines can be established.

Oil. There are two kinds of walnuts, both of which yield oil, though one far more plentifully than the other. If there were mills and other devices of the sort, large amounts of oil could be obtained. Three different kinds of oak acorns also grow there, and we were told by the inhabitants that these acorns yield very good, sweet oil. We could also get oil from the fat bears of the country, since there are great numbers of them, and their fat is so liquid that it could be used as oil for many special purposes.

Furs. All along the seacoast there are many otters, and if they could be caught by weirs and other traps, they would make us good profits. We hope also to get marten furs, for the people say that in some places they are plentiful, although during our stay in Virginia only two skins came into our hands. We also heard of lynxes, but we did not see any.

Deer skins, dressed in the manner of chamois or raw, are to be had yearly by the thou-

A YOUNG GENTLEWOMAN OF SECOTA

M*AIDENS of good family are dressed like the women of Secota, save that they wear a necklace instead of a chain around their necks. It is made of large, round pearls, interspersed with little beads of copper, or polished bones.*

They chalk their foreheads, cheeks, arms, and legs and cut their hair into two fringes and draw it into a knot at the back. They have large mouths and comely black eyes. As a sign of maidenly modesty they often put their hands upon their shoulders, thus covering their breasts.

sand from the natives through trade for trifles. And even so, there would be no more waste or spoil of deer than there has been in the past.

Civet cats. In our travels we found a civet cat, which was killed by one of the natives. In another place we came upon the smell of them. From this evidence, as well as from what the people told us, we know that these animals are found in the country, and much profit could be made from them.

Iron. In two places especially, one about fourscore, the other sixscore miles from our fort, the ground near the water's edge was rocky. When our mineral man tested it, he discovered that it held iron in rich amounts. Not only there but also in many other parts of the country iron is found. I believe this will become a good marketable commodity, considering the infinite stores of wood for smelting and the small cost there of labor and food, especially if one compares it with the scarcity and high cost of wood in England. Another manner of profiting from it would be to use it as ballast for ships.

Copper. A hundred and fifty miles inland we found that the inhabitants of two towns had several small plates of copper. They told us these had been made by the natives farther up in the interior, where, they say, are mountains and rivers that yield copper and also white grains of metal, which we deemed to be silver. In confirmation of this I may say that when we first arrived in Virginia we saw two small pieces of roughly beaten silver about the weight of a testone[1] hanging in the ears of a *Weroans,* or chief, who lived about fourscore miles from us. Upon inquiring from him how many days' journey and in what direction the place was, I learned that it was near where the copper and white grains of metal had been found. We tested this copper and discovered that it contained silver.

Pearls. There were often pearls in the mussels we ate. But they are always pied in color. We have not yet discovered where the better pearls in greater abundance are. One of our company, a man skilled in such matters, had gathered about five thousand from the savages. Out of these he chose enough to make a rare chain of pearls, uniform in roundness, luster, and size, and of a variety of excellent colors. The chain would have been presented to Her Majesty had we not lost it, along with many other things, in a terrible storm as we were leaving the country.

Sweet gums of different kinds and many other apothecary drugs can be found there. I have learned more about them from men who have knowledge in these matters and have had time to examine them more carefully. For want of the samples lost in the storm, I cannot now describe them.

Dyes of different kinds. There is *shoemake* [sumac], well known in England and used for black; the seed of a herb called *wasewówr;* a small root called *cháppacor;* and the

1. Henry VIII's shilling.

A CHIEF OF ROANOKE

THE chiefs of the island and of the town of Roanoke wear their hair cut in a coxcomb on top, but the rest they allow to flow long, and tie it in a knot at the nape of their necks. They string pearls on a thread and hang them in their ears, and on their arms they wear bracelets of pearl or small copper or bone beads, which they call minsal. *They do not paint or pumice themselves, but as a sign of honor and authority wear a chain of large pearls or copper or polished bone beads around their necks; a copper plate is hung from the waist to the thighs. They cloak themselves, as the women do, in a handsomely dressed and fringed deerskin. When they walk or talk they cross their arms one above the other as a sign of wisdom.*

The island of Roanoke is very pleasant, and the waters surrounding it abound in fish.

bark of the tree called by the inhabitants *tangomóckonomindge*. These dyes are for different shades of red, and their suitability for our English clothes remains yet to be proved. The inhabitants use them for dyeing hair and for coloring their faces, also for deer skins and for dyeing rushes to make patterns in their mats and baskets. If they should not prove marketable, there is no doubt the planters will find uses for them and also for the other colors which we know to be there.

Woad. This dyestuff is largely sold and used among English dyers. There is never enough of it in our own country, as we lack space for growing it. But in Virginia, where there is land enough, it could be planted easily. It will grow there without any doubt, since the climate is the same as that of the Azores, where woad and madder grow plentifully.

Sugar canes we took with us to plant, but since they were not as well preserved as they should have been and the time of year for setting them was past when we arrived, we could not make the experiment we wished. Nevertheless, seeing that they grow in a similar climate in the southern part of Spain and in Barbary, we can reasonably hope they will grow in Virginia. The same holds true for oranges, lemons, and quinces. From these, in reasonable time and if the undertaking is diligently prosecuted, no small commodities in sugars, sweetmeats, and marmalades may develop.

Many other goods, which I leave to your discreet and gentle consideration, may be raised there. And there are also many already growing which we have not yet discovered. I might have specified two more commodities of great value, which do not have to be planted, but can be raised there and prepared in a short time. Also, I could have revealed more of these I have enumerated, told the particular places where they are found and could best be planted and prepared. And I could have said how soon they would bring profits and how great these profits would be, but I have not done so, because I fear that persons other than well-wishers might learn too much from my description and that would not be to the advantage of the enterprise. I have omitted these facts, knowing that I have revealed enough in this part for those who are well disposed toward the Virginia undertaking.

A NOBLEWOMAN OF POMEIOCK

ABOUT twenty miles from Roanoke, near the Lake of Paquippe, is another town called Pomeiock, close to the sea. The chief ladies of that town dress very much like the women of Roanoke. Their hair is worn in a knot, and their skin is pumiced. Around their necks they wear a chain of large pearls or copper beads or smooth bones five or six strands deep. This gives support to one of their arms. In the other hand they usually carry a gourd full of some pleasant drink. Their clothing is a deerskin, tied double and folded high under their breasts, reaching almost to their knees in front, while their backs are almost naked.

They are very often accompanied by their young daughters. These little girls of seven or eight years wear girdles of skin, padded with moss, which pass between their legs. But as soon as they reach the age of ten, they dress in deerskins just as the older ones do. When we gave them the puppets and dolls that we had brought from England, they were highly delighted.

HARIOT

The Second Part

CONCERNING SUCH COMMODITIES AS VIRGINIA IS KNOWN TO YIELD FOR FOOD AND THE SUSTENANCE OF LIFE, CUSTOMARILY EATEN BY THE NATIVES AND USED BY US WHILE WE WERE THERE; FIRST, CONCERNING SUCH AS ARE SOWN AND FARMED.

Pagatowr is a kind of grain. It is called *maize* in the West Indies; Englishmen name it *Guinea wheat* or *Turkey wheat,* after the countries from which a similar grain has been brought. This grain is about the size of our ordinary English peas and, while similar to them in form and shape, differs in color, some grains being white, some red, some yellow, and some blue. All of them yield a very white and sweet flour which makes excellent bread. We made malt from the grain while we were in Virginia and brewed as good an ale of it as could be desired. It also could be used, with the addition of hops, to produce a good beer. The grain increases on a marvelous scale—a thousand times, fifteen hundred, and in some cases two thousand fold. There are three sorts, of which two are ripe in ten, eleven, and, at the most, twelve weeks, when their stalks are about six or seven feet in height. The third one ripens in fourteen weeks and is ten feet high. Its stalks bear one, two, three, or four heads, and every head contains five, six, or seven hundred grains, as near as I can say. The inhabitants not only use it for bread but also make food of these grains. They either parch them, boiling them whole until they break, or boil the flour with water into a pap.

Okindgier we called *beans,* because they are like the beans in England, except that they are flatter, more varied in color, and some are pied. The leaf on the stem is also different. However, they taste as good as our English peas.

Wickonzówr. We named these *peas* to distinguish them from the beans, because they are much smaller. They differ little from the beans, though they taste different and are far better than our English peas.

Both the beans and the peas ripen in ten weeks. The natives boil them in a broth, where the beans are reduced to small pieces or boil them whole until they are soft and begin to break, as we prepare them in England. These peas are either cooked by themselves or mixed with wheat. Sometimes after they have been boiled whole they are pounded in a mortar and made into loaves or lumps of doughy bread.

Macócqwer. This is the native name for what we call pumpkins, melons, and gourds. In Virginia there are several varieties of this family, all of which taste very good. There are two varieties of *macócqwer,* one of which is ripe in a month, the other in two months.

AN OLD MAN IN HIS WINTER CLOTHES

THE old men of Pomeiock cover themselves with large skins that hang down below the knees and are tied on one shoulder, leaving the other arm free. The skins are dressed without removing the fur, and lined with other skins. The younger men do not allow hair to grow upon their faces, they pluck it out as soon as it comes in; but when they get older, they let their beards grow, which are very thin. They wear their hair in a knot at the back and cut in a crest in front, as the others do.

The country round Pomeiock is far more fruitful than England.

There is an herb which is called *melden* in Dutch. Some people to whom I have described it believe that it is a kind of *orach* [mountain spinach]. It grows about four or five feet high, and the natives make a thick fine-tasting broth of its seeds. From the stalk of the herb they produce a kind of salt by burning it to ashes. This is the only salt they know, and they season their broths with it. We ourselves have used the leaves for pot-herbs.

There is also another large herb, which resembles the marigold, about six feet high. The head is a span in width with the flower. Some believe it to be *planta solis* [sunflower]. From its seeds a kind of bread and also a broth are made.

All the commodities I have described are planted, sometimes separately, but more often mixed together in one plot. To make you understand the fertility of the soil, I will explain briefly how the natives prepare the ground and how they go about the planting.

They never enrich the soil with refuse, dung, or any other thing, nor do they plough or dig it as we do in England. They simply break the upper part of the ground to raise up the weeds, grass, and old stubs of cornstalks with their roots. This is done by the men a few days before they sow, using wooden instruments made almost like mattocks or hoes with long handles, while the women sit on the ground helping with short peckers or parers about a foot long and five inches in breadth. After the weeds have dried in the sun for a day or two, the refuse is scraped up into many small heaps and burned to ashes. This they do to save themselves the labor of carrying it away, rather than to enrich and better the ground.

Then they sow the seed. For corn they begin in one corner of the plot and make a hole with a pecker. They put four grains into each hole, about an inch apart, taking care that they do not touch one another, and cover them with soil. The seeds are planted in rows, each row spaced half a fathom or a yard from the last, and the holes in each row are the same distance apart. Thus, there is a yard of spare ground between the holes, where the natives sometimes set beans and peas or plant *macócqwer, melden,* and sunflowers.

The planted ground, compared with an English acre of forty rods in length and four in breadth, yields at least two hundred London bushels of corn, beans, and peas, in addition to the crop of *macócqwer, melden,* and sunflowers. In England we think it a large crop if an acre gives forty bushels of wheat.

So that you who will live and plant there may know how much that country's corn is to be preferred to ours, I thought it good to tell you this. Besides the many ways it may be used for food, the yield is so great that little labor is needed in comparison with what is necessary in England. Of this I can assure you, for according to our experiments we found that one man may prepare and cultivate as much ground (which has borne corn before) with less than twenty-four hours' labor as will supply him food in abundance for

HOW THE CHIEF LADIES OF THE TOWN OF DASAMONQUEPEIO DRESS AND CARRY THEIR CHILDREN

IN THE *town of Dasamonquepeio, four or five leagues from Roanoke, the women dress and paint themselves as the women of Roanoke do, except that they do not wear wreaths on their heads or paint their thighs. They carry their children in an unusual fashion, quite different from ours. While our women usually hold them in their arms, the women of Dasamonquepeio place their infants on their backs, holding its right hand and clasping its left thigh under their left arm.*

a year. This is true even though he has no other food save what was grown in that ground, and of no other kinds than those I have spoken of, and even if the plot were only twenty-five yards square. If it were necessary, two crops could be raised on the same plot. For the natives sow at any time from the middle of March until the end of June and can still plant after they have eaten from their first harvest. We have heard that in some places they do harvest two crops from the same ground.

As to English corn, whether you who will live there should wish to use it or not, you may decide as you think best after trial. You need not doubt that it will grow, for we have seen the proof with barley, oats, and peas. We did not purposely plant these; the seeds fell casually in the worst sort of ground, and yet they grew to be as fair as any we have ever seen in England. We could not try our wheat, because it was musty and had soaked up salt water, nor could we test our rye.

There is an herb called *uppówoc,* which sows itself. In the West Indies it has several names, according to the different places where it grows and is used, but the Spaniards generally call it *tobacco.* Its leaves are dried, made into powder, and then smoked by being sucked through clay pipes into the stomach and head. The fumes purge superfluous phlegm and gross humors[2] from the body by opening all the pores and passages. Thus its use not only preserves the body, but if there are any obstructions it breaks them up. By this means the natives keep in excellent health, without many of the grievous diseases which often afflict us in England.

This *uppówoc* is so highly valued by them that they think their gods are delighted with it. Sometimes they make holy fires and cast the powder into them as a sacrifice. If there is a storm on the waters, they throw it up into the air and into the water to pacify their gods. Also, when they set up a new weir for fish, they pour *uppówoc* into it. And if they escape from danger, they also throw the powder up into the air. This is always done with strange gestures and stamping, sometimes dancing, clapping of hands, holding hands up, and staring up into the heavens. During this performance they chatter strange words and utter meaningless noises.

While we were there we used to suck in the smoke as they did, and now that we are back in England we still do so. We have found many rare and wonderful proofs of the *uppówoc's* virtues, which would themselves require a volume to relate. There is sufficient evidence in the fact that it is used by so many men and women of great calling, as well as by some learned physicians.

2. According to an old medical theory man was supposedly composed of four humors: blood, phlegm, choler, and melancholy; an excess of any one of them was thought to cause disease.

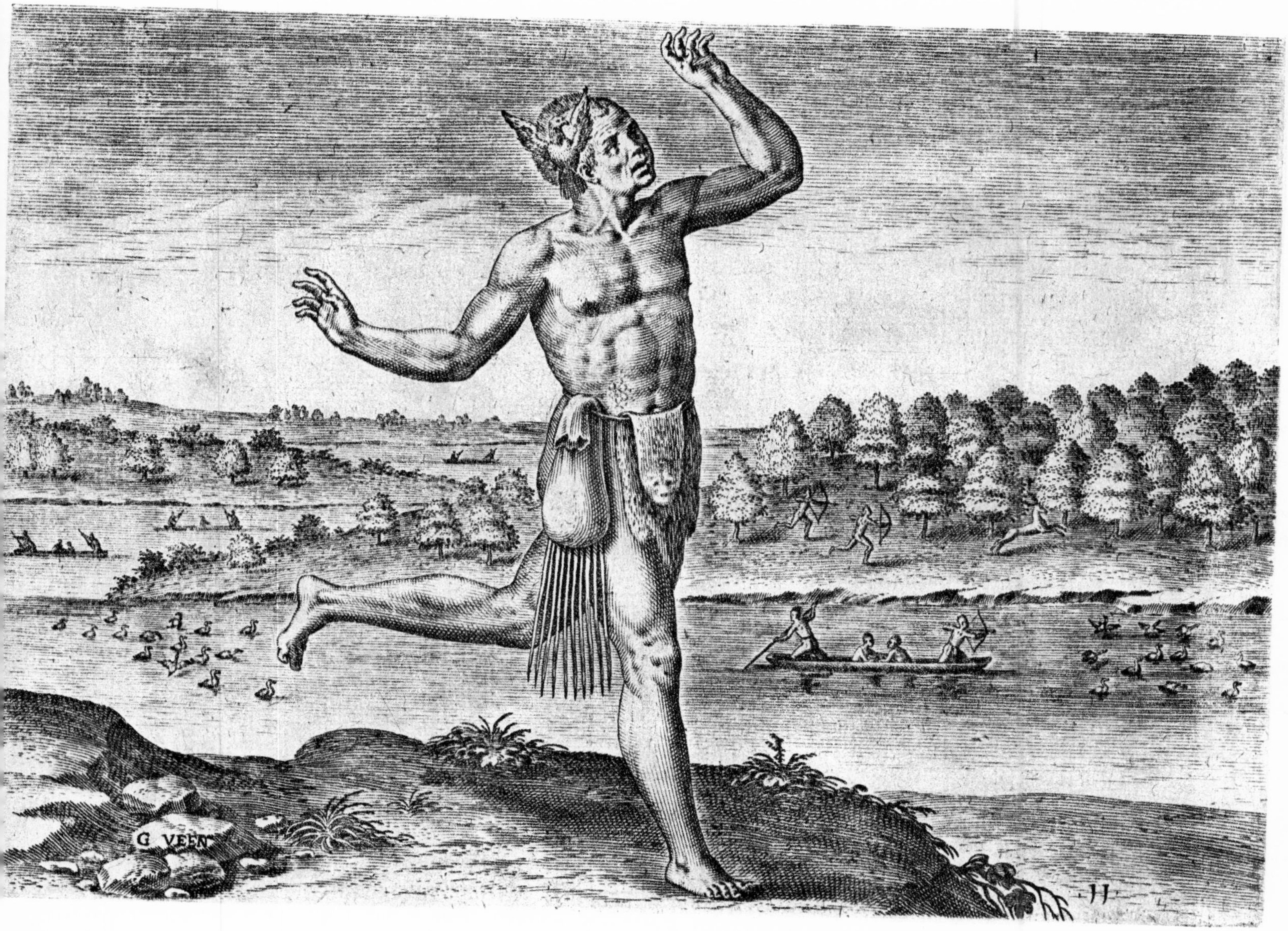

THE SORCERER

THEY *have sorcerers or jugglers who use strange gestures and whose enchantments often go against the laws of nature. For they are very familiar with devils, from whom they obtain knowledge about their enemies' movements.*

They shave their heads entirely, except for the crest, which they wear as the others do. A small black bird is fastened above one of their ears as a badge of office, and their only garment is a skin hanging from their girdle. On one side they wear a pouch.

The natives pay great attention to the sorcerer's words, which they often find to be true.

HARIOT

CONCERNING ROOTS

Openauk is a kind of round-shaped root the size of walnuts or larger. It is found in moist or marsh grounds growing together in ropes, as though fastened with string. When boiled it makes a very good food.

Okeepenauk is also round in shape, but is found in dry places. Some of these roots are as large as a man's head. They have to be eaten as soon as they are taken out of the ground, because they are dry and will neither boil nor roast. They do not taste as good as the first-named kind, but even so the inhabitants eat them with fish or meat, especially when they do not have bread or wish to vary their food. In my judgment it is as good as the English household bread made of rye.

Kaishúcpenauk is a white root about the size and shape of a hen's egg. It does not taste as good as the other; therefore we did not pay much attention to the manner of its growth. Still, the inhabitants often boil and eat it.

Tsinaw is much like the root called *China root* here in England, which is brought from the East Indies. And for all we know, it may even be the same. The roots grow in large clusters, the stalk is like that of a briar, but the leaf has a very different shape. It grows near trees, and sometimes climbs to the top of the highest. The fresh-dug roots are chopped into small pieces and pounded, and the juice formed by the adding of water is strained and used to make bread. When the root is boiled it gives a very good spoon-meat [pudding] like a jelly and is even better if the taste is tempered with oil. This *tsinaw* cannot be the same as *China root,* for it has been discovered since *China root* was brought into England; the roots are, however, very similar in shape.

Coscushaw. Some of our men believed this to be the same root which the Spaniards of the West Indies call *cassavy;* we therefore gave it the same name. It grows in muddy pools and moist ground. Prepared in the native fashion, *cassavy* makes not only a good bread but also a good spoon-meat. The juice of this root is poison, and for this reason care must be taken before anything is made with it. Either the roots must first be sliced and dried in the sun or by a fire and pounded into flour, or else they must be peeled while they are green, cut into pieces, and then beaten. The loaves made from the flour must be laid near or over the fire until they are sour. After this they are well pounded again, and the bread or spoon-meat made from them has a very good taste.

Habascon is a root like a parsnip in size and shape and hot in taste. It is not used by itself, but is boiled to flavor other foods.

There are also *leeks* in many parts of the country, differing very little from ours. We gathered and ate them, but the native inhabitants never did.

HOW THEY BUILD BOATS

THE way they build their boats in Virginia is very wonderful. For although they completely lack any iron tools such as we use, they can make boats as good as ours. And these boats are seaworthy enough to take them sailing or fishing wherever they want to go.

First they choose a tall, thick tree of the size required for the boat's frame. Then they light a fire close to its roots, feeding it bit by bit with dry moss and small chips of wood, keeping the flames from mounting too high. When the tree is almost burnt through, they make a good fire to cause it to fall. Then they burn off the top and boughs, taking care that the trunk should not be shortened.

The tree is raised upon a platform built on forked posts at a height convenient for working. The bark is stripped off with sharp shells; the inner length of the trunk is kept for the bottom of the boat. A fire is made all along the length of the trunk, and when it has burned sufficiently it is quenched and the charred wood scraped away with shells. Then they build a new fire, burn out another piece, and so on, sometimes burning and sometimes scraping, until the boat has a good bottom. Thus God has endowed these savages with enough reason to make the things they need.

CONCERNING FRUITS

Chestnuts grow in great abundance in several places. The natives eat them raw, or crushed and boiled; they also make the same kind of dough bread from the boiled chestnuts that they do from the beans.

Walnuts are of two kinds, and there is an infinite number of both. In some of their great forests a third of the trees are walnut. The one kind is very similar in taste and form to the English walnut, only harder and thicker shelled. But the other kind is larger, with a hard and ragged shell. The kernels of the fruit are very oily and sweet. The inhabitants either eat them or make a milk of them by breaking the nuts with stones and grinding the powder in a mortar with water. This they add to their spoon-meat, their boiled wheat, peas, beans, and pumpkins, thus giving the food a far more pleasant taste.

Medlars are an excellent fruit, which are not tasty until they are rotten-ripe. They are about the size of our medlars and open at the head as ours do, but otherwise they differ both in taste and color. Their color is as red as cherries, and their taste is sweet, but while the cherry's sweetness is sharp, medlars are luscious.

Metaquesúnnauk. This is a pleasant fruit, almost the same shape and size as our English pear. Its color is a perfect red, both inside and out. The plant that bears it has thick leaves full of prickles, sharp as needles. Men who have visited the Indies and seen there the kind of red dye called *cochineal* relate that its plant is very like that of *metaquesúnnauk.* Whether they speak of the true *cochineal* or of a wild variety I cannot say, as I think that true *cochineal* does not come from the fruit, but is found on the leaves of the plant.

Grapes. I have mentioned two kinds of grapes under the marketable commodities.

HOW THEY CATCH FISH

THEY have a remarkable way of fishing in their rivers. As they have neither steel nor iron, they fasten the sharp, hollow tail of a certain fish (something like a sea crab), to reeds or to the end of a long rod, and with this point they spear fish both by day and by night. Sometimes they also use the prickles and pricks of other fish. And they make traps with reeds or sticks set in the water and narrowing at the ends, as shown in the picture. They have different kinds of fish, many of them never found in our waters, and all of an excellent taste.

It is a pleasing picture to see these people wading and sailing in their shallow rivers. They are untroubled by the desire to pile up riches for their children, and live in perfect contentment with their present state, in friendship with each other, sharing all those things with which God has so bountifully provided them. Yet they do not render Him the thanks which His providence deserves, for they are savage and have no knowledge of any gods except those I have already mentioned.

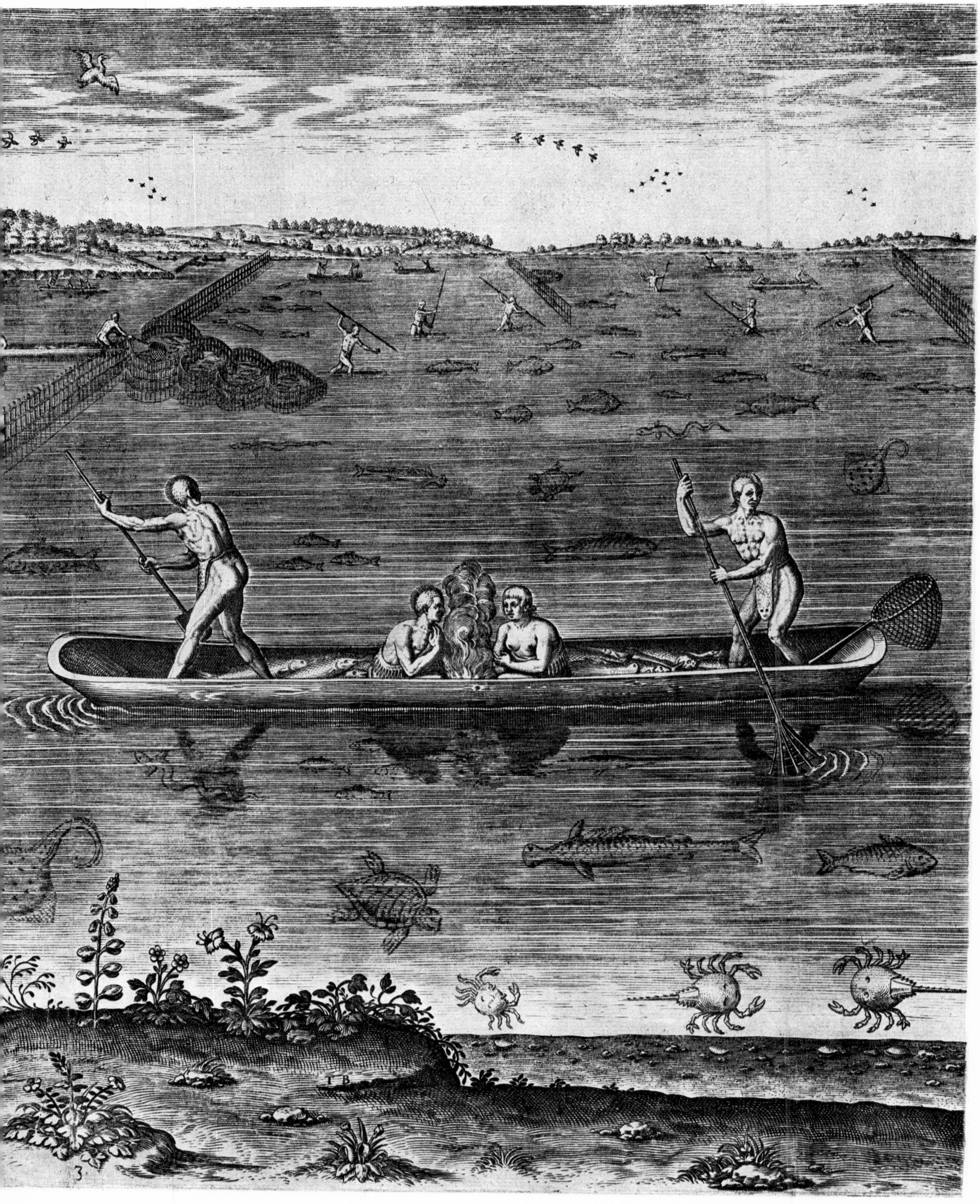
T B
3

Strawberries found in Virginia are as good and as large as those we have in our English gardens.

Mulberries, crab-apples, and whortleberries are the same as those we have in England.

Sacquenummener. These berries look like capers, but are somewhat larger. They grow in clusters on a plant or herb found in shallow waters. If boiled eight or nine hours they give good, wholesome food, but if they are eaten raw they will make a man frantic and extremely sick for a time.

There is also a variety of reed which bears a seed much like our rye or wheat and when boiled, makes a good food.

In our travels we found in some places wild peas very much like our English peas, except that they were smaller.

CONCERNING A KIND OF FRUIT OR BERRY LIKE THE ACORN

There are five different sorts of berries or acorns growing on trees. The kinds called *sagatémener, osámener,* and *pummuckóner* are dried upon a fire on a hurdle made of reeds, very much as we dry malt in England. When the berries are ready, the natives water them until they are soft, then boil them. They are eaten either raw or pounded into loaves or lumps of bread. The berries are also used for making sweet oil.

Another kind is the *sapúmmener,* which, boiled or parched, tastes like chestnuts and is eaten in much the same way.

The fifth kind is called *mangúmmenauk.* The acorns are dried like the other berries and then soaked and boiled. Not only the ordinary natives but also the chiefs themselves eat them with fish or flesh, instead of bread.

CONCERNING BEASTS

Deer. In some places there are a great number of deer. Near the seacoast their size is that of our ordinary English deer, though sometimes they are smaller; but farther inland, where there is better feed, they are larger. They differ from our deer in two ways: their tails are longer, and the snags of their horns point backward.

Conies, or rabbits, are gray in color like hares. In some places there are so many that the people of the towns make mantles for themselves of the fur or down from the skins.

Saquenúckot and *maquówoc,* two small animals somewhat larger than rabbits, make good meat. We have not caught any of them, but ate many which the natives brought to us.

Squirrels. We caught and ate gray squirrels.

Bears are black in color. In the winter the natives shoot and eat a great many, just as

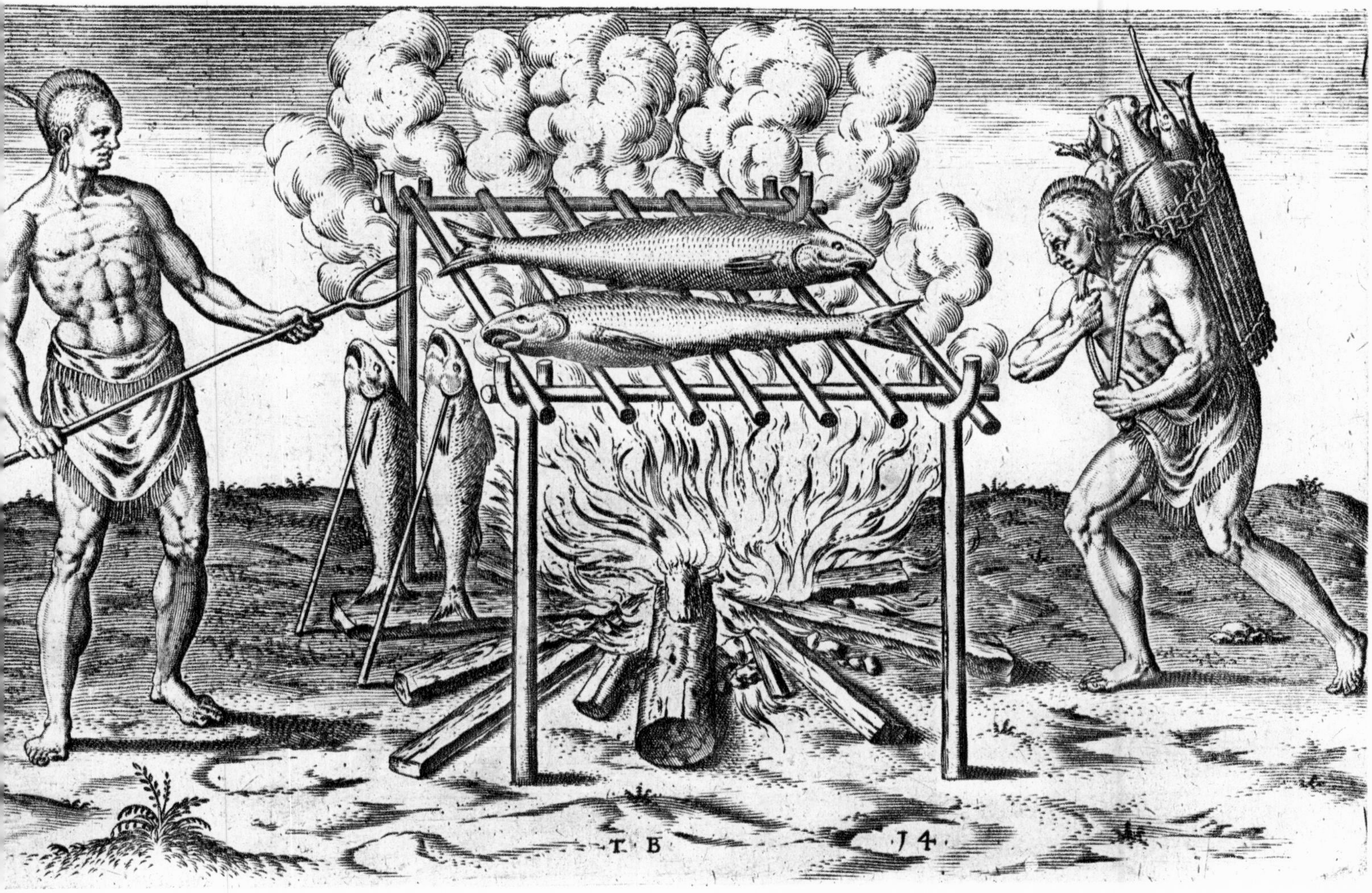

HOW THEY COOK THEIR FISH

WHEN the natives have caught enough fish, they assemble in a place where they can easily prepare them. They stick four stakes of equal height into the ground with a number of posts across them. The fish are laid upon the platform, and a fire is built beneath it.

While the people of Florida dry and cure their fish in the smoke for winter storage, these savages preserve nothing; they always use up everything at once, and whenever they need more fish, they again roast or boil them fresh.

After the platform is full of fish and will hold no more, the rest of the catch is hung at the sides, or on sticks close to the fire, until there is room for them. So they cook their whole catch at once, taking good care not to burn the fish. As soon as some are cooked, they are replaced by others; in this way they continue to cook their game until they think they have enough.

we did. They are hunted in certain islands or in places where they are especially abundant. When the bears perceive a man, they run away, and when they are chased, they climb the nearest tree, from which the natives shoot them down. We too have hunted them and killed them with our muskets.

I have the names of twenty-eight different kinds of beasts which I have been told are found in various parts of the country. Of these we have so far discovered only twelve, and those which are good for food I have already mentioned. At times the natives kill a lion and eat it, and we ourselves have eaten their *wolves* or *wolfdogs*. These I have not set down as good meat, lest my judgment in the matter be thought more simple than it is. I could describe, though, how different is the taste of the Virginia wolves from that of our English ones, for some of our company have eaten both.

CONCERNING FOWL

Turkey cocks and *turkey hens, stockdoves, partridges, cranes,* and *herons. Swans* and *geese,* which could be had in winter in great abundance, may be added to these. I have noted in the native language the names of eighty-six different kinds of fowl. Besides those I have already named, we have caught and eaten, as well as made pictures of, several different varieties of waterfowl and seventeen kinds of land fowl. We have seen and eaten many others as well, but had not the leisure to draw pictures of them. When we make further discoveries and have better examples, I shall publish all we know about the strange beasts, fish, trees, plants, and herbs there.

We found also *parrots, falcons,* and *merlins,* which we do not use for food, but I thought it would be well to mention them for other reasons.

CONCERNING FISH

For four months of the year—February, March, April, and May—there are plenty of *sturgeon* and *herring*. Some of these fish are the size of those we find commonly in England, but most of them are far larger—eighteen, twenty inches, and some two feet in length and more. We found them to be a most delicate and pleasant food.

There are also *trout, porpoises, rays, oldwives, mullets, plaice,* and many other varieties of excellent fish which we caught and ate. I know their names only in the language of the country. But we made pictures of twelve different kinds of fish while we were there.

The natives catch fish in two different ways: one is by trapping them in a kind of weir made of very strong reeds; the other is by using a pole sharpened at one end, and spearing the fish in much the same way as Irishmen cast darts. This they do either while wading in the shallows or while rowing in their boats.

HOW THEY BOIL MEAT IN EARTHENWARE POTS

THEIR *women have the greatest skill in making large earthen pots, which are so fine that not even our own potters can make any better. These are carried around from place to place just as easily as our own brass kettles. They set them up on a pile of earth and then put wood underneath and kindle it, taking great care that the fire burns evenly on all sides. They fill the pot with water, then put fruit, meat, and fish into it, and let it boil together as in a gallimaufry, which the Spaniards call* olla podrida. *When it is cooled, they serve it in small dishes and set them before the company, who make good cheer together. But they eat with moderation and thus avoid illness. I would to God that we followed their example. We should then be free of many of our diseases, caused by our too sumptuous and too frequent banquets, at which we indulge in too many kinds of rich sauces devised to arouse a gluttonous and insatiable appetite.*

There are also plenty of shellfish, *sea crabs* such as we have in England, and large and small *oysters.* They are found both in salt and brackish water, and, as in our own country, those taken from salt water are the best. Besides these, there are *mussels, scallops, periwinkles,* and *crayfish.*

Seékanauk, a kind of crusty shellfish, is a good food. It is about a foot wide, has a crusty tail, many legs, like a crab, and its eyes are set in its back. It can be found in salt-water shallows or on the shore.

Tortoises, both of the land and sea varieties, are more than a yard in breadth, with thick shells on their backs and bellies. Their heads, feet, and tails look very ugly, like those of a venomous serpent. Nevertheless, they are very good to eat, as are their eggs.

Thus, I have told about all the kinds of food eaten in Virginia that I can remember and that are worthy of mention.

The Third and Last Part

CONCERNING OTHER THINGS THE PLANTERS SHOULD KNOW OF, WITH A DESCRIPTION OF THE PEOPLE OF THE COUNTRY; CONCERNING COMMODITIES FOR BUILDING AND OTHER NECESSARY THINGS

I wish to say a few words concerning the different kinds of trees, which could be used for building and for ship's timber and also to list the lime, stone and brick we saw in that country. If I did not mention them, their existence might be doubted, or some malicious persons might say they are not found in Virginia.

Oaks grow fair, straight, and tall and make as good timber as exists. There are a great number of them, and in some places they are very large.

Walnut trees. As I have said before, there are very many walnuts; we saw some growing above fourscore feet, straight and without a bough. They make excellent timber four or five fathoms long.

Fir trees, suitable for making ships' masts, grow very large and tall.

Rakíock is a kind of sweet wood that the inhabitants in our vicinity use for their boats and canoes. They make their boats simply by the use of fire, stone hatchets, and shells for shaping them. Some of their canoes, made of a single tree, are large enough to carry twenty men and much baggage besides. The timber is thick, tall, straight, soft, and light, yet it is tough enough, I think, to be suitable also for the masts of ships.

Cedar is a sweet wood suitable for ceilings, chests, boxes, bedsteads, lutes, virginals,

HOW THEY EAT

THIS is their way of eating. They lay a mat of twigs on the ground and set their meat in the middle of it. Then they all sit around it—the men on one side, the women on the other. Their meal consists of boiled maize, which has an excellent flavor, deer flesh or some other kind of meat, and fish. As they are very temperate, both in eating and in drinking, and do not overload their constitutions, they are very long-lived.

and many other things. Some of our company, who explored places where I did not go, affirm that *cypress* is to be found there. This wood has great value, many excellent uses, and is held in high estimation.

Maple and witch hazel. The natives make their bows of this wood.

Holly is needed in making birdlime.

Willow may be used for making weirs and traps for catching fish in the English manner. The inhabitants use only reeds, which, since they are strong and flexible, serve the purpose well.

Beech and *ash* are good for cask hoops, plow work, and many other things.

Elm.

Sassafras.

Ascopo. This tree is very much like laurel, its bark spicy and hot in taste, similar to the tree which Monardus describes as *cassia lignea* of the West Indies.

Many other strange trees can be found there, whose names I know only in the Virginian language. I do not think it necessary to describe them in detail now, for I have named enough for timber and other uses. But I have no doubt that some of the woods I have not mentioned can be used to good advantage.

Stone, brick, and *lime.* Near the seacoast where we dwelt we could not find any stones save a few small pebbles about four miles away. All the stones had to be brought from the mainland. On some of our trips we saw several hard, ragged stones, great pebbles, and a kind of grey stone like marble, which the inhabitants used for their wood-cutting hatchets. When we inquired, we learned that a little farther inland there was an abundance of all kinds of stone. The natives are ignorant of quarries, and they do not keep a supply of stone. Every household has only one or two to crack nuts, grind shells, and whet copper, and also keeps a few in reserve for hatchets. They do no digging, except for their graves, which are about three feet deep. It is therefore not surprising that they have no quarries or any limestone, though both may exist near by, unknown to them.

In the meantime, until a good supply is discovered in some convenient place, you, the future planters, could use brick for building. This could be easily made, as there is

---

PRAYING AROUND THE FIRE WITH RATTLES

WHEN they have escaped some great danger on sea or land, or have returned safely from the wars, they light a great fire to celebrate. Men and women sit around it, each of them holding a rattle made of a certain kind of gourd, from which the fruit and seeds have been removed and replaced with small stones or kernels. These gourds they fasten to sticks and shake as they sing and make merry.

I thought this strange custom worth observing and noting down.

T.B.
17

THE DANCES AT THEIR GREAT FEASTS

AT A certain time of year the savages hold a great and solemn feast at which all their neighbors from the adjoining towns assemble. They come dressed in very strange fashion, wearing marks on their backs signifying the places they come from. They meet on a broad open plain enclosed by tall posts carved into faces resembling those of veiled nuns. Then, standing in a certain order, they dance and sing, making the strangest movements they can think of.

Three of the most beautiful virgins, their arms about each other, turn around and around in the center.

The festivities begin after sunset, when the air is cool and the heat of the day is gone.

Some of the savages, when they are tired of dancing, leave the circle and retire, their places being taken by others.

plenty of good clay in many places. Lime could be used for the same purpose, made of oyster or some other shells and burned as they do in the Isles of Thanet, Sheppey, and other parts of England. This kind of lime is known to be as good as any other. As for oyster shells—one can find them with the greatest ease and in great abundance in many places, particularly in one shallow sound along the coast. Here, for many miles along the shore and for three miles inland, the ground is covered with them.

A gentleman of our company found a great vein of hard, ragged stones a hundred and twenty miles from our fort, near the water in the side of a hill. I thought it good to tell you of this.

CONCERNING THE NATURE AND MANNERS OF THE PEOPLE

It remains to speak a word or two about the native inhabitants, their nature and manners, leaving detailed discourse about them until a later, more convenient time. Now it is only necessary to reassure you that they are not to be feared. I do not think they will trouble our living there or obstruct our farming. I rather believe that they will have cause both to fear and to love us.

The clothing of the natives consists of loose deerskin mantles and aprons of the same fur which they wear around their waists; they wear nothing else. In stature they differ one from another, much as we do in England. They have no edged tools or weapons of iron or steel to attack us with, nor do they know how to make them. The only weapons they possess are bows made of witch hazel, arrows made of reeds, and flat-edged wooden truncheons, which are about a yard long. For defense they wear armour made of sticks wickered together with thread, and they carry shields made of bark.

THE TOWN OF POMEIOCK

THE towns in this country are not unlike those in Florida, but they are neither so well built nor so carefully looked after. They are surrounded with poles stuck into the ground and have only a narrow entrance. Only the chief and his principal men live in houses. On the right in the picture is the temple (marked A), built without windows, the only light coming through the door. On the opposite side is the King's house (B).

These dwellings are made with posts joined to each other and covered with matting, which can be rolled up to let in light and air. Some of the houses are covered with the boughs of trees—each man builds as he likes.

Feasts and celebrations are held in the middle of the town. If the place is far from the water, they dig a pool (C), from which they fetch all the water they need.

A
B
C
T B
19

Their towns are small and few, especially near the seacoast, where a village may contain but ten or twelve houses—some perhaps as many as twenty. The largest town we saw had thirty houses. In many cases the villages are walled with stakes covered with the bark of trees or with poles set close together.

The houses are built of small poles attached at the top to make them round in shape, much like the arbors in our English gardens. The poles are covered from top to bottom either with bark or with mats woven of long rushes. The dwellings are usually twice as long as they are wide; sometimes they are only twelve or sixteen yards long, but we have seen them as much as twenty-four yards in length.

In one part of the country a *Weroans,* or chief, may govern a single town, but in other parts the number of towns under one chief may vary to two, three, six, and even to eight or more. The greatest *Weroans* we met governed eighteen towns, and he could muster seven or eight hundred warriors. The language of each chief's territory differs from that of the others, and the farther apart they are, the greater the differences.

Their manner of making war against each other is by a surprise attack, either in the dawn of day or by moonlight, by ambush, or by some such subtle trick. Set battles are very rare. When they do take place, it is always in the forests, where the natives may defend themselves by leaping behind a tree after they have shot their arrows.

If we should ever fight the inhabitants, the results can easily be imagined. We have great advantages over them, for we have disciplined soldiers, strange weapons, devices of all sorts, and especially we have large and small ordnance. So far we found their best defense against us was to turn on their heels and run away.

THE TOWN OF SECOTA

THOSE of their towns which are not fenced in are usually more beautiful, as can be seen in this picture of the town of Secota. The houses are farther apart and have gardens (marked E), in which they grow tobacco, called by the natives uppówoc. *They also have groves of trees where they hunt deer, and fields where they sow their corn. In the cornfields they set up a little hut on a scaffold, where a watchman is stationed (F). He makes a continual noise to keep off birds and beasts which would otherwise soon devour all the corn. They sow their corn a certain distance apart (H), so that one stalk should not choke the next. For the leaves are large like great reed leaves (G).*

They also have a large plot (C) where they meet with neighbors to celebrate solemn feasts, and a place (D) where they make merry when the feast is ended. In the round plot (B) they assemble to pray. The large building (A) holds the tombs of their kings and princes. In the garden on the right (I) they sow pumpkins. There is also a place (K) where they build a fire at feast time, and just outside the town is the river (L) from which they get their water.

These people live happily together without envy or greed. They hold their feasts at night, when they make large fires to light them and to show their joy.

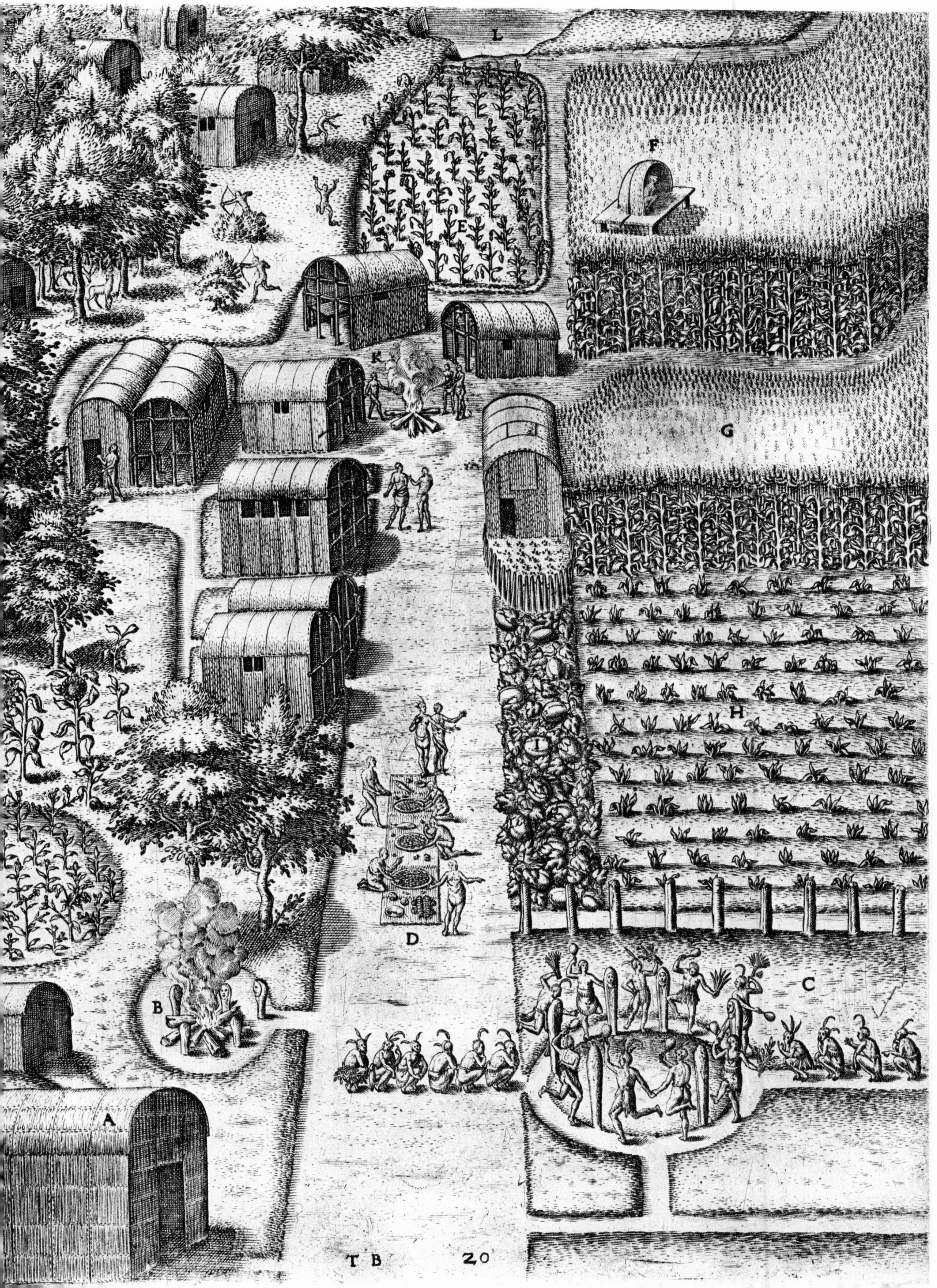

L
F
E
K
G
H
I
D
C
B
A
T B
20

Compared with us, the natives are poor. They lack skill and judgment in using the materials we have and esteem trifles above things of greater value. But if we consider that they lack our means, they are certainly very ingenious. Although they do not possess any of our tools, or crafts, or sciences, or art, yet in their own way they show excellent sense. In time they will find that our kinds of knowledge and crafts accomplish everything with more speed and perfection than do theirs. Therefore, when they realize this, they will most probably desire our friendship and love, and, respecting our achievements, they will try to please and obey us. Whereby, if we govern them well, they will in a short time become civilized and embrace the true religion.

They have already a religion of their own, which is far from the truth, yet for that reason there is hope that it may sooner and more easily be reformed.

They believe in many gods, which they call *Mantóac*. These gods are of different kinds and degrees. Their chief god has existed from all eternity. They affirm that when he created the world, he first made the other principal gods, in order to use them in the creation and government to follow. Then he made the sun, the moon, and the stars. The petty gods act as instruments of the more important ones. The natives say that the waters of the world were made first and that out of these all creatures, both visible and invisible, were formed.

As to the creation of mankind, they think that the woman came first. She conceived and brought forth children fathered by one of the gods, and in this way the natives had their beginning. But how many ages or years have passed since then, they do not know, for they have no writing or any means of keeping records of past time, only the tradition, passed on from father to son.

They believe that all the gods have human shapes; therefore they represent them by images in the form of men and call the images *Kewasówok*. A single god is called *Kewás*. These images are set up in temples which they call *Machicómuck*. Here the natives worship, pray, sing, and make frequent offerings to the gods. In some of these temples we saw only one *Kewás*, but others had two or three. Most of the natives think that the images themselves are the gods.

The natives believe also in the immortality of the soul. They say that after this life the soul departs from the body, and, according to its works in life, it is either carried to heaven, where the gods live, or else to a great pit or hole. In heaven it enjoys perpetual bliss and happiness, but in the pit, which is situated at the farthest part of their world toward the sunset, it burns continually; this place they call *Popogusso*.

In confirmation of this belief, they told me stories about two persons who had lately died and revived again. One occasion was but a few years before we came to Virginia and con-

THEIR IDOL

THEIR idol, Kewás, is four feet high and carved of wood. Its head is like those of the people of Florida; the face is flesh-colored, the breast white, and the rest all black except the thighs, which are spotted with white. Around the idol's neck is a chain of white beads interspersed with round copper beads, which they value more than gold or silver.

Kewás is placed in the temple of Secota to guard their dead kings. Sometimes there are two of these idols in their temples—sometimes three, but never more—set in a dark corner, where they have a terrifying appearance.

The savages have no knowledge of gods, although I believe they are anxious to learn about the true Lord. For when we knelt down to pray, they imitated us, moving their lips as we moved ours. They could very easily be taught the true gospel—may God in His mercy grant them this grace.

cerned a wicked man who died and was buried. The day after the burial the natives saw that the earth of his grave had begun to move, and took him up again. The man made a declaration, saying that his soul had been about to enter into *Popogusso,* when one of the gods had saved him and given him leave to return to earth to teach his friends what they should do to avoid that terrible place of torment.

The other event happened during the year we were in Virginia in a town only about threescore miles away. Again a dead man had been buried and had returned to the earth. He related that his soul had travelled far along a wide road, on both sides of which grew the most delicate and pleasant trees, bearing rare and excellent fruits of such fine qualities that he could scarcely describe them. At length he came to some beautiful houses, where he met his dead father. The father instructed him to go back to earth and to tell his friends that he was enjoying the pleasures of heaven, and after he had done so to return.

Whether or not the *Weroans* and priests use subtle devices with the common people, the belief in heaven and the fiery pit makes the simple folk give strict obedience to their governors and behave with great care, so that they may avoid torment after death and enjoy bliss. Evil-doers have to pay for their crimes in this world, nevertheless. Thievery, whoremongering, and other wicked acts are punished with fines, beatings, or even with death, according to the seriousness of the offense.

This sums up their religion. I learnt of it from some of their priests with whom I became friendly. They are not fully convinced of its truth, for in conversing with us they began to doubt their own traditions and stories. They expressed great admiration for our religion, and many showed an earnest desire to learn more than we, with our small knowledge of their language, were able to tell them about it.

THE TOMB OF THE WEROANS

UNDER the tombs of their Weroans, or chief lords, they build a scaffold nine or ten feet high, as this picture shows. They cover this with mats and upon them they lay the dead bodies of their chiefs. First the intestines are taken out; then the skin is removed and all the flesh cut from the bones and dried in the sun. When it is well dried, they wrap it in mats, which they place at the feet. Then the bones, still held together by the ligaments, are covered with the skin and made to look as if the flesh had not been taken away. They wrap each corpse in its own skin after it has been thus treated and lay it in its rightful order beside the bodies of the other chiefs. Near the bodies they place their idol, for they are convinced that it keeps the bodies of their chiefs from all harm.

Under the scaffold lives one of their priests, who is in charge of the dead and mumbles his prayers night and day. He sleeps on deerskins spread on the ground, and if it is cold, he lights a fire.

The natives are taught by their law to worship their chiefs even after their death.

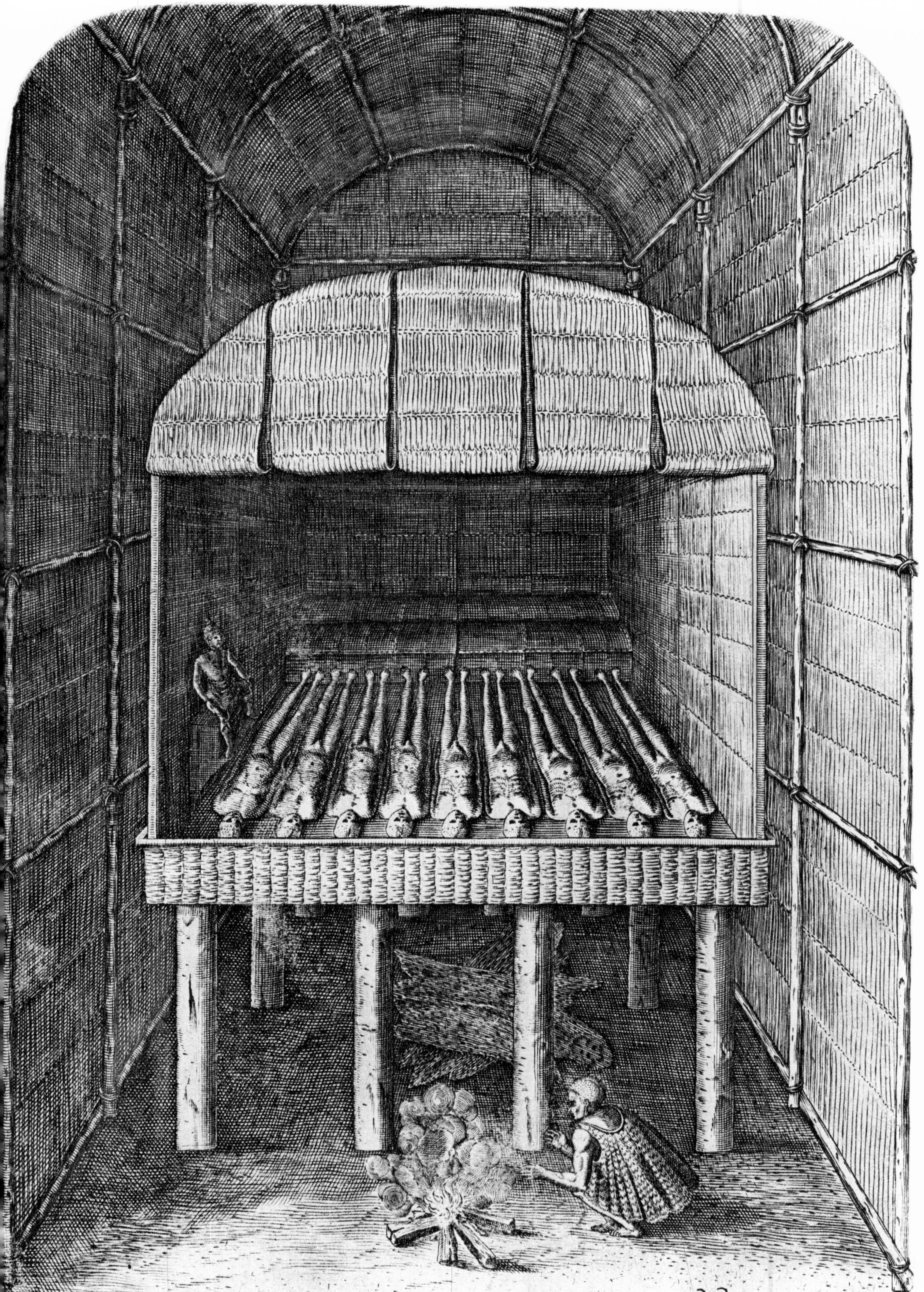

22

They marvelled at all that we had, such as mathematical instruments, mariner's compasses, the loadstone, which attracted iron, a perspective glass,[3] in which they saw many strange sights, burning glasses,[4] fireworks, guns, books, and spring clocks that seemed to go by themselves. All these things were beyond their comprehension, just as reading and writing were utterly strange to them. They could not understand how they were constructed and how they worked and thought all these things must have been made by the gods or that the gods must have presented them and taught us how to make them. Therefore they began to admire us and thought it wise to learn the meaning of the true God and the true religion. Seeing our abilities and possessions, they believed more readily in our words.

Many times and in every town I came to I described the contents of the Bible as often as I could. I told the natives that there was set forth the only true *GOD* and His mighty works, with the true doctrine of salvation through Christ. I related the miracles and the chief points of religion to them, as many as I thought fit and could recount at the time. And although I told them that the book itself had no great virtue, but only the doctrine it contained, still they wished to touch, embrace, and kiss it, and to hold it to their breasts and heads and stroke their whole bodies with it. Thus did they show their hungry desire for its knowledge.

Wingina, the chief with whom we lived, and many of his people joined us often at our prayers. He called upon us many times, both in his village and in other villages where he accompanied us, to pray and to sing Psalms, hoping thereby to benefit from the effects we also expected from those means.

On two different occasions this *Weroans* was so seriously ill that he seemed likely to die. As he lay languishing, he doubted that his own priests could help him; therefore he sent for us and asked us to pray to our God that he might either live or dwell in bliss with Him after death. And not only he but also many other natives asked us to pray for them.

Another time their corn began to wither because of an unusual drought. They feared that this had come to pass because they had displeased us in some way. A few of them came to us asking that we should pray to our English God that he should preserve their corn, and they promised that when it was ripe they would share the harvest with us. Whenever they suffered from some sickness, loss, accident, or other misfortune, they believed that this came to pass because they had offended or displeased us.

Before I come to the end of my narrative I want to mention one other rare and strange occurrence which moved the inhabitants of the whole country to a wonderful admiration for us. When trickery was practiced against us in any town, we were careful to leave it

3. Probably a spyglass.

4. Magnifying glasses.

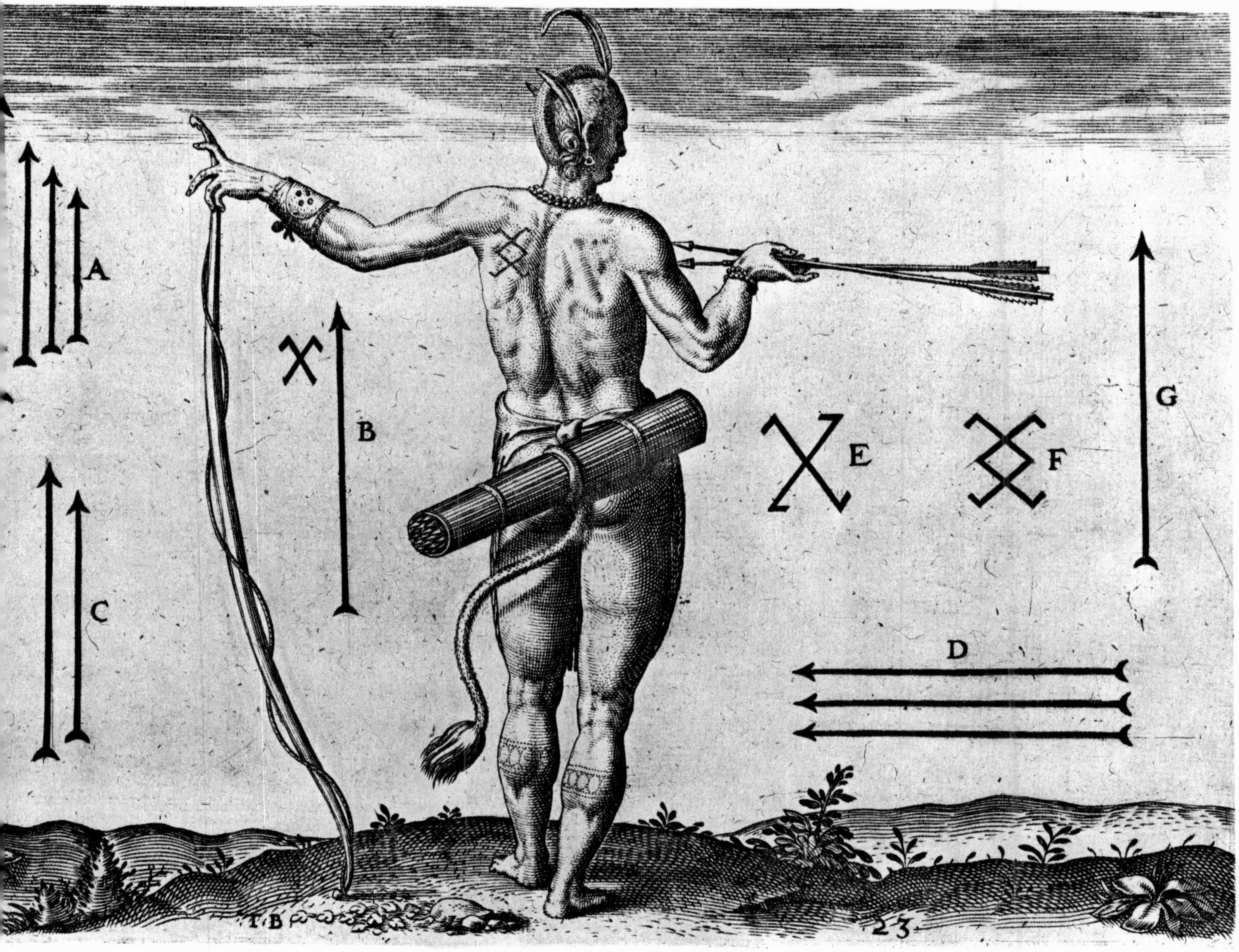

THE MARKS OF THE CHIEF MEN OF VIRGINIA

ALL the inhabitants of this country have marks on their backs to show whose subjects they are and where they come from. I therefore copied these marks in this picture, together with the names of the places, so that they might more easily be seen.

God has made these savages a wonderfully industrious people, although they are rough and simple. To speak truly, I cannot remember that I have ever seen a better or gentler folk than these.

The marks which I found among them I have set down in the following order: A is the mark of Wingina, the chief of Roanoke; B is the mark of Wingina's brother-in-law; C and D belong to various chiefs of Secota; E, F, and G belong to certain chiefs of Pomeiock and Aquascogoc.

unpunished, because we wanted to win the friendship of the natives through gentleness. But strangely it happened that within a few days of our departure the people began to die very fast. In some towns twenty people died, in some forty, in some sixty, and in one sixscore; this was a large portion of the inhabitants. And the strange thing was that this occurred only in towns where we had been and where they had done some mischief against us, and it happened always after we had left. The disease with which they were stricken was so strange a one that they did not know anything about it or how to cure it. Even their elders could not remember the like ever having happened before.

After this disease had struck in four or five places, some of our native friends, especially Chief Wingina, were persuaded that it was we who brought it about, helped by our God. They thought that through Him we were able to slay anyone at any place and without the use of weapons.

From that time on, whenever they heard that any of their enemies had abused us on our journeys and that we had not punished them, they begged us to let our God bring about the death of these enemies. This they alleged would be to our credit and profit, as well as to theirs, and they hoped we would grant their request because of the friendship we professed for them. We explained that such entreaties were ungodly and that our God would not be ruled by such prayers and requests from men; rather, all things are done according to His pleasure and as He ordains. We said that we ought to pray to Him, on the contrary, to show ourselves His true servants and ask that these enemies might know His truth and serve Him in righteousness, so that they could live together with us. And we told them that everything would be done in accordance with the divine will and pleasure of God, as He ordained to be best in His wisdom.

It happened that shortly after this the disease struck their enemies just as they had desired. They thought we had brought it about, disguising our intentions from them. They thanked us profoundly for fulfilling their wish even though we had not promised to do so.

Because of this marvelous accident all the natives throughout the country began to have a wonderful opinion of us, and they were not sure whether to consider us gods or men. Their wonderment increased when they saw that not one of our number became ill during their sickness, nor did any of us die. They also noted that we had no women with us, nor did we care for any of theirs. Some of them were of the opinion that we were not born of woman and were therefore not mortal but were men of a past generation who had risen again to immortality.

They prophesied that more of our generation would yet come to this country to kill them and to take away their homes. They imagined that these men who were to arrive after us were already in the air, invisible and without bodies, and that they shot invisible bullets into the victims who died in their villages, inflicting this punishment at our instigation because they loved us.

And as their medicine men could not cure the strange disease, they tried to excuse their ignorance by shamefully encouraging the simple people to believe that the death was caused by invisible bullets. To prove it they sucked strings of blood out of the sick bodies and said these were the strings to which the bullets were attached.

Yet some of the natives did not believe in the invisible bullets. They thought that we shot our enemies from a distance, killing anyone who offended us, no matter how far away he was. Still others said it was the work of God for our sakes, and we ourselves had reason to agree with them, no matter what other causes there might be. Astrologers believed that the reason of these strange happenings might be the eclipse of the sun which we saw during our outward voyage, or it might be caused by a comet which appeared a few days before the sickness began. But I do not myself think that these outward causes brought about these special accidents. There must have been other reasons, on which I will not speculate at present.

Thus, I have given the opinions of the native inhabitants in detail to show you that there is good hope that they may be brought to embrace the truth through discreet handling and wise government and consequently will come to honor, obey, fear, and love us. Although towards the end of the year some of our men were too harsh with them and killed a few of their number for offenses which might easily have been forgiven, still the natives thought the punishment just and did not change their friendly attitude toward us. I do not believe that they are likely to change their general good opinion of us, and if we are careful at all, they need not be feared. Nevertheless, we must hope for the best and try to do our best, taking care to remove the causes for any discontent among them.

THE CONCLUSION

I hope I have related enough about the country so that those who have been indifferent to it will like it, even if they do not know any more than I have mentioned. Without doubt there is much still to be discovered, as to both the commodities and the soil itself.

Everything I have spoken of was found not far from the seacoast where we lived. Sometimes we made journeys farther into the mainland, and there we found the soil richer, the trees taller, the ground firmer, and the topsoil deeper. We saw there more and larger fields and finer grass, as good as any in England. In some places the ground was high, rocky, and hilly, fruits grew plentifully, beasts lived in greater abundance, the country was more thickly populated, the towns and houses larger, and the communities better ruled.

HONI SOIT QVI MAL Y PENSE
V I
N
S E C O
T A N
Mongoack
Cwareuuoc
Panauuaioc
Neuusiooc
Secota
Cotan
Aquscogoc
Paquuip
Pomeiock
Tramas
Dasamong
Autore Ioanne. With Sculptore Theodoro de Bry, Qui et excud
Promontorium tremendum
Wokokon
Croatoan
Paquwoc
Scala leucarum . 25
5 10 15 20 25
Scalle of . 25 . leages

Americæ
pars, Nunc Virginia
dicta, primum ab Anglis
inuenta. sumtibus Dn. Walteri
Raleigh, Equestris ordinis Viri
Anno Dñi · M · D LXXXV regni Vero
Serenifs: nostræ Reginæ Elisabethæ
XXVII
Hujus vero Historia peculiari
Libro discripta est, additis
etiam Indigenarum
Iconibus
CHAWA
NOOK
RGIA
Ramishouwo
Ohaunoock
Catokinge
Waratan
Mascoming
Skicoak
WEAPE
MEOC
Chepanuu
Chesepiooc
Apasus
Chesepiooc sinus
Comokee
Pasquenoke
Trinety harbor
OCCIDENS
MERIDIES
SEPTENTRIO
ORIENS

Why, then, may we not expect even more and greater plenty from the inland parts? The Spaniards found this to be the case when they discovered the mainland of the West Indies. I am sure that the mainland of this country, Virginia, extending in some directions many hundreds of leagues, will yield many excellent commodities which we have not yet seen. We have certain knowledge that the country is vast—and this is not only from the tales of the inhabitants—although no Christian ruler has any trade or possessions there.

From the nature of the climate we gather that the land is similar to Japan, China, Persia, Jerusalem, the Islands of Cyprus and Candy, the southern parts of Greece, Italy, and Spain, and other famous countries. Not to be tedious, I leave to your own consideration what hopes this gives us.

The air is much warmer there in all seasons than it is in England, yet it is always temperate, never so violently hot as near the tropics. As to the wholesomeness of the climate, I need say only that we lived entirely on the food and water of the country for all but twenty days.

The foods were at first very strange to us and might have been expected to change our body temperatures and to bring about grievous and dangerous diseases, yet this was not so. Nor did we have our own means of catching beasts, fish, and fowl, and we had to depend upon native devices. Therefore we could not quickly and easily procure these foods in sufficient quantities or choice as would have satisfied and contented us. We also suffered for lack of clothing. Furthermore, in all our travels, even in winter, we lived in the open and slept on the ground. Yet despite all these discomforts, out of the hundred and eight men of our company only four died during the entire year of our stay. These four men died toward the end of the year, and none because of privation and hardship. They had all been sickly when we left England, and the wonder was that they ventured to travel and lived as long as they did.

I hope there no longer remains any reason for disliking the Virginia project. The air is temperate and wholesome there, the soil is fertile and yields the commodities I have listed, and the voyage over the ocean has been so many times performed that we now know it can be done three times a year in any season. Moreover, Sir Walter Raleigh has been liberal in granting large tracts of land there. The least he has given to any man has been five hundred acres, besides many other aids.

Those travelling to Virginia to live and plant there need carry only provisions for the first year, as the last expedition did. Then, with reasonable diligence and care, they can easily supply themselves with plenty of excellent food thereafter. More English cattle should be transported; likewise our varieties of fruits, roots, and herbs may be planted there. Some of them have already been sown and have grown well. And in a short time the planters may raise the commodities I have described. These will enrich themselves and those who trade with them.

This is all the fruits of our labors that I have thought necessary to tell you at the present. As to more concerning the nature and manners of the inhabitants of Virginia, the number and particularities of the voyages made thither, the undertakings of the men employed there and in the project by Sir Walter Raleigh, this matter I shall publish later.

Many of the men of our company are worthy to be remembered: the first discoverers of the country; Sir Richard Grenville, our General at that time; Ralph Lane, his successor and our Governor; and others who worked under their government. Besides these, the captains of our vessels and the masters of the supply ships should be mentioned, as well as the present Governor and Assistants. I have a discourse ready, written in the manner of a chronicle, dealing with all these and many other persons and occurrences, and when the time is convenient it will be published.[5]

Thus, referring my discourse to your favorable reception, awaiting the good success of the project from Him who is the acknowledged Author and Governor, not only of this but of all things else, I take my leave of you this month of February, 1588.

5. It never was published. Hariot's manuscript has not yet been found.

THE ORIGINAL TITLE PAGES OF THE NARRATIVES

BREVIS NARRATIO
EORVM QVÆ IN FLORIDA AMERICÆ PROVĨCIA
Gallis acciderunt, secunda in illam Nauigatione, duce Renato de Laudõniere classis Præfecto:
Anno M D LXIIII.
QVAE EST SECVNDA PARS AMERICAE.
Additæ figuræ et Incolarum eicones ibidem ad vivũ expressæ: brevis item Declaratio Religionis, rituum, vivendique ratione ipsorum.
Auctore
Iacobo le Moyne, cui cognomen de Morgues, Laudõnierum in ea Nauigatione sequuto.
Nunc primùm Gallico sermone à Theodoro de Bry Leodiense in lucem edita: latio verò donata a C.C.A.
Cum gratia & privil. Cæs. Maiest. ad quadriennium.

De Bry's *Florida,* published in 1591 in Frankfurt, printed Le Moyne's narrative in Latin.

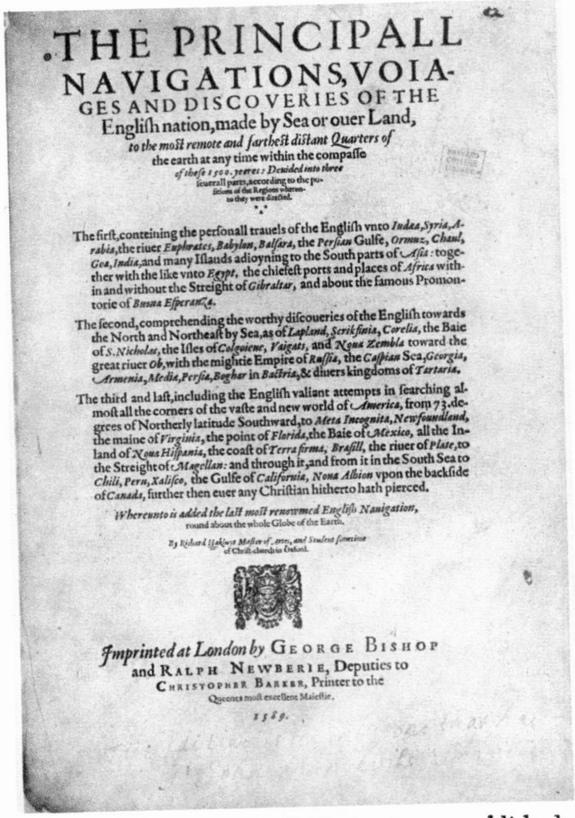

THE PRINCIPALL NAVIGATIONS, VOIAGES AND DISCOVERIES OF THE English nation, made by Sea or ouer Land,
to the most remote and farthest distant Quarters of the earth at any time within the compasse *of these 1500. yeeres: Deuided into three* seuerall parts, according to the positions of the Regions whereunto they were directed.

The first, conteining the personall trauels of the English vnto *Iudæa, Syria, Arabia,* the riuer *Euphrates, Babylon, Balsara,* the *Persian* Gulfe, *Ormuz, Chaul, Goa, India,* and many Islands adioyning to the South parts of *Asia:* together with the like vnto *Egypt,* the chiefest ports and places of *Africa* within and without the Streight of *Gibraltar,* and about the famous Promontorie of *Buona Esperanza.*

The second, comprehending the worthy discoueries of the English towards the North and Northeast by Sea, as of *Lapland, Scrikfinia, Corelia,* the Baie of *S. Nicholas,* the Isles of *Colgoiene, Vaigats,* and *Noua Zembla* toward the great riuer *Ob,* with the mightie Empire of *Russia,* the *Caspian* Sea, *Georgia, Armenia, Media, Persia, Boghar* in *Bactria,* & diuers kingdoms of *Tartaria.*

The third and last, including the English valiant attempts in searching almost all the corners of the vaste and new world of *America,* from 73. degrees of Northerly latitude Southward, to *Meta Incognita, Newfoundland,* the maine of *Virginia,* the point of *Florida,* the Baie of *Mexico,* all the Inland of *Noua Hispania,* the coast of *Terra firma, Brasill,* the riuer of *Plate,* to the Streight of *Magellan:* and through it, and from it in the South Sea to *Chili, Peru, Xalisco,* the Gulfe of *California, Noua Albion* vpon the backside of *Canada,* further then euer any Christian hitherto hath pierced.

Whereunto is added the last most renowmed English Nauigation, round about the whole Globe of the Earth.

By Richard Hakluyt Master of Artes, and Student sometime of Christ-church in Oxford.

Imprinted at London by GEORGE BISHOP and RALPH NEWBERIE, Deputies to CHRISTOPHER BARKER, Printer to the Queenes most excellent Maiestie.
1589.

Hakluyt's *The Principall Navigations*... published in 1589, includes all the English narratives.

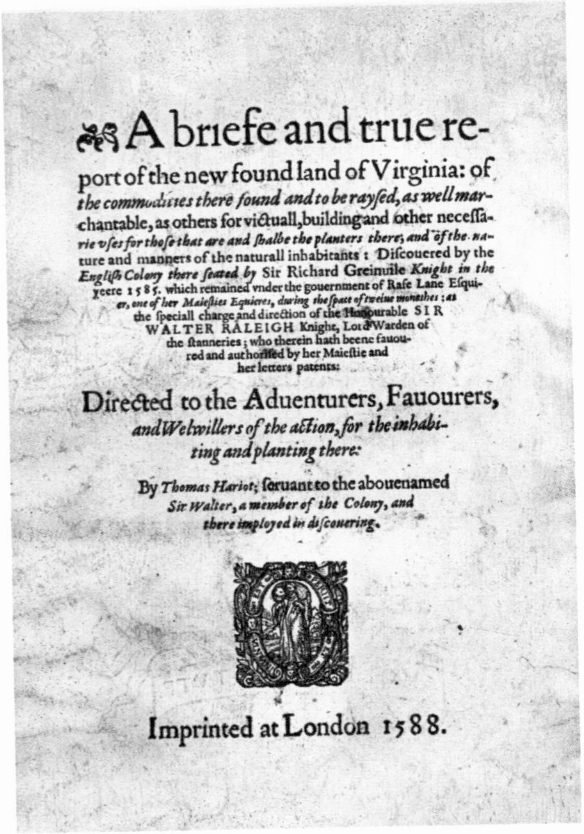

A briefe and true report of the new found land of Virginia: of *the commodities there found and to be raysed, as well mar*chantable, as others for victuall, building and other necessa*rie vses for those that are and shalbe the planters there; and of the na*ture and manners of the naturall inhabitants: Discouered by the *English Colony there seated by* Sir Richard Greinuile *Knight in the* yeere 1585. which remained vnder the gouernment of Rafe Lane Esquier, *one of her Maiesties Equieres, during the space of twelue monethes:* at the speciall charge and direction of the Honourable SIR WALTER RALEIGH Knight, Lord Warden of the stanneries; who therein hath beene fauoured and authorised by her Maiestie and her letters patents:

Directed to the Aduenturers, Fauourers, *and Welwillers of the action, for the inhabiting and planting there:*

By *Thomas Hariot;* seruant to the abouenamed *Sir Walter, a member of the Colony, and there imployed in discouering.*

Imprinted at London 1588.

Hariot's *Briefe and True Report,* published in 1588—was reprinted by Theodore De Bry in 1590.

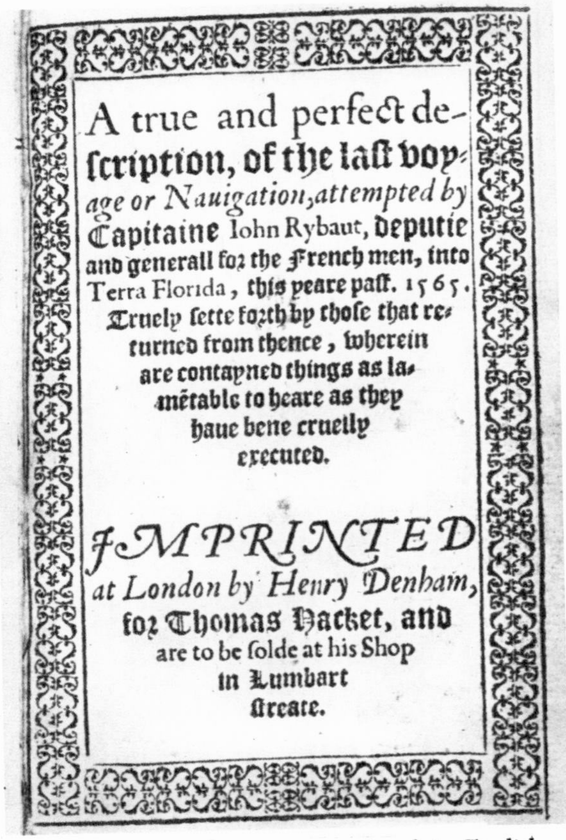

A true and perfect description, of the last voyage or Nauigation, attempted by Capitaine Iohn Rybaut, deputie and generall for the French men, into Terra Florida, this yeare past. 1565. Truely sette forth by those that returned from thence, wherein are contayned things as lamentable to heare as they haue bene cruelly executed.

IMPRINTED at London by Henry Denham, for Thomas Hacket, and are to be solde at his Shop in Lumbart streate.

Le Challeux's *Discourse* was printed in English, in 1566, the same year as the French edition.

BIBLIOGRAPHY

THE FRENCH IN FLORIDA

General History and Biography

BOURNE, EDWARD GAYLORD, "Spain in America; French and Spaniards in Florida," *The American Nation* (New York, 1904).

BRINTON, DANIEL GARRISON, *Notes on the Floridian Peninsula; Its Literary History, Indian Tribes and Antiquities* (Philadelphia, 1859).

DELABORDE, LOUIS JULES, COMTE, *Gaspard de Coligny* (Paris, 1879-1882).

GAFFAREL, PAUL, *Histoire de la Floride française* (Paris, 1875).

HAAG, E., and E. HAAG, *La France Protestante* (Paris, 1861).

KELLOGG, LOUISE PHELPS, "René Goulaine de Laudonnière," in *Dictionary of American Biography* (New York, 1935), XI, 30.

——— "Jean Ribaut," in *Dictionary of American Biography,* XV, 533.

LESCARBOT, MARC, *Histoire de la Nouvelle France* (Paris, 1609).

LOWERY, WOODBURY, *The Spanish Settlements Within the Present Limits of the United States; Florida,* 1562-1574 (New York, 1905).

MENENDEZ DE AVILES, PEDRO, "Translations of the Letters of Menéndez to Philip II in 1565," in Massachusetts Historical Society, *Proceedings,* 2d ser., Vol. VIII (1894).

PARKMAN, FRANCIS, *Pioneers of France in the New World* (Boston, 1865).

RIBAUT, JEAN, *The Whole & True Discouerye of Terra Florida;* with notes by H. M. Biggar, and a biography by Jeannette Thurber Connor (De Land, Florida State Historical Society, 1927).

SHEA, JOHN GILMARY, "Ancient Florida," in Justin Winsor, ed., *Narrative and Critical History of America* (New York, 1886), II, 231-298.

——— *The Catholic Church in Colonial Days* (New York, 1886).

SOLÍS DE MERÁS, GONZALO, *Pedro Menéndez de Avilés,* tr. from the Spanish with notes, by Jeannette Thurber Connor (De Land, Florida State Historical Society, 1923).

SPARKS, JARED, "John Ribault," in *Lives of John Ribault* . . . (Boston, 1848). The Library of American Biography, 2d ser., Vol. VII.

Original French Sources

Coppie d'une lettre venant de la Floride, envoyée à Rouen, & depuis au Seigneur d'Eueron; ensemble le plan & portraict du fort que les Françoys y ont faict (Paris, 1565), is a short anonymous narrative, probably written by one of the men who accompanied Laudonnière in the summer of 1564. It was published in Paris in 1565 and is reprinted with eleven other contemporary documents by Ternaux-Compans, ed., in *Recueil de pièces sur la Floride inédites,* and also by Paul Gaffarel, in *Histoire de la Floride française.*

FOURQUEVAUX, RAIMOND DE BECCARIE DE PAVIE, BARON, *Dépêches de M. de Fourquevaux, ambassadeur du Roi Charles IX en Espagne, 1565-1572* (3 vols., Paris, 1896-1904), contains De Fourquevaux's letters to Charles IX and Catherine de' Medici, written while he was French ambassador in Madrid. Many of these letters report on the Florida controversy. Some of De Fourquevaux's papers are printed in Paul Gaffarel, *Histoire de la Floride française,* while his unpublished correspondence and other papers are in the Bibliothèque Nationale, Paris.

GOURGUES, DOMINIQUE DE, *La Reprinse de la Floride* contains a detailed account of his expedition against the Spaniards in 1567-1568. Five different manuscripts of this narrative exist. One version is printed in Henri Ternaux-Compans, ed., *Recueil de pièces sur la Floride* and also in Paul Gaffarel's *Histoire de la Floride française.*

De Gourgues' narrative is reprinted in English in Richard Hakluyt's *Principal Navigations* (Vol. III, 1600).

LAUDONNIÈRE, RENÉ GOULAINE DE, wrote three long letters on the French expedition to Florida in 1562, 1564, and 1565. These narratives, with the above-mentioned account of the De Gourgues expedition in 1567 (written probably by the editor Basanier) were published under the title *L'Histoire notable de la Floride . . . contenant les trois voyages faits en icelle par certains capitaines et pilotes françois descrits par le Capitaine Laudonnière . . . a laquelle a esté adjousté un quatriesme voyage fait par le Capitaine Gourgues* (Paris, 1586). It was dedicated to Sir Walter Raleigh. Richard Hakluyt, who had induced the French publication, translated the volume into English and published it in 1587 under the title "A Notable Historie Containing Foure Voyages Made by Certayne French Captaynes unto Florida."

LE CHALLEUX, NICHOLAS, *Discours de l'histoire de la Floride* . . . (Dieppe, 1566), is a naïve and straightforward story by a sixty-year-old carpenter from Dieppe. Le Challeux, an eyewitness of the events at Fort Caroline, describes what he saw there, and he incorporates in his narrative the story of the sailor Christophe le Breton, who escaped the massacre.

Le Challeux's book was translated into English and published by Thomas Hacket on May 25, 1566, in the same year that the French edition appeared, under the title *A True and Perfect Description, of the Last Voyage or Navigation, Attempted by Capitaine John Rybaut . . . into Terra Florida, This Yeare Past 1565.*

The French text was printed twice—the first time on 54 pages, the second time on 62 pages—and was republished the same year at Lyons with some slight changes. It can be found in Henri Ternaux-Compans, ed., *Recueil de pièces sur la Floride,* and also in Paul Gaffarel, *Histoire de la Floride française.*

There are only two known copies of the first English edition, one in the John Carter Brown Library, Providence, R. I., the other in the British Museum. One of the copies was photostated by the Massachusetts Historical Society, Americana Series No. 13.

LE MOYNE DE MORGUES, JAQUES, *Brevis narratio* . . . , was written in London about twenty years after Le Moyne returned from Florida. The artist accompanied his narrative with sketches of scenes he remembered.

The publisher Theodore de Bry acquired Le Moyne's pictures and narrative from his widow in 1588 and printed them in Latin and later in German as the second part of his *Great Voyages* under the title "Brevis narratio eorum quae in Florida Americae . . ." (Frankfurt, 1591).

An English translation of the Latin text by Frederick B. Perkins, together with reproductions of the De Bry engravings, was published by James R. Osgood & Company, in the *Narrative of Le Moyne* (Boston, 1875).

A modern French reprint of the De Bry engravings (crudely colored) is called *La Floride française* (Paris, 1928), ed. by Charles de la Roncière, and published in two volumes in a limited edition of 500 copies. Another French reprint, containing not only the Florida engravings but also the Virginia pictures of De Bry, is *Voyages en Virginie et en Floride* (Paris, 1927).

MEDICI, CATHERINE DE', *Lettres,* ed. by Hector de la Ferrière, were published in Paris (1880-1909) in ten volumes.

"UNE REQUÊTE AU ROY, faicte en forme de complainte par les femmes, veufves, petits enfans, orphelins et autres, leurs amis, parents et alliez de ceulx qui ont esté cruellement envahis par les Hespagnols en la France antharctique dicte la Floride" is a petition of the widows and orphans of the massacred Frenchmen to Charles IX. The petition, first published in August, 1565, is known as the "Epistola supplicatoria," and it is incorporated in Chauveton's French edition of Benzoni and in Le Moyne's narrative.

The Massachusetts Historical Society made a photostatic reproduction of the original.

The text of the petition is reprinted in Gaffarel, *Histoire de la Floride française,* p. 447.

RIBAUT, JEAN, *The Whole and True Discouerye of Terra Florida,* the first detailed account of his voyage to the shores of North America, was published in London in the spring of 1563 for Thomas Hacket. The first edition must have been very small, for nineteen years later Richard Hakluyt complained that the book was "not to be had, unlesse I had caused it to be printed againe." So he incorporated the Ribaut narrative in his *Divers Voyages Touching the Discouerie of America* . . . (London, Thomas Woodcocke, 1582). However, in Hakluyt's *The Principal Navigations, Voiages, Traffiques and Discoueries of the English Nation* . . . (London, 1598-1600, 3 vols.), the Ribaut narrative is not included.

The fate of Ribaut's original French manuscript is unknown, nor is there a known copy of a French edition. Probably the book was never printed in French. When Paul Gaffarel published his *Histoire de la Floride française* (Paris, 1875), he named Ribaut's account "Histoire de l'expédition française en Floride."

However, in 1917 the original English translation of the narrative was discovered by Dr. H. P. Biggar among the Sloane manuscripts at the British Museum and published in the *English Historical Review* for April, 1917, pp. 253-

270, under the title "Jean Ribaut's Discoverye of Terra Florida." In his footnotes Dr. Biggar noted the differences between the original manuscript and the printed book and cleared up numerous printing errors.

There are only two copies of the first English edition in existence. One is in the British Museum, the other in the Lambeth Palace Library. The British Museum copy was photostated by the Massachusetts Historical Society, and copies of the photostats are available for libraries and students. The Lambeth Palace copy is reproduced in facsimile in Jean Ribaut, *The Whole and True Discouerye of Terra Florida,* ed. by Jeannette Connor (De Land, Florida, 1927). This volume also contains a reprint of the English manuscript found by Dr. Biggar.

Testimony of French Eyewitnesses

MELENECHE, one of the three Frenchmen who escaped from Fort Caroline and was captured by the Spaniards, made a deposition to Ambassador Rodriguez de Noriega in Seville. This deposition "Relación del suceso de la armada francesa que fue a poblar la tierra de le Florida," is in "Carta escrita al rey por Juan Rodriguez de Noriega, Sevilla, á 29 de marzo de 1565" (MS Direc. de Hidrog., Madrid, Col. Navarrete, tomo 14, Doc. No. 33, fols. 3b and 5b). It is reprinted in Ternaux-Compans, ed., *Recueil de pièces sur la Floride.*

MEMYN (or MENNIN), JEAN, made his deposition on October 16, 1566, to De Fourquevaux, the French ambassador in Madrid. Memyn, a member of Ribaut's last expedition, was captured by the Spaniards, but he managed to escape. His highly colored and imaginative testimony is printed in De Fourquevaux's *Dépêches* (Paris, 1896), I, 131-133.

ROJOMONTE, STEFANO DE, one of the French deserters who escaped from Laudonnière's colony in 1564 and was captured by the Spaniards, made his deposition on February 28, 1565. It is included in "Noticias de la población que habian hecho los Franceses en la Florida," 1564 (MS Arch. Gen. de Indias, Seville, Patronato, est 1, caj. 1, leg. 1/19, ro. 4, p. 1).

ROUFFI, GUILLAUME (the Spanish call him Guillermo Rufin) a French boy, who had come with Ribaut to the New World in 1562.

Rouffi remained in Florida when the half-starved colonists left Charlesfort for France, for he did not trust the sailing ability of his companions. When at the end of May, 1564, Hernando Manrique de Rojas, commanding the frigate *Nuestra Señora de la Concepción,* came to Florida to destroy Charlesfort and remove the French columns, he found the seventeen-year-old Rouffi, clothed in Indian dress, living among the Indians of Chief Audusta. From him the Spanish commander received a detailed account of Ribaut's first venture. Manrique took Rouffi to Havana, where the boy made his testimony. This is to be found in the "Relación e información de los Franceses que han ido a poblar en la costa de la Florida, San Cristobal de la Habana, 9 julio, 1564. (MS Arch. Gen. de Indias, Sevilla, est. 54, caj. 1, leg. 15.)

Original Spanish Sources

BARCIA CARBALLIDO Y ZÚÑIGA, Andrés González de (pseud., Gabriel de Cardenas y Cano), *Ensayo Cronológico para la historia general de la Florida* (Madrid, 1723). When Barcia wrote his book he had access to original documents. Some of these he used as source works; others he simply copied. Of those he copied, the most important is Solís de Merás, *Memorial. . . .*

RUIDÍAZ Y CARAVIA, EUGENIO, *La Florida; su conquista y colonización por Pedro Menéndez de Avilés* (Madrid, 1893). In Vol. II of this work Ruidíaz publishes Pedro Menéndez de Avilés' correspondence, his letters to the King, memorials, royal cedulas and patents, instructions, relations, and other documents covering the period from 1555 to 1574, chiefly relating to the conquest of Florida.

SOLÍS DE MERÁS, GONZALO, *Memorial que hizo el Doctor Gonzalo Solís de Merás de todas las jornadas y sucesos del Adelantado Pedro Menéndez de Avilés, su cuñado, y de la conquista de la Florida y justicia que hizo en Juan Ribao y otros franceses,* is reprinted in Ruidíaz, *La Florida. . . .*

Merás, the historian of the Spanish expedition, and a brother-in-law of Menéndez, wrote his book probably in 1565. It is printed in English in Connor, ed., *Pedro Menéndez de Avilés.*

BARRIENTOS, BARTOLOMÉ, "Vida y hechos de Pedro Menéndez de Avilés . . ." is published by Genaro García in his *Dos antiguas relaciones de la Florida* (Mexico, 1902, pp. 1-152). Barrientos, a professor of Latin at the University of Salamanca, completed his book in December, 1568. His material came from three independent sources. He probably used Menéndez's original report to Philip II; Barrientos quotes extensively from this document. He must have had access also to Menéndez correspondence and to some other documents, as he mentions incidents which are omitted by both Merás and Barcia.

MENDOZA GRAJALES, FRANCISCO LOPEZ DE, the chaplain of the Spanish expedition, was, like Merás, an eyewitness of the events he describes in "Relación de la jornada de Pedro Menéndez de Avilés en la Florida" (Documentos inéditos del Archivo de Indias, III, 441). The text is in Ruidíaz, *La Florida*... while a French translation of it is in Ternaux-Compans, ed., *Recueil de pièces sur la Floride.*

MENÉNDEZ DE AVILÉS, PEDRO AND ALONSO DE LA CAMPA, "Sieta cartas escritas al rey, años de 1565 y 1566," are the dispatches of Menéndez to Philip II, which were first used by Francis Parkman in his *Pioneers of France in the New World*. They consist of 72 closely written pages.

PHILIP II, *Correspondencia de Felipe II con sus embajadores en la Corte de Inglaterra 1558-1584*. In Colección de documentos inéditos para la historia de España (Madrid, 1842-1895), Vols. LXXXVII, LXXXIX-XCII. The English translation is in Great Britain, Public Record Office, Calendar of Letters and State Papers Relating to English Affairs . . . ed. by Martin A. S. Hume (London, 1892).

JOHN WHITE AND ROANOKE COLONY

ADAMS, RANDOLPH G., "An Effort to Identify John White," *American Historical Review,* XLI (October, 1935).

——— *Raleigh's Roanoke Colony of 1585* (Ann Arbor, Mich., 1935); a guide to an exhibition upon the three hundred and fiftieth anniversary of Roanoke.

BIGGES, WALTER, *Expeditio Francisci Draki . . .* (Leyden, 1588). In English it is called *A summarie and true discourse of Sir Frances Drakes West Indian Voyage . . .* (London, 1589).

BINYON, LAURENCE, "The Drawings of John White, Governor of Raleigh's Virginia Colony," in the Walpole Society *Publications,* Vol. XIII (Oxford, 1925).

——— "Governor John White, painter and Virginia pioneer," *Putnam's Magazine* (July, 1907).

BRITISH MUSEUM

——— *Catalogue of drawings by British artists . . . in the British Museum* by Laurence Binyon (London, 1907). In Volume IV, pp. 326-37, Binyon describes all the White drawings.

——— "Pictorial Postcards (coloured). Set B72" (London, 1934). Six cards by John White with a four-page leaflet by A. M. Hind.

——— *Catalogue of British Drawings, XVIth and XVIIth Centuries* by Edward Croft-Murray and Paul Hulton (London, 1960). A revision of Laurence Binyon's 1907 work.

——— *The American Drawings of John White,* a two-volume limited edition publication (600 copies, of which half were offered for sale in the United States for $225 the set) by Paul Hulton and David Beers Quinn. Volume 1: "A catalogue raisonné and a study of the artist"; Volume 2: "Reproductions of the originals in colour facsimile and of derivatives in monochrome." (London, 1964).

BUSHNELL, DAVID I., JR., "John White—the first English Artist to visit America, 1585," *Virginia Magazine of History and Biography,* Vols. 35 and 36 (Richmond, Va., 1927-1928).

CORBETT, SIR J. S., ed., *Papers Relating to the Navy during the Spanish War, 1585-1587,* Navy Records Society Publications (London, 1898).

CRAVEN, WESLEY F., "John White," in *Dictionary of American Biography* (New York, 1936).

——— *The Southern Colonies in the Seventeenth Century, 1607-1689* (Baton Rouge, La., 1949).

CUMMING, W. P., "The Identity of John White . . ." in the *North Carolina Historical Review,* Vol. XV (Chapel Hill, N. C., July, 1938).

EGGLESTON, EDWARD, "John White's drawings," in *The Nation,* Vol. II (New York, April, 1891).

——— "The beginning of a nation," "Indian War in the Colonies," and "The Aborigines and the Colonists," in *Century Illustrated* (1882-83).

HAKLUYT, RICHARD, *The principall navigations, voiages and discoveries of the English nation* (London, 1589) and 3 vols. with changed title (London 1598-1600). This work was reprinted in 12 volumes (Glasgow, 1903-05). Volume 8 contains the original narratives of Arthur Barlowe, Ralph Lane, Thomas Hariot, John White, also Laudonnière's letters.

——— *Hakluyt's Voyages.* An eight-volume abridgement in the Everyman edition with an introduction by John Masefield (London and New York, 1908 and 1927).

——— *Hakluyt's Voyages.* A one-volume synthesis, edited by Irwin R. Blacker (New York, 1965).

HALE, EDWARD E., "John White's Drawings in the Sloane Collection of the British Museum," in the American Antiquarian Society, *Transactions and Collections,* LV (Boston, 1860).

HAWKS, FRANCIS L., *History of North Carolina* (Fayetteville, N. C., 1857-1858).

MALONE, E., "Correspondence between E. Malone and Lord Charlemont," in the Historical Manuscripts Commission, *Thirteenth Report,* Part 8, Letters 81-82, Vol. LXI (London, 1894).

MOFFET, THOMAS, *Insectorum sive minimorum animalium theatrum* (London, 1634).

——— *The history of four-footed beasts and serpents ... whereunto is now added, the theater of insects ...* by Edward Topsell (London, 1658) contains the English version of the Moffet work. Both books carry a woodcut of the common American tiger swallow-tailed butterfly (Moffet, p. 88; Topsell, p. 967) after a John White original. Curiously, both books omit the reference to White which is in the original manuscript.

MORGAN, EDMUND S., "John White and the Sarsaparilla," in *The William and Mary Quarterly* (Williamsburg, Va., 1957).

PARKS, GEORGE B., "Richard Hakluyt and the English Voyagers," in the *American Geographical Society Special Publications* (New York, 1928).

QUINN, DAVID BEERS, *Raleigh and the British Empire,* (London, 1947).

——— (ed.), *The Roanoke Voyages* 1584-1590, 2 vols. (London, 1955).

SECCOMBE, THOMAS, "John White," in the *Dictionary of National Biography* (London, 1900).

STEVENS, HENRY, *Bibliotheca Historica* (Boston, 1870). On pp. 223-226 Stevens relates the sale of the White drawings to the British Museum.

VERNER, COOLIE, "The first maps of Virginia, 1590-1673," in *The Virginia Magazine of History and Biography* (Richmond, 1950).

WEITENKAMPF, FRANK, "Early pictures of North American Indians ..." in the *Bulletin of the New York Public Library* (New York, 1949).

THOMAS HARIOT

CLERKE, A. M., "Thomas Hariot," in the *Dictionary of National Biography.*

HARIOT, THOMAS, *A Briefe and True Report of the New Found Land of Virginia ...* (London, 1588). Facsimile reprints of the rare quarto edition were published by Dodd, Mead & Co., in 1903 and by Edward Brothers, Ann Arbor, in 1931. The Huntington Library supplies photostats of its copy.

Hakluyt included Hariot's report in his *Principal Navigations.*

The folio edition of Hariot's book, with De Bry's engravings, published in Frankfurt in 1590, was reprinted in facsimile in a limited edition of 100 copies by J. Sabin & Sons, New York, in 1871. Another facsimile reprint was published by the Holbein Society in Manchester, England, in 1888.

STEVENS, HENRY, *Thomas Hariot, the Mathematician, the Philosopher and the Scholar* (London, 1900). Privately printed.

THEODORE DE BRY AND HIS WORK

Great and small voyages

Theodore de Bry's *Great and small voyages* were published between 1590 and 1634. Forty-five years passed before the work was complete. Theodore de Bry himself issued only six parts of the series. After his death, in 1598, his widow and his two sons continued the publication. Between 1599 and 1602 they issued three more parts.

The publication of the *Small voyages* was begun in 1598. By 1607 De Bry's sons had completed eight parts. When Jean-Israel, the younger of the two brothers, died, in 1611, the elder, Jean-Theodore, continued the work and published two more parts during the next two years.

After Jean-Theodore's death, in 1623, his publishing business was inherited by his sons-in-law. One of them, Mathieu Merian, brought out the remaining parts of the *Great voyages,* and in 1634 he issued a fresh edition of the completed work, consisting of fourteen parts. The other son-in-law, William Fitzer, published the last two parts of the *Small voyages* in 1628.

A complete set of De Bry's voyages comes to 57 volumes. These are: 13 parts of the America series in Latin; 13 parts of the India series in Latin (including the Appendix, Congo); 14 parts of the America series in German; 14 parts of the India series in German; 1 part (Virginia) in English, 1 part (Virginia) in French, and the "Elenchus" (table of contents, etc.), in Latin.

There is a voluminous bibliography on De Bry's monumental work. This chronological list enumerates some of the important ones.

ROTHELIN, CHARLES D'ORLEANS DE, *Observations et details sur la collection des grands et petits voyages* (Paris, 1742).

CAMUS, ARMAND GASTON, *Mémoire sur la collection des grands et petits voyages*...(Paris, 1802).

BEDFORD, JOHN RUSSELL, *Description de l'exemplaire de la collection des grands voyages* (Paris, 1838).

WEIGEL, T. O., *Bibliographische Mitteilungen über die deutschen Ausgaben von De Bry's Sammlungen*...(Leipzig, 1845).

TIELE, PIETER ANTON, *Mémoire bibliographique sur les journaux des navigateurs néerlandais*... (Amsterdam, 1867).

BRUNET, JACQUES CHARLES, *A Bibliographical Description of the Collection of "Grands voyages" of De Bry* (New York, 1869).

BROWN UNIVERSITY, JOHN CARTER BROWN LIBRARY, *A Bibliographical Description of a Copy of the Collection of the Great and Small Voyages of De Bry, in the Library of the Late John Carter Brown;* by John Russell Bartlett (Providence, R. I., 1875).

HUTH, HENRY, *A Description and Collation of the Series of De Bry's Voyages* (London, 1880).

CRAWFORD, JAMES LUDOVIC LINDSAY, 26th Earl of, *Grands et petits voyages of De Bry,* Bibliotheca Lindsiana, Collations and Notes, No. 3 (London, 1884).

CHURCH, ELIHU DWIGHT, *A Catalogue of Books Relating to*...*America, Forming a Part of the Library of E. D. Church;* compiled...by George Watson Cole (New York, 1907).

BROWN UNIVERSITY, JOHN CARTER BROWN LIBRARY, *Bibliotheca Americana; Catalogue of the John Carter Brown Library* (Providence, R. I., 1919-1931). De Bry's collection of voyages appears Vol. I, p. 381.

BRITISH MUSEUM, *General Catalogue of Printed Books,* XXVII, pp. 417-418 (London, 1939).

ARENTS, GEORGE, *Tobacco; Its History, Illustrated by the Books*...*in the Library of George Arents, Jr.* Limited edition in 4 volumes (n.p., 1937-1941). Vol. I, pp. 311-317, contains a Bibliography on Theodore de Bry and Thomas Hariot.

Articles on De Bry

CATE, CHESTER M., "De Bry and the *Index Expurgatorius,*" in Bibliographical Society of America, *Papers,* XI, pp. 136-140 (1917).

GIUSEPPI, M. S., "The Work of Theodore de Bry and His Sons, Engravers," in Huguenot Society, *Proceedings,* pp. 204-226 (London, 1916).

STEVENS, HENRY N., "The De Bry Collector's Painefull Peregrination along the Pleasant Pathway to Perfection," in *Bibliographical Essays; a Tribute to Wilberforce Eames* (Cambridge, Mass., 1924).

JACQUES LE MOYNE DE MORGUES AND HIS WORK

ALLEN, ELSA G., "Jacques Le Moyne, First Zoological Artist in America," in *The Auk* (Lancaster, Pa., 1938).

——— "Some sixteenth century paintings of American birds," in *The Auk* (Lancaster, Pa., 1936).

BUSHNELL, DAVID I., JR., "Drawings by Jacques Lemoyne de Morgues of Saturioua . . . in *Smithsonian Miscellaneous Collections,* Vol. 81, No. 4 (Washington, D. C., 1928).

Narrative of Le Moyne . . . translated from the Latin of De Bry by Frederick B. Perkins (Boston, 1875).

INDEX

INDEX

INDEX

INDEX

INDEX

INDEX

Engraved and printed in black and white and three-color sheet-fed gravure by
The Beck Engraving Company, Inc. · Philadelphia · New York · Boston

Autore Ioanne With Sculptore Theodoro de Brÿ, Qui et excud
Mongoack
V N
I
SECOTAN
Cwareuuoc
Panauuaioc
Nëuustooc
Secota
Cotan
Aquscogoc
Paquuiyp
Pomeiock
Wokokon
Promontorium tremendum
Croatoan
Paquiwoc
Dasamo
Tram
Scala leucarum 25
5 10 15 20 25
Scalle of 25 leages

Americæ
pars, Nunc Virginia
dicta, primum ab Anglis
inuenta sumtibus Dn. Walteri
Raleigh, Equestris ordinis Viri
Anno Dñi. M.D LXXXV regni vero
Sereniss: nostræ Reginæ Elisabethæ
XXVII
Hujus vero Historia peculiari
Libro descripta est, additis
etiam Indigenarum
Iconibus
CHAWANOOK
ROANOAC (fragment: R)
WEAPEMEOC
Ramushouuog
Ohaunoock
Catokinge
Waratan
Mascoming
Skicoak
Chepanuu
Chesepiooc
Pasquenoke
Chesepiooc sinus
Apasus
Comokee
Trinety harbor
OCCIDENS
MERIDIES
SEPTENTRIO
ORIENS

EX LIBRIS MARK FABIAN CHERNIAVSKY
CHÂTEAU DU FEŸ